C0-CFV-057

# RESIDENTIAL ABANDONMENT

# RESIDENTIAL ABANDONMENT

## The Tenement Landlord Revisited

GEORGE STERNLIEB
ROBERT W. BURCHELL

Center for Urban Policy Research
Rutgers University—The State University of New Jersey
New Brunswick, New Jersey
1973

The Urban Renewal Demonstration Project and the publication of this report were made possible through an Urban Renewal Demonstration Grant awarded by the Department of Housing and Urban Development, under the provisions of Section 314 of the Housing Act of 1954, as amended, to Rutgers University.

**Photo Credits**

**Newark Star Ledger 50, 51, 52, 178, 235, 267, 321**
**Newark Fire Department 52, 77, 86, 91, 136, 179, 180, 220, 268**
**Newark Public Library 96, 134, 135, 234, 236**
**New Jersey Photos 96, 134**
**Newark Housing Authority 266**

# TABLE OF CONTENTS

# LIST OF EXHIBITS

# ACKNOWLEDGEMENTS

This study is unusually dependent on a variety of data. Acknowledgements on this point must go to two principal sources, the first, Dr. George Brown, Director of the Census, who, in the midst of severe demands upon his time, provided the study group with all information which was available for Newark in its preliminary state. The second source of unlimited support was Mayor Kenneth Gibson of Newark whose personal staff and department chiefs were more than cooperative at all times.

In Newark, particular mention must be given Police Director John L. Redden who completely embraced our efforts and provided staff personnel for our assistance. Similar enthusiasm was reflected in the efforts of John Caulfield, Director of the Newark Fire Department. Special thanks go to Chief Elias J. Swerida and Fireman Peter Barrone of the Newark Fire Department Combustibles Division, Joseph V. Nellegar, Chief I.D. Officer of the R&I Bureau, and Manager Robert McCale and Assistant Manager William Zuzzio of the Newark Police Data Processing Division for their continuing patience and unselfish expenditure of time. In the former case, Chief Swerida and Fireman Barrone provided the study group with vacant building records, lists of 1970 and 1971 fires, and applicable photos; in the latter, Robert C. McCale and William Zuzzio made 90,000 incidents of 1971 police data available in a format compatible with our processing equipment and pulled photos of applicable incidents of crime within abandoned buildings. Special thanks must also go to Arthur Dornbush, Esq., and Herbert Fried of the Newark Tax Department. Both of these individuals committed extensive amounts of their time probing dated records to determine both current and 1964 tax delinquency and additionally provided corroborated lists of parcels sold at annual tax sales during the period 1967 to 1971.

Richard Turtletaub of the David Cronheim Realty Company enabled our researchers to spend a week probing back issues of the *Essex County Real Estate Directory* to determine current and past levels of private interest in purchasing tax title liens within the City of Newark.

Sheila Chasen and George Chranewycz of the Newark Housing Authority delineated specific areas of the city where urban renewal/rehabilitation/code enforcement were taking place and further checked our parcels to ascertain whether any were subject to the "fruits" of such programs during the interval between studies.

Alan Shapiro and his staff of the Newark Planning Department provided this office with maps, charts, and tabular information concerning planning activity in Newark, and additionally supplemented the fire department's list of abandoned buildings with a listing which had been completed as a result of their efforts.

While it is easy to recognize the efforts of external personnel, the efforts of those within the research organization are sometimes overlooked. This should not be the case. We must thank Mildred Barry of the Center staff and now on loan to the office of Newark's mayor, where she is Program Director for the Mayor's Policy and Planning Office. Mrs. Barry directed the resampling of the original residential parcels. Her experience in the handling of interviewers was essential to the successful completion of this project. A significant input into the accomplishments of interviewers was made by Guy Sicora of the Rutgers Urban Planning Department who himself completed in excess of 100 successful interviews. In addition, he was personally in charge of securing interviews for a small resampling of owners who abandoned their buildings.

Dominic Salluce, another former staff member, now with the Plainfield, New Jersey, Planning Department, was in charge of both original data collection in 1971 and maintaining it in forms comparable to the information which was already tabulated for 1964. William Dolphin, the Center's computer specialist, processed the raw data and performed the sometimes maddeningly numerous statistical manipulations requested by the authors.

Our colleagues at the Center, James W. Hughes, Lynne Sagalyn, and David Listokin, reviewed the work as it progressed and made many valuable suggestions. Franklin James' advice on statistical methods was particularly useful; the structure of the regression analyses employed a great many of his ideas.

Mention must also be made of the contributions of the principal Center research assistants who worked on this study. Of particular note are the efforts of Alan Salinger and Adolfo Lopez-Videla and Glenn Parish, who participated heavily in both data retrieval and analysis in the sections on financial institutions and fire and crime, respectively. Michael Pepper is responsible for any clarity or precision which the graphic work affords.

Finally, mention should be made of the work of Joan Frantz and Mona Levine whose typing skills, under the direction of Mary Picarella, enabled this work to proceed through several drafts; and to Gloria Cook, who edited the final document.

Any errors, omissions, and misinterpretations remain the responsibility of the authors.

September, 1973

George Sternlieb
Robert W. Burchell

# INTRODUCTION AND SUMMARY

Residential abandonment is the end product of all the urban ills of our modern society. While it has become an urban commonplace, it is a phenomenon about which little is known or understood. The poverty of available research on the subject is due, in part, to the fact that the very definition of abandonment is far from precise. It has been defined as a condition in which buildings are vacant of tenants; commonly this is coupled with the virtual disappearance of the owner either *de jure* or *de facto*. But this definition fails to recognize that abandonment appears to be a process, a reflection of a much deeper-seated and extensive phenomenon — the disinvestment of private capital in core cities.[1]

An abandoned structure frequently represents a positive token of housing betterment. Through the filtering-down process, the development of new and better housing has precipitated the successive shifting of families into increasingly better accommodations; the vacant buildings they have left behind are no longer competitive within the market. But the obvious anomaly is that in many instances, despite substantial housing shortages, abandonment has swept away both good housing and substantial shells which are much needed. The current abandonment process, then, cannot be explained simply in terms of the "normal market" forces.

The reality of abandonment is challenging the theoretician's capacity to explain the phenomenon or predict its growth. Analysts of the reasons for the decline of blighted areas and of their prospects for renewal have brought their entire theoretical arsenal to bear on the subject but the dynamics have evaded the state of the art. Intrametropolitan job dispersal; shifting transportation facilities; changes in the level and distribution of income and consequent change in housing and neighborhood demand; demographic and racial turnover; local government fiscal systems; housing obsolescence; and the numerous other factors which have been unearthed are more symptoms than basics.[2]

Unfortunately, the range of processes impacting on neighborhood change is much beyond the organizing capability of present urban theory. Edgar Hoover and Raymond Vernon presented a rough scheme of neighborhood evolution, the basis of which was an empirical melding of the joint operation of these factors. Their evolutionary scheme carried a neighborhood from its initial development in single family homes, through density increase and apartment construction, to obsolescence and decay, but the behavioral forces guiding this evolution are unclear. So, much as in other work, the forces guiding neighborhood change are presented as a catalogue rather than a coherent theoretical structure.[3]

While the social costs of the decay of blighted areas have been recognized as potentially enormous, useful policies for coping with the processes at work are elusive. In part, this results from theory running behind market reality. Over a decade ago, Chester Rapkin raised the question of "what shall we do with physical assets that retain economic value long after they cease to serve social purposes judged by other than market criteria?"[4] Today, after enormous renewal effort and expenditure, in an increasing number of metropolitan areas the question is no longer appropriate. Actual abandonment of blighted neighborhoods by landlords has reached shockingly high levels. Housing in such neighborhoods is apparently no longer judged profitable even by market standards. The question raised by Rapkin a decade ago might be appropriately reversed. The enormous social concern over the phenomenon suggests that the question being asked by policy makers in all levels of government is: "What shall we do with physical assets that retain social value long after they have ceased to serve economic purposes judged by market criteria?"[5]

Those who have written in the area have attempted to explain the abandonment phenomenon in terms of supply and demand. (Of course, neither of these forces, nor explanations derived therefrom, can be viewed in isolation.)[6] The supply explanation usually revolves about the parcel's operation and the relationship of its owner and occupant. Abandonment occurs as a result of lower priced housing being available elsewhere while increases in the operating schedule cannot be matched by the local rental levy. A large portion of these costs may be assigned to either parcel, tenant, or owner in terms of age of structure, construction material, location of the parcel, the presence of large families, tenant induced vandalism, racial intolerance of the owner, or finally an increased level of profit deemed necessary by the owner to remain in the urban area.

The demand explanation of abandonment begins with the premise that the existing core housing stock is durable, fixed, and difficult to transform from one use to another. The environment and desirability of this housing has lessened due to rising incomes and increasing desires for suburbanization making housing in these neighborhoods economically obsolete. The effective demand for these units declines so much that it is no longer profitable to operate them and they cease to have economic value in their present use.

In accordance with these views of housing abandonment the research design, whose results are presented here, is fashioned with the basic purpose of *explaining* abandonment and its thrust combines both the supply/demand approaches. From the supply side a sample of 567 buildings originally surveyed in 1964 were revisited in 1972. Over the period a portion of these buildings had become abandoned, some were taken for public purposes, while others remained viable within the existing housing stock. Using the buildings that were abandoned and those that were retained, an effort was made to explain a parcel being abandoned in 1972 by delving deeply first into the physical characteristics of the abandoned parcels, second into their operating procedures, and finally into relations between owners and tenants that were taking place some eight years previously at the time of the original interview. In effect, the question to be answered was whether there were any early warning indicators which could be isolated that might signal sometime in advance the future abandonment of a residential structure.

Similarly, from the demand side, were there changes taking place within a city's environment that would lessen its desirability, stimulate housing obsolescence, and promote residential abandonment? To answer this question, 1960 and 1970 socio-economic data, as well as abandonment levels, were tabulated on a census tract base. What were the dominant characteristics of neighborhoods in 1960 in which abandonment was rampant in 1970? Were there changes which these neighborhoods had undergone from 1960 to 1970 that might have contributed to the high abandonment statistics evident in 1970?

Certain aspects of the supply/demand view of abandonment, however, require more scrutiny than gross statistical manipulations can provide. On the demand side, in-depth analysis was undertaken to view the "environment of abandonment." What elements comprise the matrix of change in a city which is abnormally losing a substantial portion of its residential stock? Is this situation unique to a single city? To other secondary industrial cities of the Northeast and Midwest? To all cities?

Similarly, how does the resident's view of personal safety contribute to the spread of residential abandonment? Is it cause or consequence? What is the magnitude of the problem and are urban residents viewing this problem in proper perspective? Each of these contributes to the decision on the part of the urban dweller to continue or discontinue his urban residence.

The final in-depth examination of the demand view of abandonment focusses upon the "low end" real estate sector. Are there institutional or program blockages here which would at all alter the demand for core housing? Participants in the transfer process of marginal properties are examined and their impact on local housing demand gauged. The question to be answered here is not whether the existence of illegal profit taking or excesses by banks, mortgage companies, and/or brokers is sufficient to damage the local market but rather is there sufficient *interest* in core realty by potential buyers which would render institutional foul play an annoyance rather than a devastation.

In-depth analysis also must be afforded to key elements for the supply explanation of abandonment. Analysis, therefore, is directed both to those who seem to be abandoning parcels (the slumlords of old) and also to those who are retaining parcels — the new minority home buyers.

Are the abandoners of residential properties of a certain age, race, and income, i.e., are they the elderly whose retention rate of oversized structures would have been marginal in any case or are the abandoners young, urban employed families to whom urban residence would have been a reasonable decision?

In the case of the minority homebuyer the question of the retention of a wasting asset also must be broached. Are those who are retarding abandonment and stabilizing the urban environment receiving equitable rewards for exercising a positive decision to remain? Or are they, in comparison to those who flee to the suburban frontiers, falling farther and farther behind in the capital accumulation aspect of individual home ownership?

The final supply aspect of residential abandonment which must be examined is tax delinquency. Is the illegal avenue of reduced operating expense available to those who shun annual property tax requirements being used in a positive fashion to maintain or retain structures? Are tax delinquent structures better maintained and more often found in a non-abandoned state?

The summary which follows presents pertinent findings in these areas. Similarly, the larger study is keyed both in direction and order of presentation to this basic research design.

## SUMMARY

### Supply Aspects of Residential Abandonment

In Newark, New Jersey, a key to the abandonment process appears to be prior property tax arrearage. Also contributing to the abandonment process is the heavy presence of nonwhite tenants resident in white-owned structures whose cost schedule includes funds allocated for "arm's length" operation, that is, either professionally managed or employing a professional rent collector.

Following this selection criteria in order of importance is a locational variable which expresses abandonment as a function of areas of increasing adjacent housing deterioration, i.e., once the tax arrearage, the fact of arm's length operation, and the tenant/owner racial profile of rental urban housing have been established as corollaries of abandonment, then location of the parcel seems to play an important part. Another important index which arises in areas of increasing abandonment is the lack of a mortgage or significant monetary interest in the property.

It appears, after examining this and previous indices, that abandonment may well be the nail in the coffin of the "classic" view of the tenement landlord. The reality is that the white owner in an urban core area increasingly is unable to rent his mortgage-free structures to poor blacks and still derive the necessary income to meet expenses (prime among them are taxes) and turn the necessary profit to remain solvent. It may well be, however, that the tenants themselves have partially caused the dissolution of this market. It can neither be said that the abandoned structures in Newark, as detailed later in this work, were in relatively worse condition eight years previously than their surrounding nonabandoned neighbors nor were they of a certain "tenement type" in terms of either construction or number of units. Further, the owners of abandoned buildings were not particularly aged, nor did they evidence any notable lack of real estate know-how.

It also does *not* appear to hold that succeeding waves of tenement landlords were milking parcels and from this deriving substantial income. It may well be that if there were once a tenement landlord, in the classic sense, he is fast disappearing. There appears to be a greater tendency for abandoned parcels to have been owned by people who had at least ten years' experience in the real estate market and who had incomes in 1964 in excess of $8,000, largely contributed to by their real estate holdings. These current owners wanted to sell their buildings eight to ten years prior to abandonment and could not. Today they bitterly complain that the tenantry, and not taxes or other city ills, is preventing them from improving upon or recouping all or a portion of the parcel's value.

## Demand Aspects of Residential Abandonment

Residential abandonment in terms of environment appears to increase in areas of high black and Puerto Rican concentration and thus becomes a part of the dismal social and environmental conditions which are normally associated with these subpopulations, i.e., persons in these areas suffer loss of housing through abandonment, in addition to being characterized by lack of education, lack of resources, and both high crowding and large numbers of children.

The presence of affluence, expressed in terms of neighborhood family income, education, and monthly housing cost, is associated with a lack of abandonment. What is being stated here to some degree seems obvious, i.e., that residential abandonment occurs more frequently in areas of decreasing economic demand — those areas judged socially and economically substandard regardless of specific criteria. In the opposite case, abandonment is less frequent in areas where people of higher socioeconomic status reside and consequently, where housing demands to a substantial degree are more durable.

## The Relationship of Supply to Demand

It is necessary now to return once more to the supply aspects of abandonment to gain a perspective for the *relationships* in evidence between these two indices. It should be noticed that within the supply set, the locational variable appeared to be demonstrably of secondary importance to those variables representing characteristics of both tax arrearage and those of the owner and tenant. Thus while it is easy to surmise that "slums breed abandonment" or vice versa, it may well be true that this may be said *only* to the degree that both tax arrearage and owner/tenant characteristics also vary significantly across these areas. In other words, high abandonment would only be synonymous with slum neighborhoods if one also found in these neighborhoods increased levels of tax arrearage and the combination of a white owner/black tenant in a rental relationship where structural repairs were explicitly out of pocket rather than of a self-help kind. One may be just as likely to discover within a slum neighborhood a white cooperative or townhouse where sweat equity, the cooperative arrangement, or the uniqueness of the structure has preserved the shelter in the face of diminishing area demand.

## The Environment of Residential Abandonment

The pace of urban decay, exemplified by secondary industrial cities, has outrun all the remedies that have been applied. It is easy to rail against the faulty administration of many of the remedial programs, of layers of graft or mismanagement, of sins of commission and irrelevance. Certainly they have existed and perhaps still continue. But they tend to hide rather than typify the underlying reality, providing a false feeling of assurance that, given a better administration, or more comprehending funding agencies, or some magic inspiration of imagination, all could be made well.

Certainly all of these inputs are most important, and great strides have been taken in their accomplishment. However, the basic changes in the city's reason for being, its economic base, its service as a focal point for jobs, residences, shopping, and entertainment have all been altered substantially and perhaps irremediably.

The out-migration of wealth and the in-migration of poverty in individual city after city has yet to generate an overall understanding. Certainly the reality is shared by most of our older, northeastern municipalities. The problems of a declining economic base, increasingly called upon to provide greater and more varied forms of social support, are the common denominator of every meeting of central city mayors. Public assistance rolls have increased by no less than 15 percent in the five major northeastern cities from 1971 to 1972. There is little indication that in the future gross welfare totals will be reduced significantly.

Municipalities in which abandonment is rampant are those whose absolute populations are declining, whose more affluent minority members, as fair housing legislation becomes broadened, are voting with their feet — out of the city. There is a new way of life in the suburbs, and with increasing fiscal capacity and choice, many of America's minority families want to join it. The remnant white population is aging and is not being replaced.

In few areas of social concern are the reality and the publically held image at further distance than they are in the field of urban housing. The image is one of an essentially economically productive, private housing market in which for any of a variety of reasons (and these latter, in any case, open to governmental policy) the balance between profits and quality of service delivered has been aborted.

Public intervention has taken a variety of forms; most of them have been concerned with clearing the encumbrances which seemingly deny the basic profitability of combining the provision of good housing both for the renters and owners. These efforts are essentially bankrupt in many cities. Code enforcement, for example, when private owners are fleeing the market, becomes self-defeating.

The concept of urban renewal assumed a basic level of private demand for redeveloping urban core areas, frustrated by the difficulties of securing large parcels with a clear title. The basic weakness of the market in these cities has made it ineffective. Where urban renewal has been consummated between public players, i.e., a new government General Services Administration building, a government guaranteed and financed housing project, or the like, it has not been contagious. There has been no ancillary growth generated by the governmental act — whose inspiration was derived from the hopes of essentially providing pump priming. In many cases private abandonment is outrunning public renewal. Even in 1964-1965 it was clear that in the front-runner cities the "smart" money was leaving. Now it is largely gone. The bulk of those who have not abandoned are in possession by default rather than by intent. Alternate avenues of escape have been closed. The classic slumlord remains in only the most hard core areas; there resident ownership is negligible as few buyers purchase for residence purposes. Minority landlords, the new hope for retarding abandonment, are shunning these areas. The only possible purchasers are large scale operators buying (or sometimes practically being given) parcels very, very cheaply. Their major motivation is not improvement and long-term operations, but rather windfall profits through urban renewal, highway landtaking, or the like. And if this does not come about they, too, will abandon. In the true hard core, other than this melancholy speculation, the city is the only property "buyer" and purely by default.

## Public Safety and Abandonment

There can be few aspects of urban life in which myth and reality are as inextricably interwoven as that of public safety. Regardless of the proportion of each of these, their results in consumer response, whether tenant or owner, is all too evident. Unless the impact of this basic insecurity can be allayed, no measure of physical rebuilding, no improvement in other services, can have any lasting measure of success.

Within the statistics of *crime* in urban areas, the subject of abandoned parcels plays a central role. The occurrence of abandonment functions in the same geographic areas as high crime. Rising incidence of crime and abandonment appear to be the characteristic traits of neighborhoods undergoing rapid and malign social change. Care must be taken, however, not to draw causal relationships between specific types of crime and abandoned buildings. Vacant parcels may not cause crime, but rather provide an opportunity for its occurrence — they serve as facilitating locations as well as inspiration.

In Newark, of all the Index Crimes taking place within the city, nearly 4 percent now take place within abandoned buildings. In this city, ten murders, fifteen rapes, and close to 150 incidents of assault and battery occurred in 1971 within vacant buildings. For lesser crimes, the same year saw close to 200 incidents of malicious mischief or disorderly conduct violations and 100 incidents of narcotics offenses. Finally, police assistance was required for at least twenty-three natural deaths and close to fifty cases of falls, animal bites, sicknesses, and the like.

Since it is almost an impossible task to account for the real number of criminal acts committed in vacant structures, the figures on criminal activity in abandoned parcels must be seen as extremely conservative. The abandoned structure in its standing vacant state, is thus a haven for criminal activity, both premeditated and spontaneous.

The measure of the social disintegration which characterizes the core area is the trivia which often instigates deliberately-set *fires:* two men quarrel — the loser sets fire to the other's home; a man is ejected from a tavern — he returns at night and sets fire to it; children are playing in an abandoned building and set it afire — adjacent structures are caught up in the conflagration and another fifty families lose the pitifully small collection of lifetime treasures which they may have accumulated and are forced to find new housing, often leaving behind either maimed or killed members.

Severe fires in vacant residential buildings in Newark constitute 21.2 percent of all severe fires that occurred in the city during the period 1970-1971. The number of standing, vacant buildings, though rapidly increasing, amounts to less than 5 percent of the total number of structures in the city. The frequency of severe fires occurring in them is four times the rate occurring within the city's population of structures. From these figures it would appear that the rate of severe fires within abandoned buildings is roughly equivalent to the incidence of all fires (major and minor) within generally occupied structures. To place this statement in perspective one must realize that three-fourths of the fire activity in the population of structures at large are minor fires which occur much less frequently in abandoned structures.

The magnitude of the figures previously discussed is contributed to significantly by the phenomenon of recurring fires in abandoned buildings. Again in Newark, among eighty-four buildings classified as abandoned within an interviewed sample subset, 22 percent experienced at least one instance of minor or major fire after complete vacancy, and 11 percent suffered multiples of two to five instances.

This would indicate that in the 2,000 vacant buildings standing in that city, there is a good chance that in excess of 440 will have to be serviced annually by the Fire Department at least once, and half that number on multiple occasions. Looking at it another way and expanding this relationship to other cities, roughly one fire call annually for every two standing, vacant buildings may be anticipated. In addition, since the buildings are unoccupied and in most cases the nature of the incident is not obvious, by definition, fire officials must anticipate an arson investigation in some 90 percent of the cases.

## The Participants in Abandonment

### *The "Abandoners": The Tenement Landlords*

The whole web of governmental intervention in the private housing sphere, as well as a substantial part of private investment, operates in great measure through the matrix of the landlord. With the exception of public housing, alternative approaches to the ownership and management of low income housing have been much more frequent in the verbal than in the physical, i.e., much more talked about than built. Low income housing cooperatives are just beginning to make a significant impact on the market; the vast bulk of central city housing remains in forms of ownership and management which have changed little over the last hundred years.

One of the more satisfying folk figures of our time is that of the slumlord. This is an individual who popularly is supposed to dominate the low income private housing stock, and who has not only grown wealthy historically because of his tenure, but is currently securing a more than adequate return on his properties. The myth is satisfying because it leads to the belief that the major input necessary to provide more adequate standards of maintenance and operating behavior is to get this overfed individual to disgorge some of his excess earnings; the basic pie of rents is adequate both to support owner interests in holding on to his parcels and continuing their operation while still providing the tenants with adequate service inputs. The bulk of governmental measures in the older housing sphere has revolved around this concept, whether it is tax abatement in order to assure the owner that improvements will not be overassessed, long-term inexpensive loans for essential repairs in line with code enforcement efforts, or any of the more localized activities along these same lines. All of them essentially are based on the belief in the desirability, not only from a social point of view but also from the owner's economic point of view, of holding onto his properties. They presume a basic economic viability in operating low income housing. Thus governmental intervention has essentially been enabling legislation not to change present yields, but rather to permit better services and improved structures without altering the basic rent/expense ratios.

Many of these efforts at intervention have been disappointing in their results. In many cases there have been considerable problems in administering the programs. The legal work, for example, involved in the 312 Program* which has been a mainstay in providing twenty-five year, 3 percent interest financing for capital improvements and code standard maintenance in Urban Renewal and Concentrated Code Enforcement areas has inhibited its use. But in some cases even the Grant-in-Aid Program† which gives grants without repayments of up to $3,500 to resident owners in buildings with less than four units, has been substantially underutilized.

Clearly the vision of the owners, their sophistication, their readiness to see their own best interests, is brought into question. Or is it perhaps that the public vision of their best interests and their private vision of reality are really at odds?

While the large-scale, nonresident slumlords are far from an insignificant proportion of total ownership, as previous research indicates, the degree of concentration is much overstated.

In reality the changes in form and function of the older city and the folkways of its inhabitants, the great migration patterns which have dominated the demographic considerations in and about the United States metropolitan areas for decades, and, more recently, urban racial unrest, have occasioned a housing market situation of virtual stagnation. The combination of risk, decreasing profitability, and loss of potential for capital gains has substantially restricted the kinds of professional owners who are willing to invest in slum properties. It takes a highly insensitive individual to become a professional nonresident owner of slum property, in the light of present societal attitudes. This is not an individual who is easily influenced to invest his money unless an appropriate return can be secured.

---

*Section 312 of the 1964 Housing Act provides long-term loans for extensive rehabilitation within designated program areas.

†Section 115 of the 1965 Housing Act is a grant program for persons of limited income for the purpose of correctiong minor code violations.

*There is as yet, however, no adequate replacement for these hard core tenement owners.* The minority owner (to be discussed subsequently), frequently buying for residence rather than income purposes, is avoiding the worst areas of the city. This leaves a definite gap as to who will manage hard core, urban realty. City-employed bureaucrats have characteristically done a poor job at housing management. The condition and solvency of housing run by local authorities attest to this.

Yet, annually, private ownership in northeastern and midwestern urban core areas is turning over to any taker, 1 to 2 percent of the extant housing stock. It may well be that to put this hard core housing to use the city must employ in quasi-public fashion those who were in business before and left, i.e., the tenement landlords.

## *Those Who Remain: The New Minority Landlords*

One of the most provocative and potentially important developments of our time is the increased level of minority group ownership of central city real property. This is a trend which parallels that of all the other earlier immigrant groups into the city — first as tenants, then as owners, typically of the most marginal of parcels, then with the formation of capital, the movement into the middle class mainstream. Will this sequence be replicated for our present minority group owners, both Spanish and black?

From the overall society's point of view the most crucial question of all is whether the new owners can make it, whether there is a potential for capital accumulation and for success in the future through this type of acquisition. The vigor of private ownership in a decaying city clearly is dependent upon the future growth of such activity. How then do these minority group owners view the future? What are their problems and are there any ways that society can optimize the turnover mechanisms?

Certainly for many of the minority group homeowners interviewed in the Newark study, the suburban one-family house typically is much too expensive an investment. They rather require income producing properties: the three-family house and the small tenement of Newark — these are the possible alternatives. If the sweat and savings of these kinds of families are to be utilized by society to stabilize the city, how can we insure an appropriate reward mechanism? If we do not, the results will be very evident.

The new owners of the sixties may have had little romance about their prospects, but they had great confidence in their capacity to maintain and improve the properties which they had acquired, to secure good living within them, both for themselves and their children. These same owners of the early 1970s still preserve some level of spark. Their buildings are better maintained, their hopes for the future still more considerable than for longer-term white holders in the same areas, but this positive feeling is fast ebbing, based on experience within the city.

This experience is several-fold. On the one hand, the basic parameters are degenerating: fear of crime, fire, and drugs may be far from abstractions to suburbanites, but to the central cityite and particularly in parts of the city dominated by minority group home buyers, they are deadly realities. In addition, the minority home buyer of a decade ago now finds his investment at a dead end — there are no potential buyers. How can society cope with this?

The problem is not merely one of equity, it is rather central to the preservation of the city. If a new, stable, middle class resident operating group cannot be secured — then the private residential market in the city is doomed. But, as yet, governmental action in this frontier has been confined to the awkward giant of acquisition — providing financing for the purchase of a property, and in that very act often inflating the costs — rather than necessarily imparting the skill for successful operation or, even more important, ensuring a take-out mechanism, a resale after a period of years which will serve as a reward for sustained care and demonstrably competent operating procedures.

One thing is clear, it must be governmental intervention in this frontier. Primary lenders in urban areas — commercial and mutual savings banks, savings and loan associations, insurance companies, and even individuals — are getting out of the inner city mortgage lending business. They are replaced by mortgage companies which deal almost exclusively in insured loans. Given the excesses which have been attributed to some of the procedures under the latter, even the mortgage companies may soon be leaving the scene.

The substantial default rates that are characteristic of the urban real estate market are, within conventional lending procedures, only encompassed with great difficulty. Given the risks involved and the potential for abandonment, normal profit standards and limited operating and supervisory margins may be inappropriate. What is required are completely new financial operating mechanisms, new means of property acquisition from the reluctant to new operating owners, from the owner by default to one of positive intent. Again, for this, there must be a reward mechanism — a take-out mechanism — after a period of years of good operation for the new owner operator.

Minority home ownership appears to be increasing within urban areas. In 1972 for many secondary, older industrial cities, there were probably more minority home purchasers than white ones. These new owners frequently differ from their predecessors in that their equity is low, their financial capacities limited. But their relative youth and a high level of resident ownership, the latter several times the proportion of white buyers, tend to yield better operation and maintenance of structures.

But where is public policy to be directed in this regard? *While minority home ownership is good for the building and for the municipality, is it good for the owner?* This group typically is buying for the purpose of residence rather than business; it provides stability for the neighborhood and unquestionably is invaluable to the city, but certainly in terms of the individual the situation is more complex.

One of the primary functions of home ownership in our society over the last generation has been for the purpose of capital accumulation. For most of the lower and even middle socio-economic groups, it is the long-term holding of a house, the paying down of a mortgage and the building up of equity, coupled with increasing value through inflation, which has provided the major form of securing a nest egg. The black home buyer in Newark of the 1960s has seen his investment at a standstill, while suburban equivalents doubled and tripled over the same length of time.

## Tax Delinquency/The "Low End" Real Estate Sector and Abandonment

### *Tax Delinquency*

Although all abandoned buildings may not be tax delinquent, and vice versa, the frequency with which tax delinquency signals owner abandonment (and the preceding or subsequent departure of tenants) means that the two must be discussed as an interrelated problem. In pursuing the relationship it has been found that *an abandoned property is likely also to be a tax delinquent property in at least two out of every three cases.*

Having suggested the presence of an associative relationship between these two phenomena, it then becomes necessary to examine those conditions that tend to produce tax delinquency. It has been found in this study that tax delinquent parcels are more likely to be of poorer absolute quality in terms of an interviewer's evaluation of the condition of other structures with which he/she is familiar, to be operated by landlords who have higher proportions of tenants who are on welfare, to have higher vacancy rates, to be one of multiple parcels owned by a landlord, and to be of less relative quality than surrounding neighbors.

Given the resulting lack of cash flow in the rental situation, the owner, in order to maintain the building as a viable entity, must eliminate a significant recurring cost. Frequently, therefore, he turns to municipal tax delinquency — an avenue of illegal credit engendering the slowest and least severe form of reprimand. Obligations often go unpaid for a period of up to four years with little censure and almost complete assurance that, due to waning private market interest, there will be no property loss. Yet the building ultimately becomes abandoned.

The result is that the city, through tax default, is becoming the unwilling owner of an increasing share of urban realty. Since the city steps in to purchase abandoned structures, it unwittingly encourages owners to *destroy through nonimprovement.* In other words, tax delinquency becomes the incentive for abandonment.

Through tax delinquency the landlord is in effect guaranteed a selling price equal to or greater than he could obtain through the private market. A landlord stands to benefit further by failing to improve his property, thereby being able to pocket the savings. Specifically, there is no indication that a well maintained property in Newark would bring its owner substantially more money than a property in a state of disrepair. Why then should a landlord bother maintaining a property for ultimate sale if he knows that only a limited market exists and that he can do as well in an unlimited market (municipal purchase) with no further outlay of cash for improvements?

## *The Low End Real Estate Sector*

At the time of this study, investigations in Newark and indictments in New York City and other urban communities are being undertaken involving speculators who exceed prudent risk/reward returns. The scenario at question is often repeated. A speculator, usually affiliated with a real estate broker, finds a prospective seller, often white, and aged, owning a house in a changing neighborhood. An offer is made to the seller by the broker often well *below* the actual market value of the parcel. In the owner's desperation to leave the deteriorating neighborhood the offer is accepted, and the property is taken over by the speculator. Improvements which must be made in order to qualify under a specific governmental program are not made, yet an inspection approval is granted from the overseeing federal agency and the parcel receives top heavy mortgage reflective of both substantial profits to the broker and the inclusion of closing costs for the buyer. The latter in the central city is frequently a member of a minority group, in many cases with numerous children. Within a short period of time the building is found to be in a gross state of disrepair and abandonment is frequently in the offing.

The pathos of the act and the illegitimate actions of its participants tend to mask the real question, i.e., is participation in the local real estate market sufficiently strong to sustain such excesses. The feeling is that it is not. The central city housing market is weak and those who pay for its sustenance are discontented. Finagling in this sector, if unchecked, will ultimately lead to a permanent discontinuance of interest in urban and publicly assisted housing.

## The Situation in Brief

Why then is residential abandonment taking place? In a limited economic sense it simply is a reflection of a market reality wherein revenues do not equal or exceed costs. There is a limited level of rent available to a landlord within the core, yet at the same time he is faced by uncontrollable increases in operating costs: taxes, repairs, insurance costs, security of repair, and collection personnel, all combined to make immediate yields precarious. And even when the latter are relatively generous, they are offset by the difficulties of dealing with problem tenants, not infrequently the belligerent acts of interracial conflict, as well as a dim view of the future worth of the parcel. *The key fact of life here is not owners giving up the business, that is a constant in any form of enterprise, the unique element is rather the fact that there are so few alternate buyers — regardless of price.*

What are the statistical linkages of abandonment? They are hard core locations, parcels in tax arrears, white owners who would like to sell but cannot and who frequently rent to black tenants, about whom they have mounting complaints. These are characteristics of shelter well down the road to forced retirement.

Why are there no alternate buyers? The environment of abandonment is the key here. This is illustrated by both a growing fiscal incapacity of the city and by a fear on the part of remaining residents that they will be victimized by either crime or fire.

Urban tax delinquency functions in the same general areas as abandonment, and is contributed to and linked to similar indices, i.e., basic poverty, high welfare tenantry, nonresident multi-parcel owners, and high neighborhood transiency. The whole fiscal base of the city is hostage to the weakness of its basic market reality.

Crime and fire are harsh facts both preceding and following abandonment. They provide an environment in which marginal rates of return simply are outweighed by risk; an environment in which even the well maintained parcel is swept away by neighborhood dangers. Strangely enough, in a semi-biological way, crime and fire both conspire to convert neighborhoods and buildings and shells of buildings to a form which in turn is even more conducive to premature abandonment.

There is evidence that both mainstays of low-end urban realty, i.e., minority and white tenement landlords, are leaving the city, both as owner/operators and investors. To a certain degree this must be expected, yet the tide must be abated. *The city and its future are no longer a prime concern to much of our society. A generation of post-World War II suburbanites is rising that has little of the ties of memory, of shopping or even of job location which assured its earlier psychological primacy. But the city and, much more important, its people must be helped. Dramatic success stories in the arena may be few — the essentials of continuous grinding effort, however, must be maintained. We have no other choice.*

## Notes

1. George Sternlieb, "Some Aspects of the Abandoned House Problem" (New Brunswick, N.J.: Rutgers University, Center for Urban Policy Research, 23 July 1970).

2. Franklin J. James, Robert W. Burchell, and James W. Hughes, "Race, Profit and Housing Abandonment in Newark," *Proceedings of the American Real Estate and Urban Economic Associations*, vol. 5 (1972) forthcoming.

3. Edgar M. Hoover and Raymond Vernon, *Anatomy of a Metropolis* (New York: Doubleday Anchor, 1962):183-198.

4. Chester Rapkin, letter in *Journal of Housing*, vol. 17 (May 1960):191.

5. George Sternlieb, Robert W. Burchell, Franklin J. James, and James W. Hughes, "Housing Abandonment in the Urban Core," *Journal of the American Institute of Planners* (forthcoming).

6. Gregory K. Ingram and John F. Kain, "A Simple Model of Housing Production and the Abandonment Problem," *Proceedings of the American Real Estate and Urban Economics Associations*, vol. 5 (1972) forthcoming.

# 1

# THE ENVIRONMENT OF ABANDONMENT: NEWARK — A DECADE'S CHANGE

Newark, New Jersey, a city of 380,000 inhabitants, is a focal point in the megalopolis which stretches from Boston to Norfolk, Virginia, a location which historically made it a center of manufacturing and distribution (Exhibit 1-1).

In 1950 it was economically viable and looked back at ten years of growth. Two decades later it has been deserted by much of its retailing, distribution, and manufacturing interests and a large share of its white middle and upper income populations. Now it is in the last stages of the cycle of changes being experienced by central cities.

The election of Newark's first black mayor in 1970 reflects the racial shift in the city over the last twenty years. In 1950 the city's population was 17 percent black; by 1970 this proportion had increased to 54 percent. Accompanying the racial shift have been the characteristic black-white problems of our time. Newark has had its share of both urban riots (Exhibit 1-2) and the embittered political battles between militants and those moderates acceptable as leaders to the remaining whites.

The influx of rural, low income families has overburdened municipal services and facilities. As the ratable base has deteriorated the local tax rate has been driven upward in an unsuccessful attempt to maintain fiscal stability (Exhibit 1-3). This effort has not been sufficient and municipal services have been curtailed to the point of bare

# EXHIBIT 1-1
## NEWARK, NEW JERSEY — A CORRIDOR CITY IN MEGALOPOLIS

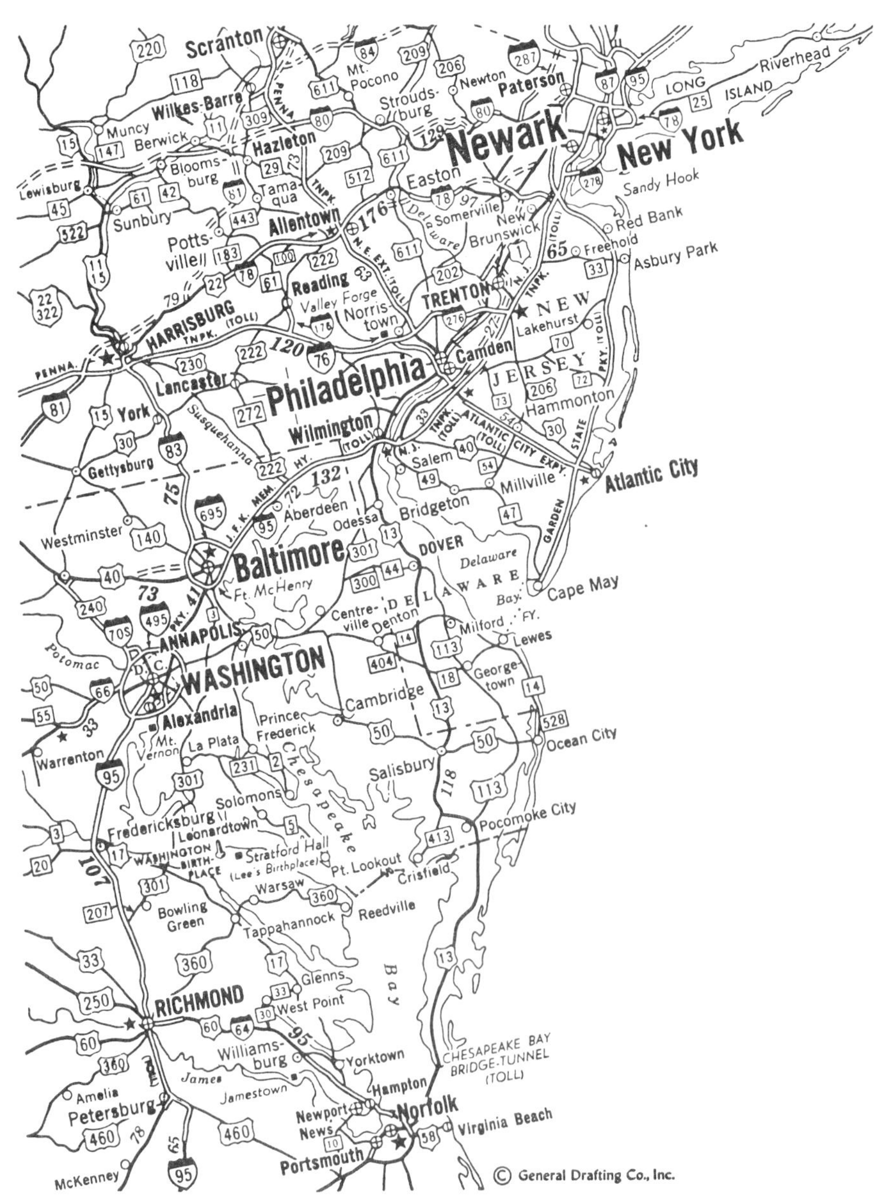

# EXHIBIT 1-2
## NEWARK'S RACIAL CONFRONTATIONS_ JULY 1967

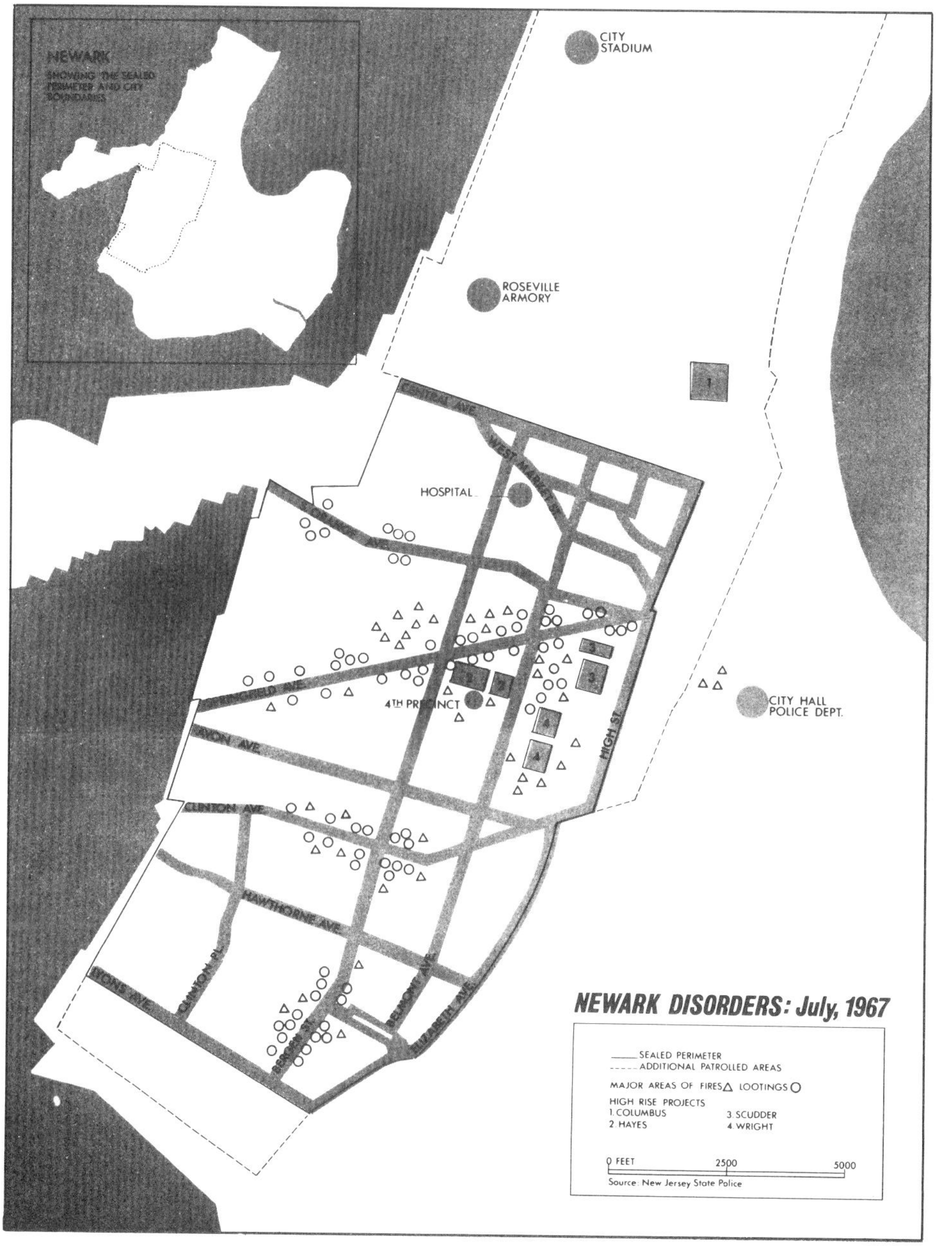

Source: Robert D. Lilley. Report for Action (Trenton, N.J., Governor's Select Committee Commission on Civil Disorder, State of New Jersey, February 1968).

existence in the face of ever increasing demands. Furthermore, Newark has had more than its share of graft and corruption, which obviously does not contribute to fiscal stability.

A statement by Newark's current mayor sums up his city's situation most perceptively: "Wherever the nation's cities are going, Newark is going to get there first."

EXHIBIT 1-3

LOCAL PROPERTY TAX RATE AND NET VALUATION TAXABLE OVER TIME, NEWARK, 1960-1972

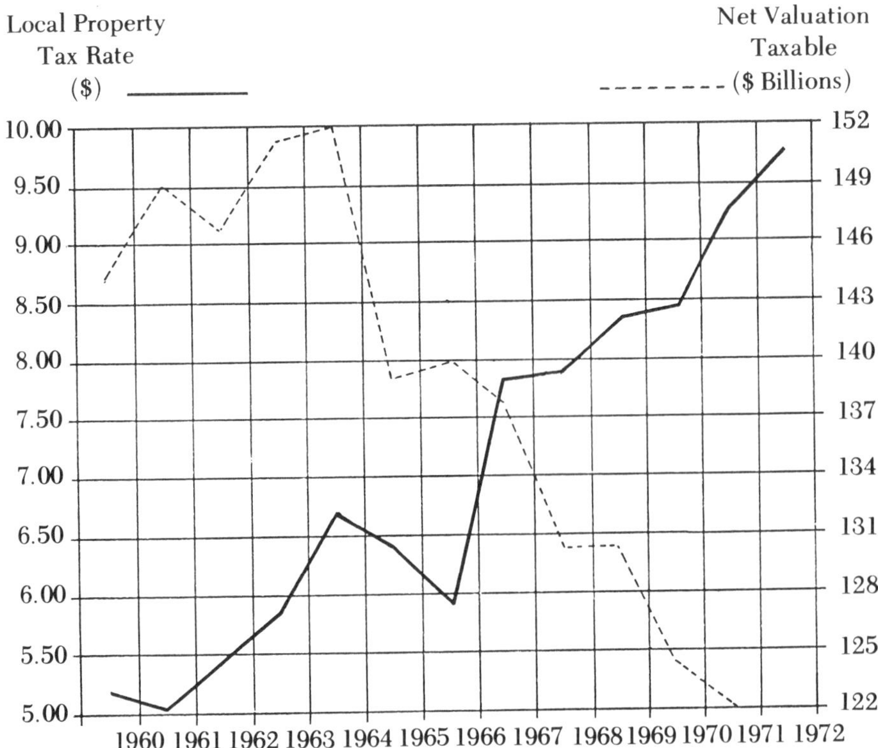


Source: City of Newark, Tax Assessor's Office. State of New Jersey, *Annual Report,* Division of Taxation (1960-1972).

## PEOPLE AND THE CITY
### Gross Population Changes and Racial Shifts

By far the most dramatic changes in the city over the decade were in its ethnic subpopulations. The out-migration of Newark's white population coupled with the in-migration of blacks and Puerto Ricans produced a considerable shift in the ethnic composition, both of core-area neighborhoods and, to a substantial degree, of the city as a whole.[1]

In 1960 approximately 62 percent of Newark's 400,000 population was white, another 35 percent was black, and the remaining 3 percent was distributed between Asian and Spanish-speaking populations, less than a third of whom were Puerto Rican. A decade later, Newark's combined black and Puerto Rican population had risen close to the previous white population level (59 percent), with the non-Puerto Rican white population now just over 40 percent of a total population which had been depleted by 22,000. In the 1960 to 1970 decade alone roughly 100,000 whites left Newark, many for the peripheral suburban areas.

The population depletion in the forty census tracts which make up the central core of the city (Areas 1-3) is phenomenal (Exhibits 1-4 and 1-5). The most severely impacted area in 1960 (Area 1), based on a variety of census categories, now contains less than half of its former residents. The core areas in general have experienced a net loss of 33,000 people while the balance of the city has actually shown a slight population gain of about 11,000.

The changing racial composition of the city is as obvious as the gross population shifts. In the study area for example, two of the three groups of census tracts (Areas 1 and 2) now have a combined black and Puerto Rican population exceeding 90 percent compared with 70 percent in 1960. Area 3, which experienced a large influx of Puerto Ricans, also had the greatest relative increase of combined black and Puerto Rican populations, i.e., a 31 percent absolute increase over the ten-year period.

The shifts in the racial composition in the balance of the city were nearly as great. Newark's North and West Wards, once a bastion of southern European ethnic solidarity, have more than doubled their concentrations of black and Puerto Rican populations. This is coupled with a general decline both in the percent of their populations who are foreign born and those who are married. The immigrant staging ground phenomenon, typified by large European families spending

EXHIBIT 1-4

SAMPLE AREA DETAIL (1964, 1971) REFLECTING 1960 HOUSING CONDITIONS IN NEWARK

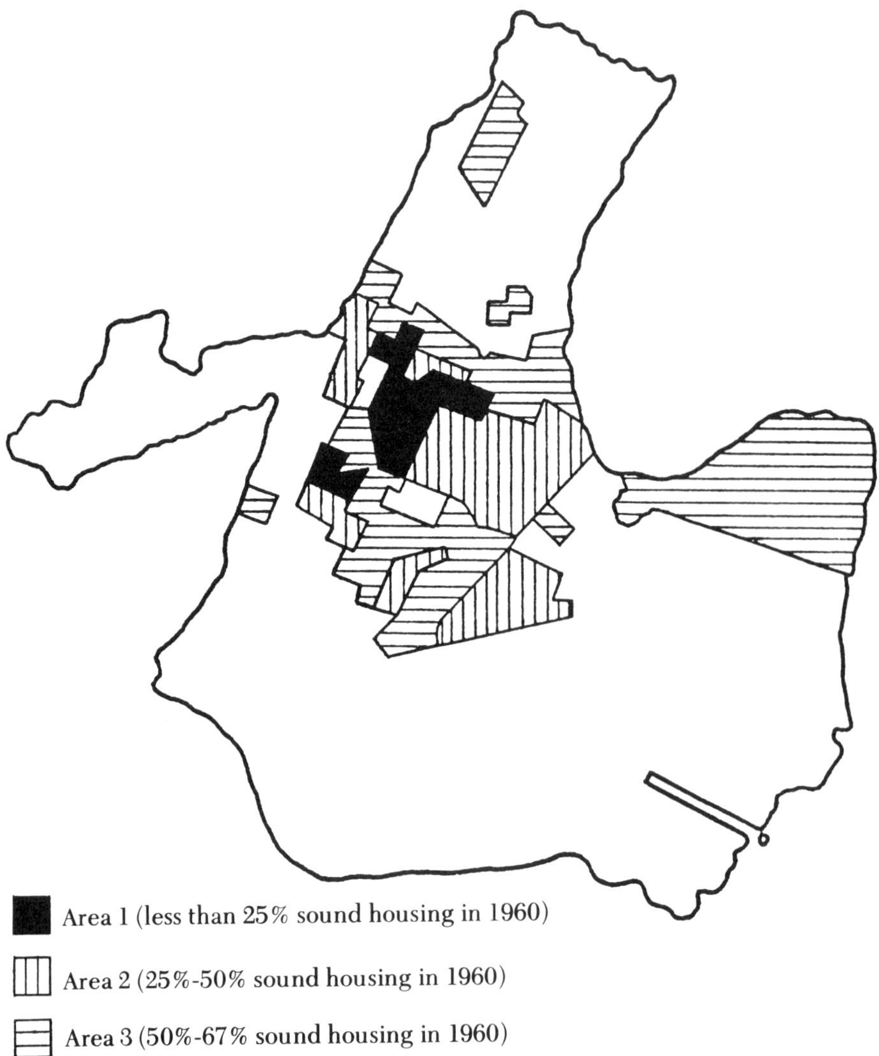


Source: U.S. Census of Housing, 1960.

## EXHIBIT 1-5
## SELECTED CHARACTERISTICS OF THE POPULATION BY AREA, NEWARK, 1960, 1970

| Population Indicators | | AREAS OF THE CITY | | | | | |
|---|---|---|---|---|---|---|---|
| | | Area 1 | Area 2 | Area 3 | Total 1-3 | Balance of City | Total Newark |
| Household population | 1960 | 24,900 | 47,600 | 54,200 | 126,700 | 272,600 | 399,300 |
| | 1970 | 10,400 | 40,100 | 42,800 | 93,360 | 284,000 | 377,300 |
| Percent of the population Negro | 1960 | 76.40 | 64.80 | 46.50 | 59.20 | 23.10 | 34.60 |
| | 1970 | 90.90 | 87.00 | 70.60 | 79.90 | 46.80 | 54.00 |
| Percent of the population Puerto Rican | 1960 | 0.80 | 0.60 | 1.60 | 1.10 | 0.50 | 0.70 |
| | 1970 | 3.20 | 5.70 | 10.50 | 7.60 | 7.20 | 7.30 |
| Percent of the population foreign born | 1960 | 5.20 | 6.20 | 10.80 | 8.00 | 14.60 | 12.50 |
| | 1970 | 2.00 | 2.30 | 7.00 | 4.40 | 12.70 | 10.60 |
| Percent of the population married | 1960 | 42.70 | 44.30 | 43.30 | 43.60 | 48.90 | 47.20 |
| | 1970 | 26.50 | 27.40 | 28.50 | 27.80 | 36.90 | 34.70 |

Source: Percentages derived from tract data, U.S. Census of Population 1960, 1970.

their child rearing years in urban areas, is long past for Newark.

The city today is the transient home of the rural and small town in-migrant. This migratory population is generally young, poor, and of minority group ethnicity. Newark's out-migrants, both black and white, are almost all married. The replacement households are more varied in composition, resulting in a decade's net loss in married population within the city.

## Household Age Structure

Newark's population over 65 years old is decreasing. This is most noticeable in the core areas yet is paralleled to a lesser degree in the rest of the city (Exhibit 1-6). The most noticeable shift, however, is the core area's specific inability to retain its elderly white residents. In these areas the city's 1970 proportion of elderly whites is barely a third of that in 1960. Changing ethnic neighborhoods and increasing center-city crime and fire have apparently occasioned a large portion of the elderly whites to leave the core. This shift is far greater than in the more ethnically homogeneous and secure peripheral areas of the city (Exhibit 1-6).

Another area of considerable decennial change is the age structure of the female population. The median-aged female in 1970 is five years younger than in 1960. In the black dominated general population this magnitude of change exists in all areas of the city. Among white females, however, a similar age structure shift is apparent only in the central core areas.

Another piece of data which may significantly influence the stability of the city as a social system is the incongruity of age structure between sexes (Exhibits 1-7 to 1-14). The exhibits compare age structure of male/female in a predominantly white suburban community to that in Newark's most hard core areas. The differences are apparent.

The most obvious variation is in the gross male/female totals for each case. While in the white working class community there is a rough balance of both male and female throughout the age structure, in Newark there are 10 percent more females than males with the greatest imbalance occurring in the labor force stages of the life cycle (Exhibits 1-9, 1-10, 1-13 and 1-14).

Figures for the period 1960 to 1970 show that the white suburban neighborhood male/female balance was relatively stable while the inner

## EXHIBIT 1-6
## SELECTED CHARACTERISTICS OF AGE STRUCTURE OF THE POPULATION BY AREA, NEWARK, 1960, 1970

| Population Age Characteristics | AREAS OF THE CITY Area 1 | Area 2 | Area 3 | Total 1-3 | Balance of City | Total Newark |
|---|---|---|---|---|---|---|
| Percent of the population over 65 years | | | | | | |
| 1960 | 7.00 | 7.80 | 8.20 | 7.80 | 9.80 | 9.10 |
| 1970 | 4.90 | 5.60 | 5.40 | 5.40 | 8.60 | 7.80 |
| Percent of the white population over 65 years | | | | | | |
| 1960 | 3.80 | 5.10 | 6.70 | 5.50 | 8.90 | 7.80 |
| 1970 | 1.10 | 1.60 | 2.50 | 1.90 | 6.80 | 5.60 |
| Percent of the population under five years | | | | | | |
| 1960 | 13.40 | 12.30 | 13.40 | 13.00 | 10.10 | 11.00 |
| 1970 | 12.40 | 12.70 | 13.10 | 12.90 | 10.20 | 10.90 |
| Percent of the population in elementary school | | | | | | |
| 1960 | 15.50 | 13.40 | 14.60 | 14.30 | 14.70 | 14.60 |
| 1970 | 17.90 | 21.00 | 20.60 | 20.50 | 16.40 | 17.40 |
| Median age female | | | | | | |
| 1960 | 29.58 | 29.43 | 28.86 | 29.22 | 34.58 | 32.88 |
| 1970 | 24.48 | 22.80 | 23.27 | 23.20 | 29.73 | 28.12 |
| Median age white female | | | | | | |
| 1960 | 41.01 | 38.47 | 33.46 | 36.83 | 37.43 | 37.24 |
| 1970 | 25.51 | 34.70 | 29.85 | 31.45 | 37.10 | 35.70 |

Source: Percentages derived from tract data, U.S. Census of Population 1960, 1970.

## EXHIBIT 1-7
### POPULATION HISTOGRAM STABLE BLACK SUBURB EAST ORANGE, NEW JERSEY, 1960

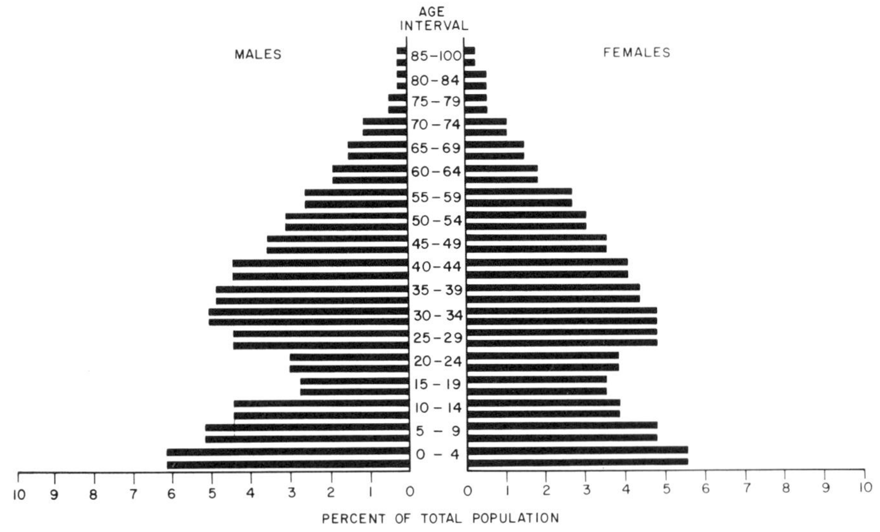


## EXHIBIT 1-8
### POPULATION HISTOGRAM STABLE BLACK SUBURB EAST ORANGE, NEW JERSEY, 1970

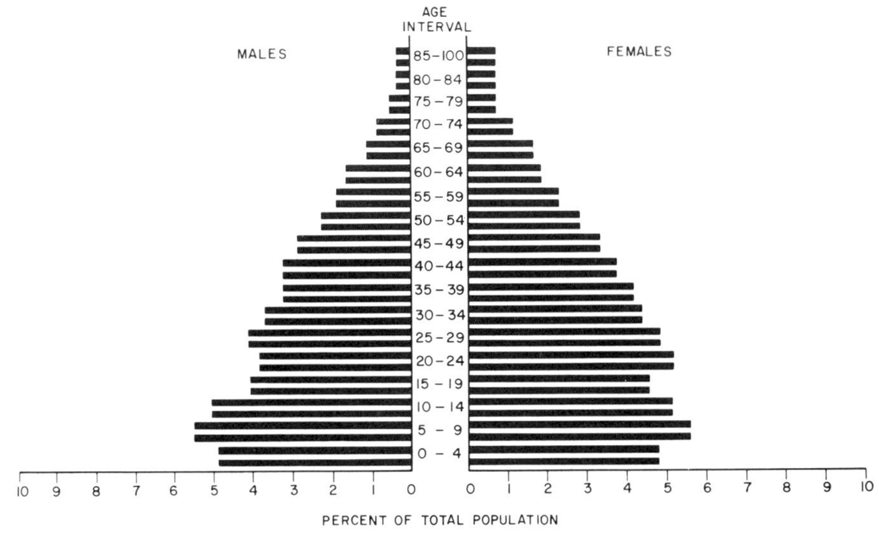

# EXHIBIT 1-9

## POPULATION HISTOGRAM STABLE WHITE SUBURB BLOOMFIELD, NEW JERSEY, 1960

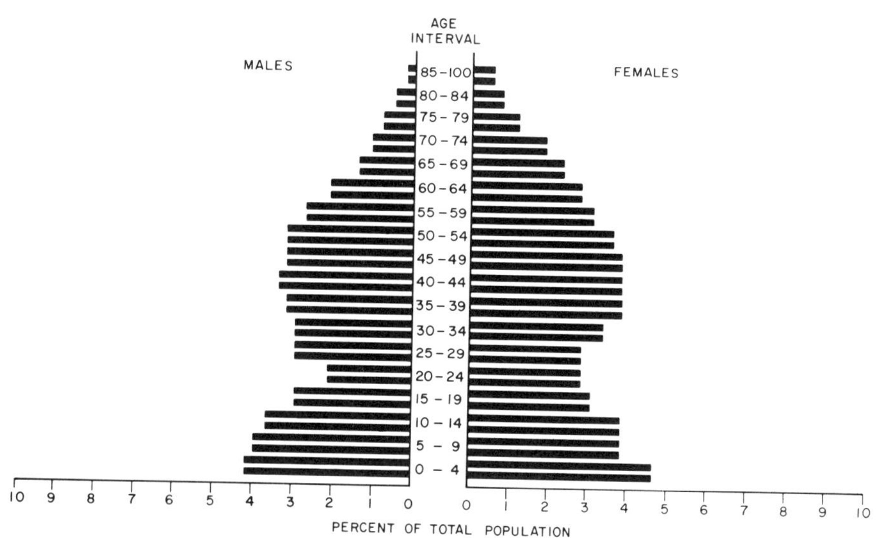


# EXHIBIT 1-10

## POPULATION HISTOGRAM STABLE WHITE SUBURB BLOOMFIELD, NEW JERSEY, 1970

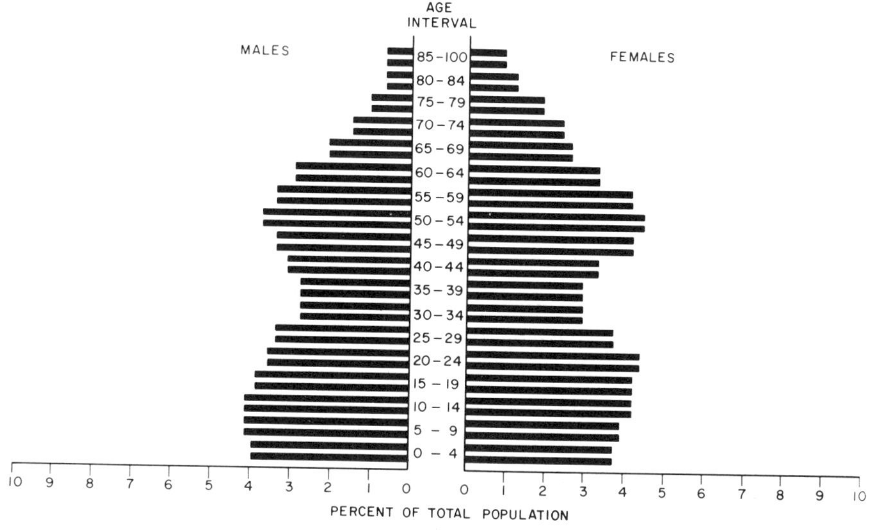

## EXHIBIT 1-11
## POPULATION HISTOGRAM CHANGING BLACK POPULATION NEWARK, NEW JERSEY, 1960

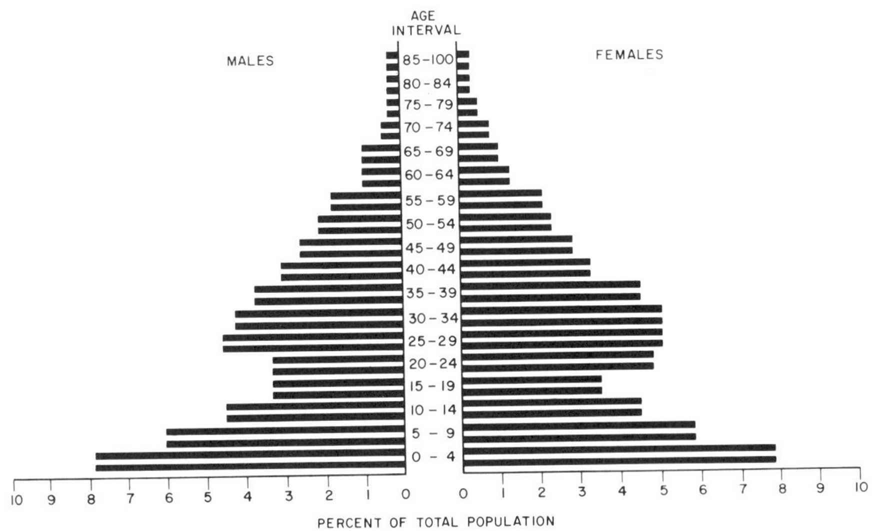


## EXHIBIT 1-12
## POPULATION HISTOGRAM CHANGING BLACK POPULATION NEWARK, NEW JERSEY, 1970

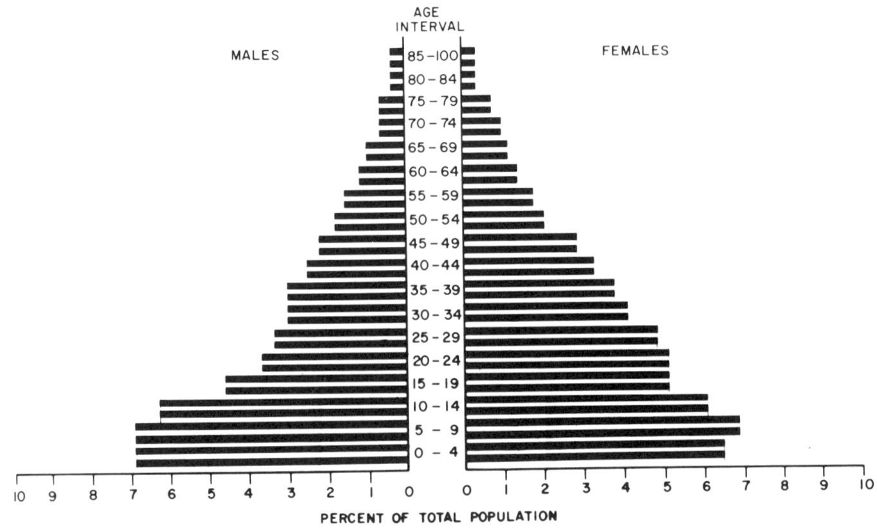

# EXHIBIT 1-13

## POPULATION HISTOGRAM CHANGING WHITE POPULATION NEWARK, NEW JERSEY, 1960

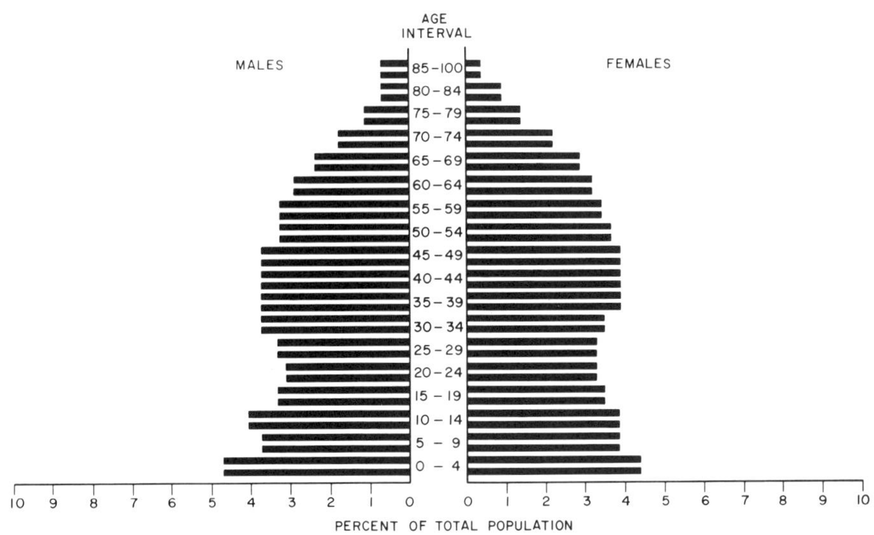


# EXHIBIT 1-14

## POPULATION HISTOGRAM CHANGING WHITE POPULATION NEWARK, NEW JERSEY, 1970

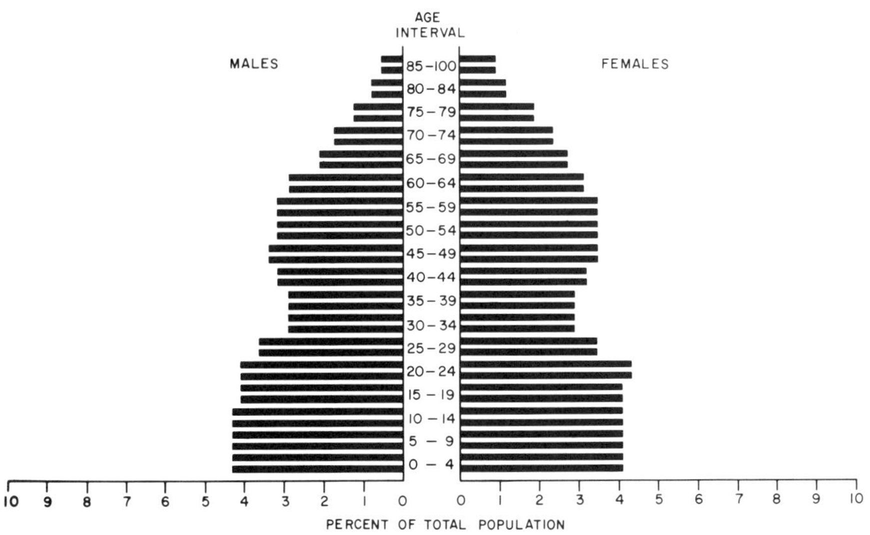

city became more unbalanced, particularly for blacks. A search of equivalent data back to 1940 reveals that the sex gap in the 19 to 34 range among blacks is widening and may indicate a decline in the dominance of the traditional modular family. While the background elements causing this phenomenon are beyond this study, the data raise questions about social trends, and changes in conventional standards.

The final segments of age structure data pertain to measures of youth. From 1960 to 1970 the core areas of Newark increased their elementary school population by nearly a third. This placed significant demands on the center-city primary educational servicing capabilities. There is gross evidence of an obvious lag in gearing up to meet these new demands.

Yet, once the demand has been met, there is a real question as to whether the increased service levels will be necessary for the post-1975 period. Another measure of youthful age structure, the proportion of children under five years old, indicates that the current pressure of center-city educational needs may be a temporary one; the 1970 proportion of pre-school children is almost identical to that which existed and was being serviced in 1960. This factor lends some additional credibility to the thesis that the staging function of the central city, i.e., as an interim residence for large, young, upward mobile families, is being reduced.

## Income and Education

The median household income for the city at large increased annually by 4 percent (barely 1 percent above inflation), which, to some degree, reflects a rise in the proportion of middle income families (above $12,000). The fact remains, however, that the proportion of lower income families (below $4,000) has also increased. This latter finding holds for almost all of Newark's inner-city areas, except for the most hard core. In Area 1 extensive urban renewal has replaced the poorest housing with several developments of desirable, low-rise cooperative units, thus changing the character of the area from low income to lower-middle income.

If Newark is compared to other urban communities within its constituent Standard Metropolitan Statistical Area (SMSA) (Exhibit 1-15) it becomes clear that the city's median household income

## EXHIBIT 1-15

### MEDIAN FAMILY INCOMES OF CONSTITUENT MUNICIPALITIES OF THE NEWARK SMSA 1960-1970 BY TOTAL POPULATION, BLACK POPULATION

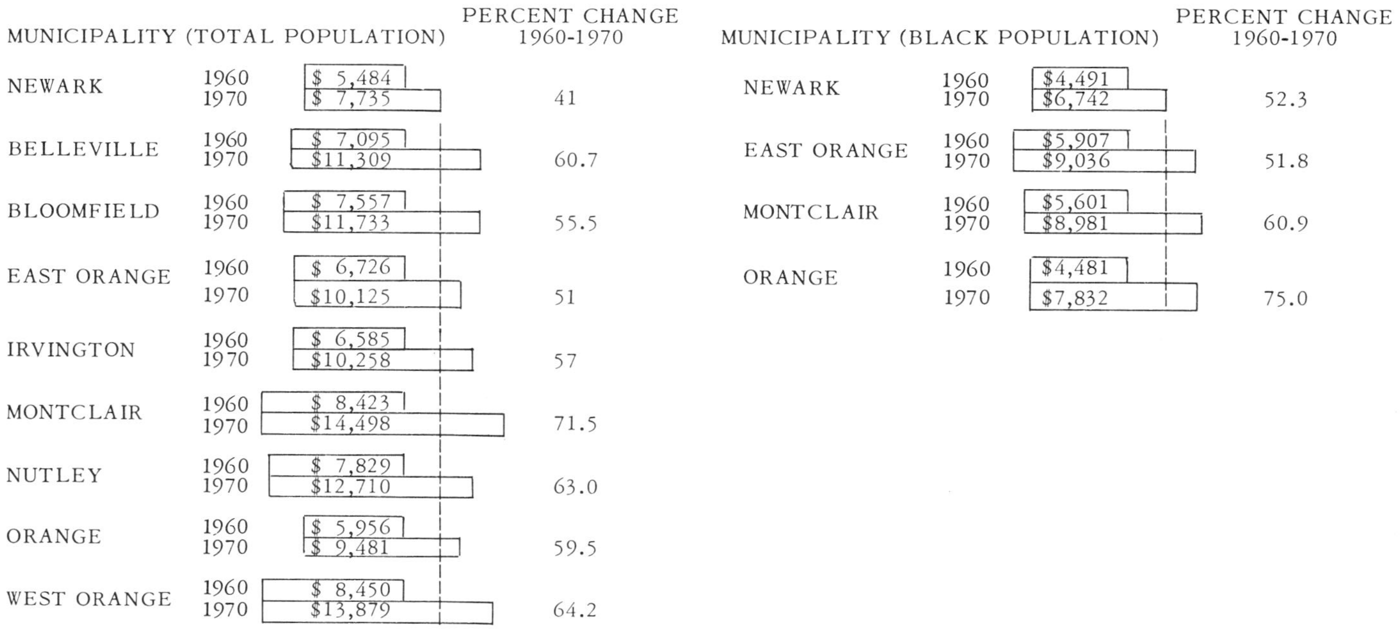

| MUNICIPALITY (TOTAL POPULATION) | Year | Income | PERCENT CHANGE 1960-1970 |
|---|---|---|---|
| NEWARK | 1960 | $ 5,484 | |
| | 1970 | $ 7,735 | 41 |
| BELLEVILLE | 1960 | $ 7,095 | |
| | 1970 | $11,309 | 60.7 |
| BLOOMFIELD | 1960 | $ 7,557 | |
| | 1970 | $11,733 | 55.5 |
| EAST ORANGE | 1960 | $ 6,726 | |
| | 1970 | $10,125 | 51 |
| IRVINGTON | 1960 | $ 6,585 | |
| | 1970 | $10,258 | 57 |
| MONTCLAIR | 1960 | $ 8,423 | |
| | 1970 | $14,498 | 71.5 |
| NUTLEY | 1960 | $ 7,829 | |
| | 1970 | $12,710 | 63.0 |
| ORANGE | 1960 | $ 5,956 | |
| | 1970 | $ 9,481 | 59.5 |
| WEST ORANGE | 1960 | $ 8,450 | |
| | 1970 | $13,879 | 64.2 |

| MUNICIPALITY (BLACK POPULATION) | Year | Income | PERCENT CHANGE 1960-1970 |
|---|---|---|---|
| NEWARK | 1960 | $4,491 | |
| | 1970 | $6,742 | 52.3 |
| EAST ORANGE | 1960 | $5,907 | |
| | 1970 | $9,036 | 51.8 |
| MONTCLAIR | 1960 | $5,601 | |
| | 1970 | $8,981 | 60.9 |
| ORANGE | 1960 | $4,481 | |
| | 1970 | $7,832 | 75.0 |

Source: U.S. Census of Population, 1960, 1970.

increases have lagged behind by a minimum of 10 to 20 percent.

The relative disparity between blacks who leave for the suburbs and those who remain is also apparent. In all but neighboring East Orange, black median income increases in suburban locations within the SMSA have been 10 to 60 percent greater than that of Newark. Thus, it appears that the income-lagging central city of 1960 has fallen even further behind in 1970.

*Black incomes have risen in the decade but the more upwardly mobile of the blacks leave the city.*

Comparative education data for the city are perhaps open to question, but there is almost a full year's gap in terms of median years of education between the core area and the balance of the city. However, if relative progress since 1960 is measured, the core area appears to have made the largest gains (Exhibit 1-16). On review, the bulk of these gains must be attributed to the census, counting students as part of Newark's inner-city resident population and growth in this grouping over the period 1960 to 1970. This is seen in both the median years of education and percent of high school and college graduates of Area 1. Yet if other inner-city locations (Areas 2 and 3) are compared to the balance of the city, the relative position of the core in improvements in educational achievements is still strong.

## JOBS AND THE CITY

The future of the city in great part depends on the jobs available there, but between 1960 and 1970 the Newark economy suffered major employment declines in its two main sectors: manufacturing and trade. Almost one-quarter of the jobs in these industries disappeared during the decade. Employment gains were registered in the rest of the private economy. However, these were too minute to counter the decline or maintain the city's share of even these growing activities within the SMSA. The city's share of SMSA employment in every private sector declined significantly over the decade except in the case of contract construction (Exhibits 1-17 to 1-19).

The residence choices of employees in the Newark economy in 1960 were typical of those made by workers in other metropolitan areas. Not surprisingly, employees in higher paid occupations tended to be less likely to reside in the central city than those in lower paid occupations. Only one-quarter of Newark's professional and managerial

## EXHIBIT 1-16
## SELECTED EDUCATION CHARACTERISTICS OF THE POPULATION, NEWARK, 1960, 1970

| Education Indicators | AREAS OF THE CITY | | | | | |
|---|---|---|---|---|---|---|
| | Area 1 | Area 2 | Area 3 | Total 1-3 | Balance of City | Total Newark |
| Median Education | | | | | | |
| 1960 | 8.38 | 8.83 | 8.99 | 8.81 | 9.66 | 9.39 |
| 1970 | 9.23 | 10.21 | 9.51 | 9.78 | 10.35 | 10.21 |
| Percent of the population college graduates | | | | | | |
| 1960 | 0.50 | 1.30 | 1.50 | 1.20 | 3.00 | 2.00 |
| 1970 | 0.70 | 1.20 | 0.60 | 0.80 | 2.70 | 2.20 |
| Percent of the population high school graduates | | | | | | |
| 1960 | 9.20 | 12.60 | 11.20 | 11.30 | 17.00 | 15.20 |
| 1970 | 10.90 | 13.90 | 11.20 | 12.40 | 18.90 | 17.30 |
| Percent of the population enrolled in elementary school | | | | | | |
| 1960 | 15.50 | 13.40 | 14.60 | 14.30 | 14.70 | 14.60 |
| 1970 | 17.90 | 21.00 | 20.60 | 20.50 | 16.40 | 17.40 |

Source: Percentages derived from tract data,
U.S. Census of Population, 1960, 1970

employees in 1960 chose to live in the city. At the same time, well over two-thirds of the city's private household workers, laborers, and service workers lived within the city's boundaries.

Very little systematic variation appears to exist in the proportion of residents of the city in various occupations who are employed in the city. Professional workers living in Newark were nearly as likely to reverse commute to jobs outside the city as were operatives. On the average almost two-thirds of the residents of the city worked within it in 1960. The decline in Newark's economy over the past decade reduced this proportion significantly. In 1970, only 56 percent of the residents of

## EXHIBIT 1-17
## SELECTED LABOR FORCE CHARACTERISTICS OF NEWARK'S POPULATION, 1960, 1970

| Labor Force Indicators | AREAS OF THE CITY | | | | | |
|---|---|---|---|---|---|---|
| | Area 1 | Area 2 | Area 3 | Total 1-3 | Balance of City | Total Newark |
| Percent of the labor force employed in manufacturing | | | | | | |
| 1960 | 36.60 | 35.50 | 41.00 | 38.10 | 36.40 | 36.90 |
| 1970 | 31.40 | 37.30 | 40.40 | 38.10 | 37.40 | 37.60 |
| Percent of the labor force employed as professional/managers | | | | | | |
| 1960 | 4.40 | 6.10 | 6.10 | 5.80 | 12.60 | 10.40 |
| 1970 | 5.00 | 7.20 | 6.00 | 6.40 | 12.70 | 11.10 |
| Percent of the labor force female employed | | | | | | |
| 1960 | 40.70 | 36.80 | 36.40 | 37.40 | 35.70 | 36.20 |
| 1970 | 43.60 | 40.50 | 39.60 | 40.40 | 42.20 | 41.70 |
| Percent of the labor force male unemployed | | | | | | |
| 1960 | 11.85 | 8.06 | 7.83 | 8.70 | 7.21 | 7.69 |
| 1970 | 6.53 | 8.76 | 7.42 | 7.90 | 5.37 | 5.99 |
| Percent of the labor force female clerical | | | | | | |
| 1960 | 3.70 | 4.70 | 6.20 | 5.10 | 10.60 | 8.90 |
| 1970 | 10.90 | 9.60 | 11.00 | 10.40 | 13.80 | 13.00 |

Source: Percentages derived from tract data, U.S. Census of Population, 1960, 1970.

## EXHIBIT 1-18
## WAGE AND SALARY EMPLOYMENT IN NEWARK AS PERCENT OF SMSA

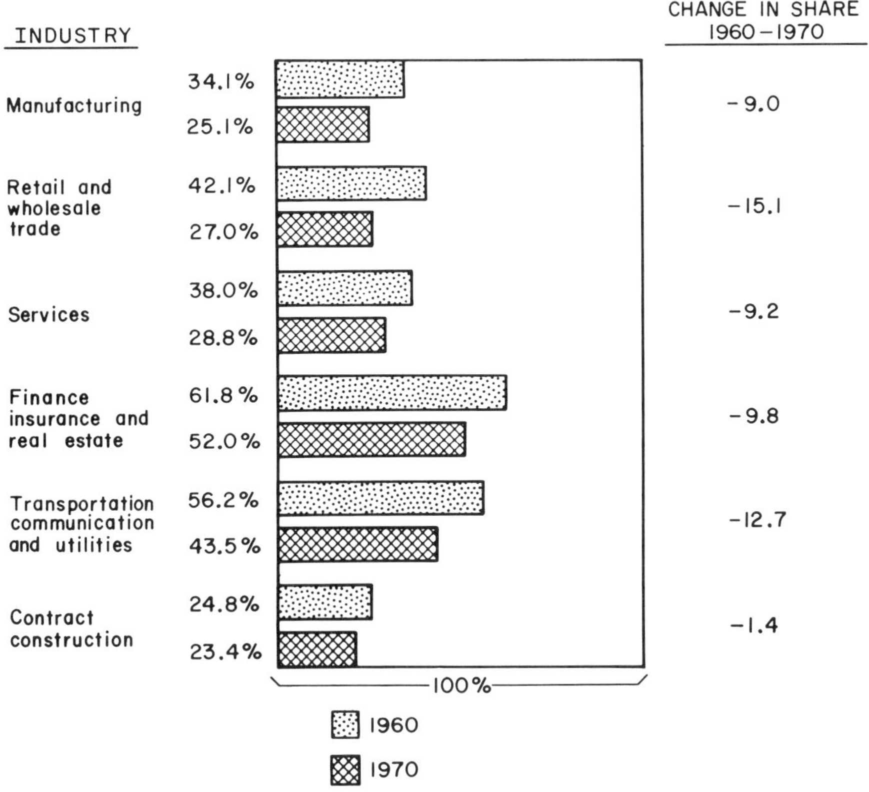

## EXHIBIT 1-19
### WAGE AND SALARY EMPLOYMENT GROWTH IN NEWARK, 1960-1970

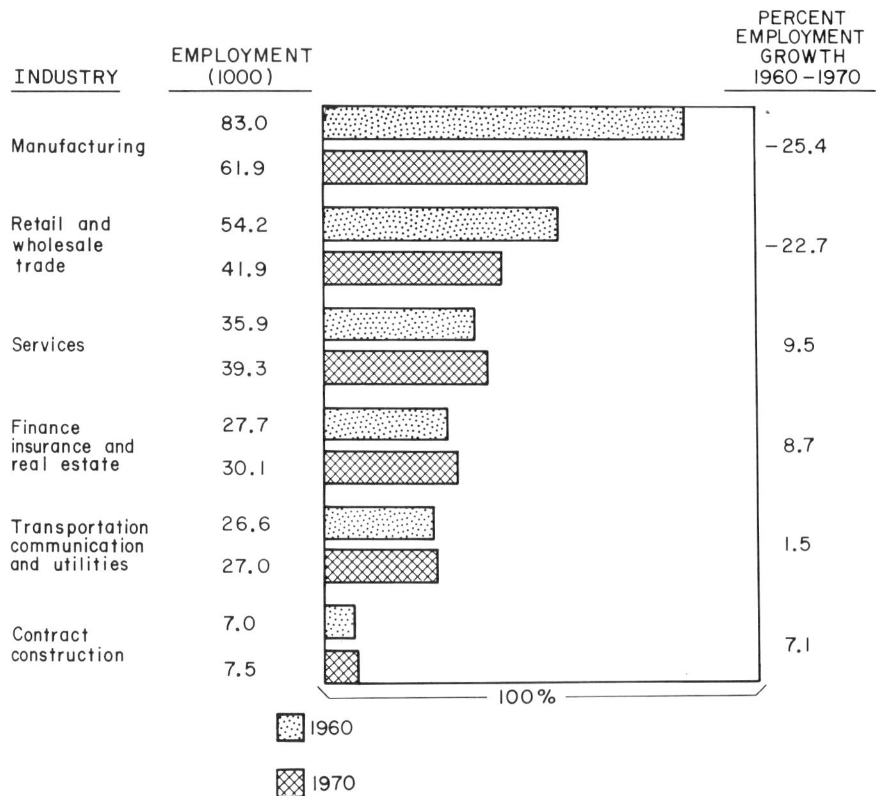


Newark holding jobs held jobs within the city. It appears that the labor force of the city was much less dependent on the city's employment opportunities in 1970 than it was in 1960.

Reverse commuting grew in importance over the last decade in Newark (Exhibits 1-20 through 1-22 summarize the major parameters). Based on a 1967 study by the Center for Urban Policy Research, minority residents of the city were more likely to be reverse commuters than were whites. As relative newcomers to a depressed job market, they had to find employment outside the municipality.

## EXHIBIT 1-20
## 1960 WORKPLACE LOCATION PATTERNS OF NEWARK RESIDENTS BY OCCUPATION

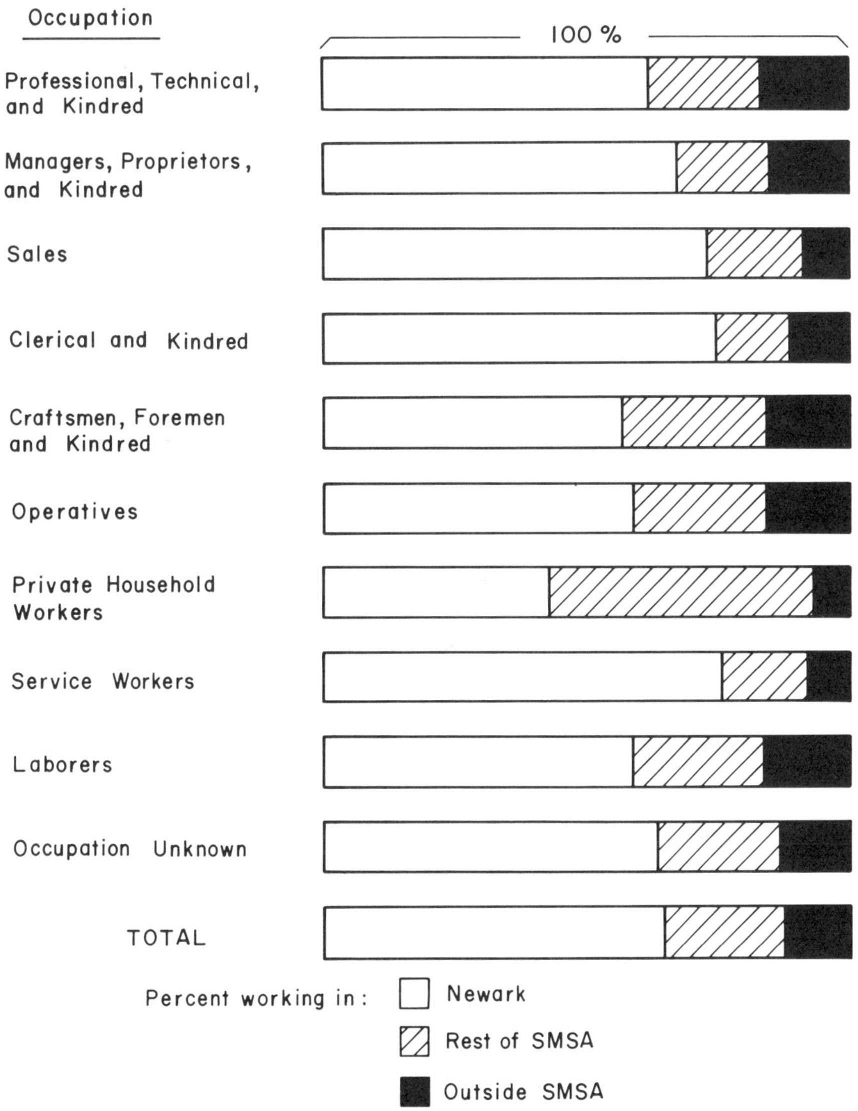

Occupation

100 %

Professional, Technical, and Kindred

Managers, Proprietors, and Kindred

Sales

Clerical and Kindred

Craftsmen, Foremen and Kindred

Operatives

Private Household Workers

Service Workers

Laborers

Occupation Unknown

TOTAL

Percent working in:

Newark

Rest of SMSA

Outside SMSA

## EXHIBIT 1-21
### 1960 RESIDENCE LOCATION PATTERNS OF WORKERS IN NEWARK BY OCCUPATION

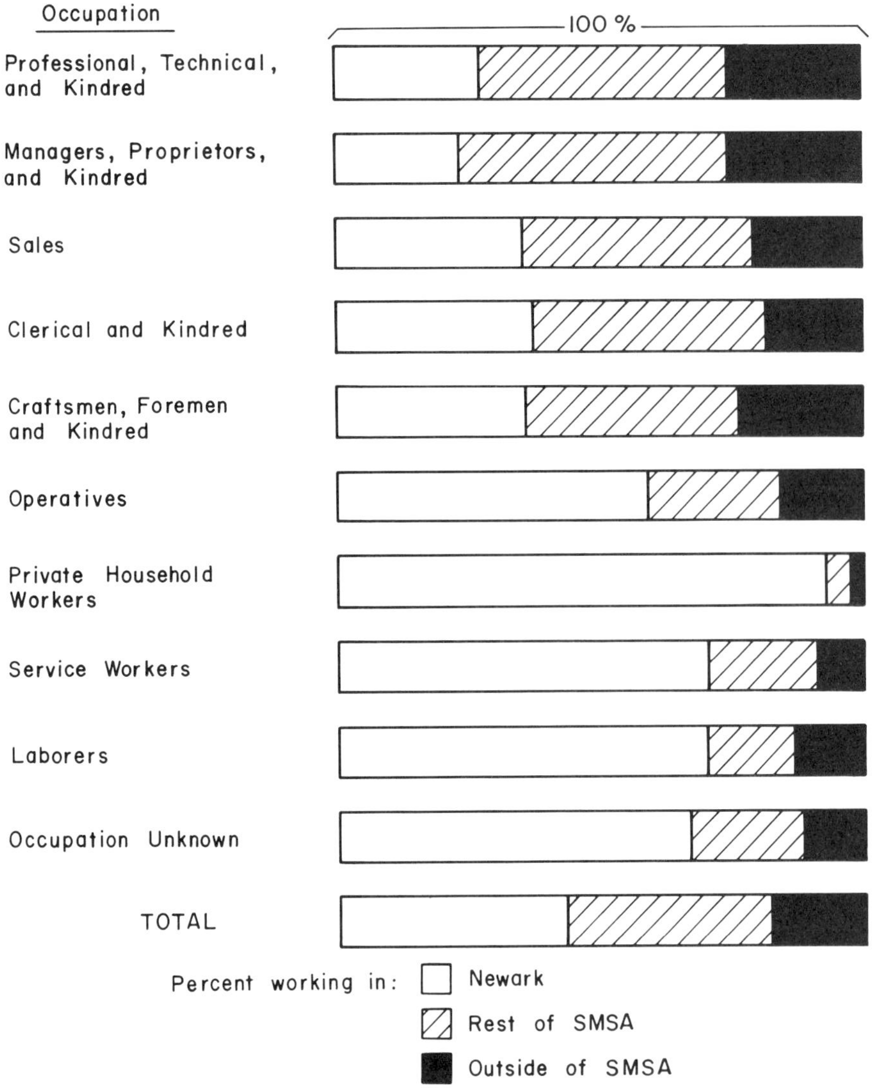

Occupation

100 %

Professional, Technical, and Kindred

Managers, Proprietors, and Kindred

Sales

Clerical and Kindred

Craftsmen, Foremen and Kindred

Operatives

Private Household Workers

Service Workers

Laborers

Occupation Unknown

TOTAL

Percent working in:
Newark
Rest of SMSA
Outside of SMSA

EXHIBIT 1-22
WORKPLACE LOCATIONS OF NEWARK'S EMPLOYED POPULATION 1960-1970

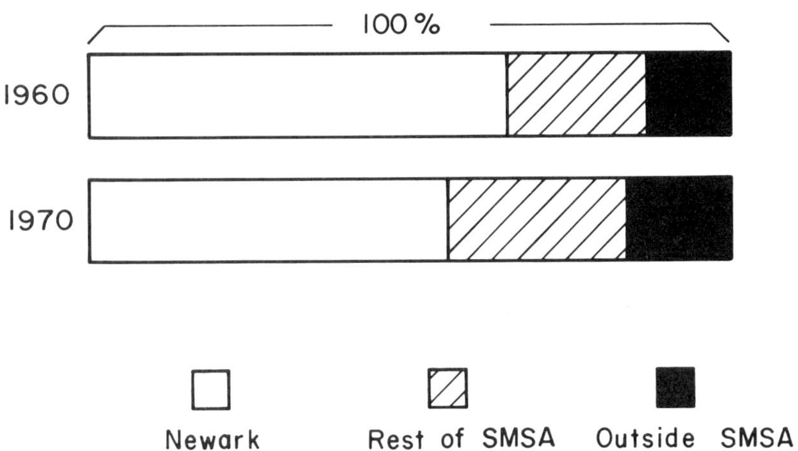


## HOUSING AND THE CITY

### Supply and Demand

Exhibit 1-23 demonstrates that the supply portion of the Newark housing market has not been overgenerous. From 1967 through 1971 there were few, if any, non-publicly assisted net additions to the standing stock while, as shown later, approximately 10 percent of the private supply had been lost through owner abandonment.

In terms of the public and publicly assisted markets as much housing has been torn down in Newark as has been replaced. *In the last four-year span 6,901 housing units were demolished while only 3,345 were replaced.* Earlier in the decade new housing outpaced demolition; now it has fallen behind. Currently there are no urban renewal programs in the active stage of housing generation in Newark nor are there substantial areas in the preconstruction process of site acquisition.

## EXHIBIT 1-23
### PRIVATE, PUBLIC CONSTRUCTION AND DEMOLITIONS
### NEWARK, 1960-1971

| Year | Construction | | | | | | | Demolitions |
|---|---|---|---|---|---|---|---|---|
| | Single Family | Two Family | Three and Four Family | Five or more | Private Total | Public Total | All Total | |
| 1960 | 28 | 76 | 9 | 803 | 916 | 0 | 916 | 414 |
| 1961 | 54 | 38 | 16 | 151 | 249 | 2,398 | 2,647 | 192 |
| 1962 | 15 | 54 | 10 | 137 | 216 | 0 | 216 | 157 |
| 1963 | 4 | 58 | ° | 257 | 329 | 0 | 329 | 1,300 |
| 1964 | 6 | 40 | 0 | 1,635 | 1,681 | 0 | 1,681 | 185 |
| 1965 | 4 | 74 | 3 | 476 | 557 | 0 | 557 | 537 |
| 1966 | 2 | 26 | 3 | 471 | 502 | 1,000 | 1,502 | 420 |
| 1967 | 2 | 16 | 0 | 319 | 337 | 1,000 | 1,337 | 4,286 |
| 1968 | 2 | 16 | 8 | 539 | 619 | 486 | 1,105 | 1,480 |
| 1969 | 0 | 4 | 4 | 643 | 651 | 0 | 651 | 471 |
| 1970 | 0 | 14 | 0 | 12 | 26 | 0 | 26 | 512 |
| 1971 | 0 | 0 | 0 | 226 | 226 | 0 | 226 | 352 |
| Total | 117 | 426 | 43 | 5,723 | 6,309 | 4,484 | 11,193 | 9,355 |

Source: New Jersey Department of Community Affairs, *Annual Summary of Building Permits* 1960-1971.

## Urban Renewal

Newark has been the scene of massive urban renewal efforts. In 1969 the city boasted that it was third nationally in the per capita federal resources that have been allocated for that purpose. The current virtual standstill of the program has enormous impact. For example, 119 of the 382 sample parcels (31 percent) that are still standing, for which information was available, were in urban renewal areas. The distribution, by area however, is quite different. In Area 1, 80 percent of the 89 structures still standing are in urban renewal areas. In Area 2 it is 33 out of 137 or 24.1 percent while in Area 3 it is only 15 parcels out of 156 or 8.3 percent. Included in Newark's Model Cities Program are 45 of the 89 parcels in Area 1, or 50.1 percent. Only 1 of 137 structures in Area 2, and 13 out of 156, or 7.2 percent, in Area 3 are under this program. Until the future of urban renewal is decided, these structures are in limbo as far as major capital improvements or alternate uses are concerned.

While the situation is far from unique on the national scene, it is of the utmost importance in Newark, given the scale of the operation and the unique local legal problems that slow down the program. The dilemma of the landlord or prospective landlord of these parcels is all too clear. Simply stated, four out of five parcels, based on the sample in Area 1, are scheduled for ultimate demolition under renewal. But ultimate is a long time away; in the meantime the parcels stand.

A variety of grant-in-aid programs, of generous rehabilitation loan funding, and so on, are available for structures grouped under urban renewal and Model Cities. But, in turn, by the very act of defining the structures as eligible their future is locked into both the vitality and the limitations of the programs and removes them from market forces.

Though more than 200 acres of land in Newark have been cleared, largely through urban renewal, the rate of new construction is slow. Not only has residential development faltered, but so have job producing commercial and industrial developments. On the other hand, suburban equivalents boom and even office functions leave.[2]

The problems of securing clear title on much of this property as well as other elements which are further down the pipe line leading to construction are fearfully obstructive. *Re-evaluation of urban investment programs by the federal government is perhaps long overdue. What must be given serious attention is not whether the programs were right in their initial formulation, but how urban renewal can be brought to a viable conclusion. The present stalemate is absolutely intolerable.*

Most of the following chapters illustrate some of the problems related to this point.

## Rent Levels

The cost element of housing again is difficult to view in isolation. Not only is it necessary to compare housing cost within a city but also across the larger region as well.

Within the city itself median contract rents have increased by over 60 percent as compared with a 41 percent increase in family income. The situation is even more acute in the core areas where median income increases have lagged behind cost of shelter increases by close to two to one (Exhibit 1-24).

Rent levels in cities such as Newark are subject to a variety of parameters which are not often found in the conventional economics textbook.

> Parcel number 004, a four-story, five-family plus store structure in a commercial area of Newark, illustrates the dichotomy that sometimes exists between black and white rents. When the owner, who is also the operator of the store, was first interviewed in 1964, the building had all white tenantry. There are now three black tenants and two white ones. He explained: "I can only keep them (the latter) because I am only charging them $50 a month, but I don't want to be all alone."

Fear of tenant moves to avoid higher rent payments sometimes keeps landlords from charging what the market will bear. Parcel number 130, for example, which could certainly bring higher rents in terms of the market, has rents of only $60 a month. The landlord thinks that he can get more, but he is fearful of difficulties in rent collection and of tenants leaving without paying rents, which would mean more potential vacancies. The latter in his experience (and this was a common point made by many other owners) leads to vandalism of the vacant units.

The owner in question is keeping this parcel because he has a business attached to it. Basically his major goal in terms of the

## EXHIBIT 1-24
## SELECTED CHARACTERISTICS OF HOUSING COST AND OCCUPANCY BY AREA, NEWARK, 1960, 1970

| Housing Indicators | AREAS OF THE CITY | | | | | |
|---|---|---|---|---|---|---|
| | Area 1 | Area 2 | Area 3 | Total 1-3 | Balance of City | Total Newark |
| Cost | | | | | | |
| median contract rent | | | | | | |
| 1960 | $ 54.42 | $ 61.68 | $ 60.03 | $ 59.55 | $ 69.52 | $ 66.35 |
| 1970 | 89.05 | 97.27 | 93.26 | 94.52 | 108.48 | 105.03 |
| median house value | | | | | | |
| 1960 | 11,768.00 | 11,171.00 | 11,563.00 | 11,456.00 | 13,591.00 | 12,913.00 |
| 1970 | 13,354.00 | 13,040.00 | 13,885.00 | 13,463.00 | 16,170.00 | 15,501.00 |
| Occupancy | | | | | | |
| vacancy rate | | | | | | |
| 1960 | 4.40% | 4.00% | 2.50% | 3.40% | 3.30% | 3.40% |
| 1970 | 8.40 | 6.00 | 6.60 | 6.60 | 2.70 | 3.60 |
| owner occupancy | | | | | | |
| 1960 | 11.90 | 18.30 | 15.30 | 15.70 | 26.00 | 22.80 |
| 1970 | 9.60 | 13.00 | 11.00 | 11.80 | 22.70 | 20.00 |

Source: Percentages derived from tract data, U.S. Census of Population, 1960, 1970.

residential rents is merely to keep the units occupied. The fear of vandalism, of losing the tenants he knows, or the fear of unknown tenants that the market may bring (even if they are at a higher rent level) is a frequent refrain on the part of both black and white owners.

## Welfare and Rent

As noted elsewhere in this work, the impact of increases in the proportion of welfare recipients to the total city population is worthy of a study in itself. The phenomenon is clearly widespread; the capacity of cities to deal with it, particularly in view of changes in employment characteristics and locale (Exhibit 1-25), is far from certain.[3] In the limited context discussed here, it should be noted that much of core housing is occupied by welfare recipients. Unfortunately the limitations of the data available from the welfare department and landlord lack of familiarity with the tenant characteristics in many cases prevent a definitive figure from being given. But certainly with nearly 105,000 people on welfare in Newark out of the total population of 380,000, its impact is of much consequence.

At the time of the 1971 interviews both the county and municipal welfare allowances segregated housing support from the basic family budget. This permitted some flexibility in rent payments without impacting other household expenditures. It is too early to evaluate the new system of a rigorous ceiling on allowances for rents in New Jersey. These typically are $100 a month, except in certain exceptional cases, as against the former system of essentially having a separate allowance for rents set at whatever the market required. Certainly, however, with the median rent pushing the legislated limit, its impact may be very substantial.[4]

## House Values

*If a homeowner in Newark encounters a cash flow situation wherein revenues just meet costs, in the long run he is losing money in constant value dollars by retaining the property.*

This point will be returned to as the role of tenement ownership in providing upward mobility to newcomers to the market is pursued in a later chapter. In any case this is a far cry from the remaining Essex County suburban areas where a decade of house value increases have

# EXHIBIT 1-25
## PERCENT OF TOTAL POPULATION RECEIVING PUBLIC ASSISTANCE
Feb. 1972 vs. Feb. 1971

| City | Percent receiving public assistance | Percent increase over 1971 |
|---|---|---|
| Boston | 20.5 | 23.5 |
| Baltimore | 17.3 | 13.8 |
| Philadelphia | 17.0 | 14.9 |
| St. Louis | 17.0 | 15.6 |
| New York City | 16.0 | 6.7 |
| New Orleans | 15.6 | 5.4 |
| San Francisco | 14.3 | 0.7 |
| Newark | 27.6 | 8.2 |

sufficiently passed the general rate of inflation to make housing a worthwhile capital investment.

Housing value comparison across urban places within Newark's same SMSA (Exhibit 1-26) makes it apparent that Newark's deficiency in 1960 has been accentuated over the intercensal period. The other communities' housing in 1960 was valued at 10 to 90 percent more than Newark's, but it has increased in value at one and one-half to two and one-half times Newark's rate. The average housing value in Newark in 1970 was a minimum of 25 percent less than neighboring urban places in the immediate region, i.e., a backslide of 15 percent over the decade.

## Vacancy Rates

Two other indices of the local housing market are ominous for the city's future. The 1970 housing vacancy rate of 3.6 percent, up 0.2 percent from 1960, masked a core vacancy rate of 6.6 percent, almost double the case a decade before. Mean core vacancy in 1970 (Areas 1, 2, and 3) is at least twice the peripheral vacancy rate and in the most severe case (Area 1) over three times as large.

The gross levels of vacancies, particularly in areas such as that of Newark's core, should not be synonymized with housing which is available for rent. A sample survey, for example, of quality of vacant structures in the spring of 1967 in Newark indicated that, even by generous standards, barely half of the housing units which were nominally vacant were available for rent with the balance being in the process of being demolished, abandoned, or converted to nonhousing uses. Of those which were available for rent a small fraction (under 20 percent) were evaluated as being in fair to good condition.[5] Again and again the point was made by owners that their vacancy rates were nonexistent, because so many competing buildings had been destroyed. The owner of parcel number 20 pointed out that his was the only occupied building on the entire block and added, "Our apartments are all occupied because they're the only available ones. There is such a large number of burnt-out buildings, places are at a premium." And yet another owner repeated an often heard refrain, "Our vacancies are usually due only to lack of notice of intention to move. There's no place to go."

This marks a radical shift in landlord attitudes as expressed in the earlier survey in 1964. Then, when owners were asked whether the

## EXHIBIT 1-26
### MEDIAN HOUSING VALUE OF CONSTITUENT MUNICIPALITIES OF THE NEWARK SMSA, 1960, 1970

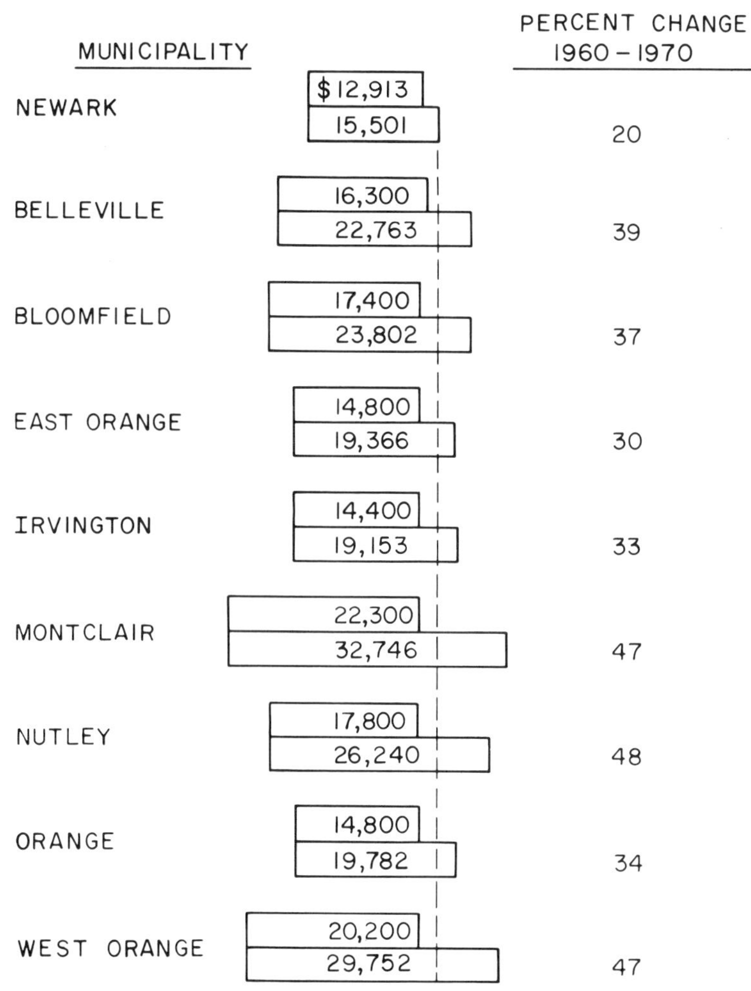

general vacancy rate in the area in which the sample parcel was located had changed, nearly 60 percent replied that it had gone up. The equivalent current vacancy increase response is barely a third of the previous figure. All the current volunteered responses reflected on the fact that burnt-out and demolished buildings have concentrated population in those structures which were still operating.

### Owner Occupancy

Citywide owner occupancy in 1970 was 10 percent less than it was in 1960. The greatest relative decrease in owner occupancy was in the originally less severely impacted of the core areas, i.e., Areas 2 and 3, which are currently only at 40 to 75 percent of the owner-occupancy levels that existed in 1970. This fact, perhaps more than others, poses a serious threat to the stability of the housing stock in areas which appear to be on the brink of both massive housing deterioration and structure abandonment.

### Housing Quality

As discussed more fully in the methodology (Appendix I) there were two major probes used to establish the quality of the structure. One was to compare the sample parcel with its immediate neighbor. The other was to rate it in terms of absolute quality aspects. These variables will be discussed at substantial length in the course of the work that follows.

In addition to the foregoing probes of quality, owners were asked to evaluate their own parcels. The results of this process are shown in Exhibit 1-27 for the three areas into which the data are grouped. The owners in Area 1 are least sanguine about the condition of their parcels, 28.8 percent of these owners versus 12.7 percent in Area 2 and 10.3 percent in Area 3 said their parcels were not in good condition, or literally said that they were very poor. While this type of observation is far from precise, there was a high level of correlation with our own evaluation of the structures.

### Quality of Housing and Ethnicity of Tenants

Based on both criteria established for 1964, there seems to be clear evidence that the housing that blacks have moved into since that date

# EXHIBIT 1-27
## OWNER'S VIEW OF OPERATING CONDITION OF THE PARCEL (1964) BY SAMPLE AREA OF THE CITY (1964/1971)

| Operating Condition of the Parcel | AREAS OF THE CITY Area 1 | Area 2 | Area 3 | Total |
|---|---|---|---|---|
| Very good | 21 | 44 | 36 | 101 |
| Moderately good | 17 | 47 | 51 | 115 |
| Livable | 16 | 7 | 14 | 37 |
| Poor | 15 | 14 | 12 | 41 |
| Very poor | 2 | 1 | 0 | 3 |
| Other | 3 | 2 | 1 | 6 |
| NA | 2 | 2 | 0 | 4 |
| DK | 2 | 1 | 3 | 6 |
| Total | 78 | 118 | 117 | 313 |

PERCENT DISTRIBUTION

| | Area 1 | Area 2 | Area 3 | Total |
|---|---|---|---|---|
| Very good | 26.9 | 37.3 | 30.8 | 32.3 |
| Moderately good | 21.8 | 39.8 | 43.6 | 36.7 |
| Livable | 20.5 | 5.9 | 12.0 | 11.8 |
| Poor | 19.2 | 11.9 | 10.3 | 13.1 |
| Very poor | 2.6 | 0.8 | 0.0 | 1.0 |
| Other | 3.8 | 1.7 | 0.9 | 1.9 |
| NA | 2.6 | 1.7 | 0.0 | 1.3 |
| DK | 2.6 | 0.8 | 2.6 | 1.9 |
| Total | 100.0 | 100.0 | 100.0 | 100.0 |

$X^2 = 0.025$

Source: Newark Area Resurvey, spring 1972

has been basically random in quality aspects, i.e., the proportion of positively rated housing newly occupied by minority groups is representative of the sample as a whole. In addition, observation was undertaken of exterior improvements such as storm windows, new porches, front steps, siding, painting, trim painting, and other external improvements that were observed in the course of the 1971 interviews. There is no great dissimilarity when these are appraised as a function of tenant ethnicity.

## Other Quality Indices

Three other housing indices provide insight in viewing the City of Newark's decennial change. Due to the massive demolition of multiple family units in core areas, the percentage of single family units within the entire city has actually increased slightly. The marked changes in the gross single/multi-family ratio occasioned by demolition is particularly noticeable in the most acutely impacted area of the core. In this area the 1970 percentage of single-family units has doubled as a result of neighboring multi-family demolition.

Crowding has also risen by approximately 10 percent from 1960 to 1970. This holds true in all areas of the city, including the periphery. The most severe change was in the least impacted of core areas (Area 3) where the number of units with greater than 1.01 persons per room actually is now one-quarter greater than it was in 1960. This must be viewed, of course, with the realization that crowding as a general U.S. urban phenomenon has decreased over the decade.

Finally, again due to the extensive demolition of the city's worst portion of its housing stock, the percent of the units which have no bath or which have shared baths is barely one-third of what it was in 1960 (Exhibit 1-28). This is a phenomenon frequently associated with cities undergoing extensive urban renewal efforts.

## Commercial Occupancy

Retail stores are common on the ground floors of buildings in older areas. In Exhibit 1-29 the degree of commercial occupancy by area is shown. Notice that nearly one out of five of the sample parcels that are standing in Area 1 have some level of commercial occupancy while in the other two areas it's less than one in ten.

Commercial space, in terms of the economics of the structure, may have a positive effect but sometimes the reverse is the case. An example of the former is parcel number 216, a masonry structure with a ground floor retail garment store and seven apartments above it. The owner, who revealed his operating data, is not making a profit on the parcel though it is reasonably well maintained. He purchased it in 1946. A check of the title reveals that the purchase price was $24,000 involving $6,000 in cash with the balance secured by a first mortgage from a bank. The parcel now in the owners words is "unmortgageable." He said, "If

I didn't have this store I would abandon the whole thing. There are simply no buyers."

In a number of other cases, as will be noted in more detail later in this study, the presence of small retail facilities which are obsolete in the age of supermarkets and discount houses has much more negative implications for the vitality of older city structures which house them.

EXHIBIT 1-28

SELECTED CHARACTERISTICS OF HOUSING CONSTRUCTION AND QUALITY BY AREA, NEWARK, 1960, 1970

| | AREAS OF THE CITY | | | | | |
|---|---|---|---|---|---|---|
| Housing Indicators | Area 1 | Area 2 | Area 3 | Total 1-3 | Balance of City | Total Newark |
| Percent of the housing units which are single family | | | | | | |
| 1960 | 3.90 | 10.20 | 6.60 | 7.40 | 13.60 | 11.70 |
| 1970 | 7.70 | 10.60 | 7.90 | 9.00 | 13.20 | 12.20 |
| Average number of rooms per unit | | | | | | |
| 1960 | 4.26 | 4.03 | 4.28 | 4.18 | 4.47 | 4.38 |
| 1970 | 4.33 | 4.46 | 4.35 | 4.40 | 4.41 | 4.40 |
| Percent of the housing units with 1.01 persons per room | | | | | | |
| 1960 | 20.80 | 20.30 | 17.70 | 19.30 | 11.20 | 13.80 |
| 1970 | 20.10 | 21.50 | 21.60 | 21.40 | 13.40 | 15.30 |
| Percent of the housing units with no bath or a shared bath | | | | | | |
| 1960 | 30.50 | 21.40 | 17.10 | 21.40 | 8.20 | 12.40 |
| 1970 | 3.90 | 5.70 | 5.30 | 5.30 | 3.30 | 3.80 |

Source: Percentages derived from tract data, U.S. Census of Population, 1960, 1970.

EXHIBIT 1-29
EXTENT OF PARCEL'S COMMERCIAL OCCUPANCY (1971)
BY SAMPLE AREA OF THE CITY (1971)

| Extent of Commercial Occupancy | Area 1 | Area 2 | Area 3 | Total |
|---|---|---|---|---|
| None | 74 | 128 | 145 | 347 |
| Minor — less than 30% of total rent | 15 | 11 | 11 | 37 |
| Significant — 30% or more of unit | 3 | 1 | 4 | 8 |
| Total | 92 | 140 | 160 | 392 |
| PERCENT DISTRIBUTION | | | | |
| None | 80.4 | 91.4 | 90.6 | 88.5 |
| Minor — less than 30% of total rent | 16.3 | 7.9 | 6.9 | 9.4 |
| Significant — 30% or more of unit | 3.3 | 0.7 | 2.5 | 2.0 |
| Total | 100.0 | 100.0 | 100.0 | 100.0 |

$\chi^2$ = n/s @0.05

Source: Newark Area Resurvey, spring 1972

## A FACTOR ANALYTICAL SUMMARY OF A DECADE'S CHANGE

The previous cross tabulation analyses provide a rather disjointed view of urban change: the black solidification within the city; a changing general age structure of the population; and finally, increased rents, higher male unemployment, and more extensive crowding in the core.

It is difficult to view these forces in isolation and for that reason a grouping mechanism, factor analysis, is employed to study their combined effect. See the Methodology for more on this approach (Appendix I).

The use of this mathematical tool in the investigation of the spatial structure of urban areas has been discussed and demonstrated in a number of publications.[6] Social area analysts confirm that the complexity of urban social structure in an industrial society can be described by three independent constructs (social rank, urbanization [family life style], and segregation [ethnicity/race] ) which indicate the way in which urban populations are differentiated.[7] This implies that there is great variation of social rank and family life style within each ethnic/racial segment, great variation in ethnicity/race and family life style at each level of social rank, and great variation in social rank and ethnicity/race within each family life style.[8]

While the use of a center city rather than an SMSA for this analysis may alter the traditional forms of analysis, the establishment of their presence or nonpresence, and an analysis of this change over time, is invaluable in viewing both current and past roles of urban areas.

## The City in 1960

If one looks at the factor structure of Newark in 1960 a traditional pattern of center city social structure presents itself. This is the 1960 view of the urban role, i.e., the scene of the invasion-succession phenomenon: younger, poorer family-raising black and Puerto Rican immigrants replacing more affluent, aged, white out-migrants.

This is particularly apparent in the first factor which identifies three elements of city structure: household resources, age of structure, and race. A high positive score in this dimension is associated with census tract populations characterized by aging white families, in many cases foreign born, having substantial economic resources, and owner occupants of single family homes. High negative scores reveal populations of just the reverse conditions, i.e., predominantly black, low income, with large numbers of children living, for the most part, in severely crowded housing conditions. Thus, it is evident that a dimension which explains 1960 city structure includes a white aged/black poverty factor *(Race and Resources)*, representing a disproportionate number of aging white families associated with higher economic status and a similarly disproportionate number of black families clustered at the lower end of the economic wealth continuum (Exhibit 1-30).

# EXHIBIT 1-30

## FACTOR ANALYSIS OF SELECTIVE 1960 SOCIO-ECONOMIC VARIABLES EMPLOYING NEWARK CENSUS TRACTS AS DATA BASES

| | Variable | Race and Resources | Social Status | Stage in the Life Cycle | Puerto Rican Segregation | Housing Stability | Male Unemployment |
|---|---|---|---|---|---|---|---|
| 1 | Percent housing units: occupied | | | | | .723 | |
| 2 | Percent population: Negro | —.919 | | | | | |
| 3 | Median age female | .807 | | | | | |
| 4 | Median age white female | | .471 | | | | —.616 |
| 5 | Percent housing units: no bath or share | | | | | —.713 | |
| 6 | Percent housing units: >1.01 persons/rm | —.767 | —.413 | | | | |
| 7 | Median contract rent | | .775 | | | .422 | |
| 8 | Median house value | | .732 | | | | |
| 9 | Percent housing units: single family | .444 | | | | | |
| 10 | Percent population: >65 years of age | .771 | .400 | | | | |
| 11 | Percent white pop.: >65 years of age | .872 | | | | | |
| 12 | Percent population: married | .685 | | | | | |
| 13 | Percent population: <5 years of age | —.837 | —.400 | | | | |
| 14 | Percent housing units: owner occupied | .705 | | | | .458 | |

| | | | | | | | |
|---|---|---|---|---|---|---|---|
| 15 | Median rooms/unit | | | | .658 | .488 | |
| 16 | Percent labor force: female | | | | .684 | | |
| 17 | Percent population: Puerto Rican parentage | | | | —.736 | | |
| 18 | Median education | | .774 | | | | |
| 19 | Median family income | .579 | .401 | | | | |
| 20 | Percent labor force: male unemployed | | | | | | —.787 |
| 21 | Percent labor force: female clerical | .722 | | | | | |
| 22 | Percent labor force: professional managerial | | .777 | | | | |
| 23 | Percent population: foreign born | .817 | | | | | |
| 24 | Population per household | | —.458 | .472 | | | |
| 25 | Percent population: elementary school enrollment | | | .776 | —.463 | | |
| 26 | Percent population: high school graduate | | .746 | | | | |
| 27 | Percent population: college graduate | | .849 | | | | |
| 28 | Percent population: income < $3,000 | —.646 | | | | | |
| 29 | Percent population: income > $10,000 | .609 | .595 | | | | |
| 30 | Percent labor force: manufacturing | | —.787 | | | | |
| | Variance explained by factor (%) | 29.6 | 21.5 | 8.9 | 8.3 | 5.3 | 4.6 |

Source: U.S. Census of Population, 1960.
< less than
> greater than

Another index of the city in 1960 is a qualitative, *Socio-Economic Status* factor. High positive scores on this factor differentiate areas of comparative affluence where inhabitants had high educational levels and incomes, employment in white collar occupations, and expensive residential accommodations. Tracts with low socio-economic levels were revealed by high negative scores: populations characterized by large, young, and crowded households whose primary employment was concentrated in manufacturing.

A third characteristic in the 1960 Newark city structure reveals the presence of a *Puerto Rican Poverty* dimension. This dimension, substantially less intense than the black poverty factor *(Race and Resources)* associates a high proportion of Puerto Rican residents among a relatively low income populace. The Puerto Rican factor is a frequent dimension in other city structure analyses.

A factor which did not emerge in 1960 is the *Stage in the Life Cycle* or *Age Distribution* factor. This may have been caused by a concentration of both young black and young white families in 1960 which prevented somewhat a balanced family spread throughout the age-structure categories. (In 1960 this dimension is subsumed within the *Race and Resources* factor.)

## The City in 1970

The urban *role* in 1970 may be a somewhat different one. The city, while still maintaining a limited staging capacity for the potentially upwardly mobile, may now be the final repository for a substantial group who are incapable of upward mobility. In Newark there is evidence of the beginnings of a culture of poverty in its most negative sense. This is reinforced by the first real presence in American cities of a "squatter" population.

In 1970, Newark's city structure was characterized again by its two principal dimensions, *Race and Resources* and *Socio-Economic Status;* by the final emergence of a *Stage in the Life Cycle* factor, and the continued separation of its Puerto Rican population (Exhibit 1-31). The 1970 prevalence of the *Race and Resources* factor shows that Newark's resident black population is still strongly associated with a lack of economic resources. Yet this also seems to indicate a total lack of black economic mobility which other studies over the decade have stated as definitely not the case. *What appears to be showing through, however, are the realities of black out-migration. As blacks move up the economic ladder they too make a spatial readjustment out of Newark into such surrounding emergence zones as East Orange and Montclair, New Jersey.*

The extreme stability of the *Socio-Economic Status* dimension further reinforces a segregation of census tracts according to the socio-economic condition of their resident populations. Areas of white affluence, whose residents have greater educational achievements, who pay higher rents, and whose housing has more value, remain a characteristic part of the city's structure.

The emergence of the *Stage in the Life Cycle* factor and the continuance of the separate *Puerto Rican* dimension also prove interesting. In the latter case in 1970 the Puerto Rican population also seems to be less associated with the socio-economic dimensions; thus a preliminary statement may be made to the effect that there are either Puerto Ricans at all levels of the socio-economic continuum or they reside in census tracts whose dominant characteristics are independent of resource deprivation. If the second condition is so, then access to better residential neighborhoods within Newark may be less restricted for this ethnic subpopulation.

## The City from 1960 to 1970

Perhaps the best summary of structural changes taking place in Newark over a decade may be had by a factor analytical examination of the 1970/1960 change quotient (Exhibit 1-32). In this analysis, variable change, as expressed by 1970 characteristics divided by 1960 characteristics, is used to describe the city.[9]

From the factor analysis significant dimensions of city structure change appear to be described by: an *Age Succession* index, i.e., significant age and family size changeovers within constituent census tracts; a *Social Status* index, i.e., substantially increasing and decreasing incomes within census tract areas; and finally, a *Racial Composition* index which indicates that perhaps the black compositional change over the decade is a dual rather than singular phenomenon. In this latter case two factors *(Young Black Families* and *Black Poverty)* indicate that components of urban racial change principally involve the appearance of: (1) young black families, living in crowded conditions yet employed

## EXHIBIT 1-31

### FACTOR ANALYSIS OF SELECTIVE 1970 SOCIO-ECONOMIC VARIABLES EMPLOYING NEWARK CENSUS TRACTS AS A DATA BASE

| | Variable | Race and Resources | Social Status | Stage of Life Cycle | Puerto Rican Segregation | Dual Worker/ Housing Quality |
|---|---|---|---|---|---|---|
| 1 | Percent housing units: occupied | .579 | | | | .613 |
| 2 | Percent population: Negro | —.716 | | —.536 | | |
| 3 | Median age female | .635 | | .721 | | |
| 4 | Median age white female | | | | —.511 | |
| 5 | Percent housing units: no bath or share | | | | | —.845 |
| 6 | Percent housing units: >1.01 persons/rm | —.673 | | —.453 | | |
| 7 | Median contract rent | | .776 | | | |
| 8 | Median house value | .473 | .582 | | | |
| 9 | Percent housing units: single family | .642 | | | | |
| 10 | Percent population: >65 years of age | | | .893 | | |
| 11 | Percent white pop.: >65 years of age | .538 | | .740 | | |
| 12 | Percent population: married | .864 | | | | |
| 13 | Percent population: <5 years of age | —.695 | | —.580 | | |

| | | | | | | |
|---|---|---|---|---|---|---|
| 14 | Percent housing units: owner occupied | .870 | | | | |
| 15 | Median rooms/unit | | | —.548 | | .602 |
| 16 | Percent labor force: female | | | | | .769 |
| 17 | Percent population: Puerto Rican parentage | | | | .790 | |
| 18 | Median education | | .893 | | | |
| 19 | Median family income | .787 | .400 | | | |
| 20 | Percent labor force: male unemployed | —.527 | | | | |
| 21 | Percent labor force: female clerical | | | | | .565 |
| 22 | Percent labor force: professional managerial | | | .862 | | |
| 23 | Percent population: foreign born | .679 | | | | |
| 24 | Population per household | | | —.824 | | |
| 25 | Percent population: elementary school enrollment | —.594 | | —.513 | | |
| 26 | Percent population: high school graduate | | .802 | | | |
| 27 | Percent population: college graduate | | .845 | | | |
| 28 | Percent population: income < $4,000 | —.834 | | | | |
| 29 | Percent population: income > $12,000 | .848 | | | | |
| 30 | Percent labor force: manufacturing | | —.490 | | .609 | |
| | Variance explained by factor (%) | 28.2 | 16.9 | 16.4 | 10.5 | 7.2 |

Source: U.S. Census of Population, 1970.

# EXHIBIT 1-32

## FACTOR ANALYSIS OF SELECTIVE CHANGE VARIABLES (1960-1970) EMPLOYING NEWARK CENSUS TRACTS AS DATA BASES

| | Variable° | Age Succession | Social Status | Young Blacks | Black Poverty | Ethnic Neighbor-hoods | Multi-Unit Female Employment | Poverty | Young Puerto Ricans |
|---|---|---|---|---|---|---|---|---|---|
| 1 | Percent housing units: occupied | | —.856 | | | | | | |
| 2 | Percent population: Negro | | | —.676 | .522 | | | | |
| 3 | Median age female | .743 | | .406 | | | | | |
| 4 | Median age white female | .428 | | | | | | | —.683 |
| 5 | Percent housing units: no bath or share | | | | .624 | | | | |
| 6 | Percent housing units: > 1.01 persons/rm | | | —.872 | | | | | |
| 7 | Median contract rent | | —.792 | | | | | | |
| 8 | Median house value | | | | | .601 | .401 | | |
| 9 | Percent housing units: single family | | | | | | —.711 | | |
| 10 | Percent population: 65 + years of age | .864 | | | | | | | |
| 11 | Percent white population: >65+ years of age | .897 | | | | | | | |
| 12 | Percent population: married | .579 | | | | .619 | | | |
| 13 | Percent population: <5 years of age | —.472 | | —.786 | | | | | |
| 14 | Percent housing units: owner occupied | | | | | .841 | | | |

| | | | | | | | | | |
|---|---|---|---|---|---|---|---|---|---|
| 15 | Median rooms /unit | —.585 | | | | | | | |
| 16 | Percent labor force: female | | | | | | .683 | | |
| 17 | Percent population: Puerto Rican parentage | | | | | | | | .740 |
| 18 | Median education | —.416 | —.632 | | | —.476 | | | |
| 19 | Median family income | | | | | | | —.761 | |
| 20 | Percent labor force: male unemployed | | | | | | | .600 | |
| 21 | Percent labor force: female clerical | | | | | —.697 | | | |
| 22 | Percent labor force: professional managerial | | —.821 | | | | | | |
| 23 | Percent population: foreign born | .652 | | | | .501 | | | |
| 24 | Population per household | —.764 | | | | | | | |
| 25 | Percent population: elementary school enrollment | —.689 | | | | | | | |
| 26 | Percent population: high school graduate | | —.632 | | | | | | |
| 27 | Percent population: college graduate | | —.821 | | | | | | |
| 28 | Percent population: income < $ 3,000 — $ 4,000 | | | | .754 | | | | |
| 29 | Percent population: income > $10,000 — $12,000 | | —.416 | | —.495 | | | | |
| 30 | Percent labor force: manufacturing | | | —.808 | | | | | |
| | Variance explained by factor (%) | 18.2 | 12.9 | 10.1 | 9.7 | 6.8 | 5.5 | 5.0 | 4.5 |

Source: U.S. Census of Population — 1960, 1970.

°Change Quotient: The ratio of the 1970 percentage to the 1960 percentage for each variable characteristic. (Maximum quotient allowed = 5.00)

in manufacturing and not noticeably stigmatized by low income, being clearly separable from (2) other, older blacks who are definitely poor, appear to be immobile, and who receive less than adequate housing services.

## Summary: The City in Change

The invasion-succession dynamics, in which an aging white population is rapidly vacating to the young, the poor, and the maturing nonwhite families, have been the critical determinants of the evolving social structure of Newark. This may be explained by the great wave of southern migration to the urban north.

During the 1960s the mass movement of blacks from the rural villages and open country of the south to the urban centers of the north slowed considerably relative to its former magnitude. The great American drama was coming to an end after a fifty-year run. Yet, despite the slowing of in-migration, disturbing societal inequalities remained in Newark in 1970. The *Race and Resources* phenomenon is still cast in a powerful construct, reemphasizing the continued concentration of the nonwhite populace at the lower levels of socio-economic status. Moreover, members of the black population who are rising up the social ladder have made a corresponding lateral transition out of the city. The least economically viable remain, inheriting neighborhoods abandoned by the white aged. This reveals the potential synthesis of a permanent lower class in Newark, substantially different from a lower working class subpopulation which is only temporarily immobile.

While the concentration of economic deprivation has remained essentially unchanged over the intercensal period, a transition in family patterns has occurred. The gradual aging of the Negro population and the young white flight has resulted in the dissipation of the 1960 concentration of Newark families in the younger stages of the family life cycle. Nor is this solely a white phenomenon. As shown in Exhibit 1-33, the twenty-five to forty-four-year group increased only 23.6 percent in the decade of the 1960s while the group as a whole expanded 53.6 percent. The implications of both of these changes are troublesome.

Despite the greatest efforts in social investment programming in this nation's history, there seems to be a massive concentration of poverty among a population which can no longer comfortably be

# EXHIBIT 1-33
## DECENNIAL CHANGE IN THE AGE STRUCTURE OF THE POPULATION — BY RACE, NEWARK — 1970

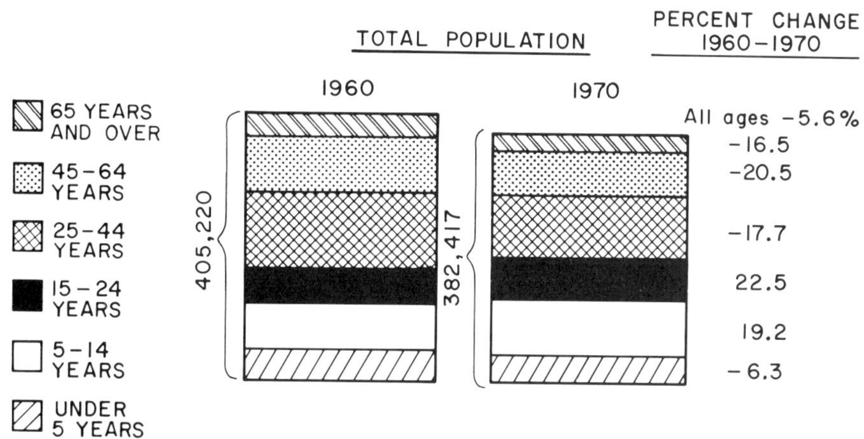


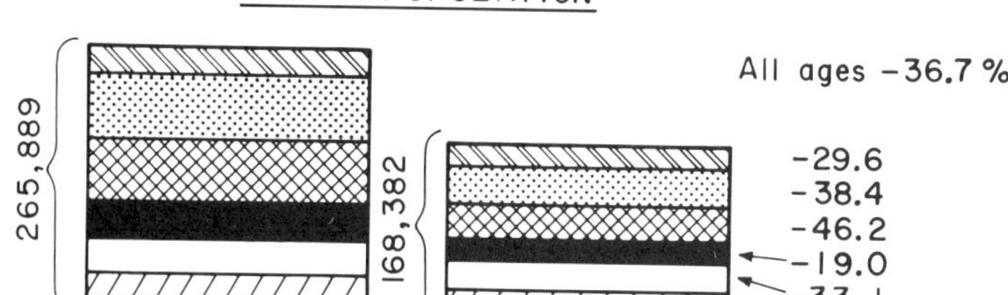


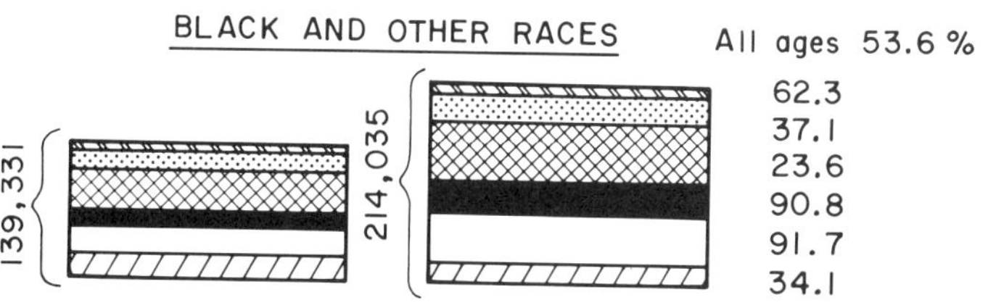

classified as purely in-migrant. Seventy-five percent of the heads of households who are newcomers to the Aid to Dependent Children category of welfare recipiency were born in the city. Newark no longer serves as an effective entrepot to middle class life. Now there is a population whose lives appear to have been largely unaffected by various job training efforts within the state of the art as practiced. Racially linked poverty, and its deep interpenetration into once economically sheltered affluent neighborhoods, has presented the dismal reality of mass human tragedy and urban decay.[10]

Moreover, the evolving social structure of Newark is bearing witness to the final tragic aspect of the black urban migration — the functional irrelevance to the United States economy of a mass of unskilled individuals. The arrivals to the city during the 1950s and 1960s were of decreasing utility to an evolving post-industrial system. While some are able to "bootstrap" themselves out, witness the outward migration, the remnant and their children, an economically incapacitated class, remain in the empty shell of a city.

## Notes

1. See Jack Chernick, Bernard Indik, and George Sternlieb, *Newark, New Jersey: Population and Labor Force* (New Brunswick, N.J.: Institute of Management and Labor Relations, Rutgers University, 1967).

2. For the extent of this outmigration in the Newark area, see: Rutgers University, Center for Urban Policy Research Staff, "Suburban Office Space: The Continued Demise of the Central City," mimeographed (New Brunswick, N.J.: Center for Urban Policy Research, Rutgers University, 1972).

3. "Jersey's Relief Rolls Rose 2-1/2 Times from '66 to '71," *The New York Times*, 23 April 1972, p. 61.

4. George Sternlieb and Bernard P. Indik, *The Ecology of Welfare* (New Brunswick, N.J.: Transaction Press, 1973).

5. See George Sternlieb and Bernard P. Indik, "Housing Vacancy Analysis," *Land Economics*, vol. 45, no. 1 (February 1969):117-121.

6. For a summary see: Janet Abu-Lughod, "Testing the Theory of Social Area Analysis: The Ecology of Cairo, Egypt," *American Sociological Review* 34 (April 1969):198-212; Brian Berry and Frank E. Horton, *Geographic Perspectives on Urban Systems* (Englewood Cliffs, N.J.: Prentice-Hall, 1969); George W. Carey, "The Regional Interpretation of Manhattan Population and Housing Patterns through Factor Analysis," *Geographical Review* 56 (October 1966):551-569; Mattei Dogan and Stein Rokkan, *Quantitative Ecological Analysis in the Social Sciences* (Cambridge, Mass.:

MIT Press, 1969); B. T. Robson, *Urban Analysis: A Study of City Structure* (London: Cambridge University Press, 1969); D. W. G. Timms, *The Urban Mosaic: Towards a Theory of Residential Differentiation* (London: Cambridge University Press, 1971).

7. See Eshref Shevky and Wendell Bell, *Social Area Analysis: Theory, Illustrative Application, and Computational Procedure* (Stanford, Calif.: Stanford University Press, 1955).

8. Scott Greer, "Urbanism Reconsidered: A Comparative Study of Local Areas in a Metropolis," *American Sociological Review* 21 (February 1956):19-24.

9. See Albert Hunter, "The Ecology of Chicago: Persistence and Change, 1930-1960," *American Journal of Sociology* 77 (November 1971): 425-444 and Robert Murdie, *The Factorial Ecology of Metropolitan Toronto 1951-1961* (Chicago: University of Chicago, Dept. of Geography, 1969).

10. James W. Hughes, "Changing Urban Social Structure: Black Differentiation in Newark," (New Brunswick, N.J.: Center for Urban Policy Research, Rutgers University, 1972, Processed).

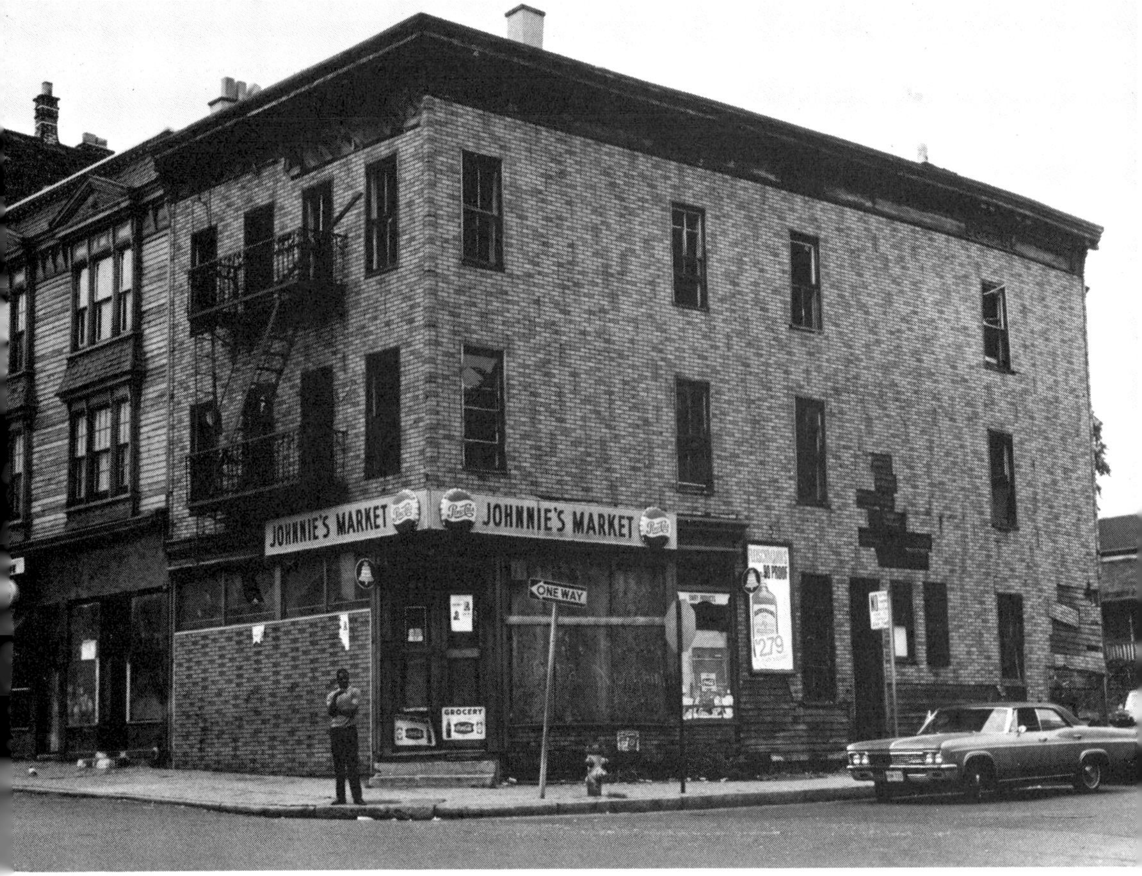
JOHNIE'S MARKET
JOHNIE'S MARKET
ONE WAY
GROCERY

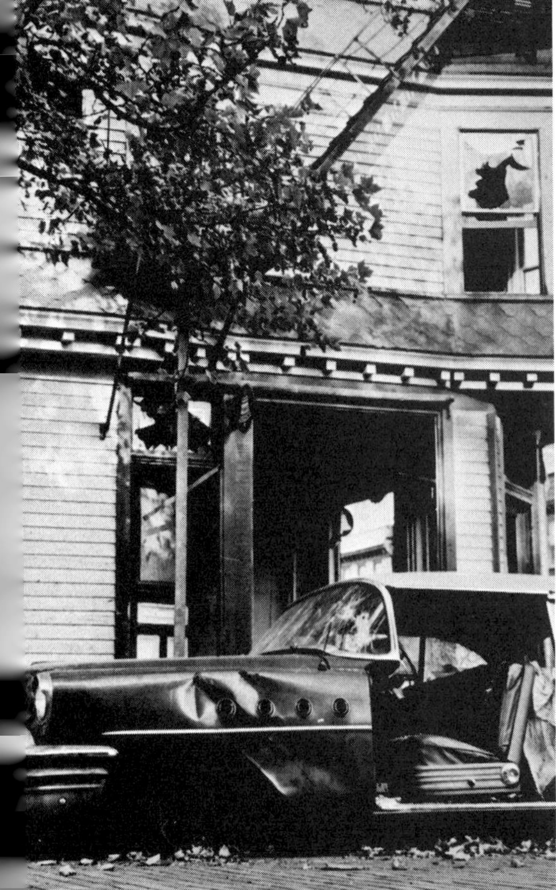

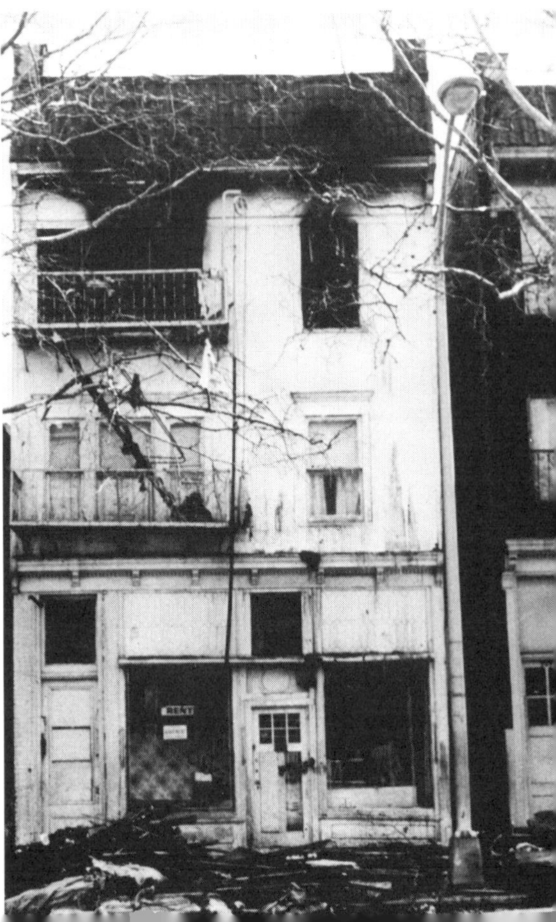

# 2

# THE "ABANDONERS:" THE FABLED TENEMENT LANDLORD

## THE MYTH OF THE URBAN LANDLORD

The whole web of governmental intervention in the private housing sphere, as well as a substantial part of private investment, operates in great measure through the matrix of the landlord. With the exception of public housing, alternative approaches to the ownership and management of low income housing have been much more frequent in the verbal than in the physical, i.e., much more talked about than placed in the ground. Low income housing cooperatives similarly are little beyond the experimental stage; the vast bulk of central city housing remains in forms of ownership and management which have changed little over the last hundred years.

One of the more satisfying folk figures of our time is that of the slumlord.[1] This is an individual who popularly is supposed to dominate the low income private housing stock, and who has not only grown wealthy historically because of his tenure, but is currently securing a more than adequate return on his properties.[2] The myth is satisfying because it leads to the belief that the major imput necessary to provide more adequate standards of maintenance and operating behavior is to get this overfed individual to disgorge some of his excess earnings; the basic pie of rents is adequate both to support owner interest in holding on to his parcels and continuing their operation while still providing the tenants with adequate service inputs. The bulk of governmental measures in the older housing sphere have revolved around this concept, whether it is tax abatement in order to assure the owner that improvements will not be over-assessed, long-term inexpensive loans for essential repairs in line with code enforcement efforts, or any of the more localized activities along these same lines. All of them are based essentially on the belief in the desirability, not only from a social point of view but also from the owner's economic point of view, of holding onto his properties. They presume a basic economic viability in operating low income housing.[3] Thus, governmental intervention has essentially been enabling legislation not to improve present yields, but rather to permit better services and improved structures without altering the basic rent/return ratios.

Many of these efforts at intervention have been disappointing in their results. In many cases there have been considerable problems in administering the programs. The legal work, for example, involved in the 312 Program* which has been a mainstay in providing twenty-five year, 3 percent interest financing for capital improvements and code standard maintenance in Urban Renewal and Concentrated Code Enforcement areas (Federally Assisted Code Enforcement [FACE] areas) has inhibited its use. But in some cases even the Grant-in-Aid program† which gives grants without repayment of up to $3,500 to resident owners in buildings with less than four units, has been substantially under utilized.

Clearly the vision of the owners, their sophistication, their readiness to see their own best interest, is brought into question. Or is it perhaps that the public vision of the landlord's best interest and the latter's private vision of reality are at odds?

In the chapter which follows the owners of the sample parcels which are still standing are examined in some depth. As detailed in the methodology (Appendix I) there were 314 responses given in the interviews conducted during September 1971. The goal was to define just who the owners were. Sections of this chapter will deal with their personal attributes and their business characteristics — when they entered the market, why they bought their parcels, and some aspects of the operating mechanisms used to run them. Most important, their attitudes and their problems as they see them will be scrutinized. The

---

*Section 312 of the 1964 Housing Act provides long-term loans for extensive rehabilitation within designated program areas.

†Section 115 of the 1965 Housing Act is a grant program for persons of limited income for the purpose of correcting minor code violations.

chapter will include a brief section on the public policy problem of both the aged owner and the owner by default. There are three sections which follow the basic presentation: the first is a statistical analysis of specific variables associated with well maintained and poorly maintained properties, the second discusses the universe of owners interviewed in 1964 versus those interviewed in 1971 for changes over time, and the third takes those sample parcels for which there were bonafide transfers during the period 1964 to 1971 and compares the two sets of owners, i.e., those who left and those who stayed, in terms of their overall characteristics.

The reader will notice that this chapter is followed by one specifically addressed to the problems and potential of minority ownership. So important is this subject that it has been given separate consideration.

## CURRENT OWNERS OF URBAN REAL ESTATE

### Who Are They?

As shown in Exhibit 2-1, the city has become by far the largest single owner of sample parcels. One hundred forty-two of the 562 (includes demolishments) for which data are available, or 25.3 percent, are owned by the municipality. The proportion in Area 1 (for definition of the area see the methodology) is 43.6 percent, in Area 2 it is 21.2 percent, in Area 3, 12.2 percent. If those parcels owned by the city are excluded, the modular form of ownership tends to be individual including joint ownership by husband and wife. Such parcels make up nearly half (47.9 percent) of the total group and two-thirds of the non-municipally owned ones.

### Date of Title by Area

The classic vision of slum tenement operation is one of high turnover, of accelerated depreciation aided by rapid transfer of title in order to renew the high level of tax coverage base. In Exhibit 2-2 is shown the date of title by area for those non-municipally held parcels for which this could be determined. It is clear from the exhibit that longevity of holding is much more considerable than would normally be projected. Nearly 40 percent (39.7) have been in the same hands for eleven or

EXHIBIT 2-1
CATEGORY OF OWNERSHIP (1971)
BY SAMPLE AREA OF THE CITY (1971)

| Category | Area 1 | Area 2 | Area 3 | Total |
|---|---|---|---|---|
| Individual (including joint ownership by husband and wife) | 57 | 96 | 116 | 269 |
| Two or more individuals | 10 | 10 | 23 | 43 |
| Realty corporation | 8 | 10 | 8 | 26 |
| Financial institution | 2 | 1 | 4 | 7 |
| Nonfinancial institution | 24 | 28 | 22 | 74 |
| Estates | 1 | 0 | 0 | 1 |
| City | 79 | 39 | 24 | 142 |
| Total | 181 | 184 | 197 | 562 |

PERCENT DISTRIBUTION

| Category | Area 1 | Area 2 | Area 3 | Total |
|---|---|---|---|---|
| Individual (including joint ownership by husband and wife) | 31.5 | 52.2 | 58.9 | 47.9 |
| Two or more individuals | 5.5 | 5.4 | 11.7 | 8.7 |
| Realty corporation | 4.4 | 5.4 | 4.1 | 4.6 |
| Financial institution | 1.1 | 0.5 | 2.0 | 1.2 |
| Nonfinancial institution | 13.3 | 15.2 | 11.2 | 13.2 |
| Estates | 0.6 | 0.0 | 0.0 | 0.2 |
| City | 43.6 | 21.2 | 12.2 | 25.3 |
| Total | 100.0 | 100.0 | 100.0 | 100.0 |

$\chi^2 = 0.001$

Source: Newark Area Resurvey, spring 1972

more years, with a third (33.2) changing hands in the last four years.

The pattern of acquisition shown in this exhibit may give a feeling of even more recency than is really the case. While we tried to correct wherever possible for variations between the title and the interview data, some mistakes probably slipped through. For example, parcel number 485 shows a transfer with substantial consideration accompanied by bank mortgage as recently as June 1971. Actually it has

EXHIBIT 2-2

DATE OF PROPERTY TITLE (1971) BY SAMPLE AREA OF THE CITY (1971)

| Years Held | Area 1 | Area 2 | Area 3 | Total |
|---|---|---|---|---|
| 0-1 | 10 | 15 | 21 | 46 |
| 2-4 | 26 | 39 | 37 | 102 |
| 5-6 | 6 | 16 | 23 | 45 |
| 7-10 | 17 | 29 | 30 | 76 |
| 11-15 | 19 | 20 | 23 | 62 |
| 16-20 | 8 | 15 | 10 | 33 |
| 20 or more | 25 | 20 | 37 | 82 |
| Total | 111 | 154 | 181 | 446 |

PERCENT DISTRIBUTION

| Years Held | Area 1 | Area 2 | Area 3 | Total |
|---|---|---|---|---|
| 0-1 | 9.0 | 9.7 | 11.6 | 10.3 |
| 2-4 | 23.4 | 25.3 | 20.4 | 22.9 |
| 5-6 | 5.4 | 10.4 | 12.7 | 10.1 |
| 7-10 | 15.3 | 18.8 | 16.6 | 17.0 |
| 11-15 | 17.1 | 13.0 | 12.7 | 13.9 |
| 16-20 | 7.2 | 9.7 | 5.5 | 7.4 |
| 20 or more | 22.5 | 13.0 | 20.4 | 18.4 |
| Total | 100.0 | 100.0 | 100.0 | 100.0 |

$\chi^2$ n/s @ 0.05

Source: Newark Area Resurvey, spring 1972

been in one family's hands since 1944, with the same individual presently listed on the title having held specific ownership for a number of the intervening years prior to its sale to another member of the family, then its return to the original party. The question of whether this is part of a pattern simply of trading, or whether it relates to renewing depreciation allowances is moot. In any case the data shown in the exhibit are probably a minimum statement of the functional longevity of ownership.

## Experience of Owners in the Real Estate Market

The time when a sample parcel was first bought may be an inadequate measurement of owner experience in real estate. When this was examined there was relatively little variation by area (Exhibit 2-3). Notice, however, that there is a surprising dearth of recent owners in Area 1, with only 17.1 percent of owners having gone into business in

EXHIBIT 2-3
TIME OF OWNER'S FIRST ENTRANCE INTO REAL ESTATE (1971) BY SAMPLE AREA OF THE CITY (1971)

| First Entered Real Estate | Area 1 | Area 2 | Area 3 | Total |
|---|---|---|---|---|
| Pre-1930 | 5 | 5 | 5 | 15 |
| 1930-40 | 7 | 1 | 5 | 13 |
| 1940-50 | 11 | 9 | 17 | 37 |
| 1950-55 | 11 | 21 | 12 | 44 |
| 1955-60 | 16 | 25 | 15 | 56 |
| 1960-65 | 13 | 22 | 23 | 58 |
| 1965-67 | 5 | 12 | 11 | 28 |
| 1967-Date | 8 | 18 | 25 | 51 |
| NA/DK | 0 | 5 | 4 | 9 |
| Total | 76 | 118 | 117 | 311 |

PERCENT DISTRIBUTION

| | | | | |
|---|---|---|---|---|
| Pre-1930 | 6.6 | 4.2 | 4.3 | 4.8 |
| 1930-40 | 9.2 | 0.8 | 4.3 | 4.2 |
| 1940-50 | 14.5 | 7.6 | 14.5 | 11.9 |
| 1950-55 | 14.5 | 17.8 | 10.3 | 14.1 |
| 1955-60 | 21.1 | 21.2 | 12.8 | 18.0 |
| 1960-65 | 17.1 | 18.6 | 19.7 | 18.6 |
| 1965-67 | 6.6 | 10.2 | 9.4 | 9.0 |
| 1967-Date | 10.5 | 15.3 | 21.4 | 16.4 |
| NA/DK | 0.0 | 4.2 | 3.4 | 2.9 |
| Total | 100.0 | 100.0 | 100.0 | 100.0 |

$\chi^2$ n/s @ 0.05

Source: Newark Area Resurvey, spring 1972

1965 or later as compared with a quarter of the owners in Area 2, and three out of ten owners in Area 3. In part, this reflects the stagnation of the market in the hard core and may be the result very specifically of black home buyers, the principal newcomers other than the municipality, avoiding the central core. This point will be touched on in a later chapter.

## Size of Holding

There is some indication that the scale of operations that are typical of core owners is being reduced. In Exhibit 2-4 the size of owners' holdings by area of the city is shown. Nearly 2 out of 3 (64.6 percent) of the 313 parcels for which data are available are in the hands of people who at most own 1 or 2 parcels in addition to their sample holding. Ten percent are in the hands of owners of thirteen or more parcels, with an additional 5 percent owning seven to twelve. When the latter owners were questioned, the typical size and location of their other parcels were quite similar to those in the sample.

Given the relative modesty of the individual structures here, typically of no more than six or eight units, it is evident that the typical scale of Newark tenement owners is relatively small, with the dominant group being single parcel owners. Notice the bifurcation of distribution in Area 1. While single parcel owners are represented in proportion to their presence in the total sample, there is a distinct skew toward very large owners being heavily represented in the balance, with 18 percent of the parcels in the hands of owners of thirteen or more units. Again this may well be a reflection of the fact that only large scale operators are buying in the central core. The data presented below tend to confirm this point.

## Who Collects the Rents by Area

As would be guessed from these data it is Area 1 that is much more substantially the arena of professional management services, with a third of the parcels having owners who claim that they use managers or rent collectors versus 22.5 percent and 22.3 percent in Areas 2 and 3, respectively. Similarly, the relative scale of operations in the several areas is shown by the fact that 37.2 percent of the owners of parcels in Area 1 said that they had full-time employees who did their repairs contrasted with 26.3 percent and 21.4 percent in Areas 2 and 3, respectively. (Notice that the size of structures is nearly equivalent regardless of area.) Nearly 30 percent of the owners in Area 1 said that they were full-time real estate operators as compared to only 20 percent in the other two areas.

EXHIBIT 2-4
OWNER'S SIZE OF HOLDING (1971)
BY SAMPLE AREA OF THE CITY (1971)

| Size of Holding | Area 1 | Area 2 | Area 3 | Total |
|---|---|---|---|---|
| No other holdings | 32 | 55 | 49 | 136 |
| Other holdings — 1 or 2 units | 11 | 24 | 31 | 66 |
| 3-6 units | 10 | 14 | 10 | 34 |
| 7-12 units | 6 | 6 | 5 | 17 |
| 13-75 units | 13 | 7 | 8 | 28 |
| 76 plus units | 1 | 3 | 1 | 5 |
| Previously owned | 0 | 0 | 1 | 1 |
| Number not known | 4 | 2 | 2 | 8 |
| NA/DK | 1 | 7 | 10 | 18 |
| TOTAL | 78 | 118 | 117 | 313 |

PERCENT DISTRIBUTION

| Size of Holding | Area 1 | Area 2 | Area 3 | Total |
|---|---|---|---|---|
| No other holdings | 41.0 | 46.6 | 41.9 | 43.5 |
| Other holdings — 1 or 2 units | 14.1 | 20.3 | 26.5 | 21.1 |
| 3-6 units | 12.8 | 11.9 | 8.5 | 10.9 |
| 7-12 units | 7.7 | 5.1 | 4.3 | 5.4 |
| 13-75 units | 16.7 | 5.9 | 6.8 | 8.9 |
| 76 plus units | 1.3 | 2.5 | 0.9 | 1.6 |
| Previously owned | 0.0 | 0.0 | 0.9 | 0.3 |
| Number not known | 5.1 | 1.7 | 1.7 | 2.6 |
| NA/DK | 1.3 | 5.9 | 8.5 | 5.8 |
| Total | 100.0 | 100.0 | 100.0 | 100.0 |

$\chi^2$ n/s @ 0.05

Source: Newark Area Resurvey, spring 1972

## Owner Residency by Area

In Exhibit 2-5 is shown the residence of owner by area of the city. Notice the relatively small proportion of resident owners in Area 1, with only 13 percent versus 27.1 percent of the owners in Area 2 and 36.8

EXHIBIT 2-5
OWNER'S ADDRESS OF RECORD (1971)
BY SAMPLE AREA OF THE CITY (1971)

| Residence | Area 1 | Area 2 | Area 3 | Total |
|---|---|---|---|---|
| Resident in parcel | 10 | 32 | 43 | 85 |
| Within a block of parcel | 4 | 3 | 1 | 8 |
| Newark (other) | 22 | 34 | 30 | 86 |
| New Jersey (20-mile radius from Newark) | 21 | 24 | 23 | 68 |
| Balance of New Jersey | 1 | 4 | 5 | 10 |
| New York | 0 | 2 | 0 | 2 |
| Non-New Jersey (Other than New York) | 4 | 2 | 0 | 6 |
| NA/DK | 15 | 17 | 15 | 47 |
| Total | 77 | 118 | 117 | 312 |

PERCENT DISTRIBUTION

| Residence | Area 1 | Area 2 | Area 3 | Total |
|---|---|---|---|---|
| Resident in parcel | 13.0 | 27.1 | 36.8 | 27.2 |
| Within a block of parcel | 5.2 | 2.5 | 0.9 | 2.6 |
| Newark (other) | 28.6 | 28.8 | 25.6 | 27.6 |
| New Jersey (20 mile radius from Newark) | 27.3 | 20.3 | 19.7 | 21.8 |
| Balance of New Jersey | 1.3 | 3.4 | 4.3 | 3.2 |
| New York | 0.0 | 1.7 | 0.0 | 0.6 |
| Non-New Jersey (Other than New York) | 5.2 | 1.7 | 0.0 | 1.9 |
| NA/DK | 19.5 | 14.4 | 12.8 | 15.1 |
| Total | 100.0 | 100.0 | 100.0 | 100.0 |

$\chi^2 = 0.05$

Source: Newark Area Resurvey, spring 1972

percent in Area 3. These data bear out the other findings of the increasing scale of operation and professionalism being much more prevalent in the more central areas of the city.

## Motivation for Purchase

Are there significant variations in owner's motivation for purchasing parcels which vary as a function of their location? In Exhibit 2-6 the variations in response to the question "Why did you buy your parcel?" are shown by area. The most significant variation is in the proportion of buyers for the purpose of residence. In Area 1 less than one out of seven of the owners bought for this reason while in the other areas it was approximately 40 percent each.

It is clear that the potential home buyer is bypassing the hard core. Increasingly this is the domain of the large scale rental owner; the professional who will buy on speculation at a very low price. And even this type of owner is in short supply, judging from the level of municipal take-overs and abandonments. More typically, these are parcels that are moving into a never-never land of nondesirability.

The private purchases in Area 1 were typically acquired for rental return or investment as were the nonhome acquisitions in the other areas. When these owners were asked whether their initial reason was still the reason for keeping their parcel, in Area 1 there was a great level of disillusionment with less than a third, 32.1 percent, answering in the affirmative versus roughly half in each of the other two areas. *In essence, therefore, in hard-core Area 1, which once housed 30,000 people, the private market now finds little role.*

## Potential for Improvement

Earlier in this chapter reference was made to the underlying concept of governmental support for urban bootstrapping. This presumes a basic will to improve, which may have been impeded by any of a variety of limited market defects. In turn, the governmental approach is to minimize the impact of these factors; whether fear of tax increases on improvement, or providing financing for areas in which conventional sources have dried up. How realistic is this approach?

One of the weakest areas of research involves asking people questions along the line of "Would you, if?" particularly when positive

## EXHIBIT 2-6
## OWNER'S REASON FOR PROPERTY PURCHASE (1971) BY SAMPLE AREA OF THE CITY (1971)

| Why Did You Buy? | Area 1 | Area 2 | Area 3 | Total |
|---|---|---|---|---|
| Home | 11 | 47 | 51 | 109 |
| Rental return (Investment) | 48 | 49 | 45 | 142 |
| Speculation | 0 | 0 | 2 | 2 |
| Inheritance | 6 | 4 | 8 | 18 |
| Debt | 1 | 1 | 0 | 2 |
| Commercial purposes | 4 | 6 | 0 | 10 |
| Home plus income | 3 | 4 | 0 | 7 |
| Other | 4 | 5 | 9 | 18 |
| Mortgage foreclosure | 1 | 2 | 2 | 5 |
| Total | 78 | 118 | 117 | 313 |

PERCENT DISTRIBUTION

| Why Did You Buy? | Area 1 | Area 2 | Area 3 | Total |
|---|---|---|---|---|
| Home | 14.1 | 39.8 | 43.6 | 34.8 |
| Rental return (investment) | 61.5 | 41.5 | 38.5 | 45.4 |
| Speculation | 0.0 | 0.0 | 1.7 | 0.6 |
| Inheritance | 7.7 | 3.4 | 6.8 | 5.8 |
| Debt | 1.3 | 0.8 | 0.0 | 0.6 |
| Commercial purposes | 5.1 | 5.1 | 0.0 | 3.2 |
| Home plus income | 3.8 | 3.4 | 0.0 | 2.2 |
| Other | 5.1 | 4.2 | 7.7 | 5.8 |
| Mortgage foreclosure | 1.3 | 1.7 | 1.7 | 1.6 |
| Total | 100.0 | 100.0 | 100.0 | 100.0 |

$\chi^2 = 0.01$

Source: Newark Area Resurvey, spring 1972

answers require nothing but their verbalization and places the respondent in a societally approved role. Obviously this is the case when owners are asked such questions as "Would you improve a parcel given relief from taxes or given mortgaging?" There is a clear built-in bias toward affirmative answers here.

Given this bias the results that have been secured, when analyzed by area, are very negative. Nearly a third of the owners in Area 1 (32.7 percent) when asked if they would improve (given no increase in taxes) said simply that their properties were not worth it. This compares with 14.5 percent in Area 2 and 12.5 percent in Area 3. In the latter two areas, about a quarter of the respondents in each case stated that their parcels did not need improvements and an equivalent proportion that they could not afford them. Area 1 on the contrary secured approximately half that level for each response. The bulk of the balance of the responses indicated they didn't know.

A similar question on the utilization of government financing for purposes of rehabilitation and maintenance of structures secured the same results. Again in Area 1 there was basically a dominant negative tone with the other two areas giving answers slightly more positive and thus quite similar to the tax response.

## Owners' Expectation of the Worth of Their Parcels Five Years From Now

*It is not only the current year's results which determine landlord behavior, his willingness to improve, to make additional capital investment, and to maintain. Perhaps even more important is his expectation of future value. If the projections are positive then holding a parcel presents a relatively assured investment. If they are in the negative, however, the owner rightly or wrongly sees himself as a holder of a wasting asset. His response to this latter supposition is to maximize immediate yield, minimize investment, and, perhaps, even in the very act of preparing for the worst, generate its fulfillment.*

And in Newark the answers to questions on "Do you think your parcel is going to be worth more or less five years from now?" are such as to raise some very real questions about public policy. In Area 1, for example, 45.5 percent of the owners said their parcels would be worth less five years in the future. This compares with 37.3 percent in Area 2 and 23.9 percent in Area 3 who had similar prophesies. When asked why, the answers tended to be quite similar; the bulk of them in every case referred to area characteristics, neighborhood problems, and the like.*

## Increased Rent or Resale Potential

When owners were asked what it would cost to repair their parcels and whether they could get rent increases that would cover such repairs, only a quarter of the owners in Area 1 versus approximately a third of the owners in Areas 2 and 3 answered in the affirmative, i.e., that the tenants could or would pay rents commensurate with the cost of improvement. The gaps, however, are substantial and the level of positive feeling in securing the additional rents is low at best. When, in addition, owners were asked if they were to make improvements could they get their money back on resale, the answers in all cases were terribly somber, with only 15.4 percent of the owners in Area 1 answering yes, definitely or probably, as compared with 20.4 percent of the owners in Area 2, and 24.8 percent of the owners in Area 3.

## The Landlords and Welfare Tenantry

As pointed out earlier, welfare recipients now comprise more than a quarter of the city's population. While no specific data are available for location within the municipality, undoubtedly there is an even higher concentration of such individuals in the core areas under consideration here. In an earlier study of landlords' opinion and behavior in New York City, the welfare variable, i.e., the proportion of tenants receiving welfare in particular buildings, correlated negatively with the condition of that building, holding constant all other factors, including rent levels, costs of repairs and maintenance, landlord characteristics, and tenant ethnicity.[5] What is the situation in Newark?

Only one out of five parcel owners in Area 1 answered that he had no welfare tenants, with about a third of the balance simply saying they didn't know. The equivalent figures for Areas 2 and 3 are very similar with about a third of the parcel owners indicating that they had no welfare tenants and about one out of five responding that he did not

*Areas 1, 2, and 3, as indicated previously, denote increasing percentages of housing soundness (compared to other census tracts) as observed in 1960.

know. Taking these figures at face value and assuming that all the "don't knows" reflect buildings without welfare tenants, which is undoubtedly a gross oversimplification, would lead to a finding that approximately half of the buildings in Area 1 had at least some welfare tenants, and at least 40 percent of the buildings in Areas 2 and 3 were similarly occupied.

What do the owners say about the impact of such tenantry? In general the responses are quite negative. With substantial emphasis in Area 1 and relatively little change in the other two areas, the comments were that welfare tenantry had a very deleterious impact on the maintenance of property. This answer was given by half the owners in Area 1, 46 percent of the owners in Area 2, and 43 percent of the owners in Area 3 (Exhibit 2-7).

When questioned further as to the impact of welfare tenants on rent levels, there was no indication that such tenantry had a significant impact either in raising or lowering overall rent levels. The responses, therefore, are substantially aimed at operating problems rather than nominal rental levels. The open ended responses showed a considerable variation of opinion on welfare recipients. Some owners pointed to the fact that it is tenants, regardless of whether they are on welfare or not, who occasion grief. In some cases owners actually prefer welfare recipients as tenants. In one case, the owner pointed out:

> "Welfare tenants make things easier as far as being able to collect rents at all — if the manager can get there soon after the welfare checks arrive. It's a much more reliable source of rental income, unless the tenants are employed."

It should be pointed out that the owner in question, a white pharmacist who used to live in the building but who has since moved away, at one time collected his own rents. Now monthly payments within the three-family house are secured by a rent collector. The owner, who is afraid to go to the parcel, stated that within the last week there had been a shooting on the premises.

A more negative opinion was expressed by one of the major operators still active in Newark, who, referring to a parcel in the hard core which has six apartment units (all of which are occupied by blacks on welfare) said:

EXHIBIT 2-7

RELATIVE IMPORTANCE OF VARIOUS INHIBITORS TO PARCEL MAINTENANCE AND IMPROVEMENTS (1971) BY AREA (1971)

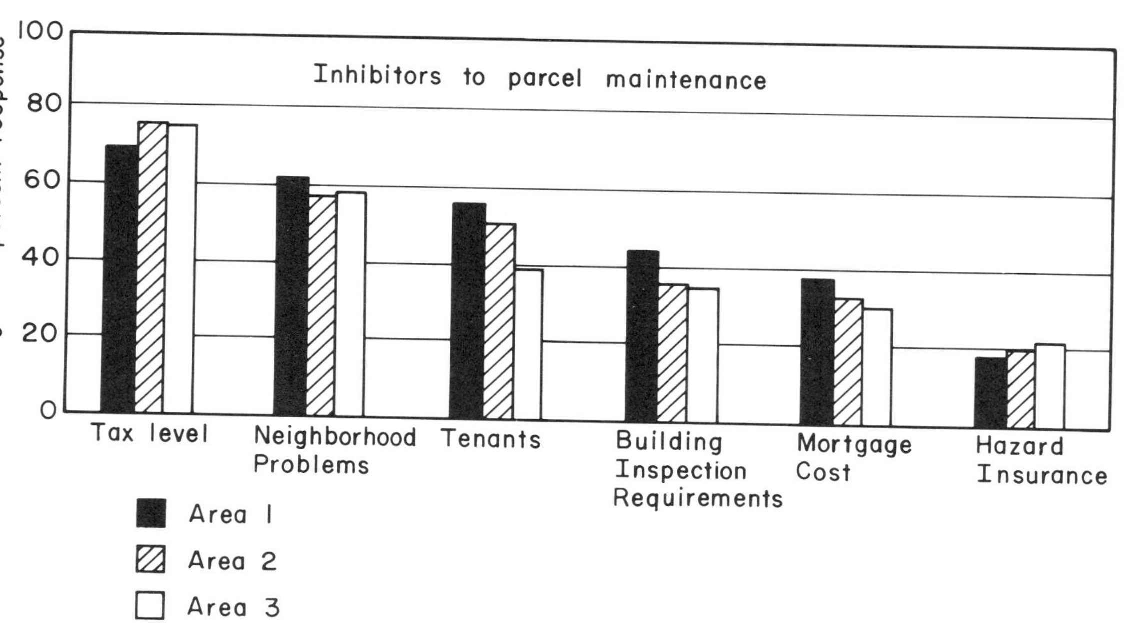

> "They're the worst — they bring in more children than they tell you, and both parents and children are totally destructive. Since they don't have to pay out of their own pockets, they don't realize the value of property."

Nor, as pointed out in more detail in the chapter on minority owners, is this purely a white affectation. The black head of a store-front Baptist Church which is involved in running three parcels with eighteen apartments stated:

> "Those welfare tenants have less respect for property and it's more difficult to collect the rent."

A number of the major holders mentioned close relationships with the welfare department in securing tenantry. As one of them pointed out:

> "They're always calling me up whenever they have a burnt out family or somebody has got to find rooms for some reason or another."

Whether, given the limitations on the welfare budget, as well as the scarcity of good apartments, the welfare department could secure more in the way of amenities for their clients is an open question. There seems to be very little indication that presently much is being done along these lines. In any case, welfare tenants are severely underrepresented in well kept parcels.

## OWNERSHIP CHARACTERISTICS LEADING TO WELL MAINTAINED STRUCTURES

Later in this chapter the linkage of condition of parcel and the variables associated with ownership will be discussed, using a variety of integrative statistical techniques. In this section, however, a few of the distinct variations will be considered.

### Longevity of Holding

There is a degree of linkage between the length of time that an owner has been in the real estate business, the length of time which he has owned a sample parcel, and its condition. But the former variables, it should be noted, are interlinked with many others; first entry into real estate operations, for example, is strongly correlated with both white owners and professional operators.

## Home Ownership

*Sixty-nine percent of the parcels that were well kept were bought for reasons of home ownership. This compares with barely half that for the sample as a whole (37.4 percent).* And when owners were asked whether their original motivation for purchase was still their reason for keeping the parcel, there was a very high level of correlation between positive answers and well kept parcels. Conversely, for poorly kept parcels, there was a relatively low positive response. The figures are 33.7 percent for the latter versus 81.3 percent for the former.

## Operating Patterns

Well kept parcels tend to be owner managed and to be in the hands of people who had no other holding, with a third of the poorly kept versus two-thirds of the well kept in such hands. Full-time real estate owners tended to be slightly underrepresented among well kept parcels but made up for this in reasonably kept units; the variation, however, was slight. Rent collection and furnished versus unfurnished procedures did not seem to make too much of a difference here.

## Landlord/Tenant Relationships

The dominance of tenantry and tenantry problems among resident and nonresident owners is outstanding; both the problems of adjusting to large families and the suspicion of the unknown are widespread. The fear of losing the tenants you know for those you don't know is exemplified by the response of the owner of parcel number 280:

> This six-family frame house is in reasonably good condition. The landlord, who feels considerable pride in it, points to the fact that his most recent tenant moved in six years ago. When asked what improvements he would make in the property if he was sure of not getting a boost in taxes, he said, "Central heating is the only service that isn't available in the building. . . . Even with tax stabilization I wouldn't put it in since the building is too old and the rents would have to be raised, and I don't want to do this, because I don't want

> to lose any of my long-term tenants. You don't know who will move in."

Notice that all the tenants, as well as the owner, are black. The problem, therefore, is clearly not a racial one.

The complexity of these issues is exemplified by parcel number 366:

> The black owner of this building purchased it through a VA mortgage twenty years ago. He now owns it free and clear. The building is beautifully maintained; it is on a rather good street in the middle of a marginal neighborhood in Newark. The owner presently is renting just one apartment while leaving the attic vacant. He is securing only $85.00 a month for the apartment, though he points out (and this was confirmed in the area) he could get $125.00 easily. His problem as he put it was, "Now I have just one person living there and this house is beautiful. If I raise it to $125.00, I have to take in a family with a lot of kids, and that's murder on a house."

The house clearly needs no repairs, but the attitude expressed here is exemplified by a number of other owners who would probably not be interested in government mortgage programs which involved any risk of losing present tenantry through increases in rent levels. There is a very strong feeling expressed throughout the survey results that if one has good tenants one tries to keep them, even accepting a lesser rent if necessary. This is particularly evident in interviews with resident landlords, perhaps even more so than absentees.

In hard core areas this is combined with the fear of securing tenants who may be drug addicts, or of an apartment becoming a hangout for neighborhood gangs and junkies with resulting damage not merely to the apartment but also the loss of all the residual tenants and ultimately the abandonment of the building. A case in point is parcel number 238.

> This twelve-family frame house is assessed for a total of slightly over $30,000. It was purchased in 1961 by a medium scale white operator for $28,000, subject to a $12,500 mortgage held by a savings and loan. A second mortgage for $8,000 was given by the previous owner. The present owner took title in 1970 with a complete purchase money mortgage given by his predecessor for the full total price of $28,000. He is presently trying to sell the parcel, with no potential buyers and is in the process of permitting the city to foreclose on it since he finds it unprofitable to run the building.

> According to the Haitian owner, it's difficult to collect rent. He feels that the junkies in the area (there are four abandoned buildings on the same block) discourage good tenantry and in turn are bringing about the ruin of the building. When interviewed he was evicting four of his tenants for rent evasion. (There is some indication that rather than contracting for their apartment through him they had merely squatted in vacant units.) This is a building that is well on its way to abandonment.

Owners' statements of their problems were further cross tabulated by condition of parcel. Among poorly kept parcel owners, it was the tenant problem which was given the highest order of priority with 44 percent of the respondents giving it either the first or second priority. Among reasonably kept parcels the equivalent was only 22 percent, with the well kept parcels a shade under that. The sample for the purposes of three-way cross tabulations is relatively small, but the ethnicity of tenantry did not seem to play a major role.

## The Impact of Real Estate Taxes

The enormous bite that real estate taxes take of the rent dollar in Newark (upwards of 35 percent) is explained in the chapter on taxes. How does this affect landlord behavior? There is really a dichotomy here between the more recent, more sophisticated owner who buys a parcel particularly cheaply because the high tax rates have been capitalized, and essentially deducted from the nominal selling price of a parcel, as against the longer term owner, particularly resident owners on fixed incomes who find that their operating costs as a function of tax increases begin to press their budgets, sometimes to a point of losing the house in question. Certainly there is a real and genuine fear that observable improvements may result in reassessment.

That this intimidation is not purely a mental fabrication is reinforced by the experience of one black owner of a semi-abandoned two-family house, parcel number 131P.

> The owner presently has only two squatters in the house, but when he bought it some five years ago, he felt that he was immediately reassessed. He feels now that this was a penalty for bringing improvements to the property. His tax bill went up $200 because he admitted in court that he put in new plumbing fixtures, sinks and bathtubs, etc., rather than having bought the parcel with them.

> While the owner may have minimized the level of capital improvement made in the parcel, a search of the records does indicate some building improvement permits.

*This is not the same, however, as saying that a rollback in taxes would necessarily generate improvements in parcels.* Discussed earlier was owner response to the levels of improvements that he would make if given an assurance against reassessment. One may well scant the owner's responses here by saying that this shows a basic insecurity about the quality and the longevity of the protection against increased taxes; still the overwhelming refusal to envision additional improvements cannot be scoffed at. The open end responses to this area are sometimes confusing. Not atypically, however, they run along the line of the response given by the owner of parcel number 475:

> He said that, if given the assurance against getting a boost in taxes, he would put central heat in his four-family house. He then paused and continued, "But that costs a lot of money and I wouldn't get it back." Note that this refusal is in the face of current rents of only $70.00 a month.

Tax stabilization is a very necessary input if any level of substantial capital improvements is to be made, but it is merely an enabling act, it would have to be complemented by drastic action and assurances on a number of fronts as to the future of the city.

Among poorly kept parcel owners 51 percent gave taxes first or second priority as a problem. For owners of reasonably kept parcels it was fully 70 percent, and this was matched by the well kept parcel owners.

(As noted in the Methodology, owners' self evaluation of parcels tended to agree with those of our interviewers. When asked whether their parcels were in good condition, this was the case as well as in the evaluation of responses toward a variety of questions; whether they would make repairs if given financing or guarantee against tax increases. The response levels indicating no repairs necessary in the latter two cases were largely in accord with our own evaluation of the parcels in question.)

## The Availability of Financing

Owners of well kept parcels tended to be much more certain about securing mortgages on resale. More than half of the group (56 percent versus only 18 percent of the poorly kept parcel owners and a third of the reasonably kept parcel owners) indicated that if they sold their parcels now, they could get a mortgage. Does this measure the fact that better parcels can secure mortgaging or is it that owners who think they can get mortgaging approved, maintain their properties? These questions will be discussed in a later chapter. Even in the moderately kept and well kept parcels, however, a significant proportion of the owners were not at all sanguine about securing financing.

## Level of Rent Increase Necessary for Maintenance

When owners were asked what level of rent increase would be needed to make their buildings a good investment, about 20 percent of the poorly kept parcel owners said either that no one would pay the necessary rent or that they were satisfied with the present level. For those who did give figures, the range tended to be quite broad, with somewhere on the order of \$20. to \$50. a month per unit providing the largest cluster. The bulk of the owners of well kept parcels answered that they were satisfied with present rent levels. The latter, however, were also much more certain that they could secure rent increases if they wanted them, compared to the poorly kept parcel owners. These owners said that they probably could not get necessary rent increases. As pointed out in another context, poorly kept parcels tended to have lower rent levels.

## Improvement Return on Resale

Owners were not at all sure that they could get their money back if they made improvements. Some 60 percent of the poorly kept parcel owners said definitely not, with only 16 percent giving a positive answer.

In general, while the samples are too small for definitive analysis, the well kept parcel owners were much more hopeful, with the reasonably kept parcel owners intermediate. When asked about government financing legislation, regardless of quality of structure, about three-fifths of the respondents showed some knowledge of government programs with no specific program singled out.

## Financing Terms

There is no variation in what they would have to pay for financing or sources of potential financing which would account for variations in conditions of parcel. The same held true for urban renewal both in terms of whether the owners thought they were in a designated area and also whether they would, if taken, secure an appropriate recompense.

## Resident Ownership and Condition

Eleven percent of the poorly kept parcel owners were resident owners with 60 percent evenly divided between Newark residents outside of the core area and suburbs within twenty miles of Newark. Fifty-six percent of the well kept parcel owners and 38.4 percent of the reasonably kept parcels were owned by people who were residents.

## Ethnicity of Owner and Condition

This factor is touched on later, but it is worth noting here that there is some indication that blacks are more than holding their own as to the condition of the parcels which they own. Only 30 percent of the poorly kept parcels are held by blacks versus 40 percent of the reasonably kept and an even larger proportion of the well kept.

When asked whether they would improve their parcel if given mortgages, the great bulk of the respondents answered negatively regardless of condition of the parcel. Typically the reasons for this were lack of return, bad neighborhood characteristics, and the like.

## Owner Forms and Condition

As would be guessed from the residence pattern, individual ownership was overrepresented in the well kept parcels with 63.8 percent of the total sample in such hands versus 50 percent of those poorly kept. Contrarily, nonfinancial institutions were overrepresented among the owners of the poorly kept parcels holding 22.4 percent of them versus half that for the reasonably kept and well kept.

Structures with outstanding indentures tended to be in significantly better condition than those without. This parallels findings in the abandonment section wherein abandoned parcels seemed to be less likely to have mortgages.

## The Problem of the Aged Owner

In a recent statewide conference on the problems of code enforcement in New Jersey, there was a sympathetic murmur of assent when one of the building inspection supervisors from a major municipality raised the question of what was to be done in terms of the aged, frequently impoverished, owners of less than standard buildings. As the speaker commented, "If we push the code, we're just moving an old person from his home into the poor house."

While the Grant-in-Aid program (Section 115 of the 1964 Housing Act) makes possible the provision in federally assisted code enforcement areas, as well as those under urban renewal and several other designations, of grants up to $3,500 to low income resident owners, as well as long term inexpensive loans for rehabilitation, these frequently are difficult to secure. The level of local legal expertise required to implement the program, limitations on its funding, and perhaps more than anything else, the inertia that sometimes characterizes the owners, have limited the effectiveness of such programs in providing the supplement which the elderly proprietor frequently needs.

The problem of the aged owner in coping with building ownership is exemplified by parcel number 062, a three-story, three-family frame house.

> Its owner who is black and sixty-five years of age is a widow whose husband died five years ago. When asked about repair work, she said, "I'm too old to do much in the way of repairs, and licensed repairmen are too expensive. I only make repairs when I have to, because of the inspector." The owner in question had purchased the parcel with her husband back in 1950 for $8,500 with a $7,000 mortgage from a local savings and loan association. This is now paid off. The taxes on the parcel are slightly over $800.00 a year, the total rent roll is $2,400 plus the apartment in which the proprietor lives. With no charges for debt service, the owner is securing a free apartment; on the other hand, she does not have either the resources in cash or, perhaps even more important, in energy to undertake anything in the nature of a much required repair and maintenance program.

The facts of age frequently play a role in the abandonment of a unit.

> Parcel number 593, for example, was foreclosed in 1969 by a savings and loan association which held a small remnant of a mortgage on the property. Its owner in 1964 was a retired real estate broker and perhaps the words of our interviewer at that time best describe the situation: "This is an old man of sixty-five, not perhaps chronologically, but physically and mentally. He is in poor health, semi-retired. He spends his time keeping track of his properties. He owns six buildings in addition to this three-family frame structure. This occupies him quite fully and in his own words he's glad to have an income from them as he is too tired to sell them or to do anything particularly to alter them. He is maintaining them as is, and not complaining about taxes or seeking to improve. He is just playing end game. The owner secured the parcels in description on a foreclosure; he had sold them in 1957 on a single blanket transaction to another realty operator and ended up taking back the parcels in 1963.
>
> By 1969 the savings and loan company which had mortgages on them foreclosed and bought the parcels at the sheriff's sale. The sample building is boarded up, the bank is simply waiting for proposed highway construction to take it off their hands. It should be noted, by the way, that in a later check of the tax records, the building had fallen into real estate tax arrears indicating that, with the probability of the highway land-taking being put off, the bank would let the building go to the city. By this time, however, it has fallen into a condition which probably means that demolition is its sole possible future.

*Investment in income producing real property has been one of the classic forms of old-age financial planning. The problem of the aged owner who may have bought a building a generation ago as a form of annuity for these reasons is evident.*

> Parcel number 279, for example, is an eight-family, two store, masonry structure with four stories on a major traffic artery. It was purchased in 1951 for $36,000, with a first mortgage secured from a bank for $24,000. The aged couple who own it, live on social security. They find great difficulty in collecting the rents and the building, by their own admission, is run down. In the words of our interviewer, "The couple desperately want to sell, but selling is a real problem, since there are no buyers, so they're keeping the building. They want to be completely free of the structure and

therefore will not sell unless they do not have to take back the mortgage. Their great fear, if they were to do the latter, is that they would have to end up taking back the building after selling it, with all that might happen in the interim." In the meantime, the building goes no place.

The rent roll in this structure, assuming that all the units were fully occupied and rents were fully collected, would amount to nearly $1,200 a month at present levels. With allowance for noncollection and vacancies, gross rents should be on the order of $12,000. Taxes, however, are over $4,600 with insurance and heating bills amounting to $3,000. Allowing a $100 a month for janitorial and management services and a minimum of $1,200 for basic maintenance and other operating expenses means that the building has perhaps $2,000 left over as a return on equity. It simply is not a commercial property at any price much in excess of one and a half times the basic rent. This, in turn, means that the parcel is worth perhaps less than half of its present assessment of $8,700 for land and $43,000 for the building.

The owners have no resources, feel the building slipping deeper and deeper into a never-never land of unrentability, yet they have no alternative since there are no substantial buyers, nor anything in the nature of institutional financing which could bridge the gap between potential purchasers' equity and the sale value of the parcel. This structure too, judging from its condition may well be on its way to abandonment.

Unless there are buyers, legitimate buyers with a capacity to secure institutional financing, there is no market, and in default of the market, parcels maintained for their return must sooner or later slip into decline.

# STATISTICAL ANALYSES OF VARIABLES AFFECTING THE ABSOLUTE QUALITY OF A STRUCTURE

## BACKGROUND

The object of this section is to present briefly statistical linkages between the absolute quality of a structure and several of the other descriptive factors of the parcels or respective owners/tenants which directly bear upon this quality. Initially, one to one relationships will be established between absolute quality as the dependent variable and each of twenty-five indices as independent variables. Further on, the independent variables will have their combined effect on absolute quality viewed through multiple regression.

In terms of the analysis of variance model, the dependent variable is an 0 or 1 dichotomous choice while the dependent variables are grouped data frequently comprising four to seven intervals. In the multiple regression model both dependent and independent variables are dichotomous and the exercise is nothing more than a 1 by 25 analysis of variance used to gauge both strength and direction of association for the complete variable array.

It should be realized that no attempt is being made to establish a causal relationship between housing quality and selected variates, but rather to survey associative relationships which exist in Newark at a single point in time. What is being attempted initially is to develop patterns of association between 1971 characteristics of buildings/owners/tenants and buildings currently classified as being reasonably or well maintained.

### Statistical Significance Via the Analysis of Variance

Employing the analysis of variance, Exhibit 2-8 shows that in sixteen out of the twenty-five cases, specific parcel variables explain an amount of variance in absolute housing quality sufficiently in excess of what would have been expected from sampling variation and thus may be adjudged to have a significant effect on the sample data (F statistic — 0.05 level).

The most closely linked factors (significant at the F 0.01 level) appear to be the relationship of better *absolute* housing quality and: (1) better *relative* quality of the structure as compared with immediate neighbors, (2) location in a peripheral rather than a core area of the city under a rental relationship in which the owner is resident, (3) being of masonry rather than frame construction with an absence of both problem and welfare tenantries, (4) having taxes up-to-date (this is occasioned in many cases by their inclusion within scheduled mortgage payments), and finally, (5) location in areas of minimal surrounding nuisances (bars, junkyards, etc.) and purchased for reason of residence rather than income.

Of somewhat less significance (0.01-0.05), yet still strongly linked, are the one to one relationships of well maintained parcels and owners who do *not* have extensive real estate holdings yet who are not novices to the real estate business. Finally there seems to be a positive relationship between better absolute quality of structures and neighborhoods in which vacancy rates are lower.

## Statistical Significance and the Relative Effect Of Variables Via Multiple Regression

If the F test at the 0.10 level is chosen for significance (Exhibit 2-9), it may be seen that when all variables are simultaneously taken into account, housing quality is explained most significantly by the association of this phenomenon with a similar array of variables that dominated the singular variate analysis. Masonry parcels, which are in better condition relative to their neighbors, are located in more peripheral areas of the city and have resident landlords, and are much more likely to be of better absolute condition than buildings which do not possess these attributes. Similarly, if a building has a mortgage and an owner with real estate experience, yet one who has not held the specific building for a great period of time, it tends also to be well maintained. Furthermore, its taxes will be up to date and more than likely it will probably not fall prey to abandonment.

These findings are not dissimilar from the information presented in earlier cross tabulations or what will follow in the next section on characteristics of buildings which have recently been sold. Structures that turn over frequently ultimately ending in the hands of an owner who will abandon are those of poorer absolute quality. They are structures which have been owned for shorter periods of time; they were purchased with other similar structures for rental return rather than residence; and are owned by owners who frequently complain about tenants. Abandonment, given such ownership patterns, may well be in the offing.

## EXHIBIT 2-8
## INDIVIDUAL SIGNIFICANCE OF 1971 PARCEL COROLLARIES OF ABSOLUTE QUALITY

### ANALYSIS OF VARIANCE

003. DEPENDENT VARIABLE: POOR QUALITY(0)/REASONABLE OR BETTER QUALITY(1)STRUCTURES

| Variable Number | Variable Name | Direction of Coding[a] | Individual Significance | Direction of Significance |
|---|---|---|---|---|
| 001 | Size of parcel | (Increases with size) | No | |
| 002 | Type of construction | (Increases toward masonry) | Yes | + |
| 004 | Relative quality | (Increases with better quality) | Yes | + |
| 005 | Commercial occupancy | (Increases with degree of occupancy) | No | |
| 006 | Nuisances nearby | (Increases with various nuisances) | Yes | — |
| 007 | Length of real estate experience | (Decreases with length) | Yes | + |
| 008 | Why purchased | (Increases with income motive) | Yes | — |
| 009 | Want to sell | (Increases with desire to sell) | Yes | + |
| 010 | Professional manager | (Increases with degree of professional management) | No | |
| 011 | Size of holding | (Increases with size) | Yes | — |

| | | | | |
|---|---|---|---|---|
| 012 | Make living from real estate | (Increases with percent R.E. involvement) | No | |
| 013 | Race of tenants | (Increases toward black) | Yes | — |
| 014 | Neighborhood vacancy rate | (Increases with larger) | Yes | — |
| 015 | Problem tenants | (Increases with severity rating) | Yes | — |
| 016 | Abandonment | (Increases with degree of abandonment) | Yes | — |
| 018 | Residence of owner | (Increases with nonresidency) | Yes | — |
| 019 | Race of owner | (Increases toward white) | No | |
| 022 | Type of owner | (Increases with nonindividuals) | No | |
| 023 | Length of ownership | (Increases with term) | No | |
| 026 | Location in U.R. area | (Increases with location in U.R. area) | No | |
| 027 | Multiple mortgages | (Increases with one or more mortgages) | Yes | + |
| 028 | Location of parcel | (Increases with better locations) | Yes | + |
| 029 | Tax arrearage | (Increases with periods of arrears) | Yes | — |
| 030 | Mortgage source | (Increases with non-institutional lenders) | No | |
| 031 | Welfare tenantry | (Increases with number on welfare) | Yes | — |

F = 0.05 or less

Source: Newark Area Resurvey, spring 1972

EXHIBIT 2-9
PARCEL COROLLARIES (1971) OF ABSOLUTE QUALITY OF STRUCTURE (1971)

| Dependent Variable | Poorly Kept (0)/Reasonably or Well Kept (1) Structures | | | |
|---|---|---|---|---|
| Variable Number | Variable Name | Regression Coefficient | F Statistic | F to Reject Randomness |
| 004 | RELQAL | 0.444 | 68.10 | 2.74 |
| 016 | ABNDON | —0.291 | 19.63 | 2.74 |
| 018 | RESLAN | 0.128 | 3.63 | 2.74 |
| 002 | FRMCON | —0.194 | 13.02 | 2.74 |
| 029 | TAXARR | —0.161 | 6.53 | 2.74 |
| 017 | NOWELF | 0.117 | 4.99 | 2.74 |
| 028 | LOCATN | —0.139 | 7.11 | 2.74 |
| 011 | NOHOLD | 0.100 | 3.47 | 2.74 |
| 023 | LENOWN | —0.176 | 8.57 | 2.74 |
| 007 | RELEXP | 0.158 | 5.48 | 2.74 |
| 024 | NOMORT | —0.090 | 3.06 | 2.74 |

F = 0.10

Source: Newark Area Resurvey, spring 1972.

# OWNER CHARACTERISTICS OF PARCELS SOLD 1964 TO 1971

## OWNER CHARACTERISTICS

### Residence of Owner

In 1964, of the ninety-one later transferred parcels, 26.4 percent were in the hands of resident owners; this has declined to 17.6 percent. On the other hand, the proportion living within Newark but not resident in a sample parcel has moved from 24.2 percent to 40.7 percent with an equivalent decline in out-of-Newark owners.

### Owner Ethnicity

Of the ninety-one parcels that changed hands for which there are complete data for 1964 to 1971, 24.2 percent were owned by blacks on the earlier date, 68.1 percent by whites, 2.2 percent by Spanish-speaking individuals, and for 5.5 percent either there were no data or the parcels were held by corporate shells that could not be traced. The equivalent figures currently are 41.8 percent black owned, 53.2 percent white owned, and 5.1 percent in Spanish-speaking hands. This indicates an increase in nonparcel resident, multi-parcel owner blacks who live in Newark.

### Amount of Experience in Real Estate

As of 1964, of the same ninety-one parcels, 53.9 percent were in the hands of owners with nine or more years of experience in owning real estate. The equivalent figure for the owners in 1971 was 29.7 percent. Clearly in terms of change of title there has been a shift to less experienced hands though conceivably more youthful and energetic ones, as shall be seen later.

### Motivation for Purchase

There was little variation in the motivation of people who owned the houses which were sold in the seven years subsequent to 1964 and those who bought them. Purchase for a home or home plus some level of income was relatively minor, representing barely a quarter for both cases. This may indicate some of the problems in generating continuing home buying for residence purposes in Newark. The expansion of suburban housing alternatives for minority groups has diminished the potential strength of Newark as a residential locus.

When the responses are compared to the question of whether the original motivation is still the reason for keeping the parcel, if anything, the current owners are more disillusioned than their predecessors. In the first survey, 64.8 percent of the ninety-one parcels had owners who answered in the affirmative. Now it is only 44 percent. In the first survey, 26.4 percent wanted to sell their parcels, now it is 37.4 percent. The new owners, i.e., of the ninety-one parcels that changed titles subsequent to the 1964 survey, were less sanguine than long-term holders, of whom only 27.4 percent wanted to sell in 1971.

### Degree of Ownership: Making A Living From Real Estate

There has been a marked reduction (not so much in full-time operators who hover around the 20 percent mark for both periods) in those who claim they made a quarter to three-quarters of their living from realty operations. In 1964 it was 18.7 percent; now it is down to 8.8 percent. The bulk of the shift is made up in a slight increase in proportion of those who claim that they derive either no income or a minor income supplement from their real estate holdings.

Why is there the shift downward in the scale of operation and yet, if anything, a greater detachment, i.e., more use of rent collectors and the like? Perhaps this indicates some of the difficulties of amateur operation in Newark.

## OPERATIONAL CHARACTERISTICS

### Trends Toward Professionalization

In 1964 only 14.6 percent of the ninety-one parcels had owners who used outside managers. The bulk of the rent collection, 82.9 percent, was owner-conducted. Now the equivalent figures are 28.2 and 57.6, indicating a higher level of professionalization. Perhaps, as a tribute to this, the frequency of rent collection on a nominally monthly-but-must-collect-more-frequently base has gone down from 12.1 percent to 1.1 percent. While the questionnaire contained no direct question on this point, more owners now insist on tenants mailing their rents in, or bringing them in, rather than personal collection.

### Scale of Operation

Slightly more than half of the ninety-one transferred parcel owners, for whom data are available for both periods, owned at most one or two other parcels. There has been, moreover, a substantial decrease in very large scale operators. In 1964, 19.8 percent of the ninety-one parcels were held by operators with twelve or more structures. The equivalent figure in 1971 was half that (9.9 percent).

### Tenantry

The great majority of the ninety-one transferred parcels had all black tenantry with 72.5 percent in 1964 and 78 percent at the time of the latter interview. There has been an increase from zero to 6.6 percent in

Spanish-speaking tenant occupied structures, with an equivalent increase in those structures which are completely vacant. All the shrinkage has taken place in the proportion of purely white, non-Spanish-speaking occupied structures. In 1964 these made up 19.8 percent of the parcels later transferred; now they make up 1.1 percent.

### Welfare Tenantry

Unfortunately the question on the welfare status of tenants was not asked in 1964, thus there are no comparable data. It is interesting to note, however, that in 1971 only 24.2 percent of the ninety-one transferred parcels had no welfare tenants, according to their owners, as against 38.5 percent of the nontransferees. Of the post-1964 owners, 40.7 percent indicated that welfare tenantry had a very serious negative effect on property values and operation, as compared with only 23 percent of the nontransferees.

### Vacancy Rate

In 1964 42.9 percent of the respondents indicated that vacancy rates in the neighborhood were up; the rate has now shrunk to 19.8 percent. A similar disproportion responded to questions about vacancy rates within their own parcels. Notice that there seems to be no distinction between holders and sellers in either period based on their vacancy response.

### Who Does the Repairs?

The response to this question provides some insight into the bifurcation that is taking place on both ends of the operational spectrum. In 1964, 8.8 percent of the respondents said that they did practically all the repairs themselves, with 62.6 percent saying they rarely or never did repair work. This compares with 23.1 percent and 62.4 percent, respectively, in the latter interview. In the first interview only 12.1 percent said that they had full-time employees who did their repairs while in the latter interview the response was at the 33 percent level. This gives evidence of a decrease in the smaller scale, directly involved multiple parcel owner. The arena is left to the professionals and to the residents.

## Attitudes Toward the Making of Capital Investments

The essence of owner attitudes was summarized in the variation in response in 1964 as against 1971 to the question, "Would you make improvements if you were guaranteed against a tax increase?" In 1964, 7.7 percent of the ninety-one transferred parcels had owners who said they could not afford improvements and would not make any regardless of tax elements. The equivalent figure now is 32 percent.

At the earlier date, 12.1 percent said their parcels weren't worth improving; now 20 percent do. And remember, these responses are confined to those people who bought parcels in the seven years subsequent to 1964. In the earlier interview 30.8 percent said bluntly that their apartments did not need capital investment, that they were in good condition; now it is 22 percent. And when asked whether, if they made improvements the resale market would support their cost in 1964, 44 percent said definitely *no* (compared with 34.1 percent of the people who kept their holdings); now it is 53 percent.

There is no comparison over time on the response to the question of whether a parcel would be worth more in five years. However, in 1971 of those owners who predated 1964, about 39 percent felt that their parcels would be worth more in the next five years. Among the more recent buyers, the equivalent figure was only 30 percent, with 43 percent of the latter versus the 29 percent of the former saying definitely *no*. Why the difference? The variation seems to be accounted for by negative feeling toward area characteristics on the part of more current buyers.

# CHANGES IN OWNERSHIP: THE SAME PARCELS, 1964, 1971

## Transfers Within A Fixed Sample Set

It is difficult to compare the total sample of parcels in 1964 and that secured in 1971. The degree of attrition both through urban renewal, highways, and the like, as well as abandonment, prohibit clearcut conclusions. In addition, in some cases, we were not able to interview the owners of the same parcels at each time. For that reason, a special analysis was undertaken of the 225 parcels for which there are complete data, both in 1964 and in 1971, including landlord interviews.

In Exhibit 2-10, the total transfer rate is shown by area. It is Area 1, the hard core, which has the lowest rate of transfers with less than a third of the parcels (32.7 percent) changing hands. Area 2 and 3 hover close to the 40 percent mark at 45.6 percent and 39.8 percent, respectively. This may indicate the fact that potential home buyers are

EXHIBIT 2-10
RESIDENTIAL TURNOVER
BY SAMPLE AREA OF THE CITY

| Residential Activity | Area of the City | | | |
|---|---|---|---|---|
| | Area 1 | Area 2 | Area 3 | Total |
| | NUMBER | | | |
| Turnover | 17 | 41 | 33 | 91 |
| Stable | 35 | 49 | 50 | 134 |
| Total | 52 | 90 | 83 | 225* |
| | PERCENT DISTRIBUTION | | | |
| Turnover | 32.7 | 45.6 | 39.8 | 40.4 |
| Stable | 67.3 | 54.4 | 60.2 | 59.6 |
| Total | 100.0 | 100.0 | 100.0 | 100.0 |

*Cases with both 1964 and 1971 interviews

$\chi^2$ n/s @ 0.05

Source: Newark Area Resurvey, spring 1972

avoiding the hard core. The bulk of the owners there are residuals, large scale operators many of whom are seeking outlets, as shall be seen later, only through urban renewal and Model City property acquisition.

## Degree of Occupancy

Of the parcels for which there are data in both interview sets, and which had transferred ownership, 86.8 percent were occupied at the time of the last survey compared with 95.5 percent of those for which there are no transfers. This may indicate the habit of a transfer, sometimes nebulous in nature, before abandonment or virtual abandonment.

## Quality of External Appearance

Eleven percent of the parcels that were transferred were rated in 1964 as poorer than their immediate neighbors versus only 6 percent of the nontransfers. The difference is small, but it gives some insight into the condition.

In terms of absolute quality, only 17.6 percent of the parcels that were subsequently to be transferred were rated as well kept versus 29.9 percent of those that did not change hands.

Of those that were later transferred, 15.4 percent were rated poorer than their street or block as compared with 5.2 percent of those that were not transferred.

## Commercial Occupancy

Commercial occupancy seems to have some significant influence, with only 6.6 percent of the transferees having commercial occupancy versus 17.9 percent of the nontransfers.

## Propensity to Sell by Longevity of Holding

It is the less experienced owners who had the highest propensity to sell their parcels, with 26.4 percent of the parcels that were subsequently sold in the hands of owners in 1964 who had first gotten into the game in the four years prior to the survey. This compared with 17.8 percent of the holders.

## Date of Title

There is a higher propensity to sell as a function of recent ownership than of long-term. More than one out of three (35.2 percent) of the owners who sold in the seven-year period from 1964 to 1971 had held their parcels for periods of up to but not exceeding four years as compared with 24.1 percent of the keepers. Indeed, nearly a third (33 percent) of the keepers had held their parcels for over fifteen years at the time of the earlier survey (more than twenty-two years by the time of the later survey), as compared with 25.3 percent of the sellers.

## Reason for Buying by Propensity to Sell

Of the holders, 45.5 percent had bought for home or home plus some income versus only 29.5 percent of the sellers. The bulk of the latter, 56.8 percent, had purchased strictly for rental return against 36.6 percent of the holders.

When they were asked whether this was still their reason for keeping the parcel, 26.4 percent of the sellers versus 17.7 percent of the keepers replied that they wanted to sell. This gives a pretty good handhold on a forecast for turnover.

## Do You Use A Manager or Rent Collector?

There was trivial variation here though a slightly higher proportion of keepers (87.7 percent versus 82.9 percent) did their own rent collection. There was a significant variation in the frequency of rent collection; 72.5 percent of the sellers collected rent purely monthly versus 82.2 percent of the keepers. Fully 19.8 percent of the former said that they collected their rents weekly, or at best nominally monthly, while really collecting more frequently, versus only 9.7 percent of the keepers.

The number of furnished units is generally small in any case, but it should be noted that 8.8 percent of the sellers maintained purely furnished operations versus only 3.7 percent of the keepers.

## Size of Holding by Propensity to Sell

As Exhibit 2-11 denotes, there is a substantial propensity to sell as a function of size of operation. The greater the size of holdings, the greater the number of parcels, the greater is the tendency for a specific parcel *not* to be in the same hands over the seven years separating the two studies.

As would be guessed from this, among full-time real estate owners, or those at least deriving a substantial part of their income (more than a third) from real estate operations, there is a higher proportion of sellers than is true of the keepers' group. In the former, such individuals make up 39.6 percent of the sample; in the latter they make up only 28.1 percent.

### Tenant Ethnicity and Propensity to Sell

There was only small variation in tenant ethnicity as a forecaster of whether a parcel was sold or not sold. Nor was there any significant variation in the estimation of vacancy rates, either in the general area or in the specific properties, as a function of propensity to sell.

## What Problems Did Landlords See as Function of Propensity to Sell?

When tenantry was posed to owners as one of a series of operating and maintenance problems, a third of the holders had no response whatsoever versus 19 percent of the sellers, i.e., *for the keeper of property tenantry presents less of a problem than for the seller.* There was little variation of consequence in any of the other variables which were probed including tax levels, nor was there any variation in the levels of improvements that would be made if the landlord was guaranteed freedom from reassessment.

When asked whether the resale market was such that they could get potential improvement investments back, there was a significant difference in response. Slightly over 23 percent of the sellers versus 34.1 percent of the keepers answered in the positive. A similar disproportion answered in the affirmative on the question of whether they could get increased rents commensurate with the investment. Notice, however, that in both cases it was still a minimum of the respondents.

There is little variation in the level of response to investment potential if given a long-term mortgage nor is there any significant response on the impact of building inspectors.

## EXHIBIT 2-11
## RESIDENTIAL TURNOVER BY SIZE OF HOLDING (1964 AND 1971)

| Residential Activity | Size of Holding 1964 | | | | | | | |
|---|---|---|---|---|---|---|---|---|
| | No other | 1 or 2 more | 3-6 more | 6-12 more | Over 12 more | Used to own more than one but no longer | No answer Don't know | Total |
| Turnover | 30 | 18 | 14 | 8 | 18 | 1 | 2 | 91 |
| Stable | 71 | 27 | 7 | 11 | 17 | 0 | 2 | 135 |
| Total | 101 | 45 | 21 | 19 | 35 | 1 | 4 | 226 |
| | | | | PERCENT DISTRIBUTION | | | | |
| Turnover | 33.0 | 19.8 | 15.4 | 8.8 | 19.8 | 1.1 | 2.2 | 100.0 |
| Stable | 52.6 | 20.0 | 5.2 | 8.8 | 12.6 | 0.0 | 1.5 | 100.0 |
| Total | 44.7 | 19.9 | 9.3 | 8.4 | 15.5 | 0.4 | 1.8 | 100.0 |

| Residential Activity | Size of Holding 1971 | | | | | | | | | |
|---|---|---|---|---|---|---|---|---|---|---|
| | No other | 1 or 2 more | 3-6 more | 6-12 more | Over 12 more | Used to own more than two but no longer | Used to own more than one but no longer | Other | No answer don't know | Total |
| Turnover | 24 | 23 | 16 | 12 | 8 | 1 | 0 | 3 | 4 | 91 |
| Stable | 76 | 25 | 9 | 3 | 9 | 0 | 1 | 5 | 7 | 135 |
| Total | 100 | 48 | 25 | 15 | 17 | 1 | 1 | 8 | 11 | 226 |
| PERCENT DISTRIBUTION | | | | | | | | | | |
| Turnover | 26.4 | 25.3 | 17.6 | 13.2 | 8.8 | 1.1 | 0.0 | 3.3 | 4.4 | 100.0 |
| Stable | 56.3 | 18.5 | 6.7 | 2.2 | 6.7 | 0.0 | 0.7 | 3.7 | 5.2 | 100.0 |
| Total | 44.2 | 21.2 | 11.1 | 6.6 | 7.5 | 0.4 | 0.4 | 3.5 | 4.9 | 100.0 |

$\chi^2 = 0.05\ (2)$

Source: Newark Area Resurvey, spring 1972

## Personal Characteristics of Owner By Propensity to Keep or Sell

There was little variation in age though a slightly lower average age level on the part of keepers.

*Residence patterns, however, were quite different.* Only 26.4 percent of the sellers lived in the sample area versus 46.7 percent of the keepers. An additional 17.6 percent of the former lived outside the study area but were within Newark versus only 11.1 percent of the keepers, while 37.4 percent of the sellers were suburbanites versus only 30.4 percent of the keepers.

Over 25 percent (25.3) of the sellers were either lawyers or real estate managers and 14.3 percent were brokers. Among the keepers there were only 8.8 percent who were lawyers and real estate managers with an additional 11.9 percent real estate brokers. Otherwise the distributions were roughly parallel.

## Owner Ethnicity

*Negroes made up 29.3 percent of the total sample but only 24.2 percent of the sellers. While they were 39.3 percent of the keepers, whites made up 68.1 percent of the sellers.* There was little variation in the workplace of the owner to account for the propensity to sell, nor was there any variation of significance in income level. Interestingly enough, there was little difference in the form of ownership, i.e., corporation, partnership, or individual holding.

## Financing

There was no variation in mortgage source of any significance with one exception: 20 percent of the parcels which were later sold had second mortgages at the time of the initial title search as compared with 12.1 percent of the keepers. The total portion, however, is still relatively small.

## Notes

1. See George Sternlieb, *The Tenement Landlord* (New Brunswick, N.J.: Rutgers University Press (1969), pp. 121-141; Michael Stegman, "The Myth of the Slumlord," *American Institute of Architects Journal* (March 1970):45-49.

2. For this view, see: Walter Blum and Allison Dunham, "Slumlordism as a Tort: A Dissenting View," *Michigan Law Review* (January 1968):451-464; Joseph Sax, "Slumlordism as a Tort: A Brief Response," *Michigan Law Review* (January 1968): 465-468.

3. National Housing Agency, *Who Owns the Slums? Where Does Money Spent for Slum Property Go?* (National Housing Bulletin 6, March 1964); Arthur D. Sporn, "Empirical Studies in the Economics of Slum Ownership," *Land Economics* (November 1960); Thomas Kniesner, "A Quantitative Analysis of Substandard Urban Housing in Ohio," *Bulletin of Business Research* 45 (September 1970):5-8.

4. Alvin L. Schorr, *Slums and Social Insecurity* (Washington, D.C.: U.S. Government Printing Office, 1966), Chapter 1.

5. See George Sternlieb, *The Urban Housing Dilemma* (New York, 1970).

# 3

# THOSE WHO REMAIN: THE NEW MINORITY OWNERS

One of the most provocative and potentially important developments of our time is the increased level of minority group ownership of central city real property.[1] This is a trend which parallels that of all the other earlier immigrant groups into the city — first as tenants, then as owners typically of the most marginal of parcels, then, with the formation of capital, the movement into the middle class mainstream. Will this sequence be replicated for present minority group owners, both Spanish and black?

In the analysis which follows the focus will be initially on the numbers and trends in the numbers of black owners over time. (As yet the Spanish-speaking portion of Newark's population is relatively small and just beginning to make its presence felt.) Who are these people; what kinds of buildings do they buy; and why do they buy them? Are there variations in operating procedures, in attitudes toward tenants and the like?

From society's point of view the most crucial question of all is whether the new owners can make it; whether or not there is a potential for capital accumulation and for success in the future through this type of acquisition. The vigor of private ownership in the city clearly is dependent upon the future growth of such activity. How then do these minority group owners view the future? What are their problems and are there any ways that society can optimize the turnover mechanisms?

Ethnicity data are available for 281 of the 312 completed interviews in the 1971 survey. Some of the balance were shell corporations for which we could not determine the ethnicity of the owner; still others were in the hands of management corporations who refused to reveal these data and the like. The bulk of the answers shown in the data that follow, therefore, refers specifically to the ethnicity of owners parcels for which there are specific data.

## THE ARRIVAL OF MINORITY OWNERS

### Where Are Blacks Buying?

In Exhibit 3-1 is shown an analysis of owner ethnicity by area of the city. Even if the data are adjusted to include the ethnicity of nonrespondents, it is evident from the exhibit that black owners are avoiding the hard

EXHIBIT 3-1
CHANGING OWNER ETHNICITY OVER TIME
NEWARK (1964-1971)

| | Owner Ethnicity (1971) | | | | Owner Ethnicity (1964) | | | |
|---|---|---|---|---|---|---|---|---|
| Area | Black | White | Spanish Speaking | Total* | Black | White | Spanish Speaking | Total* |
| Area 1 | 13 | 52 | 0 | 65 | 35 | 89 | 2 | 126 |
| Area 2 | 54 | 51 | 0 | 105 | 52 | 73 | 0 | 125 |
| Area 3 | 45 | 61 | 4 | 110 | 41 | 89 | 3 | 133 |
| Total | 112 | 164 | 4 | 280 | 128 | 251 | 5 | 348 |
| | PERCENT DISTRIBUTION | | | | | | | |
| Area 1 | 20.0 | 80.0 | 0.0 | 100.0 | 27.8 | 70.6 | 1.6 | 100.0 |
| Area 2 | 51.4 | 48.6 | 0.0 | 100.0 | 41.6 | 58.4 | 0.0 | 100.0 |
| Area 3 | 40.9 | 55.5 | 3.6 | 100.0 | 30.8 | 66.9 | 2.3 | 100.0 |
| Total | 40.0 | 50.6 | 1.4 | 100.0 | 33.3 | 65.4 | 1.3 | 100.0 |
| | PERCENT DISTRIBUTION | | | | | | | |
| Area 1 | 11.6 | 31.7 | 0.0 | 32.2 | 27.3 | 35.5 | 40.0 | 32.8 |
| Area 2 | 48.2 | 31.1 | 0.0 | 37.5 | 40.6 | 29.0 | 0.0 | 32.6 |
| Area 3 | 40.2 | 37.2 | 100.0 | 39.3 | 32.0 | 35.5 | 60.0 | 34.6 |
| Total | 100.0 | 100.0 | 100.0 | 100.0 | 100.0 | 100.0 | 100.0 | 100.0 |

* *Nonresponses* and *Other* answers excluded from the total.
$\chi^2 = 0.001$

Source: Newark Area Resurvey, spring 1972

core (Area 1). The proportion of black owners has actually decreased there, whereas in Area 2 and Area 3 (see methodology for area description) the proportion has increased. In Area 2, for example, black ownership has gone from 41.6 percent to 51.4 percent, while in Area 3 it has moved from 30.8 percent to 40.9 percent.

Separate analysis was undertaken of the ethnicity of refusals (44), no contacts (16), and owner's address unknown (38), i.e., the 98 parcels for which interviews were not secured.

Data for 92 of these were obtained as follows: Of twenty-two parcels in Area 1, ten were owned by whites, eight by blacks, one by a Spanish-speaking person, and three were in corporate name. In Area 2, there were fourteen whites, eight blacks, one in corporate name, and no Spanish-speaking. In Area 3 there were twenty-five whites, eleven blacks, two Spanish-speaking individuals, and nine in corporate name. There were six parcels distributed across the board for which there were no data securable.

## When Did Blacks Begin to Buy?

The proportion of black owners is increasing very rapidly, as tabulated in Exhibit 3-2. While 164 out of the 280 parcels for which there are ownership ethnicity data are owned by whites, only nineteen, or 11.7 percent, of the owners first entered the business during the period 1967 to date. This contrasts with the twenty-two out of 112 blacks, or 19.5 percent, who came into the business in the four-year period from 1967 to the date of the survey.

Given the variation in time span it is difficult to compare these data with that discovered in the earlier survey. In any case, in the survey conducted in 1964, thirty-three of the 128 black owners, or 25.8 percent, had gone into business in the four years preceding the 1964 survey as compared with 14 percent of the 251 white owners.

In general it is the oldtimers among the whites who show the greatest degree of attrition with 63.8 percent of the present white owners having been owners of realty for ten or more years as compared with 69.6 percent in the earlier survey. As would be guessed, the proportion of long-term black owners is relatively small. Only 12.5 percent of the respondents are in the twenty-year and over category as compared with 22.6 percent of the whites.

## EXHIBIT 3-2

### TIME OF OWNER'S FIRST ENTRANCE INTO REAL ESTATE (1971) BY ETHNICITY OF OWNER (1971)

| First Entrance into Real Estate | Black | White | Spanish Speaking | Total |
|---|---|---|---|---|
| Pre 1930 | 1 | 13 | 0 | 14 |
| 1930-1940 | 1 | 11 | 0 | 12 |
| 1940-1950 | 15 | 21 | 0 | 36 |
| 1950-1955 | 19 | 22 | 0 | 41 |
| 1955-1960 | 14 | 37 | 0 | 51 |
| 1960-1965 | 29 | 26 | 2 | 57 |
| 1965-1967 | 11 | 12 | 2 | 25 |
| 1967-Date | 22 | 19 | 0 | 41 |
| NA/DK | 1 | 2 | 0 | 3 |
| Total | 113 | 163 | 4 | 280 |

PERCENT DISTRIBUTION

| First Entrance into Real Estate | Black | White | Spanish Speaking | Total |
|---|---|---|---|---|
| Pre 1930 | 0.9 | 8.0 | 0.0 | 5.0 |
| 1930-1940 | 0.9 | 6.7 | 0.0 | 4.3 |
| 1940-1950 | 13.3 | 12.9 | 0.0 | 12.9 |
| 1950-1955 | 16.8 | 13.5 | 0.0 | 14.6 |
| 1955-1960 | 12.4 | 63.8 | 0.0 | 18.2 |
| 1960-1965 | 25.7 | 19.1 | 50.0 | 20.4 |
| 1965-1967 | 9.7 | 7.4 | 50.0 | 8.9 |
| 1967-Date | 19.5 | 11.7 | 0.0 | 14.6 |
| NA/DK | 0.9 | 1.2 | 0.0 | 1.1 |
| Total | 100.0 | 100.0 | 100.0 | 100.0 |

$X^2 = 0.005$

Source: Newark Area Resurvey, spring 1972

This has important consequences. The white owners tend to have substantially paid down parcels, to have the feeling in many cases that they essentially have "gotten their money out." In addition, as was noted earlier, they tend to be much older as a group. The blacks are newcomers to the real estate scene, without, in many cases, the build up in equity over time which characterizes the longer-term holder. Their fiscal capacities, therefore, tend to be much more limited though in their relative youth they may have much more of a will to invest.[2]

Intensive analysis was undertaken of level of turnovers and other title data as a function of ethnicity. There was little variation, 61.9 percent of the black owned structures versus 67.1 percent of the white owned structures had no turnover since 1964, and, while multiple turnovers were a bit more prominent among black owned parcels, the variation is trivial.

## Instances of Minority Group Purchases

The evidence for the transfer data will be explored in subsequent parts of the chapter. There is no question, however, that in a number of cases the functional reality of minority group ownership is a very slender one.

For example:

> Parcel number 383 is a six apartment, four-story building with two stores on the ground level. This was sold in 1965 for $26,500, subject to a $19,000 mortgage with the seller taking back an additional $8,000 mortgage, i.e., the total package was worth around $34,500 with $27,000 of it being represented by mortgages. In 1970 it was sold to a black owner for $48,600, all of it in the form of purchase money mortgages. The sale was obviously of a most nebulous character. The interview with the black owner indicates that he is not collecting rents and since the parcel is delinquent in taxes, the city is presently collecting rents in lieu of payment.
>
> Here is a parcel which has been clearly walked away from by the earlier owner. The level of sales price in 1970 is obviously fictitious. At worse, the former owner generated a substantial tax loss, at best, if the parcel is taken for urban renewal, possibly he will gain a substantial payment. The area is one of devastating abandonment; empty structures and littered lots abound. The future of the parcel is in real doubt; it is questionable whether any alternate buyer could have been found.

Even in the very midst of this decay, however, there is a potential for local people to inherit parcels from absentee owners who no longer feel capable of operating them.

> Parcel number 450 reveals something of this. This is a twenty-five family, plus six store masonry building in an area which ten years ago was thought suitable for concentrated code enforcement and rehabilitation. It has rapidly gone down hill, however. Half of the apartments are furnished, the other half unfurnished. The tenantry

> is all black with the exception of one unit which is occupied by a Puerto Rican household. At the time of our 1964 interview, the then owner had purchased the building twenty years before and paid $60,000, $35,000 of which was covered by a 4.5 percent mortgage from a savings and loan company.
>
> The present owner, who is black, secured the title in 1971. He had been the handyman of the previous owner and in the course of time had secured several parcels to operate on his own. Despite the fact of a rent roll which is currently well past the $35,000 mark, he obtained the building which "needs a lot of repairs and a lot of work, at least $50,000 worth," on a no-cash basis. The nominal sale of $55,000 was based on a 100 percent purchase money mortgage* secured from the seller. "The owner just wanted out and I couldn't resist taking it over."

The hazard to the future operation and capital investments in the building is obvious; on the other hand, the potential here should not be underestimated. This will be reviewed in a later chapter.

## CHARACTERISTICS OF MINORITY GROUP OWNERS

### Residency

There is a significant variation in the proportion of resident ownership as a function of ethnicity. Sixty-five out of the 113 black owners for whom there are data, or 57.5 percent, are resident owners, compared with only seventeen out of 163 (10.4 percent) of the white owners for whom there are similar data. The *no answer/don't know* response shown in Exhibit 3-3, which is very substantial, tends to be in the white case, corporate response.

The exhibit further details where the nonresidents live. The bulk of the nonresident black owners are residents of Newark with only 12.4 percent outside the city, but in New Jersey, and only one additional individual in another locale. White owners much more typically are resident outside the city.

The significance of these data are hard to exaggerate. For the great bulk of white owners, their Newark parcels are at most a source of additional income, at worse an encumbrance, an inconvenience, to be

---

*Purchase money mortgage: A mortgage given by the purchaser to the seller at the time the property is acquired.

## EXHIBIT 3-3
## RESIDENCE OF OWNER (1971) BY ETHNICITY OF OWNER (1971)

| Location | Black | White | Spanish Speaking | Total |
|---|---|---|---|---|
| Resident in parcel | 65 | 17 | 3 | 85 |
| Within one block of parcel | 1 | 3 | 0 | 4 |
| Other areas of Newark | 26 | 44 | 1 | 71 |
| Within 20 miles of Newark yet in New Jersey | 14 | 50 | 0 | 64 |
| Somewhere in the balance of New Jersey | 0 | 10 | 0 | 10 |
| New York | 1 | 1 | 0 | 2 |
| Other | 1 | 5 | 0 | 6 |
| NA/DK | 5 | 33 | 0 | 38 |
| Total | 113 | 163 | 4 | 280 |

PERCENT DISTRIBUTION

| Location | Black | White | Spanish Speaking | Total |
|---|---|---|---|---|
| Resident in parcel | 57.5 | 10.4 | 75.0 | 30.4 |
| Within one block of parcel | 0.9 | 1.8 | 0.0 | 1.4 |
| Other areas of Newark | 23.0 | 27.0 | 25.0 | 25.4 |
| Within 20 miles of Newark yet in New Jersey | 12.4 | 30.7 | 0.0 | 22.9 |
| Somewhere in the balance of New Jersey | 0.0 | 6.1 | 0.0 | 3.6 |
| New York | 0.9 | 0.6 | 0.0 | 0.7 |
| Other | 0.9 | 3.1 | 0.0 | 2.1 |
| NA/DK | 4.4 | 20.2 | 0.0 | 13.6 |
| Total | 100.0 | 100.0 | 100.0 | 100.0 |

$\chi^2 = 0.001$

Source: Newark Area Resurvey, spring 1972.

forgotten about or disposed of as quickly as possible. On the other hand, for the bulk of the black owners, the economics of the parcel frequently are secondary to its use as a place of residence. In addition, even when nonresident, the bulk of the minority owners live close to their holdings and are therefore in a better position to service them personally.

## Types of Ownership

As Exhibit 3-4 shows, more than four out of five of the black owned parcels (81.4 percent) are in the hands of individuals, including husband and wife teams, as against 56.1 percent for the white owned parcels. Partnerships make up only 7.1 percent of the black owned parcels while

EXHIBIT 3-4
CATEGORY OF OWNER (1971) BY ETHNICITY OF OWNER (1971)

| Category | Black | White | Spanish Speaking | Total |
|---|---|---|---|---|
| Individual (including husband and wife) | 92 | 92 | 4 | 188 |
| Two or more individuals | 8 | 22 | 0 | 30 |
| Realty corporation | 2 | 12 | 0 | 14 |
| Financial institution | 2 | 0 | 0 | 2 |
| Nonfinancial institution | 8 | 37 | 0 | 45 |
| Public institution | 1 | 1 | 0 | 2 |
| Total | 113 | 164 | 4 | 281 |
| PERCENT DISTRIBUTION | | | | |
| Individual (including husband and wife) | 81.4 | 56.1 | 100.0 | 66.9 |
| Two or more individuals | 7.1 | 13.4 | 0.0 | 10.7 |
| Realty corporation | 1.8 | 7.3 | 0.0 | 5.0 |
| Financial institution | 1.8 | 0.0 | 0.0 | 0.7 |
| Nonfinancial institution | 7.1 | 22.6 | 0.0 | 16.0 |
| Public institution | 0.9 | 0.6 | 0.0 | 0.7 |
| Total | 100.0 | 100.0 | 100.0 | 100.0 |

$\chi^2 = 0.01$

Source: Newark Area Resurvey, spring 1972.

there are nearly double that proportion (13.4 percent) for the white owned ones. Corporate holdings and institutions of one kind or another make up nearly a quarter of the white owned parcels but less than 10 percent of the black owned ones.

## Scale of Operation

All but a very few of the black operators are at most in the possession of one or two buildings aside from the one in the sample, with 86.7 percent owning less than three parcels in total. While the scale of white operators has decreased substantially since 1964, 17 percent owned more than twelve parcels, while an additional 6.7 percent owned from six to twelve.

What is happening to the proportion of full-time real estate operators? Are blacks beginning to move into this area? Given the size of the sample, the findings can only be viewed as tentative. The proportion of black full-time real estate operators has moved from 4.7 percent in the earlier survey to 7.1 percent. This is a promising if not definitive increase given the size of sample, i.e., 128 and 113, respectively. Whites, on the other hand, have been reduced, going from 26.7 percent who claimed to be full-time real estate operators in 1964 to 19.5 percent.

## Size of Structure

As discussed earlier, the bulk of Newark's buildings are small. Of the buildings for which there are owner interviews, 83.6 percent had six or fewer units, with only 10.3 percent having seven to twelve units, and the relatively small balance with thirteen or more units. Minority group ownership particularly was concentrated in the smallest buildings with blacks having 93.6 percent of their holdings in six-unit or smaller buildings. Blacks owned just seven buildings with seven or more units. And only one of these had 25 units. This shows some slight improvement, however, over the scale of holdings in black hands in 1964 when only 3.2 percent of the black owned parcels were larger than six units. All four of the Puerto Rican owned buildings (for which there are data) were at the six-unit or less category.

## Commercial Occupancy

Ninety-five and a half percent of the black owned parcels had no commercial occupancy as compared with 82.1 percent of the whites. A number of the latter group of owners, as noted earlier, were essentially interested only in their buildings because they had businesses there. While commercial occupancy may provide some form of additional income, it is increasingly vulnerable, particularly as the tide of retailing moves out of the city. This may explain some of the levels of abandonment of black versus white owned structures.

## Quality of Structure

As described in Appendix 1, there were a number of measures of quality of structure. Of those parcels which were rated as superior to their immediate neighbors in appearance, 20.0 percent were owned by blacks as against only 13.7 percent of those owned by whites (Exhibit 3-5). Basically this is the same ratio that was established in the 1964 study. Similarly, when analysis was undertaken of the absolute quality grades given the structures as evaluated by the field crew, 10 percent of the black owned parcels but only 2.7 percent of the whites were graded as well kept, while 27.3 percent of the former versus 40 percent of the latter were graded as poorly kept. Again, these ratios confirm the 1964 findings. Notice that these results seem to be specific to the parcels. When the quality of the street and block in which particular parcels were located was evaluated by field interviewers, they were given practically identical ratings both for black and white owned structures.

In general black owners were much more positive about the condition of their buildings when asked very simply whether their parcels were in good condition or not. Four out of five black owners felt that they were in either very good or moderately good condition as compared with 64 percent of the whites. In the latter group, 15.8 percent said their buildings were either very poor or simply were not in good condition as compared with 11.5 percent of the blacks.

## Motivation for Purchase

As Exhibit 3-6 makes most evident, the great bulk of the nonwhite purchasers, seven out of ten, bought their sample parcels as homes in contrast to the whites where the equivalent response is barely one out of seven. The influence of this motivation on staying power, attitudes toward fixing up the place, etc., are evident. This finding reveals very little difference from the trends extant in the earlier survey which were practically identical.

When asked why they were keeping their parcel, the bulk of the blacks answered that their motivation had not changed — 60.2 percent as compared with 37.8 percent of the whites. The bulk of the latter had been disenchanted in their original motivation which typically was for investment or capital appreciation.

EXHIBIT 3-5
QUALITY OF PARCEL'S EXTERIOR APPEARANCE (1971) BY ETHNICITY OF OWNER (1971)

| Quality of Appearance | Black | White | Spanish Speaking | Total |
|---|---|---|---|---|
| Poorer than neighbors | 23 | 32 | 0 | 55 |
| Same as neighbors | 65 | 94 | 3 | 162 |
| Better than neighbors | 22 | 20 | 1 | 43 |
| Total | 110 | 146 | 4 | 260 |
| **PERCENT DISTRIBUTION** | | | | |
| Poorer than neighbors | 20.9 | 21.9 | 0.0 | 21.2 |
| Same as neighbors | 59.1 | 64.4 | 75.0 | 62.3 |
| Better than neighbors | 20.0 | 13.7 | 25.0 | 16.5 |
| Total | 100.0 | 100.0 | 100.0 | 100.0 |

$\chi^2$ n/s @ 0.05

Source: Newark Area Resurvey, spring 1972

## EXHIBIT 3-6
## OWNER'S REASON FOR PROPERTY PURCHASE (1971) BY ETHNICITY OF OWNER (1971)

| Reason for Property Purchase | Black | White | Spanish Speaking | Total |
|---|---|---|---|---|
| Home | 79 | 24 | 4 | 107 |
| Rental return | 24 | 103 | 0 | 127 |
| Speculation | 2 | 0 | 0 | 2 |
| Inheritance | 2 | 14 | 0 | 16 |
| Debt | 0 | 2 | 0 | 2 |
| Commercial purpose | 0 | 8 | 0 | 8 |
| Home plus income | 4 | 3 | 0 | 7 |
| Other | 2 | 8 | 0 | 10 |
| Mortgage foreclosure | 0 | 2 | 0 | 2 |
| Total | 113 | 164 | 4 | 281 |

PERCENT DISTRIBUTION

| Reason for Property Purchase | Black | White | Spanish Speaking | Total |
|---|---|---|---|---|
| Home | 69.9 | 14.6 | 100.0 | 38.1 |
| Rental return | 21.2 | 62.8 | 0.0 | 45.2 |
| Speculation | 1.8 | 0.0 | 0.0 | 0.7 |
| Inheritance | 1.8 | 8.5 | 0.0 | 5.7 |
| Debt | 0.0 | 1.2 | 0.0 | 0.7 |
| Commercial purpose | 0.0 | 4.9 | 0.0 | 2.8 |
| Home plus income | 3.5 | 1.8 | 0.0 | 2.5 |
| Other | 1.8 | 4.9 | 0.0 | 3.6 |
| Mortgage foreclosure | 0.0 | 1.2 | 0.0 | 0.7 |
| Total | 100.0 | 100.0 | 100.0 | 100.0 |

$\chi^2 = 0.001$

Source: Newark Area Resurvey, spring 1972

## OPERATING PROCEDURES OF MINORITY OWNERS

### Use of the Manager

As Exhibit 3-7 reveals, less than one in ten of the black owned buildings have professional outside management. This compares with approximately four in ten of the white owned buildings for which there is this kind of interface between owner and tenant (This includes rent collections through direct mail). The difference in relationship that is engendered here, or perhaps the mere fact of the negative relationship which is implied by this arm's length approach particularly used by whites, is disclosed by the data.

The users of outside management are absentee owners, not merely in terms of residence, but also in active participation. There is, however, some indication of an increasing professionalization of black owners. In the 1964 study all 121 black owners collected the rents by themselves, as contrasted with the data in the exhibit. Similarly, in the 1964 data 77 percent of the whites collected by themselves as compared with the 54.2

EXHIBIT 3-7

OWNER'S METHOD OF RENT COLLECTION (1971)
BY ETHNICITY OF OWNER (1971)

| Method of Rent Collection | Black | White | Spanish Speaking | Total |
|---|---|---|---|---|
| Manager | 10 | 56 | 0 | 66 |
| Self | 93 | 83 | 4 | 180 |
| Mailed | 0 | 8 | 0 | 8 |
| NA/DK | 4 | 6 | 0 | 10 |
| Total | 107 | 153 | 4 | 264 |
| PERCENT DISTRIBUTION | | | | |
| Manager | 9.3 | 36.6 | 0.0 | 25.0 |
| Self | 86.9 | 54.2 | 100.0 | 68.2 |
| Mailed | 0.0 | 5.2 | 0.0 | 3.0 |
| NA/DK | 3.7 | 3.9 | 0.0 | 3.8 |
| Total | 100.0 | 100.0 | 100.0 | 100.0 |

$X^2 = 0.001$

Source: Newark Area Resurvey, spring 1972

percent shown in the 1971 data presented here. *It is clear that as the housing market degenerates in Newark, the level of resident ownership or nonresident direct participation and management-ownership is beginning to decrease.*

## The Repair Function

As would be guessed from the data on the proportion of resident owners, there is a substantial variation as a function of the proprietor's race on who does the repair work. Slightly over one quarter (25.7 percent) of the black owners do practically all the repairs themselves as against 14.6 percent of the whites. Conversely, only 14.2 percent, or one out of seven, of the blacks use a personal employee for the repair work as compared to nearly a third (32.3 percent) of the whites (Exhibit 3-8). This particular finding shows little variation from those of the earlier study.

## Rent Collection Schedules

In general, collection of rents on a weekly basis is indicative of a weak market, of poor buildings, and of tenants who find it difficult to manage on a monthly base or whom the landlord fears can't be trusted with a whole month's account receivable. For the sample total of 281, only a minority of the structures for which there are data have rent collected on a purely monthly base (37.4 percent). Only 11.5 percent of the buildings owned by blacks, but 31.7 percent of those owned by whites, have purely weekly collection. There is no question that the overall ratio has degenerated substantially since the earlier study when in both groups more than three-quarters collected on a purely monthly basis. To this degree whites have rapidly moved into the position of running more of the nonmonthly rent collection type of operation than is true of blacks. The overall implications for the housing stock are not good in any case.

The linkage between racial patterns and rent collection practice is only partly explained by the difference in the provision of furnished or partly furnished facilities which more normally rent by the week. Over a tenth (10.3 percent) of the white operated parcels, as contrasted with 5.4 percent of the black owned ones, are either furnished or have a mixture of furnished and unfurnished units in them.

EXHIBIT 3-8
OWNER'S RESPONSE TO HOW HIS REPAIR WORK WAS COMPLETED (1971) BY ETHNICITY OF OWNER (1971)

| Do You Do Your Own Repair Work? | Black | White | Spanish Speaking | Total |
|---|---|---|---|---|
| Practically all done by self | 29 | 24 | 1 | 54 |
| About half and half | 15 | 17 | 0 | 32 |
| Just a little done by self | 11 | 4 | 0 | 15 |
| Rarely or none by self | 40 | 59 | 3 | 102 |
| Employee | 16 | 53 | 0 | 69 |
| NA/DK | 2 | 7 | 0 | 9 |
| Total | 113 | 164 | 4 | 281 |
| PERCENT DISTRIBUTION | | | | |
| Practically all done by self | 25.7 | 14.6 | 25.0 | 19.2 |
| About half and half | 13.3 | 10.4 | 0.0 | 11.4 |
| Just a little done by self | 9.7 | 2.4 | 0.0 | 5.3 |
| Rarely or none by self | 35.4 | 36.0 | 75.0 | 36.3 |
| Employee | 14.2 | 32.3 | 0.0 | 24.6 |
| NA/DK | 1.8 | 4.3 | 0.0 | 3.2 |
| Total | 100.0 | 100.0 | 100.0 | 100.0 |

$\chi^2 = 0.01$

Source: Newark Area Resurvey, spring 1972.

## Owner/Tenant Relationships

Nine out of ten of the black owned buildings, as shown in Exhibit 3-9, have strictly black tenants (90.3 percent). Allowing for the 3.5 percent of the black owned buildings which were vacant, there is only one other group of substance, the 3.5 percent of mixed ethnic tenancy buildings. This is not too dissimilar from the findings in 1964. What is striking, however, is the change in the tenant ethnicity of white owned buildings. In 1964, 25.5 percent of these buildings' owners responded that their

EXHIBIT 3-9

TENANT ETHNICITY (1971) BY OWNER ETHNICITY (1971)

| Tenant Ethnicity | Owner Ethnicity: Black | White | Spanish Speaking | Total |
|---|---|---|---|---|
| Black | 102 | 90 | 0 | 192 |
| White | 0 | 14 | 0 | 14 |
| Mixed | 4 | 15 | 0 | 19 |
| Spanish-speaking | 1 | 13 | 4 | 18 |
| Black and Spanish-speaking | 1 | 8 | 0 | 9 |
| Spanish-speaking and other white | 0 | 3 | 0 | 3 |
| Vacant — no tenants | 4 | 16 | 0 | 20 |
| NA/DK | 1 | 5 | 0 | 6 |
| Total | 113 | 164 | 4 | 281 |

PERCENT DISTRIBUTION

| Tenant Ethnicity | Black | White | Spanish Speaking | Total |
|---|---|---|---|---|
| Black | 90.3 | 54.9 | 0.0 | 68.3 |
| White | 0.0 | 8.5 | 0.0 | 5.0 |
| Mixed | 3.5 | 9.1 | 0.0 | 6.8 |
| Spanish-speaking | 0.9 | 7.9 | 100.0 | 6.4 |
| Black and Spanish-speaking | 0.9 | 4.9 | 0.0 | 3.2 |
| Spanish-speaking and other white | 0.0 | 1.8 | 0.0 | 1.1 |
| Vacant — no tenants | 3.5 | 9.8 | 0.0 | 7.1 |
| NA/DK | 0.9 | 3.0 | 0.0 | 2.1 |
| Total | 100.0 | 100.0 | 100.0 | 100.0 |

$\chi^2 = 0.001$

Source: Newark Area Resurvey, spring 1972.

tenants were white, while for the sample as a whole, the figure was 17.1 percent. Now, in white owned buildings, the strictly white tenanted buildings make up only 8.5 percent of the total. As a proportion of the entire sample they are only 5 percent.

The four Puerto Rican owned buildings strictly housed members of the same group. The other Puerto Ricans in the sample are represented substantially in white owned, rather than black owned, buildings. These are relative newcomers to the sample since in total they amounted to less than 4 percent of the tenantry mentioned by landlords in our earlier survey. (For similar findings on the tenantry of minority owned buildings see *The Urban Housing Dilemma*, NYCHDA, New York, 1972.)

## Variation in Landlord Problem Areas

Is there a pattern in landlord attitude toward tenantry as a function of the landlord's own ethnicity? Findings on this point in 1964 and 1971 are shown in Exhibits 3-10 (1964) and 3-11 (1971).

The relative variation in orders of priority of problems as a function of owner ethnicity should not be taken to mean that black owners necessarily have no problems with tenants. For example, the problem of tenant nonpayment of rent was exemplified by the response given by the black owner of a bar and grill who owns a half dozen parcels in Newark. The particular one in the sample is a frame and siding, three-family house. When asked how much of a rent increase he would need in order to make major additions a good investment, he said, "If the rent was paid promptly, then I'd only need a moderate increase, even as is, I've trouble getting my tenants to pay up on time." Nor, as shall be seen later in more detail, are black owners completely free of the lack of confidence in the city which was all too apparent through many of the interviews with whites. As one black resident owner said, "I can't get insurance because of fires, although I had insurance before the riot. Even though I increased rents in the last six months, the property will be worth less five years from now because there are no improvements in the city and the people that are coming in are bad." There is no question, however, based on the chart of problems that there is a substantial difference in attitude and outlook of blacks and whites.

## Welfare Landlords

Half the black owners, but only 21.3 percent of the whites said that they had no tenants on welfare. Only 3.5 percent of the black owners said that their buildings were completely welfare tenanted as compared with 13.4 percent of the white ones. This finding is substantially at odds with

EXHIBIT 3-10

RELATIVE IMPORTANCE OF VARIOUS INHIBITORS TO PARCEL MAINTENANCE AND IMPROVEMENTS (1964) BY ETHNICITY OF OWNER (1964)

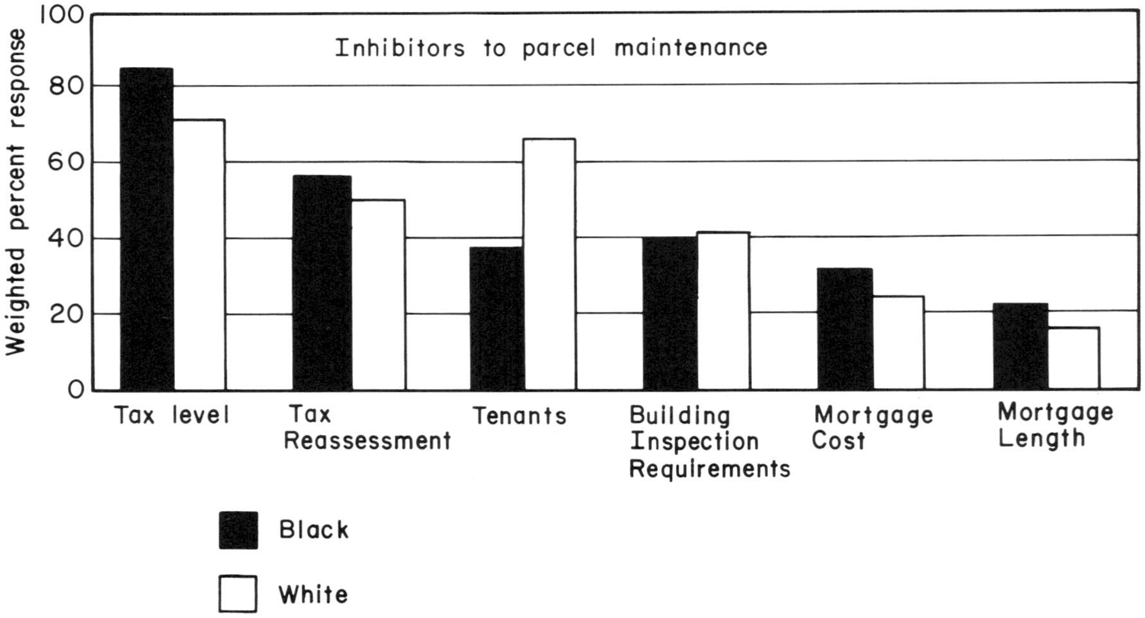

Inhibitors to parcel maintenance

Weighted percent response

100
80
60
40
20
0

Tax level
Tax Reassessment
Tenants
Building Inspection Requirements
Mortgage Cost
Mortgage Length

Black
White

EXHIBIT 3-11

RELATIVE IMPORTANCE OF VARIOUS INHIBITORS TO PARCEL MAINTENANCE AND IMPROVEMENTS (1971) BY ETHNICITY OF OWNER (1971)

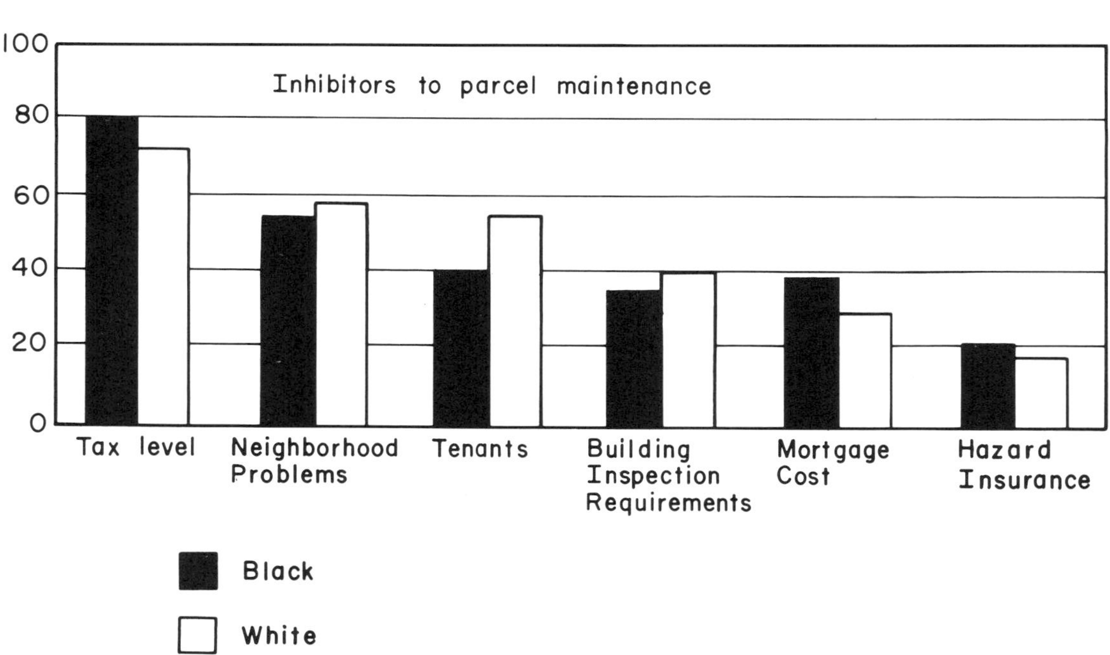

that of the study *The Urban Housing Dilemma* conducted in New York City. In that case there was a much higher degree of identity between black owners and welfare recipient tenants. The variation, in part, undoubtedly is accounted for by the large proportion of Newark's black owners who are resident but not on welfare.

When asked about the influence of welfare tenants on the maintenance of a building there is little variation as a function of owners' race in terms of either positive or no effects, with slightly over a third of each of the groups in that category. Of those owners who felt that welfare tenants were very hard on a building, i.e., exhibited very negative feelings, 31.9 percent of the blacks and 29.3 percent of the whites reported such attitudes. In sum, there was little variation in response as a function of owner ethnicity.

## What is the Long-Term Future Of Minority Tenement Landlords?

The function of residential structures, particularly multi-family ones, in the central city can be seen in any number of ways. Certainly prime among them is the role these structures play in providing accommodations for their tenants. And here from a broad societal point of view we are interested in a type of ownership which most complements this goal.

*Another facet, however, in the role of the tenement is its potential as a source of capital accumulation for local people.*[3] Earlier in this chapter reference was made to the fact that low rent central city housing had been one of the classic ladders of upward socio-economic mobility in the United States. How well is it working out currently? In this section of the chapter the focus will first be on the potential for capital accumulation with part of the section devoted to the impact of acquisition prices and patterns as well as financing. The material will then hone in on landlords' attitudes toward the future of their holdings with specific reference to the variation between ethnic minority owners and whites.

### Vacancy Rates

Part of the variation in response to tenantry problems, earlier noted as a function of the ethnicity of the owner, may be accounted for by comments made by several owners with regard to changes in vacancy rates both in their areas and in their particular parcels. Black owners were much more positive than whites in terms of vacancy rates with only 15 percent of the former versus 25 percent of the latter admitting that they had gone up. This pattern was reversed in the response indicating that vacancy rates have gone down, i.e., 5.3 percent to 15.2 percent (Exhibit 3-12). Perhaps because of the quality of their building, perhaps because of their relationship to the neighborhood or expectations, black owners were much more sanguine about general area vacancy rates in any case, certainly based on their responses. Similar findings were yielded when the question was rephrased in terms of vacancy rates in one's own building. Only four out of the 113 black owners (3.5 percent) felt that their parcel vacancy rates had gone up while 11 percent, i.e., eighteen out of 164, of the whites felt that they had moved similarly. For the very great bulk of owners, in any case, there had been no shift and it should be recalled that in the last several years Newark generally has had extremely low vacancy rates.

## Profitability Potential

Is there a potential for profitability? Much clearly depends on the acquisition price and that will be touched on later. What is the situation in terms of operating yields and saleability? Certainly despite high tax rates there is a significant potential in the former. For example:

> Parcel number 360 was purchased in 1968 by a black craftsman and his wife who live several blocks away in another parcel which they purchased in 1962. They paid $11,900 for the building which was assessed at $10,200. They put up a cash down payment of $1,300, the balance was secured through a mortgage company. The three-story frame building is in reasonable condition. Taxes are $937 a year; heat and insurance run $1,000; with basic maintenance varying somewhat but averaging roughly $300 per year. Its three apartments generate a rent roll, given no vacancies, of $4,500 a year. The mortgage cost is a 10 percent constant, i.e., approximately another $1,000 a year. The cash flow characteristics of the parcel, therefore, are adequate.

The real key, however, is whether the parcel in the future can serve as collateral either for a refinancing which would return to the owner the built up equity (in the paid down mortgage), or for that matter, even

## EXHIBIT 3-12
## OWNER'S OBSERVATIONS CONCERNING VACANCY RATE CHANGES (1971) BY ETHNICITY OF OWNER (1971)

| Is Vacancy Up? Down? | Black | White | Spanish Speaking | Total |
|---|---|---|---|---|
| Yes — up | 17 | 41 | 1 | 59 |
| Yes — down | 6 | 25 | 1 | 32 |
| No | 47 | 53 | 2 | 102 |
| Up — due to fire and abandonment | 8 | 6 | 0 | 14 |
| Up — due to widespread demolition | 2 | 6 | 0 | 8 |
| People move to projects | 0 | 1 | 0 | 1 |
| Unclassifiable "others" | 9 | 11 | 0 | 20 |
| NA | 0 | 6 | 0 | 6 |
| DK | 24 | 15 | 0 | 39 |
| Total | 113 | 164 | 4 | 281 |
| PERCENT DISTRIBUTION | | | | |
| Yes — up | 15.0 | 25.0 | 25.0 | 21.0 |
| Yes — down | 5.3 | 15.2 | 25.0 | 11.4 |
| No | 41.6 | 32.3 | 50.0 | 36.3 |
| Up — due to fire and abandonment | 7.1 | 3.7 | 0.0 | 5.0 |
| Up — due to widespread demolition | 1.8 | 3.7 | 0.0 | 2.8 |
| People move to projects | 0.0 | 0.6 | 0.0 | 0.4 |
| Unclassifiable "others" | 8.0 | 6.7 | 0.0 | 7.1 |
| NA | 0.0 | 3.7 | 0.0 | 2.1 |
| DK | 21.2 | 9.1 | 0.0 | 13.9 |
| Total | 100.0 | 100.0 | 100.0 | 100.0 |

$\chi^2 = 0.05$

Source: Newark Area Resurvey, spring 1972.

profits as part of increases in value at the time of ultimate sale. Is this the beginning of a potential real estate operation or rather a closed circuit? Will low income housing provide a bootstrap up into bigger and better things for the new black tenement operator or is it essentially a dead end?

The somber fact is that for many long-term owners, black as well as white, the latter case seems to hold. So important is this question that, at the risk of redundancy, a number of brief vignettes of these owners will be included.

> Parcel number 057 involves a retired black handyman living on social security. He is the owner of a three-story house on a major intersection. The building is in excellent condition. There are new storm windows and fresh shingling; all the framework has been freshly painted. The owner is resident and purchased the building back in 1949 "for my retirement. . . . I'm keeping the property now because I can't get rid of it; no one wants to buy. When I bought the property I hoped it would help me when I retired. But it costs too much to keep up. The taxes are just killing. The neighborhood has just gone down. The city doesn't take care of it." The owner is presently running the building as a rooming house, renting out nine rooms and securing his own apartment on the first floor. He would like to make further repairs, particularly on the ceilings, and some basic cellar work as well as on the electrical system in the building. He was unaware of any federal programs for home improvement. While he rents his rooms for $13.00 a week, he barely breaks even. Under no circumstances, as he stated very succinctly, would he ever mortgage the building, since it is his only real holding.

There is no question that the tragedy of the black owner locked into a neighborhood which is beyond the investment guidelines of institutional financing and in which there is little possibility of legitimate sales with substantial cash down payments are little different from those of whites.

> Parcel number 415 is an excellently maintained building; it has a new roof, new siding, and new storm windows. It was purchased by the present owner who had been retired for four years with asthma in 1946. He bought it because "we didn't have a place to rent; we had too many kids; and the landlords didn't want tenants with kids." The landlord has no problem with tenantry, but he is beginning to feel the squeeze in taxes and the general problems of the neighborhood. He pointed to the fact that when he bought the

> building the neighborhood was well maintained in terms of municipal services; now he indicated the car abandoned on the street in front of his home and stated that despite numerous calls which he had made, it had been sitting there for several months. When asked if he could get his money back from the improvements that had been made, his response was, "No, there's just too much trouble in this area. The building's worth nothing."

While most white owners pointed to relatively unimproved buildings as securing adequate or more than adequate returns in case of urban renewal land taking, this owner typified the pattern of answers on the part of those owners who had made significant capital investments on the buildings when he said, "You can't get your improvement money back."

At times the transition in attitude from the earlier interview to the current one with the same minority group owner is very telling. One black owner of a pleasant three-family frame house in a better section of Newark, who had bought it twelve years ago, typified the generalized disillusionment.

> The house when he was interviewed six years ago was in the process of extensive repairs. The owner now says that he doubts he can get the money back that he invested in making those improvements. "They're ripping down all of the neighborhood. Unless something is done to build up this section, I just don't know."
>
> The house was purchased on a VA mortgage; economically it's sound; the view of the future, however, is not good.

The GI Bill and VA mortgage combination played a substantial role in bringing many minority group Newarkites into home ownership in the late forties and fifties while the bulk of their white co-citizens made equivalent housing investments in the suburbs. Parcel number 546 exemplified the former pattern.

> A substantial three-story frame house, it is on a small but well landscaped lot. It was bought in 1949 by a black Newarkite who had just returned from the Army.
>
> "My parents didn't have any place to stay, so I bought this place, so that for once we'd have a place to live without being pushed around." The parcel was assessed at $10,400 and he made an excellent buy, paying only $8,000 and securing a $6,000 mortgage

> through a savings and loan. The balance was money that he had saved while in the Army.

When this owner was interviewed in 1965, he was obviously proud of his building which was very well maintained indeed. It had new storm windows, new paint, and the basic lot was neatly maintained. The owner at the time envisioned ultimately paying down his mortgage and selling the improved house. In turn, he hoped to secure enough equity for a move to a nearby prestige suburb with a small black enclave.

In the current interview, his attitude is much less positive; he does not feel that he can get his improvement money back if he sold the building and while he is hopeful that some planned highway improvement might take it, he is far from sure that in even that case he will be able to secure the money that he has invested in the building.

When asked about the future, he said, "This neighborhood's going down, the man next door bought his house a year ago and he hasn't made any repairs which as you can see it needs. If any buyers look at my place and they see what's next to the house, I won't get any kind of money out of the deal." The building next door is owned by a real estate speculator who is obviously not reinvesting in it. What we have is a trapped, black owner.

In some cases, despite the demand for housing, the deterioration of a neighborhood and its potential tenantry brings into question the very survival of long-term ownership — black or white.

> Parcel number 445 is a four-story structure with three apartments plus a store on the ground floor. The black owner, presently retired, formerly worked as a laborer in the construction trade. He secured the parcel in 1955. It was then assessed at $8,900, and he paid $12,500, securing a $9,500 first mortgage from a mortgage company and a second mortgage from the prior owner for $2,900, i.e., no real cash exchanged hands. In the seventeen years that have gone by, the mortgages have been substantially paid down, but the parcel rather than serving as a base for the owner's anticipated return to South Carolina, which he mentioned in our first interview, now is essentially a wasting asset. The store is vacant, taxes have risen substantially while the rents remain relatively static. "The people" [i.e., his tenants] "have been here too long to ask for an increase and they can't afford it." The owner felt sure that he could not get money back for repairs (which are needed) and could not sell the parcel "even if I tried."

A similar case involves an elderly blind black owner who bought his building back in 1944. He points out that when he bought it, institutional financing was available, now there is none. He would not make any improvements in his building because they would not be worthwhile. While his principal problem was the housing code and inspection requirements, he was bitter on the subject of tenants. This was specifically in reference to welfare tenantry, the only ones that would move into his structure. He said, "They tear the glass down near the door, they wreck the place." He is now tax delinquent.

The inhibiting characteristics are not merely those of a building being run down or of its owner being disabled or impoverished, and not even of the present general neighborhood characteristics, but also the negative view of the future.

> Parcel number 430 is a well maintained frame house on a tree-lined street in Newark. There are two legitimate apartments and a garret which is rented, perhaps illegally. The owner lives in one of the apartments, the other is rented for $100 a month, the garret at the moment is vacant. The owner purchased the building in 1961, when he and his wife were both working, in the post office and as an assembler in an electronic plant, respectively. They had combined incomes of $12,000. The building was assessed at $8,300 and they paid $10,500 with a first mortgage of $7,000 secured from a local savings and loan company. At the time of the original interview, three years after they had purchased it, substantial repairs had been made in the building. These included replumbing of the bathrooms and major redecoration internally as well as a fresh painting of the entire exterior. The couple at that time, were in their early 40s and discussed with us their plans for the future. These involved improving the building, paying down the mortgage, and ultimately remortgaging the building based on its improved value and, with the proceeds, moving into a one family house or keeping the older property for income. Their attitude now is one of resignation. They have no difficulty in renting out their rental units but the owner is no longer interested in seeking improvement money. "The taxes just keep going up and the neighborhood is going to go bad. The cost of improvments would easily out distance the amount of increased rent I could get." When asked whether the building would be worth more five years from now, he said, "It will be worth less because of the quality of the neighborhood and the general depreciation of the city."

A number of case studies have been presented in this section which describe long-term minority group owners who purchased at relatively reasonable cost and despite this have substantial problems. This situation, however, is even more pointed when the acquisition price has been artificially increased. And this is done sometimes, sadly enough, under a veil of well meaning governmental intervention.

## Inflated Sales Prices

It is difficult to analyze some of the older titles. The practices of posting the precise sales prices or, for that matter, the restatement of extent mortgages have varied over the years. There is some indication, however, that though minority group members may have paid more for housing than whites in the forties and early fifties, that the increases in rent levels and general inflation that have taken place since that time have tended to sustain the investments if not yield profits. In more recent years, however, the level of inflated prices at purchase is even more substantial and results sometimes are horrendous. Frequently the potential purchaser is relatively passive, with a realtor cum mortgage broker essentially seeking out potential sellers, finding purchasers who qualify under any of a variety of governmental programs, and packaging the sales transaction.

The packager's function is essential in American society; the question, however, is how much of a price must society pay for it? When it results in a parcel which is completely overpriced in terms of the market, in which the potential lack of means on the part of the buyer to improve the parcel or even to service its debt requirements is evident, the results may clearly lead to tax delinquency and abandonment. This is a far from new process:

> Parcel number 478 is owned by a black middle-aged couple. "Seven years ago, I think it was 1964, I wanted a home. The G.I. loan man came around and asked if I would like a loan for a home." The sale with a federally guaranteed mortgage of $18,400 was for $18,500 as against an assessment of $9,600 for the two-family house. The tenant in the house is on welfare, both parties are black. The current rent is $115 per month. The owner is presently having difficulty in securing fire insurance since his insurance company has dropped the parcel.
>
> Back in 1944, twenty years before the sale for $18,500 the parcel was sold for $5,000. While similar levels of inflation in prices are evident in the suburbs, this does not hold true for Newark. The

> owner is a bartender and feels very clearly that the house is not worth what he paid for it. As he stated, "The V.A. knocked off a little on the price but there is at least $4,000 water in here. I wanted the house, I've got seven kids and I needed a place to go. And besides, I looked at the purchase of the property as advancement."

It will be a very, very long time, however, before the owner, despite mortgage payments faithfully adhered to, will have developed any equity of substance in this parcel, considering the disparity between the mortgage value and the market value of the house. Based on comparable sales in the neighborhood the estimated worth of the parcel would be at most between $9,000 and $10,000.

The faith in the FHA expressed by some buyers is very substantial and some of their disappointments subsequent to involvement with the organization equally evident. For example:

> One black longshoreman bought a three-family house in one of the better areas of Newark and commented, "When I bought the house the FHA approved, and I thought the house then was in good condition because it was approved. When I took title, I realized that the roof leaked, the walls and the halls and all the floors were cracked, and there was no electrical circuitry on the top floor. It's going to cost me $2,000 to make the repairs. I'm in debt right up to my ears and besides the insurance company which presently holds the fire insurance just raised the rate an additional $111.70 on the building."

This building was purchased in June 1971. A local mortgage broker arranged the mortgage of $25,500 against the consideration of $25,900. The total assessment is $11,600 and back in 1959 this building sold for $13,500. Again in terms of comparable sale for the neighborhood it is certainly worth no more than $12,000 to $14,000.

Even with government subsidized mortgages the fiscal strains can be too much for the owner to support. Parcel number 317 is a case in point:

> This house was bought by a black machinist and his wife in 1962. While assessed at $9,900 it was purchased through a G.I. mortgage of $15,000 with first mortgage of $14,600. The owner, in our earlier interview, said that he had paid $1,200 down as well as $400 in "service fees" in the course of the transaction. As a factory worker he was unable to sustain the mortgage payments which ran to $166

> per month and the next entry on the parcel title is foreclosure by the bank holding the mortgage. It was then sold to the present incumbent three years ago by the bank which continued to hold the mortgage. The present owner is a construction worker who cannot even afford, as he put it "to have insurance on the building." The apartments have degenerated in quality and are currently vacant. The condition of the building, which in the earlier survey was marked as excellent, is now at best on the tottering side. Here is a building which can very easily become abandoned.

Yet another building indicates this same pattern which can be repeated again and again from our files — parcel number 228:

> This building was purchased in 1971 by a black handyman who presently occupies one of its three apartments and rents the other two. It is a frame and shingle house in reasonable repair on the fringes of the core slum area. It was purchased under the Federal Interest Supplement Program for $17,300, its assessment is $12,900. Comparable parcels in the area are selling for approximately the assessment figure. The present owner is now unemployed and is very frustrated with the building which needs repairs. He said, "I've got no money and I can't get any kind of mortgage from anybody to take care of it." He is presently tax delinquent and the parcel shows every indication of beginning to degenerate.

The need and the virtues of revolving patterns of ownership in the central city of minority groups entering into the entrepreneurial cycle, just as their predecessors did, should not close our eyes to the essential requirement that the dynamic be accompanied by sound financing practices. The very act of introducing generous mortgages has generated an inflation in the market which is wholly without economic basis. How can we better package this operation?

The potential of putting local people into business, though, is evident. For example:

> Parcel number 477 was purchased in 1970 by a black handyman who had worked for a medium scale white real estate operator. He paid $14,000 for the parcel with the seller taking back the first mortgage for the full amount of the parcel. The assessment of the two and one-half story frame house is $7,200. Two of the three apartments are presently rented. The present owner said, "I was collecting rent and doing handy work for Mr. ________, and I bought the parcel from him as an investment." The present rents are $135 a month. The previous owner had purchased the building

> in 1963 for $10,700 with a first mortgage secured for $8,400 from a savings and loan company. In 1969 the parcel had been sold for $10,000. The 1962 transfer was achieved through default on the mortgage in the earlier sale. At the time of the interview in 1964 the owner indicated that he wanted to get rid of the building but there were no buyers.

How does one interpret the most recent sale? From one point of view it is the exploitation of the purchaser through a sale at $14,000 for a parcel which at its best currently would only be worth about $8,500. Alternately, one can say that since the seller has not secured any cash, he is taking a rather considerable risk, but then, what options did he have? From a societal point of view there is virtue in a shift to a more locally based owner, i.e., the current operator lives around the corner from the parcel, but given the financial strains imposed by the size of the extant mortgage he is certainly in no position to borrow any additional money to repair the building. Assuming that we want to put this type of present owner in business, how do we insure that it is at a price which makes market sense? Is it worthwhile putting these people in business? What is the future of the minority owner in Newark?

## THE MINORITY OWNER'S PROBLEMS AND VIEWS OF THE FUTURE

### Views of the Future

In Chapter 7 the subject of abandonments and the variables grouped with it are examined in some substantial detail. It is noteworthy here, however, as shown in Exhibit 7-15, that it is white owners who bulk more substantially in the "abandoners."

There is a very substantial variation in the degree of positive thinking on the future of their holdings by landlords based on their ethnicity. Of the black owners, 48.7 percent felt that their parcels would be worth more, or much more, five years in the future as contrasted to only 30.1 percent of white owners. Without exception the respondents who said "worth less," regardless of their racial background, refer to area characteristics and overall municipal degeneration as the causes. While, in the absolute, neither of these figures is one to gladden the city planner's heart, optimizing the variation in positive thinking is essential if there are to be any long-run investment in and substantial care of parcels.

When owners were asked whether they could get capital investments made on their parcels returned through ultimate resale, there was substantial variation by the ethnicity of the respondent (Exhibit 3-13). Blacks were much more positive than whites with nearly one third (31.9 percent) of the former but barely half that (16.5 percent) of the latter answering either yes, definitely, or maybe. While the bulk of the response regardless of race was negative, clearly there are significant differences. Is it that the blacks have more illusions or are there several layers of opportunity within the market strata?

EXHIBIT 3-13
OWNER'S VIEW TOWARDS AVAILABILITY OF RENT INCREASES
FOR STRUCTURAL IMPROVEMENTS (1971)
BY ETHNICITY OF OWNER (1971)

| Will you get a rent increase . . .? | Black | White | Spanish Speaking | Total |
|---|---|---|---|---|
| Yes, easily | 36 | 37 | 1 | 74 |
| Yes, grudgingly | 5 | 7 | 0 | 12 |
| Could go either way | 2 | 3 | 0 | 5 |
| Not likely | 5 | 6 | 0 | 11 |
| Definitely not | 20 | 46 | 2 | 68 |
| Other | 5 | 10 | 1 | 16 |
| NA/DK | 40 | 55 | 0 | 95 |
| Total | 113 | 164 | 4 | 281 |
| **PERCENT DISTRIBUTION** | | | | |
| Yes, easily | 31.9 | 22.6 | 25.0 | 26.3 |
| Yes, grudgingly | 4.4 | 4.3 | 0.0 | 4.3 |
| Could go either way | 1.8 | 1.8 | 0.0 | 1.8 |
| Not likely | 4.4 | 3.7 | 0.0 | 3.9 |
| Definitely not | 17.7 | 28.0 | 50.0 | 24.2 |
| Other | 4.4 | 6.1 | 25.0 | 5.7 |
| NA/DK | 35.4 | 33.3 | 0.0 | 33.8 |
| Total | 100.0 | 100.0 | 100.0 | 100.0 |

$\chi^2 = 0.05$

Source: Newark Area Resurvey, spring 1972

Blacks were also much more positive than whites on the potential of securing rent increases commensurate with the level of needed capital investment on their parcels. As shown in Exhibit 3-14, there is a rather substantial range of response when owners were asked what kind of rent increases would be required to make their parcels good investments. In general the blacks were slightly lower with the mode at the $11 to $20 a month per dwelling unit figure. Whites were somewhat higher. When they were asked whether they could secure these increases, 31.9 percent of the blacks answered in the affirmative, while only 22.6 percent of the whites gave the same positive response. Conversely, 17.7 percent of the blacks as against 28 percent of the whites said definitely not. In both cases about 5 percent of the respondents replied that there was something in the nature of family relationship or fear of losing good tenants which would inhibit any effort of raising rents even if such increases were securable.

There are some ominous clouds on the horizon, however. As pointed out later, there is a higher proportion of blacks than whites with multiple periods of tax delinquencies. While some of these delinquencies clearly are the reflection of essentially paper sales of parcels far gone in the abandonment process and made over to local residents by absentee whites, there is no question that black owners as well as the whites are dependent upon the overall vitality and revival of the city.

As has been pointed out earlier, some of the responses by relatively new owners are somber indeed. A case in point is parcel number 407:

> In 1964 the building, a three-family frame home, was purchased by a black couple for $8,500 with a savings and loan taking back a $5,800 mortgage. The parcel at that time was assessed for $11,300. At the time of the first interview, the parcel was described by the interviewer as scrupulously clean. The owner's comments were as follows: "Everybody wants to get profits for rentals. When problems become too big, they sell. I want to keep the parcel nice so I can keep tenants. When the time comes that I want to sell, I want to get a good price." Both husband and wife were very proud of their new acquisition. It should be noted that they lived in a very pleasant one-family house in the suburbs, and already owned an additional five-family rental unit.

Currently, the three apartments in parcel number 407 are run-down. While apartment rents have moved up perhaps 10 percent

# EXHIBIT 3-14
## OWNER'S VIEW TOWARDS SUFFICIENT RENT INCREASES TO OCCASION IMPROVEMENT INVESTMENT (1971) BY ETHNICITY OF OWNER (1971)

| A ______ Increase is Necessary To . . . | Black | White | Spanish Speaking | Total |
|---|---|---|---|---|
| Up to $5/tenant | 0 | 4 | 0 | 4 |
| $ 6 — 10 | 15 | 15 | 0 | 30 |
| $11 — 20 | 20 | 22 | 1 | 43 |
| $21 — 30 | 19 | 8 | 0 | 27 |
| $31 — 50 | 10 | 24 | 0 | 34 |
| $51 and over | 3 | 9 | 1 | 13 |
| No one would pay rent needed | 1 | 14 | 0 | 15 |
| Satisfied with present level | 15 | 29 | 1 | 45 |
| NA/DK | 30 | 39 | 1 | 70 |
| Total | 113 | 164 | 4 | 281 |

PERCENT DISTRIBUTION

| | Black | White | Spanish Speaking | Total |
|---|---|---|---|---|
| Up to $5/tenant | 0.0 | 2.4 | 0.0 | 1.4 |
| $ 6 — 10 | 13.3 | 9.1 | 0.0 | 10.7 |
| $11 — 20 | 17.7 | 13.4 | 25.0 | 15.3 |
| $21 — 30 | 16.8 | 4.9 | 0.0 | 9.6 |
| $31 — 50 | 8.8 | 14.6 | 0.0 | 12.1 |
| $51 and over | 2.7 | 5.5 | 25.0 | 4.6 |
| No one would pay rent needed | 0.9 | 8.5 | 0.0 | 5.3 |
| Satisfied with present level | 13.3 | 17.7 | 25.0 | 16.0 |
| NA/DK | 26.5 | 23.8 | 25.0 | 24.9 |
| Total | 100.0 | 100.0 | 100.0 | 100.0 |

$\chi^2 = 0.001$

Source: Newark Area Resurvey, spring 1972.

> from earlier levels to a current $95 average, this is not commensurate with increases in operating expenses. The owner, when asked if the property would be worth more or less five years from now said, "I don't know, I think it's getting worse in Newark with the crime and the burning of buildings. People don't want to buy. I think the value of buildings will go down."

Many of Newark's black owners' possession of their properties rests upon a very delicate fabric which frequently encompasses high sale prices. In addition, there is a substantial dependence upon second incomes in the family. Third, there is the role of mortgage company fees and discounts which, over and above the face value of the mortgage, frequently inflate closing costs and deplete the new owner's immediate cash position.

The type of case vignettes presented here can be repeated practically without end. Here is a typical example:

> Parcel number 321 is a two-family house purchased in 1967 by a black couple. He works as a guard at a bank; his wife is a night cleaning woman at the same institution. The house is presently in the midst of fairly extensive repairs done by the couple themselves. The one tenant pays $125 a month rent which covers the taxes with perhaps $300 a year to spare. The owner has enclosed the porch, put in a new heating system, new roof, the stairs have been repaired, the house has been repainted, and he has done substantial wall work.
>
> The house was bought through a G.I. mortgage secured through a local mortgage company. The total sale price of $13,000 included a $12,900 first mortgage; the house's assessment is $10,200. Our appraisal would indicate that it might be worth on a cash sale on the order of $8,000. Examination of the title shows that there was no previous sale on the house after 1943 when it sold for $2,500. The owner, when asked if the house would be worth more or less in the future, said, "If the Model Cities area develops over the next five years, then maybe the value will go up; if not it is going to drop."

The problems of area decay, as earlier noted, are not exclusive to white owners by any means. Again and again, regardless of ethnicity, questions on potential of investment secured answers similar to that of one black owner who said in relation to a question on the costs of putting his building into good repair, "Hard to say until I know how much a complete overhaul would cost, but it probably wouldn't be worthwhile in this area."

## Attitudes Toward Urban Renewal

In Exhibit 3-15 the owner response to the question of whether his parcel is in an urban renewal area is shown by ethnicity. Note the very substantial level of ambivalence and uncertainty of the respondents. More than a third of the blacks (34.5 percent) and nearly a fourth (22

EXHIBIT 3-15
OWNER'S KNOWLEDGE OF HIS PROPERTY FALLING WITHIN AN URBAN RENEWAL AREA (1971) BY ETHNICITY OF OWNER (1971)

| Will Your Property Be Taken By Urban Renewal? | Black | White | Spanish Speaking | Total |
|---|---|---|---|---|
| No | 41 | 73 | 0 | 114 |
| Yes, within 1 year | 4 | 2 | 0 | 6 |
| Yes, 1 to 5 years | 3 | 4 | 0 | 7 |
| Yes, 5 to 10 years | 2 | 1 | 0 | 3 |
| Yes | 8 | 24 | 0 | 32 |
| Not sure | 39 | 36 | 3 | 78 |
| Other | 1 | 3 | 0 | 4 |
| NA/DK | 15 | 21 | 1 | 37 |
| Total | 113 | 164 | 4 | 281 |
| PERCENT DISTRIBUTION | | | | |
| No | 36.3 | 44.5 | 0.0 | 40.6 |
| Yes, within 1 year | 3.5 | 1.2 | 0.0 | 2.1 |
| Yes, 1 to 5 years | 2.7 | 2.4 | 0.0 | 2.5 |
| Yes, 5 to 10 years | 1.8 | 0.6 | 0.0 | 1.1 |
| Yes | 7.1 | 14.6 | 0.0 | 11.4 |
| Not sure | 34.5 | 22.0 | 75.0 | 27.8 |
| Other | 0.9 | 1.8 | 0.0 | 1.4 |
| NA/DK | 13.3 | 12.8 | 25.0 | 13.2 |
| Total | 100.0 | 100.0 | 100.0 | 100.0 |

$X^2$ n/s @ 0.05

Source: Newark Area Resurvey, spring 1972.

percent) of the whites said simply that they didn't know. This clearly is an area that requires some substantial attention by federal authorities and municipal ones as well, given the uncertainties of the entire urban renewal program which overhang Newark. *The owner, faced with some vague feeling that his parcel simply isn't going to be there at some finite point in the future, is probably not disposed to make a long-term investment.*

And clearly this nebulousness affects the relatively unsophisticated smaller-scale black owners even more so than whites. Blacks, in general, were less sanguine about the results of urban renewal land taking in terms of getting their investments back than were whites, with 40.9 percent of the latter as against 29.2 percent of the former positive that if their parcels were taken for urban renewal, they would be able to secure full value. Interestingly enough, this result was nearly offset by 15 percent of the blacks versus 22 percent of the white owners who said "definitely not."

The causes for this kind of dichotomy are not clear. In part, in reviewing the open-ended part of the responses to this question, it reflects some of the bitterness of white owners toward what they feel is the unfairness of government policy in regard to them. In part, also, it just indicates that three out of ten of the blacks simply didn't know. In general, they seem much less familiar with this process than is true of the white responses where only one out of eight gave this similar "don't know — no answer" response.

## Institutional Financing Potential

Black owners were much more sanguine than whites in their responses to the question: "If you were selling now would it be possible to get a mortgage from a lending institution?" While in neither case was a majority at all sure on this point, the positive figure among black owners was 40.5 percent. The white equivalent (a perhaps more realistic one) was only 19.5 percent — less than half. Nearly a quarter (23.9 percent) of the blacks felt they would not have to take back a purchase money mortgage on a sale, i.e., that the financing available plus purchaser's equity would cover the purchase. The same held true for only 9.1 percent of the whites. Among this latter group 10 percent specifically said that they would have to take back a purchase money mortgage for

100 percent of the selling price as compared with less than 2 percent of the nonwhites.

Two-thirds of the respondents regardless of race knew of no government program for financing available for rehabilitation in their particular area in which they owned their parcels. Only 5.3 percent of the blacks and 3.7 percent of the whites mentioned the Federally Assisted Code Enforcement (FACE) program specifically. An additional 10 percent of each group made some reference to the FHA. Again, much in the way of education has to be done here.

*Certainly, then, minority group ownership in and of itself cannot resolve city problems. It can provide a base of more useful, more involved ownership but the surrounding infra-structure of the city must support a decent living base.*

In that context some of the problems of the city, its building owners and tenants must be viewed in detail before policy parameters for the future are determined. Prime among these are the roles that abandonment and tax delinquency play.

## Notes

1. Jonathan Spivak, "Pride of Ownership: Government Is Testing a Plan to Help Poor Buy Their Own Homes," *Wall Street Journal*, 23 October 1970, 1.

2. For earlier work on this same area, see: William Grigsby, "The Residential Real Estate Market in an Area Undergoing Racial Transition" (Doctoral diss., Columbia University, 1958).

3. There is already recognition of this facet of policy. See: U.S. Congress, House of Representatives, Committee on Banking and Currency, *Housing and the Urban Environment* (Washington, D.C.: Government Printing Office, 1971); U.S. Congress, House of Representatives, Committee on Banking and Currency, *Interim Report on HUD Investigation of Low- and Moderate-Income Housing Programs* (Washington, D.C.: Government Printing Office, 1971); Richard Jones, "Sponsorship of Subsidized Housing for Low and Moderate Income Families under the National Housing Act," *George Washington Law Review* 38 (July 1970):1073-1090; "How Washington Is Helping More People Buy Homes," *U.S. News and World Report*, 26 October 1970.

2

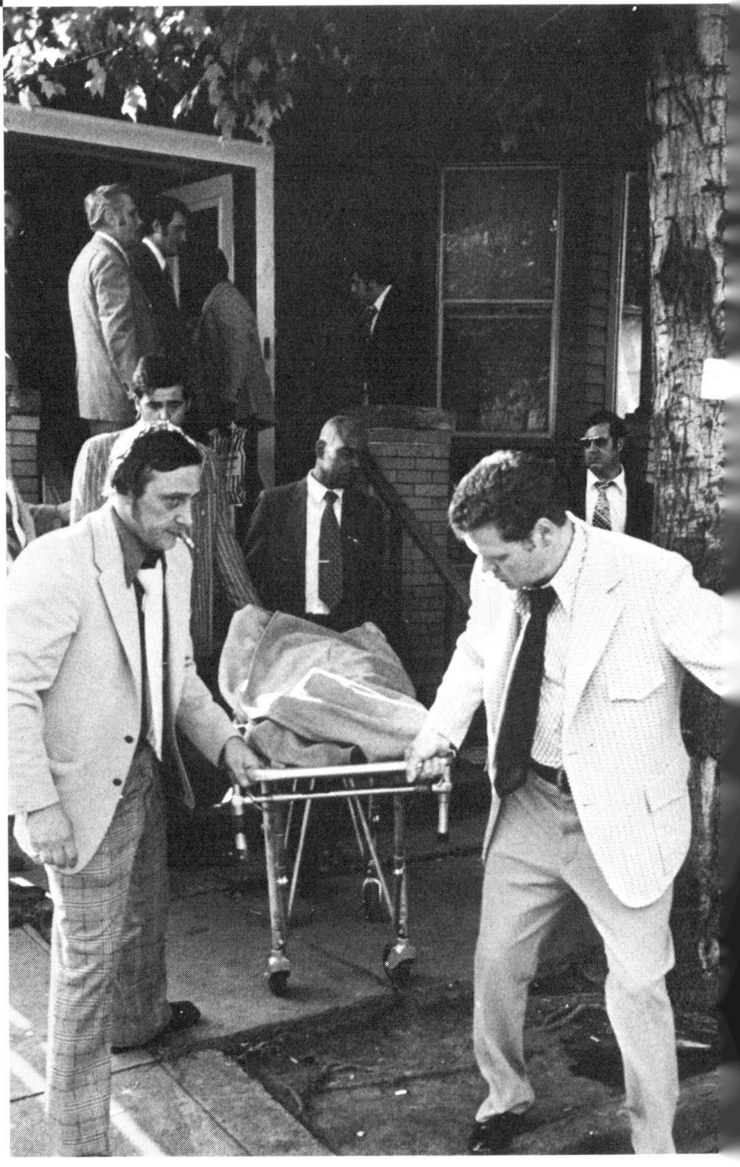

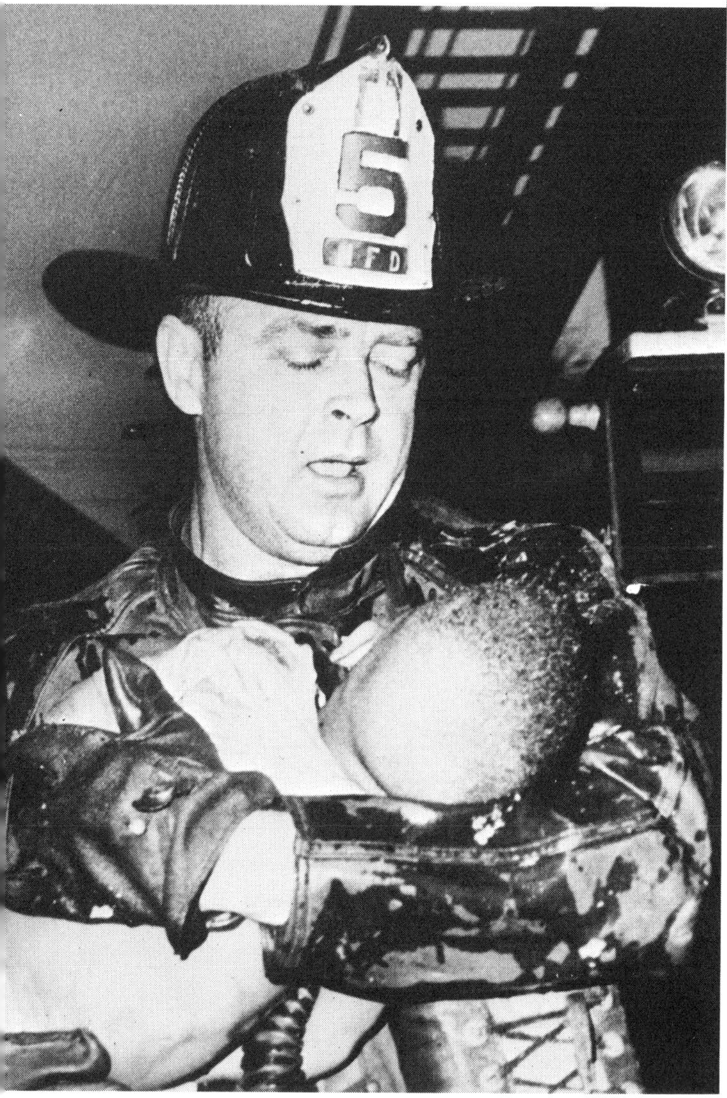

ACY
NO
STOPPING OR
STANDING
4 TO 6PM

# 4

# PUBLIC SAFETY AND ABANDONMENT

## PUBLIC SAFETY AND THE CITY

There can be few aspects of urban life in which myth and reality are as inextricably interwoven as that of public safety. Regardless of the proportion of each of these, their results in consumer response, whether tenant or owner, is all too evident. Unless the impact of this basic insecurity can be allayed, no measure of physical rebuilding, no improvement in other services, can have any lasting measure of success. In a recent survey of welfare recipients in New York City, for example, the single largest problem which the 412 respondents voiced in terms of housing problems was fear of crime and drugs.[1] And certainly this is not confined to New York; it is characteristic of Newark as well.

> It is epitomized here in the response of the white, absentee owner of parcel number 414, a three story, masonry structure, fronting on a park, which is presently in the process of being abandoned. The owner pointed to the fact of three murders in the area, one which was actually in the building itself, the other two on the same block within the prior year, as forcing his decision to walk away from his building. Or the statement of a three-family house owner (parcel number 379) who said "It is very costly to collect rents here, two of us go out to do it, one rides shotgun." Or yet another black nonresident owner (parcel number 268), who varies his rent collection dates "so the robbers won't be able to mark me." To say that these are not owners whose outlooks are conducive to long-run investment is to be guilty of the most horrendous level of understatement.

Overhanging all of these responses, accounting for much of the fear of tenants and owners alike, is the reality of drug addiction with all that it means to a neighborhood. Again and again in the course of the interviews, this problem was addressed:

> "One junkie drives out all the tenants. Even if the junkies don't live in a building but just hang around, this will happen. It's the major problem. It's number one in some buildings." (parcel number 263) And as another black nonresident owner of a three-family house said when asked about the future of his parcel, "That dope business is getting worse and worse. Who wants to own property in the middle of a dope filled area? These are places in which no one wants to live, property values just keep going down." (parcel number 94)

Would there be crime if drug addiction was resolved? Would it be as prevalent? As destructive of the basic neighborhood? These are problems which are outside the competence of this study, but the sum of the results is exemplified by an interview with a large scale property owner in Newark:

> In 1965 this operator had nearly forty parcels in the city. He is now down to two, both of which are vacant and vandalized. He secured the building (parcel number 370) in 1929 through a foreclosure. When interviewed about the parcel in 1965, he was enthusiastic about the rent potential and tenantry in its four apartments and store. Even at that time he had some hesitations, though, about the balance of his holdings in Newark. Now the parcel is located in the heart of the zone of abandonment; there are burned out structures on all sides.
>
> The owner claimed that welfare tenants and drug addicts demolished whatever repairs he could make. He pointed out that he had bought the properties for next to nothing and had gotten his money back. He had no interest in going into debt for this property in terms of repairs, since its future was clearly limited. He continues paying the taxes at a minimal base in order to avoid foreclosure, still hoping that urban renewal will ultimately take the parcel. In the meantime, his attitude is epitomized by his comments on the area, "All of ______ Avenue in Newark is vandalized and terror ridden. There are many, many vacancies and abandonments. Crime has spread throughout the neighborhood and the narcotics condition is on the rise. The houses have had all their plumbing ripped out. Nobody wanted the parcel when we tried to sell it; after the last tenants left we just decided to let the property die."

The attitudes expressed above are not limited to white owners nor to nonresidents. The decline in morale of some of the minority group home buyers, who were interviewed in 1965 and who are still residents in the same parcel, is deeply troubling. In part they have been addressed in the chapter on minority owners. Their attitudes toward crime and the fear of its reality vary little regardless of race or residence pattern.

> Survey example, parcel number 503, is owned by a black couple, who purchased the three-family frame house in 1952. At the time of the first interview, March 31, 1965, they were very enthusiastic. "They've painted the inside, finished the kitchen, dining room, and living room floors; they've also gotten storm windows and screens. They've modified the inside configuration of the house, put in new doors, new plumbing, fixed the ceiling in the kitchen, put in the fire escape that is required by the building inspector. House in excellent condition. Good tenants and the neighborhood is good." This is what the interviewer recorded.
>
> They had bought the house, which was assessed for $8,000, for $7,000 with a first mortgage of $5,000 secured from a savings and loan company. At the time of the second interview, at the end of 1971, the owners pointed out that the rents are the same that they had in 1965, in order to keep their old tenants. While taxes were troublesome, having gone from $580 a year to $800 currently, their worst problem was that of crime in the neighborhood. The owner's wife, when asked whether she would continue to put money into the building, said, "We'll never get our investment back, I just want to get out of here."

The driving out of resident owners because of fear of crime and drug addiction, unless halted, means the end of the last and best hope for a revitalization of the city as a residential center. The problem of some of the older resident owners faced with a changing locale is even more substantial.

> Parcel number 361, for example, is a very tall, gaunt frame structure peripheral to the hard core slum area. In 1965 the present owner, a welder, was resident there. Having reached his early 60s, he was essentially retired, though he put in some part-time work in small shops around Newark. He had bought the house in 1950 for $9,000, and made substantial repairs himself. The mortgage was paid off and he looked forward to a relatively free future.
>
> He still owns the house, though he no longer lives there. His response on this point was, "No, I couldn't stay there, I'm afraid of

> the neighborhood." Now his maintenance of the parcel is minimal and he has no feeling for making any significant improvements. As he pointed out "Who the hell is going to buy it." His best estimate is that at most he would get $5,000 back on the sale of the parcel currently, and even then he would have to take back a purchase money mortgage. This is a parcel that is on its way to abandonment.

These cases could be replicated time and time again. Their sheer redundancy should not minimize their fundamental impact on the realities of the city's viability.

> There is also the black home owner who refused to move back into Newark after purchasing parcel number 363 for a home. It is a three-family house which he bought for $18,000, securing a $14,900 mortgage. The owner then was living in East Orange. His family had grown and they were looking for "larger quarters." "Things got so bad in Newark, we decided not to move in, we just rent the place."
>
> There is the three-family frame structure purchased by a black family in 1951 under the GI bill (parcel number 571). They paid $15,000 with a $13,500 mortgage from a local bank at 5 percent. The parcel was bought as a place to live and they moved in immediately. The male head of household is a repairman. As he explained the purchase back in 1965, "We couldn't afford, at first, a one-family house. We needed an income property. Back in 1965 the biggest problem as seen by him was taxes. He had just rewired the house only to see his assessment increase. (The taxes since 1961 have gone from $337 to more than $1,000 per year.) The monthly rent roll per apartment was also increased; in 1951 it was $60, in 1965 it was $80, but even though it has moved up to $125 currently it is becoming more difficult to make ends meet. On the other hand, the building is now owned virtually free and clear of mortgage.
>
> In the normal course of events, under private market conditions, this is a building which would serve as a base for a move to the suburbs or to another neighborhood. The housewife's comments on the area and the building, however, indicate the problem, "This used to be a lovely neighborhood. There was a local policeman who used to walk around the block. Now the neighborhood keeps going down in value. This property will drop even if we maintain it well. I couldn't sell it, the neighborhood is so bad that nobody would want to buy it."

What should have been a basic way station to middle class life has instead turned out to be a dead end.

How can one secure understanding of the crime and fire phenomena? The section on public safety which follows is divided into three parts. The first takes up the reality of crime in Newark. The Newark Police facilitated the acquisition of over 90,000 data cards which list all police activity, whether for major or minor crime or for assistance purposes within the city during 1971. In addition, equivalent summary data were secured for 1965. These cards contain a five digit address listing. By comparing this listing with the standing, vacant building tabulations prepared by the Newark Fire Department for the two respective years, it was possible to identify both the crimes and arrests that occurred within these two specific building sets.

The first part of the analysis will touch on general crime trends within the United States, then turn to a similar analysis for New Jersey, and then to crimes in cities of similar size as Newark. Finally, the focus will turn to variations in crime data within Newark itself. These investigations provide the background necessary to uncover the role of abandoned buildings in crime.

The next major part of this section is devoted to a study of what may well be the culmination of the city's trauma — the fires which are an ever increasing accompaniment of social problems and the desertion of areas.

The last section of the chapter uses the statistical technique of factor analysis to examine in more detail the parameters which are linked with both crime and fire. The reader will note that in this last section are grouped the two phenomena earlier analysed independently. The results of the factor analysis utilized here show that both fire and abandonment are linked to a basic common denominator, *poverty*.

## CRIME AND THE CITY

The fear of crime in the city dates back to medieval days. The prevalence of strangers, the sheer critical mass of population, the hurly burly of different groups, all lent themselves to criminal acts, whether they were related to property, to personal violence, or both. In the days of the Founding Fathers, the city, portrayed as the center of the landless mob, was a thing to be dreaded. And this was true not only for the old northern aristocracy of conservatives but also for no less a populist than Jefferson. Any reader of the novels of Walter D. Edmonds on nineteenth century New York will find much that is comparable to current conditions in his description of the Five Points Area and the like. And certainly the urban riots of Civil War days were far more destructive even than their equivalent in this last decade.

In earlier times, the prevalence of crime within the city was seen as a function of the city drawing upon itself lawless individuals. The sociology of crime was seen substantially as a function of individual acts, not as the result of societal imperfections upon individuals. The literature of the second half of the twentieth century reflects a radically different understanding of the causal relations between central city life and criminal activity. This is characterized by Ramsey Clark, former attorney general of the United States, when he analyzed the urban crime relationship as follows:[2]

> "In every major city in the United States you will find that two-thirds of the arrests take place among only about two percent of the population. Where is that area in every city? Well, it's in the same place where infant mortality is four times higher than in the city as a whole; where the death rate is 25 percent higher; where life expectancy is ten years shorter; where common communicable diseases with potential of physical and mental damage are six and eight and ten times more frequent; where alcoholism and drug addiction are prevalent to a degree far transcending that of the rest of the city; where education is poorest — the oldest school buildings, the most crowded and turbulent school rooms, the fewest certified teachers, the highest rate of dropouts; where the average formal schooling is four to six years less than for the city as a whole."

Regardless of the causal relationships that are at work here, the results are beyond cavil. As shown in Exhibit 4-1, crimes in the United States, regardless of their character, have been increasing at a horrendous rate; crimes of violence have increased by 156 percent and crimes against property by 180 percent. Certainly the increase in crime can, in part, be seen as resulting from the changing age structure in the United States. Criminal activity is more prevalent among youth than any other age category. And today there is a larger proportion of persons in the 15 to 25 year age bracket than has been true for several generations. Certainly too, this is a generation in which the mass media have relentlessly pursued a path of propagating a standard of living which many of the urban poor have no hope of obtaining legitimately.

## EXHIBIT 4-1
## CRIMES IN THE UNITED STATES
## 1960-1970

### PERCENT CHANGE

(Per 100,000 Inhabitants)

| | TYPE OF CRIME | | | | | | |
|---|---|---|---|---|---|---|---|
| Absolute | Murder* | Aggravated Assault* | Forcible Rape* | Robbery* | Burglary** | Larceny** over $50 | Auto Theft** |
| Offense Increase | 76 | 117 | 121 | 224 | 142 | 245 | 143 |
| Rate Increase | 56 | 92 | 95 | 186 | 113 | 204 | 150 |

*Crimes of Violence (up 156%)
**Crimes Against Property (up 180%)

Source: U.S. Federal Bureau of Investigation. *Crime in the United States Uniform Crime Report* (Washington, D.C.: Government Printing Office, 1970), pp. 7-29.

That the resulting frustration leads not only to crimes against property but also crimes of violence, needs little exposition.

Over all of this, as earlier mentioned, is the terrible aberrant of drug addiction. There are no accurate data on its incidence in Newark. There is a consensus, however, certainly among the police in the city who were interviewed, that nearly half of all the real crime in Newark is the immediate or extended result of the drug problem.

In essence, then, the country as a whole is faced not only with an increased reported prevalence of crime, but also a much promulgated increase. Where do New Jersey and Newark stand in this dismal procession?

## Crime in New Jersey

The State of New Jersey, unfortunately, more than reflects the increased rate of crime characteristics of the 1960s (Exhibit 4-2). The general crime index rate of the *Uniform Crime Report* for the state rose 176 percent between 1960 and 1970, representing 2,744 incidents of crime per 100,000 inhabitants. (The national figure is 2,740 incidents of index crimes per 100,000 inhabitants in 1970, reflecting a 144 percent increase from 1960.) Such an *increase* over national figures can partially be explained by New Jersey's rating as the most urban state in the union by the Department of the Census in 1970. State figures reveal New Jersey's trend of crime surpasses national statistics in all categories except forcible rape.

Of even more relevance are the crime figures for New Jersey's six largest cities as measured by the seven offenses tabulated as part of the *Crime Index*[*] (Exhibits 4-3 and 4-4). From these data it is evident that Newark exceeds all large cities in the state and many of similar size in the nation in all seven indices of crime. But, characteristically, cities with populations of more than a quarter of a million have the highest rate of crime of any other category of city size. Therefore, closer examination of crime in Newark compared to the average level of crime for cities in the United States of populations over 250,000 is even more revealing. The City of Newark's combined *Crime Index* exceeds the national average for cities of 250,000 or more by almost 60 percent.

---

[*]FBI Uniform Crime Reporting Program, *Crime Index* (murder, forcible rape, robbery, aggravated assault, burglary, larceny [over $50], and auto theft).

## EXHIBIT 4-2
### 1960-1970 INCREASES IN NEW JERSEY CRIME COMPARED TO NATIONAL CRIME TRENDS

| | Type of Crime | | | | | | |
|---|---|---|---|---|---|---|---|
| | Murder | Forcible Rape | Robbery | Aggravated Assault | Burglary | Larceny over $50 | Auto Theft |
| 1960 rates per 100,000 inhabitants State of New Jersey | 2.9 | 7.9 | 46.0 | 59.8 | 438.6 | 236.9 | 201.9 |
| 1970 rates per 100,000 inhabitants State of New Jersey | 5.7 | 12.9 | 169.4 | 99.0 | 1041.4 | 855.2 | 557.4 |
| Rate increase | 97% | 63% | 268% | 65% | 137% | 262% | 176% |
| National rate increase | 56% | 95% | 186% | 92% | 113% | 204% | 150% |

Source: *Crime in the United States, Uniform Crime Reports*, 1970, p. 66 and 67 and 7-29 and *Uniform Crime Report*, 1960, p. 36.

## EXHIBIT 4-3
## CRIME IN MAJOR NEW JERSEY CITIES

| City | Year | Population | Type of Crime by Rate per 100,000 Inhabitants | | | | | | |
|---|---|---|---|---|---|---|---|---|---|
| | | | Murder* | Rape | Robbery | Aggravated Assault | Burglary | Larceny over $50 | Car Theft |
| Camden | 1960 | 117,159 | 12.8 | 25.6 | 148.7 | 183.8 | 798.7 | 512.8 | 475.2 |
| | 1970 | 102,551 | 27.0 | 41.0 | 684.0 | 266.0 | 2,726.0 | 1,046.0 | 2,214.0 |
| Elizabeth | 1960 | 107,698 | 8.0 | 9.0 | 94.0 | 106.0 | 582.0 | 164.0 | 352.0 |
| | 1970 | 112,654 | 8.9 | 28.6 | 249.1 | 280.4 | 1,575.0 | 830.4 | 1,255.4 |
| Jersey City | 1960 | 276,101 | 4.3 | .7 | 31.2 | 28.0 | 272.1 | 80.1 | 356.9 |
| | 1970 | 260,545 | 17.7 | 17.3 | 333.0 | 137.3 | 698.0 | 160.4 | 1,597.7 |
| Newark | 1960 | 405,220 | 19.7 | 41.0 | 325.0 | 424.5 | 1,775.8 | 1,056.3 | 960.5 |
| | 1970 | 377,485 | 45.6 | 67.1 | 1,237.7 | 575.6 | 3,017.2 | 1,619.4 | 1,875.1 |
| Paterson | 1960 | 143,663 | 5.6 | 3.5 | 78.3 | 80.4 | 702.8 | 77.6 | 345.5 |
| | 1970 | 144,824 | 13.9 | 12.5 | 452.8 | 205.6 | 1,878.5 | 474.3 | 1,759.0 |
| Trenton | 1960 | 114,167 | 12.7 | 13.6 | 100.0 | 72.7 | 875.5 | 385.5 | 406.4 |
| | 1970 | 104,638 | 3.0 | 38.0 | 657.0 | 239.0 | 3,333.0 | 1,785.0 | 1,345.0 |

*Includes manslaughter

Source: *Crime in the United States, Uniform Crime Report, 1960-1970.*

EXHIBIT 4-4
CRIMES PER 100,000 INHABITANTS FOR LARGE CITIES
(URBAN CRIME INDEX — 1970)

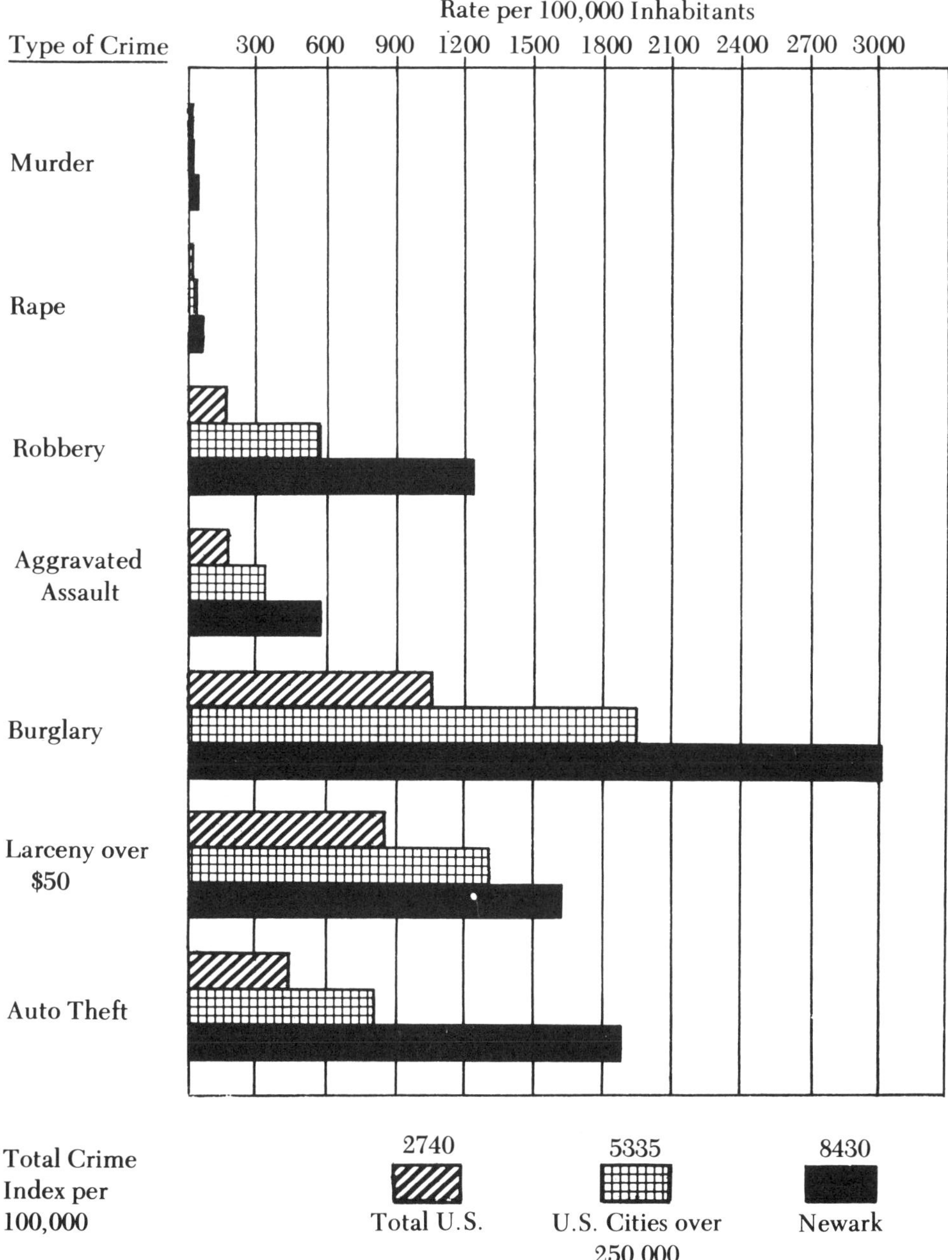


Source: *Crime in the United States, Uniform Crime Report, 1970.*

## Crime in Newark

The distribution of criminal activity throughout the City of Newark reveals a consistently high rate of crime, even the proportional distribution of types of crime for Newark's five wards shows marked similarity.

Exhibits 4-5 and 4-6 demonstrate that there is little variation in type of crime in particular wards. All have the same general distribution of crime. For example, crimes against persons /property vary by no more than 10 percent between the two wards with the highest and lowest percent of crime in this category. Closer examination of these data reveals Newark's most affluent sectors, the North and West Wards, although they have generally lower crime rates, rank second and third in the specific category of crime against persons and property (in terms of the percent distribution of *Index Crimes* versus lesser offenses). This pattern suggests the use of these wards by nonresidents for criminal acts rooted in economic gain.

The statistics also demonstrate a level of general criminal activity for all five wards of Newark above national averages. While the North and West Wards, which are the most remote sectors of the city from Newark's central business district, have the *lowest* rate of total criminal activity per 100,000 inhabitants (including crime against persons/ property, disorderly conduct, suspicious persons, and false alarms), as noted previously, bulking large here are the relatively higher percentages of crimes against persons and property. Contrastingly, the city's most deteriorating and socially depressed areas, the Central and East Wards, have the *highest* total rate of crime in the city. The crime rate in the East Ward (includes most of the downtown area and several public housing projects) is almost five times the national average and twice that of Newark's relatively safest ward, the North.

## CRIME AND RESIDENTIAL ABANDONMENT

Within the statistics of crime in the city, the subject of abandoned parcels plays a central role. The occurrence of abandonment functions in the same geographic areas as high crime. Rising incidence of crime and abandonment appear to be the characteristic traits of neighborhoods undergoing rapid and malign social change. The high level of crime occurring in certain areas of the city to some extent may

## EXHIBIT 4-5
### SUMMER EVENING CRIME SAMPLE BY WARD
### NEWARK, 1971

| Type of Crime | West | Central | North | South | East | Total |
|---|---|---|---|---|---|---|
| Crime Against Persons/Property | 44 | 48 | 50 | 72 | 73 | 287 |
| False Alarms/ Bomb Scares | 18 | 24 | 16 | 18 | 49 | 125 |
| Suspicious Persons | 30 | 56 | 31 | 65 | 70 | 252 |
| Disorderly Conduct | 33 | 33 | 35 | 31 | 65 | 197 |
| Total | 125 | 161 | 132 | 186 | 257 | 861 |
| PERCENT DISTRIBUTION | | | | | | |
| Crime Against Persons/Property | 35.2 | 29.8 | 37.9 | 38.7 | 28.4 | 33.3 |
| False Alarms/ Bomb Scares | 14.4 | 14.9 | 12.1 | 9.7 | 19.1 | 14.5 |
| Suspicious Persons | 24.0 | 34.8 | 23.5 | 34.9 | 27.2 | 29.3 |
| Disorderly Conduct | 26.4 | 20.5 | 26.5 | 16.7 | 25.3 | 22.9 |
| Total | 100.0 | 100.0 | 100.0 | 100.0 | 100.0 | 100.0 |

$\chi^2 = 0.001$

EXHIBIT 4-6
SUMMER EVENING CRIME SAMPLE BY WARD (CONDENSED)
NEWARK, 1970-1971

| CRIMES | West | Central | North | South | East | Total/ Average |
|---|---|---|---|---|---|---|
| Population 1970 | 77,371 | 54,960 | 89,985 | 88,403 | 71,211 | 381,930 |
| Aggregate crimes | 4,350 | 5,610 | 4.590 | 6,480 | 8,970 | 30,000 |
| Crimes per 100,000 | 5,649 | 10,388 | 5,157 | 7,363 | 12,633 | 8,430 |

Source: Newark Police Department, 1970-1971.

be viewed in terms of crime committed in abandoned parcels. Care must be taken, however, not to draw causal relationships between specific types of crime and abandoned buildings. Vacant parcels may not cause crime, but rather provide an opportunity for its occurrence. They serve as facilitating locations as well as inspiration.

*Of all the Index Crimes taking place within the City of Newark, nearly 4 percent now take place within abandoned buildings. Within the city in 1971, ten murders, fifteen rapes, and close to 150 incidents of assault and battery occurred within vacant buildings. For lesser crimes the same year saw close to 200 incidents of malicious mischief or disorderly conduct violations and 100 incidents of narcotics offenses. Finally, police assistance was required for at least twenty-three natural deaths and close to fifty cases of falls, animal bites, sicknesses, and the like.*

When tabulated by the fire department, 755 vacant structures were found to exist in 1965 while 3,162 (vacant plus partially vacant) stood in 1971. Aggregate reported crimes via Rutgers and Newark Police Department surveys registered 526 incidents of police activity within these buildings in 1965, while totals for 1971 were 1,882 (Exhibit 4-7). Within this six-year period, the number of reported crimes increased 257 percent, while the number of abandoned buildings increased 322

## EXHIBIT 4-7
## REPORTED POLICE ACTIVITY IN ABANDONED BUILDINGS
## NEWARK, 1965, 1971

| | Total Abandoned Buildings | Abandoned Buildings With One Or More Incidents Of Police Activity | Percent Of Total | Abandoned Buildings With One Incident Of Police Activity | Percent Of Total | Abandoned Buildings With Two Or More Incidents Of Police Activity | Percent Of Total | Abandoned Buildings With No Police Activity | Percent Of Total | Total Incidents Of Police Activity In Abandoned Buildings |
|---|---|---|---|---|---|---|---|---|---|---|
| 1965 | 755 | 385 | 51.0 | 207 | 27.0 | 178 | 24.0 | 370 | 49.0 | 526 |
| 1971 | 3162 | 932 | 29.5 | 546 | 17.4 | 386 | 12.0 | 2230 | 71.0 | 1882 |

Source: Newark Police Department, 1965, 1971.

percent. The annual rate of abandonment was 10 percent greater than the rate of crime over a similar period.

While the number of reported crimes per abandoned building has shown a relative decrease over the six-year period, the absolute magnitude of these figures remains remarkable. The gross number of crimes within abandoned buildings has more than tripled over a six-year period. Additionally, the number of buildings with one incident of crime, as well as those with multiple instances, has more than doubled. This former figure is eight times greater than the increase in general crime* which is happening within the city at large.

Analysis of the data reveals a marked similarity between the trend of crime generally in Newark and the trend of crime in vacant structures. Newark's multifold absolute rise in crime is mirrored in abandoned structures. On an equalized population basis,† incidents of murder, rape, assault and battery, burglary, arson, prostitution and sex offenses, vandalism (malicious mischief) and possession of stolen property, and incidents of non-negligent injury in abandoned buildings increased significantly. In all instances these crimes also increased throughout the city. Even more significant are the increases in incidents of larceny, weapons possession, and narcotics in abandoned buildings relative to the city at large. *In these cases the increases noted in abandoned buildings far exceeded the citywide rate.*

A more subtle trend which appears as a result of closer analysis is that as the universe of abandoned structures grows, if one continues to view the type of crime committed within these buildings as a whole, there is likely to be found a shift away from the category of crimes against persons to those of crimes against property (Exhibits 4-8 and 4-9). In 1965 the proportion of crimes against persons relative to all police activity in abandoned structures was 17 percent; for 1971 this category was reduced to roughly 9.2 percent. Countering this reduction was the proportional increase of crimes against property. Between 1965 and 1971 this category rose from 41 percent to 56 percent, an increase of 15 percent. This can be explained through the absolute rise in the number of vacant structures and attendant interior fixturing available for crimes of property and the simultaneous desertion of whole neighborhoods,

*The FBI reports an Index Crime increase of 40 percent over the period 1960 to 1970.

†Newark's household population decreased from 399,300 to 377,300 over the period 1960 to 1970.

lessening the frequency of personal contact necessary to sustain or increase levels of crime against persons. Of further note was the percentage decline in the category of assistance rendered. Between 1965 and 1971 there was a drop of 7 percent in police activity responding to accidents and mishaps in vacant structures. The decline in assistance rendered to those found within abandoned structures, according to the Newark Police Department, can be partially traced to a strong city ordinance passed in the late sixties requiring all vacant properties to be boarded and secured. It was felt that this action, while not wholly effective, at least forbade entry to both those who were the potential victims of muggers and those who were likely to fall prey to the weakness of the structure itself (children, elderly, etc.).

Finally, while similar data were not analyzed in 1971, it was apparent that abandoned buildings in 1965 seemed to serve as a refuge for those who had already committed the more traditional offenses. In the 755 buildings surveyed in 1965, there were nearly 100 arrests for major crimes against persons and property. In addition, for less than major offenses, i.e., threatening, disorderly conduct, drunkenness, etc., arrests outnumbered incidents within these buildings by a factor of two to one (Exhibit 4-8).[3]

## Conclusion

In summary, in assessing the number of crimes in these vacant structures, certain points must be kept in mind. Part of the definition of abandonment noted earlier includes the abdication of responsibility on the part of the owner of the parcel for the physical status of the building and the social interactions which take place within it. As such, concerned observation of the parcel is reduced to a minimum. Individuals, with no stake in the parcel, have little incentive to report instances of illegal behavior. Additionally, abandonment implies either no occupants or a skeleton level of squatter tenantry. Thus, these buildings offer, relative to more viable structures, alluring opportunities for crimes of property or violence. Yet abandoned structures in terms of reported crimes have a rate of criminal activity not unlike those of more economically viable structures.

Since it is almost an impossible task to account for the real number of criminal acts committed in vacant structures, the figures on criminal

EXHIBIT 4-8
POLICE ACTIVITY IN VACANT BUILDINGS
(January 1, 1965 — December 31, 1965)
BY TYPE OF ACTIVITY

| CRIME/ASSISTANCE CLASSIFICATIONS | | FREQUENCY OF INCIDENTS/ARRESTS | | | |
|---|---|---|---|---|---|
| | | NUMBER | | PERCENT | |
| | | Incidents | Arrests | Incidents | Arrests |
| MAJOR OFFENSES | | | | | |
| Crimes against persons | | | | | |
| Murder | | 4 | 1 | — | — |
| Manslaughter | | 0 | 0 | — | — |
| Rape | | 4 | 2 | — | — |
| Assault and battery /child abuse /kidnapping /abortion | | 79 | 42 | — | — |
| | Subtotal (1) | 87 | 45 | 17 | 13 |
| Crimes against property | | | | | |
| Robbery /auto theft | | 28 | 5 | — | — |
| Burglary (B&E)/burglary tools (possession) | | 143 | 29 | — | — |
| Larceny/counterfeiting/ fraud/embezzlement/extortion/ bribery /perjury | | 38 | 18 | — | — |
| | Subtotal (2) | 209 | 52 | 41 | 15 |
| Missing persons/runaways | Subtotal (3) | 16 | 0 | 3 | 0 |
| | Total (1) | 324 | 96 | 61 | 28 |

| CRIME/ASSISTANCE CLASSIFICATIONS | FREQUENCY OF INCIDENTS/ARRESTS | | | |
|---|---|---|---|---|
| | NUMBER | | PERCENT | |
| | Incidents | Arrests | Incidents | Arrests |
| LESS THAN MAJOR OFFENSES | | | | |
| Arson/attempted suicide | 6 | 1 | — | — |
| Prostitution/sex/illegitimate child | 10 | 9 | — | — |
| Malicious mischief/possession of stolen property | 42 | 22 | — | — |
| Narcotics | 18 | 38 | — | — |
| Gambling | 10 | 47 | — | — |
| Threatening/disorderly conduct/drunkenness suspicious/possession weapon | 19 | 34 | — | — |
| Subtotal (1) | 105 | 151 | 20 | 42 |
| Liquor violations | 2 | 5 | — | — |
| Material witness/contempt of court/parole violation | 0 | 63 | — | — |
| Traffic laws | 0 | 3 | — | — |
| Loitering/city ordinance violation/vagrancy | 4 | 6 | — | — |
| Miscellaneous offenses | 12 | 9 | — | — |
| Subtotal (2) | 18 | 86 | 3 | 25 |
| Total (2) | 123 | 236 | 23 | 67 |

EXHIBIT 4-8 (con't)

| CRIME/ASSISTANCE CLASSIFICATIONS | FREQUENCY OF INCIDENTS/ARRESTS | | | |
|---|---|---|---|---|
| | NUMBER | | PERCENT | |
| | Incidents | Arrests | Incidents | Arrests |
| ASSISTANCE RENDERED | | | | |
| Natural death | 12 | 0 | — | — |
| Falls/sickness/accident/ animal bite/poisoning | 48 | 0 | — | — |
| Mental case | 4 | 0 | — | — |
| Subtotal (1) | 64 | 0 | 13 | 0 |
| Lost/found property/ doors ajar | 13 | 0 | — | — |
| Assistance to other agencies | 2 | 16 | — | — |
| Subtotal (2) | 15 | 16 | 3 | 5 |
| Total (3) | 79 | 16 | 16 | 5 |
| TOTAL POLICE ACTIVITY | 526 | 348 | 100 | 100 |

Source: Newark Police Department, *Vacant Building Report*, December 1966

## EXHIBIT 4-9
## POLICE ACTIVITY IN VACANT BUILDINGS
### (January 1, 1971 — December 31, 1971)
### BY TYPE OF ACTIVITY

| CRIME/ASSISTANCE CLASSIFICATIONS | | FREQUENCY OF INCIDENTS | |
|---|---|---|---|
| | | Number | Percent |
| MAJOR OFFENSES | | | |
| Crimes against persons | | | |
| Murder | | 10 | — |
| Manslaughter | | 1 | — |
| Rape | | 15 | — |
| Assault and battery/child abuse/kidnapping/abortion | | 146 | — |
| | Subtotal (1) | 172 | 9.2 |
| Crimes against property | | | |
| Robbery/auto theft | | 269 | — |
| Burglary (B&E)/burglar tools (possession) | | 536 | — |
| Larceny/counterfeiting/fraud/embezzlement/extortion/bribery/perjury | | 250 | — |
| | Subtotal (2) | 1055 | 56.0 |
| Missing persons/runaways | Subtotal (3) | 41 | 2.2 |
| | Total (1) | 1268 | 67.3 |

EXHIBIT 4-9 (con't)

| CRIME/ASSISTANCE CLASSIFICATIONS | | FREQUENCY OF INCIDENTS Number | Percent |
|---|---|---|---|
| LESS THAN MAJOR OFFENSES | | | |
| Arson/attempt. suicide | | 17 | — |
| Prostitution/sex/illegitimate child | | 13 | — |
| Malicious mischief/possession of stolen property | | 128 | — |
| Narcotics | | 99 | — |
| Gambling | | 22 | — |
| Threatening/disorderly conduct/drunkenness suspicious/possession weapon | | 53 | — |
| | Subtotal (1) | 332 | 17.6 |
| Liquor violations | | 1 | — |
| Material witness/contempt of court/parole violation | | 11 | — |
| Traffic laws | | 83 | — |
| Loitering/city ordinance violation/vagrancy | | 5 | — |
| Miscellaneous offenses | | 10 | — |
| | Subtotal (2) | 110 | 5.8 |
| | Total (2) | 442 | 23.4 |

| CRIME/ASSISTANCE CLASSIFICATIONS | | FREQUENCY OF INCIDENTS | |
|---|---|---|---|
| | | Number | Percent |
| ASSISTANCE RENDERED | | | |
| Natural death | | 23 | — |
| Falls/sickness/accident/ animal bite/poisoning | | 46 | — |
| Mental case | | 3 | — |
| | Subtotal (1) | 72 | 3.8 |
| Lost/found property/ doors ajar | | 99 | — |
| Assistance to other agencies | | 1 | — |
| | Subtotal (2) | 100 | 5.5 |
| | Total (3) | 172 | 9.3 |
| TOTAL POLICE ACTIVITY | | 1882 | 100 |

Source: Newark Police Department, *Vacant Building Report*, December 1971.

activity in abandoned parcels must be seen as extremely conservative. The abandoned structure in its standing vacant state is a haven for criminal activity, both premeditated and spontaneous.

Abandoned structures and incidents of crime to some degree must also be viewed within the ecology of the neighborhoods in which they are located. The presence of high rates of crime and abandonment seems to be a product of the same social malaise found in areas of low personal income, high unemployment, and high racial discrimination. One cannot conclude, however, that the absence of abandoned structures would lower the instance of crime by the reported levels of crime currently found within them. Vacant structures offer a somewhat easier opportunity for crime yet at reduced economic gain. For instance, an occurrence of a murder in an abandoned structure can by no means be causally connected, although the building's presence can be related to a convenience factor. Crimes against persons or property in vacant structures can be tied to ease and accessibility for criminal behavior (although the potential economic return on property crimes in vacant parcels dwindles significantly once the structure has been gutted). Thus, generally it may be said that in the case of serious crimes of a premeditated nature, abandoned buildings represent a convenience factor for an individual who has already made a decision to commit a crime. For crimes of spontaneity which thrive despite lack of economic motivation, the abandoned building represents a relatively unobserved shell for criminal activity even though the potential gain is also lessened by the victim's fear and thus avoidance of the neighborhood.

Vacant structures in Newark and similar cities are found clustered rather than in isolated patches throughout the city. The geographic areas in which the 755 abandoned structures were found in 1965 have produced 3,162 vacant buildings in 1971. A street containing one vacant structure in 1965 had four such structures in 1971. Accordingly, where one refuge served as shelter for a single illicit incident in 1965, now there are four potential shelters for two crimes. From a micro or neighborhood perspective, abandonment may be seen by those residing there as doubling the local crime rate.

## FIRE AND THE CITY

The core of Newark is burning down. Anyone driving through the main arteries that partition the city sees the truth of this statement. Boarded buildings, burned out buildings, fire charred lots and children playing in rubble dominate the eye. Every day newspapers report multiple-alarm fires and describe families burned out. The welfare department is overwhelmed with people for whom it must find temporary housing.

One measure of the social disintegration which characterizes the core area is the trivia which often instigates deliberately-set fires: Two men quarrel, then the loser sets fire to the other's home; or a man ejected from a tavern returns at night and sets fire to it; or children playing in an abandoned building set it afire and adjacent structures are caught up in the conflagration — with the result that another fifty families lose their pitifully few treasures of a lifetime and are forced to find new housing — often leaving behind their dead or maimed victims.

The number of significant fires in cities has become so large as to numb the mind. The reality of their harm is steadily more apparent.

### Fire in the United States

In 1970 fire killed 12,200 Americans and destroyed $2.63-billion worth of property.[4] This constituted the highest per capita fire death rate and property loss rate of any industrialized nation in the world. In that same year, 1970, the National Fire Code was published in ten volumes, totaling 8,000 pages of codes, standards and recommended practices, and $2.5-billion to $3-billion were spent on more than 23,500 public fire departments. The degree of effectiveness of previous similar measures of prevention and control may be seen by comparing the fire losses in the United States over time. Because the incidence of fires bears some relation to the size of the population, statistics are given per 1,000 population. The figures in Exhibit 4-10 show that the number of fires per 1,000 population remained approximately constant during the period 1961-1970. In 1961, fire claimed the lives of 11,700 people and destroyed $1.5-billion worth of property. Although the absolute number of fire deaths per year rose by 500 between 1961 and 1970, the ratio of deaths to total population actually declined from 0.065 to 0.059 per 1,000. In contrast, the property loss increased from $1.5-billion to $2.63-billion during this period. But had there been no progress in property

EXHIBIT 4-10
BUILDING FIRES IN THE UNITED STATES
1961-1970

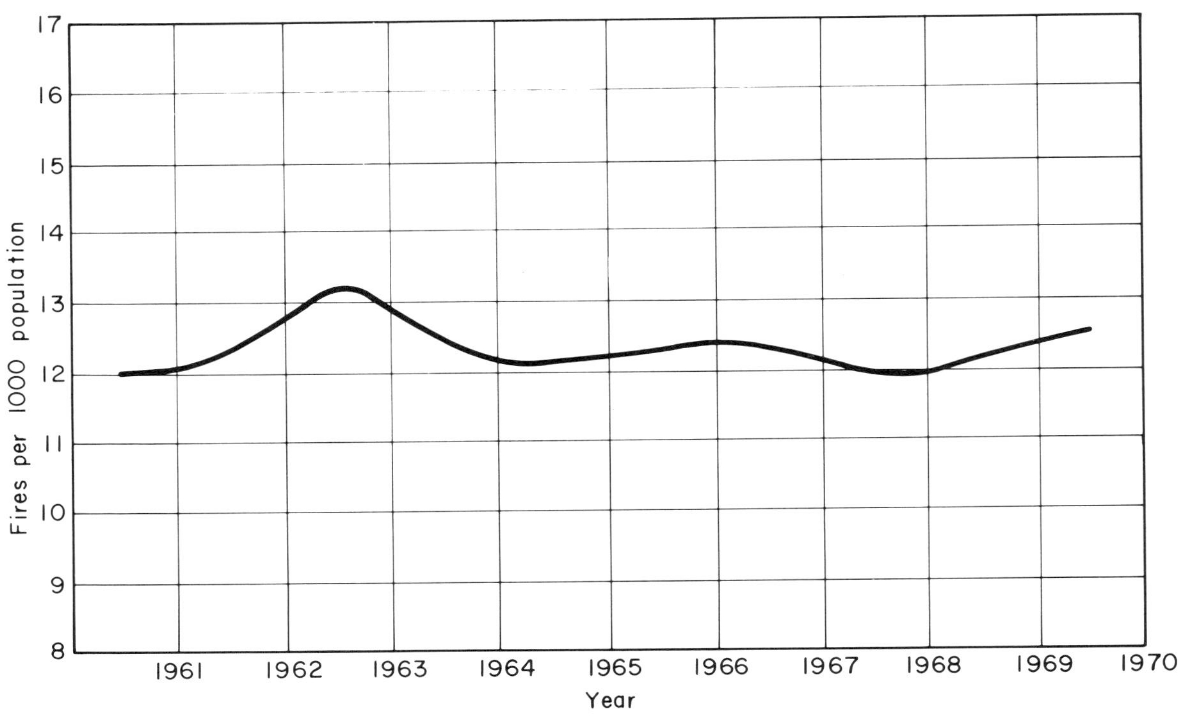

fire protection, losses would have been running at the rate of over $3-billion yearly by 1970, due to the growth of gross investment in capital goods — new buildings and equipment.

Clearly, the relative magnitude of losses caused by fire was reduced, if only slightly, during the 1960s. However, not only have the absolute losses continued to increase, but evidence will show the development of certain trends which have socio-economic rather than technological roots, and which therefore complicate the problem of fire prevention and control.

### Fire in New Jersey and Newark

With few exceptions the northern industrial cities have a higher incidence of fires than their southern counterparts. Exhibit 4-11 shows that the average number of alarms, fires, building fires, and false alarms is higher in New Jersey cities than in all U.S. cities. It shows also that the cities of Camden, Elizabeth, Jersey City, Newark, Paterson, and Trenton, which constitute New Jersey's "Big Six," have a higher average number of alarms, fires, building fires, and false alarms than all New Jersey cities. Finally, it shows that of the group, Newark has the highest incidence of all these phenomena.

Exhibit 4-11 shows the number of alarms, fires, building fires and false alarms in Newark during the period 1964-1969. The highest percent increase is in the number of false alarms (168.8 percent). In spite of a decrease in population, there has been a marked increase in the total number of alarms, fires, and building fires.

## FIRE AND RESIDENTIAL ABANDONMENT

Frequency of fires has been increasing rapidly in Newark, as in other cities during the past several years.[5] Reported annual figures for the period 1965-1971 (Exhibit 4-12) show increases in both building and nonbuilding fires. Primarily due to a fast-growing rate of vehicular fires, nonbuilding fires increased by 43.3 percent during the six-year period. And in spite of a 5.2 percent reduction in the number of structures standing within the city limits, the number of building fires grew by 13.6 percent. The number of vacant buildings, on the other hand, increased by a remarkable 319 percent, concomitantly with an

## EXHIBIT 4-11
## FIRES IN NEWARK OVER TIME—FIRES IN NEWARK COMPARED TO OTHER CITIES

| | Newark—1964-1969 | | | | | | | Newark and Other Cities 1970 | | | |
|---|---|---|---|---|---|---|---|---|---|---|---|
| Categories of Fire | 1964 | 1965 | 1966 | 1967 | 1968 | 1969 | Percent Increase 1964-1969 | Newark† | N.J. "Big Six" | N.J. Cities Over 25,000 Pop. | U.S. Cities Over 25,000 Pop. |
| Alarms per 1,000° population | 29.2 | 28.2 | 30.3 | 31.6 | 42.8 | 44.4 | 52.0 | 52.3 | 44.5 | 28.4 | 27.1 |
| Fires per 1,000 population | 13.2 | 18.2 | 18.1 | 18.2 | 21.0 | 21.0 | 59.1 | 21.6 | 20.8 | 14.5 | 12.5 |
| Building fires per 1,000 population | 8.1 | 10.4 | 10.6 | 9.7 | 11.5 | 11.0 | 35.8 | 10.5 | 8.4 | 6.2 | 4.8 |
| False alarms per 1,000 population | 3.2 | 2.7 | 2.4 | 4.2 | 7.3 | 8.6 | 168.8 | 11.2 | 13.67 | 5.58 | 4.33 |

°Steady 1960 Newark Population of 405,200
†Steady 1970 Newark Population of 375,400

Source: National Fire Protection Association.

EXHIBIT 4-12
BUILDING, NONBUILDING AND VACANT BUILDING FIRES
NEWARK, 1965-1971



Source: Newark Fire Department: *Annual Report* (1965-1971)

astonishing 538 percent increase in the frequency of fires occurring in these structures between 1965 and 1971.

The inevitable consequences of such fire frequency are correspondingly high penalties, in terms both of lives lost and of property destroyed. During this period the annual fire deaths ranged between a low of 24 and a high of 40, running at an average rate of 33 deaths per year. In 1972 through the end of September there were 28 fire deaths, 15 percent of which could be attributed to fires specifically within or spreading from vacant buildings.

In terms of the facilities required to control a fire, the Newark Fire Department classifies severe fires into the "Signal 11" and "Multiple Alarm" varieties. The Signal 11 type requires response by heavy apparatus from only one fire district, while the Multiple Alarm type requires response by heavy apparatus from more than one fire district. Within this categorization the severe fires in vacant residential buildings in Newark were predominantly Signal 11 for both 1970 and 1971 (Exhibit 4-13). *Particularly revealing is the percent distribution which shows that 27.1 percent of all the multiple alarm fires and 19.1 percent of all the Signal 11 fires occurred in vacant structures; together they constitute 21.2 percent of all the severe fires that occurred in Newark during 1970 and 1971. The number of standing vacant buildings, though rapidly increasing, amounts to less than 5 percent of the total number of structures in the city.* The frequency of severe fires in abandoned buildings is four times the rate occurring within the city's population of structures.[6]

Exhibit 4-14 further disaggregates fires in abandoned structures by type. It may be seen that when vacant/abandoned structures are isolated as a subset of all buildings, there are slight variations, i.e., approximately 15 percent, between types that are more or less prone to fire. In Newark, for instance, vacant former commercial structures have a 10 to 12 percent higher incidence of fire than their previously residential or industrial equivalents.

## Recurring Fires in Abandoned Buildings

One phenomenon contributing to the magnitude of the figures discussed above is that of recurring fires in abandoned buildings. As Exhibit 4-15 shows, among eighty-four buildings classified as

## EXHIBIT 4-13
### SEVERE FIRES, NEWARK, 1970-1971

Type of Fire by Occupancy of Structure

| Occupancy of Structure | | Type of Fire | | |
|---|---|---|---|---|
| | | Multiple Alarm | Signal 11 | Total |
| Occupied | | 103 | 190 | 293 |
| Partially occupied | | 30 | 6 | 36 |
| Vacant | | 55 | 104 | 159 |
| NA/DK | | 15 | 247 | 262 |
| | Total | 203 | 547 | 750 |

PERCENT DISTRIBUTION

| | | Multiple Alarm | Signal 11 | Total |
|---|---|---|---|---|
| Occupied | | 50.7 | 34.7 | 39.1 |
| Partially occupied | | 14.8 | 1.1 | 4.8 |
| Vacant | | 27.1 | 19.1 | 21.2 |
| NA/DK | | 7.4 | 45.1 | 34.9 |
| $\chi^2 = .01$ | Total | 100.0 | 100.0 | 100.0 |

Source: Newark Fire Department, Fire Prevention Division, Bureau of Combustibles: *Annual Report,* 1971.

abandoned, nineteen experienced at least one minor or major fire after complete vacancy, and nine suffered two to five incidents.

This would indicate that if 2,000 vacant buildings are standing, there is a good chance that over 450 will have to be serviced annually at least once, and half that number on more than one occasion. To look at it another way: Roughly one fire call annually for every two standing vacant buildings may be anticipated. In addition, since the buildings are unoccupied and in most cases the nature of the incident is not obvious, fire officials must anticipate arson investigation in 90 percent of the cases.

## EXHIBIT 4-14
### FIRES IN VACANT BUILDINGS BY TYPE NEWARK, 1971

| Type of Structure | Vacant Buildings With Fire | Universe of Vacant Buildings | Percent of Universe |
|---|---|---|---|
| Residential/residential-commercial | 882 | 1786 | 49.0 |
| Commercial | 145 | 235 | 60.0 |
| Industrial | 98 | 213 | 46.0 |
| Buildings under construction (all classes) | 10 | — | — |
| Total/Average | 1135 | 2234 | 50.7 |

Source: Newark Fire Department, Fire Prevention Division, Bureau of Combustibles: *Annual Report* 1971.

## EXHIBIT 4-15
### THE PHENOMENON OF RECURRING FIRES WITHIN ABANDONED BUILDINGS — THEIR FREQUENCY AND NONROUTINE NATURE, NEWARK

| Recurring Fires (1964-1971) | Number |
|---|---|
| Total number of buildings classified as abandoned within the sample subset | 84 |
| Total number of buildings experiencing at least one fire after complete vacancy | 19 |
| Total number of buildings experiencing two to five fires after complete vacancy | 9 |
| Total number of buildings where nature of fire was not obvious and arson squad had to investigate | 17 |

Source: Newark Fire Department, Fire Prevention Division, Bureau of Combustibles: *Annual Report,* 1971.

## The Temporal Relationship between Fire and Abandonment

The temporal relationship between fire and abandonment is a provocative subject. Did fire cause abandonment, or is fire a result of abandonment? In many cases it is difficult to find an answer because the data source often severely limits the information provided. In this case the listing of abandoned buildings came from the local fire department. One would expect the fire department's list, although supposedly an inventory of all standing vacant structures, to contain a substantial proportion of buildings vacated specifically because of fire. Within these limitations, however, the data may still be utilized.

Over the period 1970 and 1971 a total of 1,600 buildings became abandoned. During those two years the total number of abandoned buildings with instances of major fire was 325. In 265 of these, fire appeared to occur before abandonment, while in sixty, fires occurred after abandonment (Exhibit 4-16). Although one cannot establish a direct cause-effect relationship from these figures, the fact that 265 buildings were listed as occupied when fire occurred makes it likely that in a large number of cases abandonment was indeed a consequence of fire. During the same period the citywide total for severe fires (Signal 11 and Multiple Alarm) was 750. If it is assumed that there was only one instance of fire in each of the sixty buildings where fires occurred after abandonment, this would mean that 8 percent of all major fires in the city during this period occurred in listed abandoned buildings. This percentage is likely to increase to 12 percent if the 50 percent rate of recurring fires that are typical of abandoned buildings is projected.

## The Administrative Burden of Fires In Abandoned Buildings

Definite administrative problems arise with the increase of fires in abandoned buildings. The Bureau of Combustibles, which structurally houses the fire inspection staff under current fire organization, is probably hardest hit in terms of extra administrative duties. In Newark the bureau requested, and received, a local ordinance to require owners of vacant/abandoned buildings to board all first-floor means of access (windows, doors, etc.).

## EXHIBIT 4-16

THE FREQUENCY OF FIRE IN ABANDONED° BUILDINGS AND THE TEMPORAL RELATIONSHIPS OF FIRE AND ABANDONMENT, NEWARK

| Fires in Abandoned Buildings (1970-71) | Number |
|---|---|
| Total number of buildings becoming abandoned over period 1970-1971 | 1600 |
| Total number of abandoned buildings with *major*† fires 1970-1971 | 325 |
| (*a*) Fire occurred before abandonment | 265 |
| (*b*) Fire occurred after abandonment | 60 |

°In this case *abandoned* is synonymous with observed vacant.

†The citywide total for major fires 1970-1971 (Signal 11 or Multiple Alarm) was 750.

Source: Newark Fire Department, Fire Prevention Division, Bureau of Combustibles: *Annual Report*, 1971.

Fire inspectors must patrol their areas daily to list addresses where the ordinance should be invoked. Support staff must then check the address with municipal block and lot listings to obtain the name of the owner. The owner is advised by form letter of the requirement to secure his structure, and a reminder file is kept of his response. Since fire officials estimate that the average life span of plywood (for which there appears to be a tremendous local demand) as a securing device for abandoned structures is less than *one day*, both the repetitive nature of this task and waning future successes due to owner rebellion are obvious. An owner will usually board a structure on request once. Successive efforts prove futile.

Exhibit 4-17 shows the relatively high initial success in obtaining owner cooperation with the building-securing requirement of the Newark ordinance. It may also be seen that in roughly 5 percent of the cases the initial notice leads to either subsequent rehabilitation or razing of the structure. It should also be noted, however, that in both years 15 percent of the owners took no action whatsoever on the initial notice.

Exhibit 4-18 reveals one irony of the environment of decay. One of the few growing sources of revenue in the City of Newark is fines

EXHIBIT 4-17
PERFORMANCE BY OWNERS OF VACANT BUILDINGS WHO ARE INFORMED OF EXISTING FIRE VIOLATIONS

| Notification/Action | 1971 | 1970 |
|---|---|---|
| Vacant buildings in violation of fire code | 779 | 773 |
| Buildings rehabilitated in response | 56 | 27 |
| Buildings secured in response | 507 | 624 |
| Buildings razed* in response | 26 | 31 |
| No action by owner | 90 | 89 |

*Estimate of 5 percent of citywide razings in 1970 (624) and 1971 (507)

Source: Newark Fire Department, Fire Prevention Division, Bureau of Combustibles, *Annual Report,* (1970, 1971)

collected by the city for violation of the ordinance requiring the boarding of buildings. Nonexistent in 1965, those fines now represent a revenue approaching $75,000 annually. The dramatic increase in receipts exactly parallels Newark's post-1967 surge of abandoned buildings.

Fire department officials are certain that, given a choice, the city would rather be income-deficient than have as a source of income a growing inventory of derelict buildings whose owners will take no action or, having once had their action thwarted by vandals, will make no further effort.

## Summary

It may be seen that, like crime, fire in abandoned structures is mushrooming. Over 10 percent of the city's annual fires now occur in abandoned buildings. A significant percentage of fire service deaths may now be attributed solely to the presence of potentially-fired vacant buildings. The operational capacity of arson squads has been

## EXHIBIT 4-18
### COURT CASES INITIATED BY FIRE DEPARTMENT AND FINES COLLECTED — VACANT BUILDINGS NEWARK, 1960-1971

| Year | Court Cases Initiated | Fines Collected |
|---|---|---|
| 1960 | 15 | 0 |
| 1961 | 12 | 0 |
| 1962 | 20 | 0 |
| 1963 | 21 | 0 |
| 1964 | 25 | 0 |
| 1965 | 30 | 0 |
| 1966 | 29 | $ 25 |
| 1967 | 44 | $ 500 |
| 1968 | 104 | $ 4,885 |
| 1969 | 170 | $12,960 |
| 1970 | 207 | $51,452 |
| 1971 | 287 | $72,775 |

Source: Newark Fire Department, Fire Prevention Division, Bureau of Combustibles, *Annual Report 1971*

overburdened by suspicious fires in vacant buildings. Finally, the administrative tasks of fire inspectors have been greatly expanded, in efforts to prevent rampant fire spread in abandoned structures.

The fire department on an average day is in a turmoil of activity. There is no seasonal variation. In the winter the main problem is kerosene or wood fires started by transients; in the summer, opening of fire hydrants, which lessens water pressure. In all seasons false alarms (up locally 500 percent in six years) spur continuous activity. Unless completely razed, the abandoned structure continues to tempt the arsonist and thus adds one more dimension to an already demanding urban fire department schedule.

## PUBLIC SAFETY AND THE SOCIAL DIMENSIONS OF CITY STRUCTURE

The object of this section is to view two constituent elements of public safety, i.e., crime and fire, within the social structure of the city in 1970 as interpreted through factor analysis. In accord with previous use of this technique, the orthogonal solution is employed, with factors rotated if values exceed unity.

### City Structure In 1970

City structure, as indicated by the rotated factor matrix, parallels what was originally found and discussed in Chapter 1. Present is the economic/race/age structure dimension *(Race and Resources)*, wherein high negative loadings are indicative of blacks, low income, high unemployment, and large families. At the opposite extreme within this factor is a small group of foreign born whites, who have substantial economic resources and are owner occupants of their respective housing. Thus one dimension of city structure is the tracts which group due specifically to the presence or lack of economic resources. Not coincidentally, this usually follows racial lines. (See Exhibit 4-19)

A second dimension of city structure is *Social Status*. High positive scores on this factor differentiate areas of comparative affluence where those of higher education are employed in a professional rather than manufacturing capacity, earn more money, and occupy more expensive housing.

The third independent grouping according to the orthogonal solution is the *Puerto Rican Segregation* factor. This dimension comprises dichotomous elements of large Puerto Rican families whose male head of household is employed in manufacturing and at the other end of the scale, the smaller family of the young, white, working female.

The fourth element of city structure is the *Stage in the Life Cycle* factor. This factor differentiates black areas of high unemployment, containing substantial proportions of children contributing to large families, high crowding, and high numbers of rooms/people per unit. These are opposed to inclusive areas where just the reverse conditions are present, i.e., those containing high proportions of elderly whites, low numbers of children, and smaller housing units.

Finally the city, in 1970, is described by two disparate, yet in part similar housing dimensions. They are different in terms of clientele

EXHIBIT 4-19

FACTOR ANALYSIS OF SELECTIVE 1970 SOCIAL CHARACTERISTICS* EMPLOYING NEWARK CENSUS TRACTS

| Variables | Factors | | | | | |
|---|---|---|---|---|---|---|
| | Race and Resources | Puerto Rican Segregation | Social Status | Stage in Life Cycle | Housing Transiency | Housing Stability |
| 1. Percent housing units: occupied | | | | | .481 | .630 |
| 2. Percent population: Negro | —.507 | | | —.732 | | |
| 3. Median age female | | | | .822 | | |
| 4. Median age white female | | .712 | | | | |
| 5. Percent housing units: no bath or share | | | | | —.862 | |
| 6. Percent housing units: >1.01 persons/room | | | | —.596 | | —.515 |
| 7. Median contract rent | | | .791 | | | |
| 8. Median housing value | | | .695 | | | |
| 9. Percent housing units: single family | | | | | | |
| 10. Percent population: >65 years of age | | | | .934 | | |
| 11. Percent white population: >65 years of age | | | | .889 | | |
| 12. Percent population: married | .588 | | | .536 | | .500 |
| 13. Percent population: <5 years of age | —.530 | | | —.681 | | |
| 14. Percent housing units: owner occupied | .478 | | | | | .622 |
| 15. Median rooms per unit | | | | —.464 | .636 | |

| | | | | | | |
|---|---|---|---|---|---|---|
| 16. Percent labor force: female | | .710 | | | | |
| 17. Percent population: Puerto Rican parentage | | —.821 | | | | |
| 18. Median years of education | | | .919 | | | |
| 19. Median family income | .529 | | | | | .472 |
| 20. Percent population: male unemployed | —.537 | | | —.480 | | |
| 21. Percent population: female clerical | | .550 | | | | |
| 22. Percent population: professional managerial | | | .848 | | | |
| 23. Percent population: foreign born | .686 | | | | | |
| 24. Population per household | | | | —.807 | | |
| 25. Percent population: elem. school enrollment | | | | —.695 | | |
| 26. Percent population: H.S. graduate | | | .830 | | | |
| 27. Percent population: college graduate | | | .820 | | | |
| 28. Percent population: income <$4,000 | —.721 | | | | | —.510 |
| 29. Percent population: income >$12,000 | .631 | | | | | .463 |
| 30. Percent labor force: manufacturing | | —.442 | —.663 | | | |
| 31. Percent structures: abandoned | | | | | | —.736 |
| 32. Percent structures: tax delinquent | | | | | | —.787 |
| 33. Percent structures: with fire | | | | | | —.878 |
| 34. Crime per 1000 population | | | | | .788 | |

°Including indices of fire, crime, abandonment, and tax delinquency

Source: Newark Area Resurvey, spring 1972, 1970 Census of Population

served yet they are similar in that they both tend to retard housing abandonment. The first is a housing transiency dimension which clusters areas of S.R.O.* accommodations which are characterized by both lower rental levels per room and lower numbers of rooms per unit. The second is a housing stability dimension which links areas of high owner occupancy, low vacancy, and high family stability (percent married). In this second factor, as expected, elements of housing instability, i.e., tax delinquency and abandonment, load highly negative.

## Fire/Crime and City Structure

Both fire and police activity load within factors associated with either the permanency or stability of housing.

Police activity (index crimes, minor crimes, and emergency assistance) appears to be associated with areas of high transiency (large proportion of rooming houses, S.R.O. etc.), moderate vacancy, and both low numbers of persons and rooms per unit. It would appear that when serious crime is included within general police activity in terms of additional pursuit of minor offenses and emergency assistance, that the transient areas bulk large within the total police committment.

Fire activity (Signal 11 plus Multiple Alarm [i.e., serious] fires) loads heavily negative on the *Housing Stability* factor. Within this factor areas of higher owner occupancy, low vacancy, high percent married, and high income are diametrically opposed to areas of crowding, low property tax delinquency, housing abandonment, and fire. As was previously indicated in the general discussion on abandonment, in addition to the few middle income areas of the city, there appears to be a greater retention of structures in the rooming house/S.R.O. areas due to the strong market for such accommodations; correspondingly there appears in these areas fewer instances of fire.

It should be realized that the failure of fire and crime to load within recognized poverty factors to some degree may be attributed to the size of the universe considered. From a regional perspective the isolated core is a relatively homogeneous area incapable of dissection sufficient to segregate areas of specific social characteristics which are particularly akin to either fire or crime. Both fire and crime seem to transcend the slight hierarchy of social structure discernible within Newark.

*Single Room Occupancies

# NOTES

1. George Sternlieb and Bernard P. Indik, *The Ecology of Welfare* (New Brunswick, N.J.: Transaction Press, 1973), Chapter 3.
2. Joseph Lincoln Steffens, *The Autobiography of Lincoln Steffens* (New York: Harcourt, Brace and Company, 1931), Chapter 14.
3. U.S. Federal Bureau of Investigation, *Crime in the United States, Uniform Crime Reports — 1970* (Washington, D.C.: Government Printing Office, 1971), 2. Hereafter cited as *Uniform Crime Reports—1970.*
4. *Ibid.*, 104; U.S. Federal Bureau of Investigation, *Crime in the United States, Uniform Crime Reports — 1960* Washington, D.C.: Government Printing Office, 1961), 81. Hereafter cited as *Uniform Crime Reports — 1960.*
5. Ramsey Clark, *Crime in America* (New York: Simon and Schuster, 1971), 11.
6. U.S. Federal Bureau of Investigation, *Crime in the United States, Uniform Crime Reports — 1970* (Washington, D.C.: Government Printing Office, 1971), 3-4.
7. "Insurers Get Burned on Ghetto Policies," *Business Week,* November 6, 1971, 38.
8. John J. Ahern and Charles S. Morgan, "The National Fire Profile," *Fire Journal,* Vol. 66, No. 2 (March, 1972), 7-11.
9. *Ibid.*, 7.
10. Edward H. Blum, "Fire Service: Challenge to Modern Management," *Public Management,* Vol. 52, No. 11 (November, 1970), 4-7.
11. Sid Ross and Herbert Kupferberg, "The Undeclared War on the Nation's Firemen," *International Fire Fighter,* Vol. 54, No. 11 (November, 1971), 18-22.
12. Edward H. Blum, "Fire Service: Challenge to Modern Management," *Public Management,* Vol. 52, No. 11 (November, 1970), 4-7.
13. U.S. National Advisory Commission on Civil Disorders, *Report* (Washington, D.C.: Government Printing Office, 1968), 272.
14. John T. O'Hagan, *Fire Fighting During Civil Disorders* (New York: International Association of Fire Chiefs, 1968), 17.

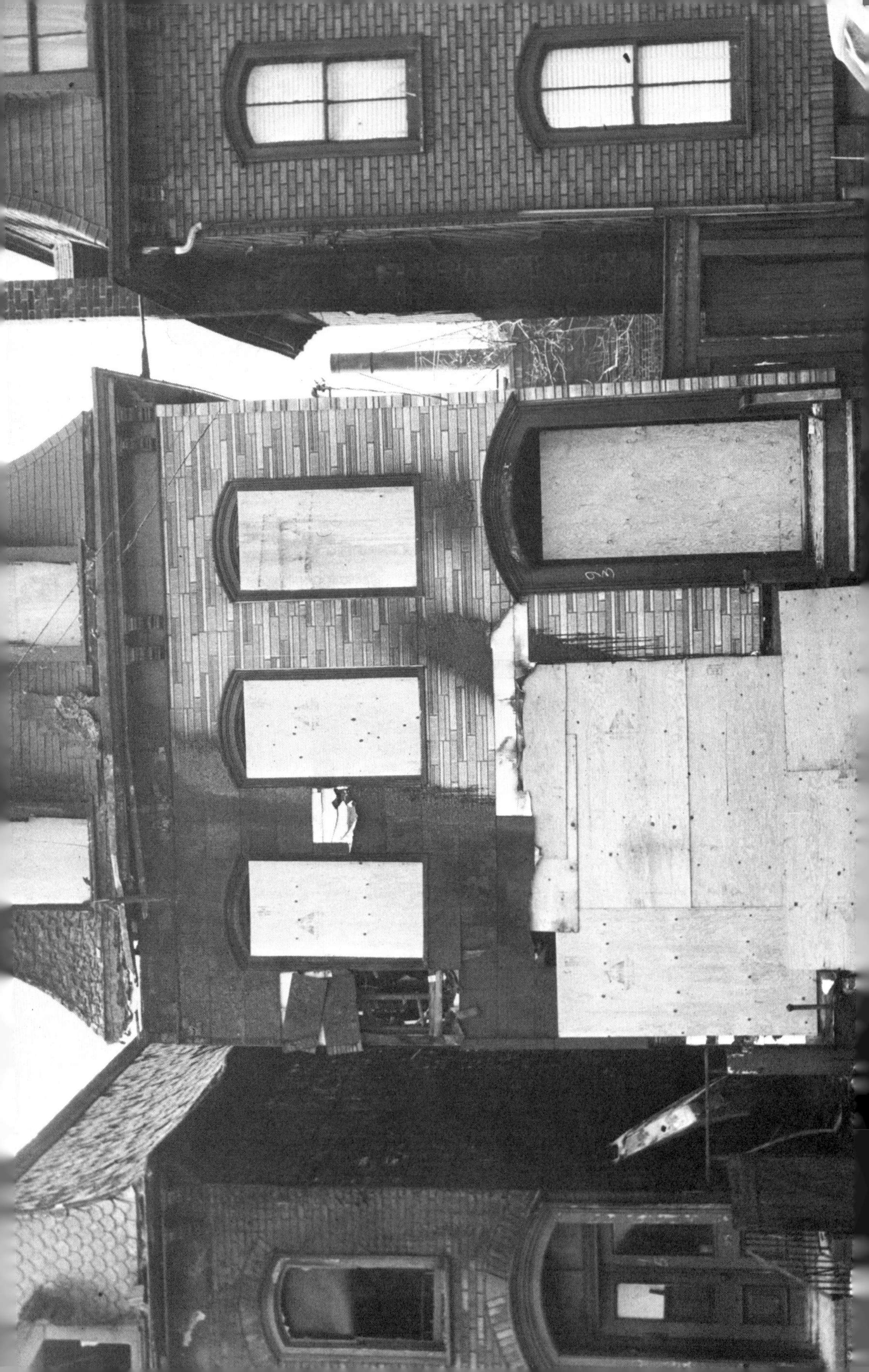

# 5

# TAX DELINQUENCY AND ABANDONMENT

Tax delinquency is not an inevitable companion of abandonment. But there are striking similarities in its incidence and the matrix of events and attitudes which cause it. The problems of the city would not go away if the tax system were radically altered. Yet, without this essential reformulation as a base condition, there can be little hope for broader efforts at reconstruction.

## THE PROBLEM

### Revenues Lagging Costs

The problems of rising levels of local expenditures as well as increasing local tax levies to support them are a constant of our time. It is far from unique to Newark or to older cities as a group. Their situations, however, are made more complex by the relative stability at best (or actual decrease) of ratables upon which to base taxes. Municipal sales taxes or income taxes though growing in number are viewed as having negative feedback effects upon the overall economy of a municipality, with jobs and retail sales moving out, in part, to escape these specific levies. While there has been some increase in the level of transfer payments from other governmental units (county, state, and federal) all too frequently, particularly in the case of this last category, these have been for the funding of new programs — Model Cities or a venture in new health or job action. The fundamental costs of municipal government, the year-to-year expenditures of line departments, have to be met by municipal revenues. As discussed earlier in Chapter 1

(Exhibit 1-1), the result has been an enormous strain on local property taxes. The Newark tax rate, based on 100 percent evaluation, has gone from 5.13 in 1960 to 6.60 at the time of the first survey in 1964 to 9.63 in 1972. The average annual increase is 7.3 percent.

## Falling Tax Collection Ratios

In very large measure increases in rates have become self-defeating. In Exhibit 5-1 are presented data on the Newark tax collection ratio as compared with the average for New Jersey. In the latter case the collection ratio, defined as total taxes collected for a specific year divided by the total taxes levied for that year, has hovered around the 94 percent level. For Newark, on the other hand, although in 1960 it was 92.78, by 1964 it had declined to 89.50, and by 1970 it was only 87.75. This simply means that Newark is now collecting less than ninety cents

EXHIBIT 5-1
TAX LEVY COLLECTION PERCENTAGES *
NEWARK, 1960-1970

| | Newark Versus Statewide Tax Collection Percentages | | |
|---|---|---|---|
| Year | Newark | New Jersey Average | Percent Difference |
| 1960 | 92.78 | 94.07 | 1.29 |
| 1961 | 92.13 | 93.28 | 1.15 |
| 1962 | 92.09 | 93.93 | 1.84 |
| 1963 | 89.92 | 94.08 | 4.16 |
| 1964 | 89.50 | 93.97 | 4.47 |
| 1965 | 89.28 | 94.00 | 4.72 |
| 1966 | 88.26 | 94.22 | 5.96 |
| 1967 | 87.44 | 94.01 | 6.57 |
| 1968 | 88.42 | 94.63 | 6.21 |
| 1969 | 89.61 | 94.59 | 4.98 |
| 1970 | 87.75 | 94.35 | 6.60 |

*Tax levy collected percentage for Year N = $\frac{\text{Total taxes collected as of December 31 of Year N}}{\text{Total taxes (levied) for Year N}}$

Source: N.J. Department of Community Affairs, Division of Local Finance, *Twenty-Third to Thirty-Third Annual Reports* (Trenton, N.J., NJDCA, 1960-1970).

out of every dollar of tax levies. Tax levels have reached the point where little in the way of new construction can be secured except with special tax deals. New commercial facilities' assessments tend to be based on levies not as a function of cost or value, but rather as a moderate percentage of gross rents. And the same holds true for housing. While certainly these improvements are essential to the city's overall health, they do little to aid the burden on older tax paying improvements. *The very size of the tax generates the dynamic which increases that size in turn, as the level of actual collection of taxes is impacted.*[1]

## Increasing Tax Liens and Property Foreclosures

When real estate taxes are not paid for a period of time the city may secure a lien on the property which stays until either the taxes are repaid or the building ultimately goes into foreclosure. In Exhibit 5-2 is a ten-

EXHIBIT 5-2
TAX TITLE LIENS OUTSTANDING °
NEWARK, 1960-1970

| | Newark as a Portion of the Statewide Total | |
|---|---|---|
| Year | Newark | New Jersey Total |
| 1960 | $ 887,371 | $16,240,356 |
| 1961 | 921,604 | 14,697,894 |
| 1962 | 835,946 | 15,182,757 |
| 1963 | 1,061,044 | 16,222,877 |
| 1964 | 1,374,895 | 18,782,405 |
| 1965 | 1,569,371 | 20,361,390 |
| 1966 | 2,317,605 | 21,136,094 |
| 1967 | 2,518,686 | 20,908,759 |
| 1968 | 3,170,262 | 24,219,124 |
| 1969 | 4,532,307 | 28,408,196 |
| 1970 | 5,941,922 | 33,079,038 |

°As of January 1 of year indicated.

Source: N.J. Department of Community Affairs, Division of Local Finance, *Twenty-Third to Thirty-Third Annual Reports* (Trenton, N.J., NJDCA, 1960-1970).

year summary of the tax liens outstanding both for New Jersey and Newark. It is evident from the data that in ten years the New Jersey total has doubled from $16-million to $33-million. Newark's, however, has gone from under $1-million dollars in 1960 to nearly $6-million in 1970. Newark contains nearly 20 percent of all the outstanding tax indentures in New Jersey, though it has only 2.7 percent of the total value of real estate.

In a process which will be described more fully later, parcels on which taxes are not paid for an appropriate time are foreclosed by the creditor municipality. In Exhibit 5-3 these data are shown for both Newark and all of New Jersey. The state figure given for purposes of comparison has been reasonably constant through the years hovering at around the $60,000,000 mark. Newark's growth in foreclosures has paralleled the trend in tax title liens, rising from only $654,000 in 1960 to nearly six times that amount, $3,415,000 in 1970.

EXHIBIT 5-3
DOLLAR VALUE OF PROPERTY ACQUIRED BY DEED OR FORECLOSURE* FOR UNPAID TAXES
NEWARK, 1960-1970

| | Newark as Compared to Statewide Total | |
|---|---|---|
| Year | Newark | New Jersey Total |
| 1960 | $ 654,300 | $59,054,968 |
| 1961 | 672,700 | 59,560,406 |
| 1962 | 695,200 | 63,684,036 |
| 1963 | 735,500 | 64,578,199 |
| 1964 | 770,000 | 64,982,706 |
| 1965 | 936,800 | 59,523,484 |
| 1966 | 933,500 | 58,087,115 |
| 1967 | 1,507,500 | 60,516,430 |
| 1968 | 1,254,400 | 64,888,030 |
| 1969 | 2,220,959 | 57,335,590 |
| 1970 | 3,415,044 | 60,671,395 |

*As of January 1 of year indicated.

Source: N.J. Department of Community Affairs, Division of Local Finance, *Twenty-Third to Thirty-Third Annual Reports* (Trenton, N.J., NJDCA, 1960-1970).

## THE SCOPE OF THE TASK

The object of this chapter is to scrutinize the process of tax delinquency in Newark and ultimately attempt to utilize the tax delinquency phenomenon as an advance indicator of structure abandonment. While abandoned buildings may not be tax delinquent, nor are all tax delinquent structures vacant, the frequency with which tax delinquency signals the abandonment of a structure by an owner, either followed or preceded by an equivalent action on the part of the tenantry, means that the two must be discussed as an interrelated problem.

Does the owner's lack of interest in a parcel ultimately occasion tax delinquency and finally foreclosure? Is abandonment generally a thought out procedure in which the owner methodically reduces inputs, particularly as evidenced by nonpayment of taxes, until the holding is finally given up? Certainly this scenario exists, but it is far from the definitive one. Though a negative market may be viewed as linked to tax foreclosure, the assumptions which accompany efficient parcel disposal, i.e., complete market knowledge and immediate, unencumbered participant reaction, while still viable in theory may be much too severe a limiting factor for the practicing public. The procedural repetition of paying taxes, the feeling that one must, under the law, bear the tax burden in good and bad times alike, or possibly, the belief that another use will eventually arrive for an income-deficient property, all contribute to a lack of determinism in the tax delinquency process. This, of course, may deter the establishment, at a point in time, of significant correlations between tax delinquency and structure abandonment. In the material that follows the dynamics of the process are explored. But first it is necessary to define the phenomenon and the data which are brought to bear on it.

## THE DEFINITION OF TAX ARREARAGE/TAX DELINQUENCY

For the purposes of the following analyses, tax arrearage within the sample of 569 parcels has been defined as the nonpayment of local municipal property taxes for two or more tax periods. A tax period in this case spans six months and itself includes two sub-periods or quarters. An owner in tax arrears at a minimum has missed payment of taxes for four quarters within one year and local tax officials have administratively recorded this delinquency on at least two separate occasions.

On a gross city basis tax delinquency is defined as sufficient tax arrearage on a property for it to be sold at tax sale for nonpayment of taxes. In terms of the sample's previous definition of tax arrearage any of the properties so defined would qualify. Thus, while a definitional distinction is being made here between tax arrearage and tax delinquency, in the material which follows, except when applying their specific association with a particular group of data, the terms are used interchangeably.

Thus, within the sample nonpayment of taxes is viewed both prior and subsequent to the fixing of a lien on a delinquent property. By definition all of these properties are sufficiently delinquent to be classified similarly yet specific municipal administrative procedures have not caught up with some. On a gross city basis, however, only properties which have liens affixed are viewed. This occurs after the local tax sale and after all procedural warning periods have expired.

## THE FREQUENCY OF TAX DELINQUENCY

Exhibit 5-4 provides a frame of reference for levels of tax delinquency within various geographical regions. It is based on 1970 municipal tax collection figures for cities in excess of 200,000 population.[2] Compared to those in other regions, tax collection percentages are lower and delinquency is correspondingly greater in both the northeastern and midwestern regions. In fact, the average urban tax delinquency rate of northeastern cities (8 percent) is twice that of their southeastern equivalents (4 percent). (The general range of annual property tax delinquency throughout the country usually varies from 0 to 12 percent.)

Exhibit 5-5 shows both the volume and composition of Newark's tax delinquent parcels during the period from 1967 to 1971. The number of tax delinquencies is on a par with abandonments since approximately 1.6 percent of the city's parcels become tax delinquent each year.

The six categories of Newark real estate examined show essentially stable trends over time. Interestingly, however, large residential and commercial structures and vacant land become tax delinquent at over two times the rate of small residential and industrial structures. Despite

## EXHIBIT 5-4
### 1970 PROPERTY TAX DELINQUENCY * IN MAJOR U.S. CITIES BY REGION

| Region | Percent Delinquent | Region | Percent Delinquent |
|---|---|---|---|
| **Northeast** | | **Midwest** | |
| New York | 5.0 | Chicago | 15.3 |
| Boston | 9.7 | Detroit | 2.8 |
| Philadelphia | 4.4 | Cleveland | 4.7 |
| Newark | 11.9 | Cincinnati | 2.8 |
| Pittsburgh | 7.4 | St. Louis | 5.3 |
| **Southeast** | | Kansas City | 2.4 |
| Miami | 2.4 | **West** | |
| Jacksonville | 2.4 | Portland | 7.3 |
| Atlanta | 4.5 | Seattle | 3.7 |
| Baltimore | 2.4 | San Francisco | 1.6 |
| Norfolk | 4.5 | Los Angeles | 2.3 |
| **Southwest** | | Oakland | 2.6 |
| Dallas | 1.5 | **Northwest** | |
| Houston | 8.3 | Portland | 7.3 |
| New Orleans | 1.9 | Seattle | 4.7 |

* Reconstructed from tax collection percentages

$$\text{Tax Collection Percentage} = \frac{\text{Total Taxes Collected}}{\text{Total Taxes Levied}}$$

Tax Delinquency Percentage = 100 Minus Tax Collection Percentage

Source: *Moody's Municipal and Government Manual, 1972*

the diminished market for both its available vacant land and its large residential and commercial structures, Newark maintains a steady local tax revenue from its industrial properties. Although it was noted earlier that structure abandonment (vacancy) is the highest for industrial land uses, it appears here that industrially zoned land offers enough economic potential to encourage owners to continue to pay taxes, hoping for a new industrial use to arise for the parcel. Their hopes may well be borne out with the advent of a statewide property tax or a federal *value added* tax, under which a suburban community would receive no revenue advantage for housing industry and commerce.

EXHIBIT 5-5
CLASSES OF NEWARK'S TAX DELINQUENT PROPERTY BY YEAR OF MUNICIPAL SALE

| Classification | 1967 | 1968 | 1969 | 1970 | 1971 | Numerical Total | Existing Stock (Parcels) |
|---|---|---|---|---|---|---|---|
| | Number of Parcels Sold at Tax Sale | | | | | | |
| Vacant Land | 32 | 94 | 112 | 77 | 136 | 451 | ( 2,369) |
| Residential (Less than 6 units) | 351 | 414 | 376 | 374 | 342 | 1,857 | (31,785) |
| Residential (6 units or more) | 39 | 148 | 121 | 132 | 124 | 564 | ( 3,571) |
| Commercial | 148 | 164 | 188 | 127 | 135 | 762 | ( 7,078) |
| Industrial | 10 | 23 | 27 | 18 | 21 | 99 | ( 1,531) |
| Not indicated | 16 | 0 | 0 | 0 | 0 | 16 | — |
| Total | 596 | 843 | 824 | 728 | 758 | 3,749 | (46,334) |
| | Percent Distribution of Parcels Sold at Tax Sale | | | | | | |
| Vacant land | 7.1 | 20.8 | 24.8 | 17.1 | 30.2 | 12.0 | (18.2) |
| Residential (Less than 6 units) | 18.9 | 22.3 | 20.2 | 20.1 | 18.4 | 49.5 | ( 5.9) |
| Residential (6 units or more) | 6.9 | 26.2 | 21.5 | 23.4 | 22.0 | 15.0 | (15.8) |
| Commercial | 19.4 | 21.5 | 24.7 | 16.7 | 17.7 | 20.3 | (14.0) |
| Industrial | 10.1 | 23.2 | 27.3 | 18.2 | 21.2 | 2.6 | ( 6.5) |
| Not Indicated | 0.0 | 0.0 | 0.0 | 0.0 | 2.7 | 0.4 | — |
| Average | 15.9 | 22.5 | 22.0 | 19.4 | 20.2 | 100.0 | ( 8.1) |

$\chi^2=0.01$

Source: Tax Sale Listings, Newark, 1967-1971.

## Citywide Tax Delinquency by Ward Location

It is difficult to develop an optimum geographic frame for viewing tax delinquency. Analysis by the city's five wards may be of use in this context. Exhibit 5-6 depicts local ward structure, Exhibit 5-7 the intensity of tax delinquency.

The most intense area of tax delinquency, both relatively and absolutely, is Newark's Central Ward; its historic core slum area. This

# EXHIBIT 5-6
## 1970 CENSUS TRACTS AND WARD DISTRICT MAP

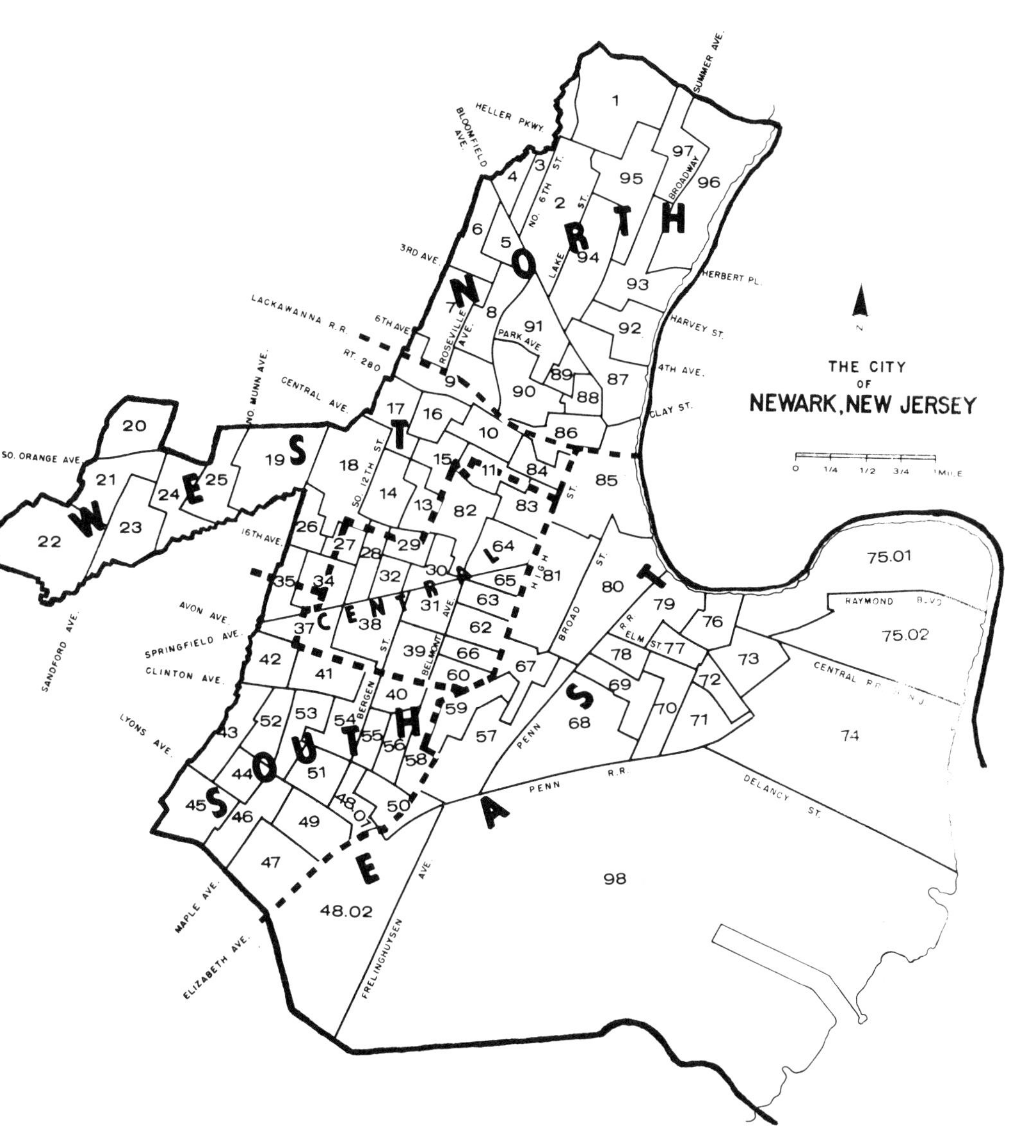


PREPARED BY
DIVISION OF CITY PLANNING

# EXHIBIT 5-7
## GROSS TAX DELINQUENCY LEVELS NEWARK, NEW JERSEY 1967-1971

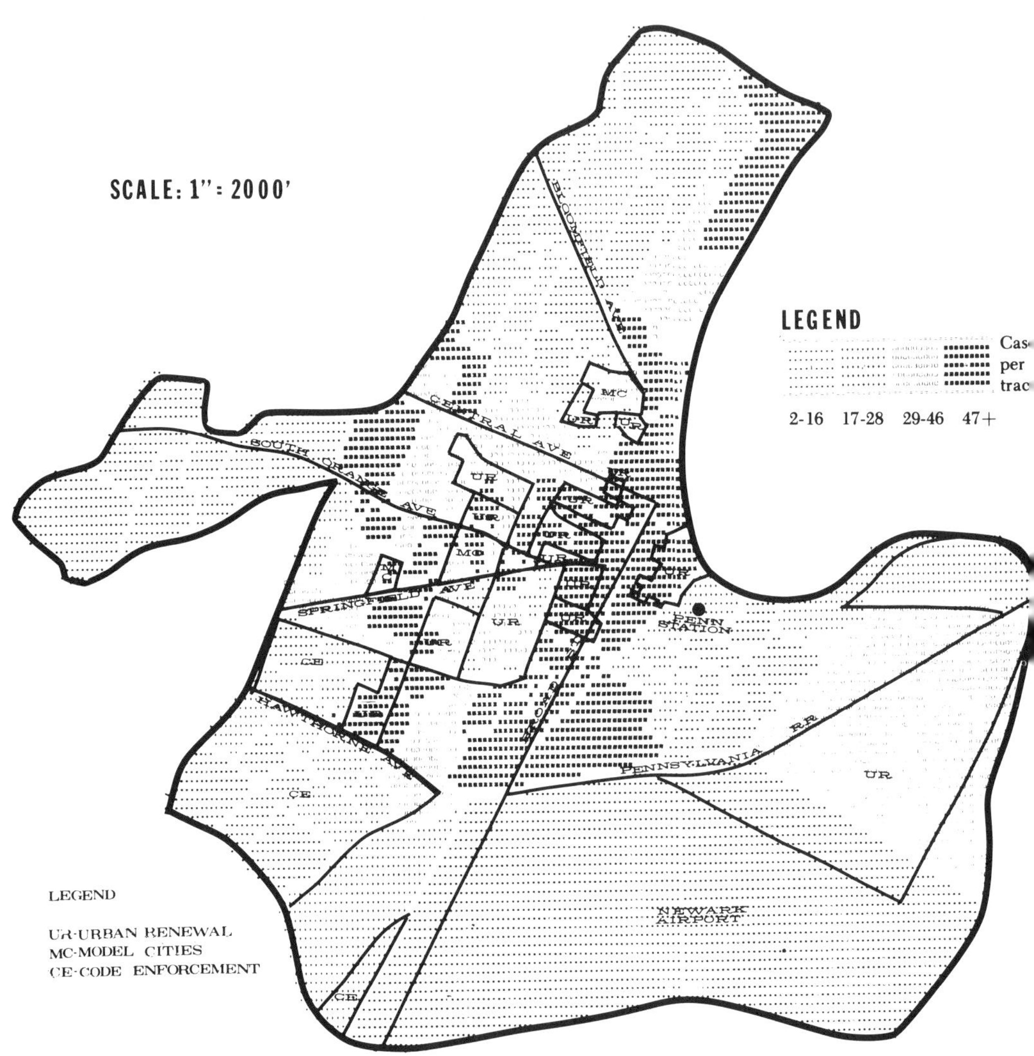

ward, west of High Street and extending to the Irvington, N.J. line, represents over 30 percent of the total tax delinquencies occurring during the period 1967 to 1971. Viewed from another perspective, almost 28 percent of this ward's stock is tax delinquent. This area alone contains 25 percent of the residential delinquencies, over 30 percent of the vacant land, commercial and industrial delinquencies, and 42 percent of the delinquencies in large residential structures (six units or more). Perhaps more significantly, this is one of the few areas of *increasing* tax delinquency. The Central Ward's property forfeitures increased by nearly half during 1970 and currently represent close to 40 percent of 1971 citywide tax delinquencies (Exhibit 5-8).

The East Ward, which includes an old ethnic enclave (the Ironbound Area), contains as well most of the downtown commercial area, and the South Ward, once a Jewish enclave and now substantially black, have very similar gross numbers of tax delinquencies. Due to the city's existing land use variations, however, the East Ward, primarily a nonresidential sector, has significantly more commercial and industrial tax delinquencies than does the South Ward, representing one-third of the former and over one-half of the latter categories. In terms of gross numbers of delinquencies, while both wards individually contribute 20 to 25 percent of citywide property forfeitures, the East Ward's delinquency appears to be diminishing while the South Ward is maintaining a peak which was reached in early 1969. This may show an outward movement of tax delinquency from the core led by a more rapid abandonment of small commercial structures. The West and North Wards, found on the Hillside/Irvington, N.J., and Belleville/Kearny, N.J., borders, respectively — both the last bastions of the European ethnic concentrations — are relatively low areas of tax delinquency. As has been shown previously, these are areas with high percentages of owner-residents, and conversely low percentages of multiply-owned, primarily rental-income properties. Because of the building configuration of these areas, the delinquency which is taking place there is in small frame residential structures of five units or less.

Perhaps the most obvious trait of these two wards is their relative stability in terms of property forfeiture. In 1971, in neither district were there appreciably more tax delinquencies than were evident in 1967 (Exhibit 5-9). This is in sharp contrast to the other locations, i.e., the South, East, and Central Wards where a delinquency "riot hump" was clearly visible.

## EXHIBIT 5-8
## CLASSES OF TAX DELINQUENT PROPERTY BY CITY WARD LOCATION OF DELINQUENCY

| Location (Ward) | Vacant Land | Residential (5 units or less) | Residential (6 units or more) | Commercial | Industrial | Type not indicated | Total / Average |
|---|---|---|---|---|---|---|---|
| | | | | NUMBER | | | |
| West | 42 | 283 | 68 | 78 | 6 | 0 | 477 |
| Central | 173 | 459 | 241 | 263 | 23 | 0 | 1,158 |
| North | 71 | 221 | 58 | 365 | 7 | 1 | 423 |
| South | 80 | 446 | 131 | 111 | 12 | 7 | 787 |
| East | 85 | 448 | 66 | 245 | 51 | 8 | 903 |
| Total | 451 | 1,857 | 564 | 762 | 99 | 16 | 3,749 |
| | | | | PERCENT | | | |
| West | 8.8 | 59.3 | 14.3 | 16.4 | 1.3 | 0.0 | 100.0 |
| Central | 14.9 | 39.8 | 20.8 | 22.7 | 2.0 | 0.0 | 100.0 |
| North | 16.8 | 52.2 | 13.7 | 15.4 | 1.7 | 0.2 | 100.0 |
| South | 10.2 | 56.7 | 16.6 | 14.1 | 1.5 | 0.9 | 100.0 |
| East | 9.4 | 49.6 | 7.3 | 32.2 | 5.6 | 0.9 | 100.0 |
| Average | 12.0 | 49.5 | 15.0 | 20.3 | 2.6 | 0.4 | 100.0 |
| $\chi^2=0.01$ | | | | | | | |

Source: Tax Sale Listings, Newark, 1967-1971.

EXHIBIT 5-9
YEAR OF TAX SALE
BY WARD LOCATION OF DELINQUENCY

| Location (Ward) | 1971 | 1970 | 1969 | 1968 | 1967 | Total |
|---|---|---|---|---|---|---|
| | | | NUMBER | | | |
| West | 91 | 94 | 96 | 109 | 87 | 477 |
| Central | 286 | 197 | 259 | 265 | 151 | 1,158 |
| North | 84 | 98 | 67 | 101 | 73 | 423 |
| South | 174 | 182 | 178 | 140 | 114 | 787 |
| East | 123 | 157 | 224 | 228 | 171 | 903 |
| Total | 758 | 728 | 824 | 843 | 596 | 3,749 |
| | | | PERCENT | | | |
| West | 12.0 | 12.9 | 11.7 | 12.9 | 14.6 | 12.7 |
| Central | 37.7 | 27.1 | 31.4 | 31.4 | 25.3 | 30.9 |
| North | 11.1 | 13.5 | 8.1 | 12.0 | 12.2 | 11.3 |
| South | 22.9 | 25.0 | 21.6 | 16.6 | 19.1 | 21.0 |
| East | 16.2 | 21.6 | 27.2 | 27.0 | 28.7 | 24.1 |
| Total | 100.0 | 100.0 | 100.0 | 100.0 | 100.0 | 100.0 |
| $\chi^2$=0.01 | | | | | | |

Source: Tax Sale Listings, Newark, 1967-1971

## Private Interest in Purchasing Tax Title Liens

The growing lack of interest in Newark as a potential place of industry, commerce, and residence is shown in Exhibit 5-10. In 1961, of the 398 parcels sold for tax purposes, 275 (nearly 70 percent), were repurchased by the private market. Clearly the belief in Newark's viability was strong enough to prompt the repurchase of available tax title liens by private investors despite their awareness that the previous owner may have realized no profit from the property.

By 1971 there was a drastic drop-off in the interest of private investors. Of the 750 tax liened parcels up for sale, *none* was purchased by the private market. In other words, there was not *one* instance where a potential buyer had enough confidence in Newark's future to make a tax property purchase. Newark's problems seem to have substantially discouraged private interest in property *repurchase. Significantly, the decline in purchaser interest was evident by 1965, reflecting a change in*

EXHIBIT 5-10
PRIVATE INTEREST IN PURCHASING TAX TITLE LIENS
NEWARK, 1957-1972

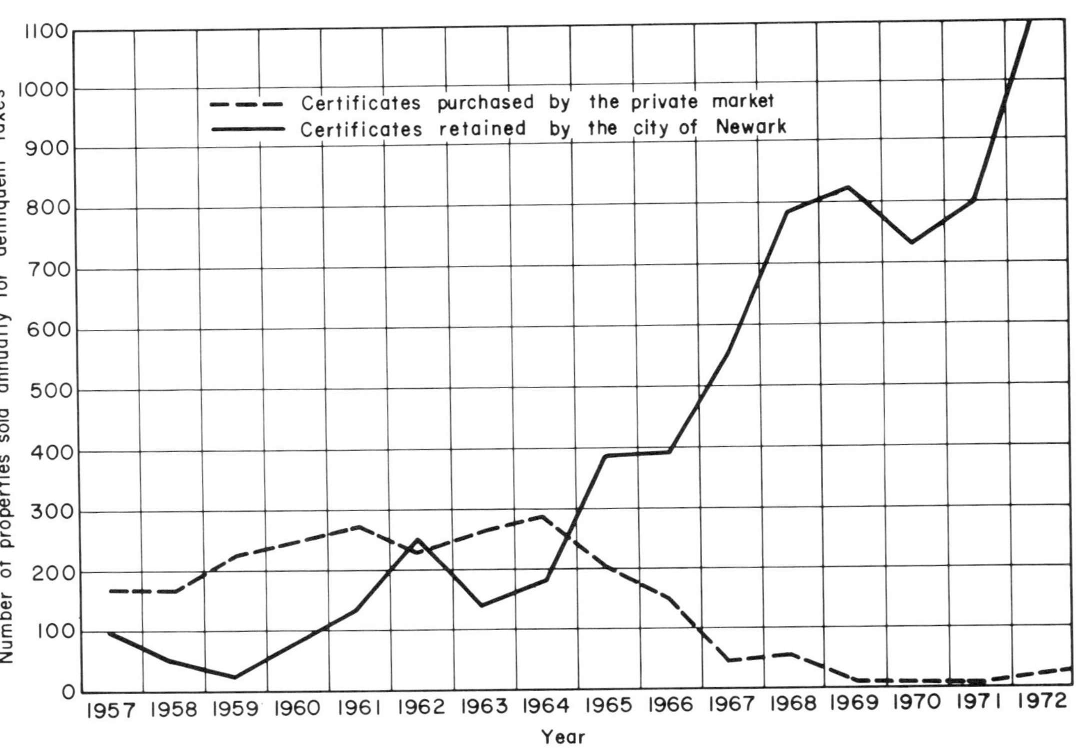

*the marketability of Newark property at least two years before the eruption of racial confrontation in central core locations.*

Thus, in ten years the number of delinquent properties has doubled with interest in their repurchase falling from near the 70 percent level to nonexistence. Later in this chapter appears a description of the tax delinquency process and its attendant economics which will clarify some of the problems.

## Tax Lien Purchase Price by Location and Property Classification

The median tax lien purchase price shows little variation by area of the city. The North, South, and East Wards are almost identical at the $370 level, or about one quarter's taxes for the average residential parcel (Exhibit 5-11). The Central Ward, experiencing substantial commercial and large multifamily delinquency, reflects this in a 25 percent higher lien purchase price. The West Ward, however, again primarily a residential area, lags in median purchase price by approximately 10 percent.

Variation in lien purchase price by property category follows the traditional value pattern assigned to various land uses. The median of the aggregate industrial and commercial liens is usually higher than all but the most intense residential category (apartment houses with six units or more). The smaller, frame residential units and vacant land follow in order of purchase price.

Can detailed analysis of the 1964 and 1971 survey data provide insight into the tax delinquency phenomenon?

EXHIBIT 5-11

MEDIAN TAX LIEN PURCHASE PRICE BY (1) CITY WARD LOCATION AND (2) PROPERTY CLASSIFICATION

| | Purchase Price (1) | | Classification | Purchase Price (2) |
|---|---|---|---|---|
| Wards | All Types | Residential | | By Type |
| West | $527 | $512 | Vacant land | $ 309 |
| Central | 633 | 600 | Residential (5 units or less) | 521 |
| North | 570 | 626 | Residential (6 units or more) | 1,020 |
| South | 665 | 699 | Commercial | 817 |
| East | 574 | 543 | Industrial | 1,036 |

Source: Tax Sale Listings, Newark, 1967-1971.

# LEAD INDICATORS OF TAX DELINQUENCY

The tight nexus between tax delinquency and abandonment has been indicated. In the material which follows, the phenomenon of tax delinquency is examined in a variety of ways. The objective here is to see if there are lead indicators of tax delinquency. Although both 1964 and 1971 sample data will initially be viewed, via cross tabulation, for their relationships to tax delinquency, the more current data will be used in attempts to develop predictors of tax delinquency via multiple regression.

## Data Description

In viewing tax delinquency within the sample set three distinct data groupings will be used. Tax information for 1971 is available for each parcel regardless of whether a 1964 or 1971 owner interview was obtained. Thus, when tax delinquency information is being cross tabulated by a variable associated with the parcel and not bound by owner interview, there will be more tax arrearage information available. For instance, there will be a maximum of 100 cases of parcels with two or more periods of arrears (Exhibit 5-12). When these 100 cases of sustained delinquency are limited to those with owner interviews fewer examples will be available, i.e., in 1964 a maximum of fifty-nine cases will be evident. Similarly, when the set is refined by 1971 owner interviews, a maximum of forty-seven instances of two or more periods of arrears is available.

## Gross Sample Tax Delinquency and Tax Delinquency by Occupancy Status

Exhibit 5-12 shows the gross level of tax delinquency for the 568 parcels for which data were available as of 1971. Three hundred forty, or 59.9 percent, of the total had no tax delinquency; 128, or 22.5 percent, were one period delinquent; while 100, or 17.6 percent, were two or more periods delinquent.

The gross pattern is troublesome and becomes even more so when occupancy status is considered (Exhibit 5-13). One out of eight, or 12.3 percent, of the occupied structures were two or more periods delinquent while the same held true for a third of the partially occupied and nearly

EXHIBIT 5-12

TAX DELINQUENCY WITHIN THE SAMPLE SET: TOTAL INSTANCE OF ARREARAGE AND PARCELS IN ARREARS WITH 1964 AND 1971 INTERVIEWS

| | | Periods of Tax Arrears | | |
|---|---|---|---|---|
| | Total | Zero | One | Two to Twenty |
| Entire sample | 568 | 340 | 128 | 100 |
| With 1964* interviews | 285‡ | 154 | 72 | 59 |
| With 1971† interviews | 314 | 181 | 86 | 47 |

*Minus 105 parcels which were taken by funded urban renewal programs and thus not included in this analysis.
†Owners of parcels taken for urban renewal purposes not interviewed in 1971.
‡One case lacks tax delinquency information.

$\chi^2=0.01$

Source: Newark Area Resurvey, spring 1972.

half of the vacant structures. The lowest proportion in the group were those buildings which were demolished either publicly or privately. And there may be some difficulties in posting errors or lack of write-offs which account for the slightly over 10 percent of these groups collectively which are still shown as two or more periods delinquent.

## Tax Delinquency Within Sample Areas

In Exhibits 5-14 and 5-15 is shown by tract category the current tax delinquency pattern within the sample areas. Tract category one had 17.3 percent of its parcels two or more periods delinquent. This area (1) in 1960 consisted of the seven census tracts with less than 25 percent of their housing units sound. Areas 2 and 2A, as shown, were the eleven tracts with 25 percent to 50 percent sound housing as of 1960. Areas 2 and 2A and 3 and 3A are differentiated on the basis of racial patterns. While in Area 1, as of 1960, the pattern of black population per census

## EXHIBIT 5-13
### PERIODS OF TAX ARREARAGE (1971) BY OCCUPANCY STATUS (1971)

| Occupancy Status | Periods of Arrears | | | |
|---|---|---|---|---|
| | Zero | One | Two to Twenty | Total |
| Occupied | 199 | 85 | 40 | 324 |
| Partially occupied | 8 | 4 | 6 | 18 |
| Vacant | 8 | 13 | 19 | 40 |
| Demolished — public | 108 | 13 | 16 | 137 |
| Squatters | 4 | 6 | 2 | 12 |
| Demolished — private (reuse) | 7 | 4 | 16 | 27 |
| Demolished — private (no reuse) | 6 | 3 | 1 | 10 |
| Total | 340 | 128 | 100 | 568 |
| PERCENT DISTRIBUTION | | | | |
| Occupied | 61.4 | 26.2 | 12.3 | 100.0 |
| Partially occupied | 44.4 | 22.2 | 33.3 | 100.0 |
| Vacant | 20.0 | 32.5 | 47.5 | 100.0 |
| Demolished — public | 78.8 | 9.5 | 11.7 | 100.0 |
| Squatters | 33.3 | 50.0 | 16.7 | 100.0 |
| Demolished — private (reuse) | 25.9 | 14.8 | 59.3 | 100.0 |
| Demolished — private (no reuse) | 60.0 | 30.0 | 10.0 | 100.0 |
| Average | 59.9 | 22.5 | 17.6 | 100.0 |

$\chi^2$=0.001

Source: Newark Area Resurvey, spring 1972

tract ran from a low of a little less than half (48.7 percent) to a high of 92.9 percent, there were substantial dichotomies in the other groups. In Area 2, for example, the proportion of nonwhites in 1960 ran from a low of 56.2 percent to a high of 84.4 percent while Area 2A went from a low of 22.1 percent to a high of 42.4. Three and 3A were similarly divided with the eleven census tracts in Area 3 running from 41.2 to 95.1 percent nonwhite and the ten tracts in Area 3A grouped from a low of

# EXHIBIT 5-14
## TAX ARREARAGE BY SAMPLE AREA

LEGEND
PARCELS IN TWO OR MORE PERIODS OF ARREARAGE (1964-71)

● RESIDENTIAL—4 units or less
○ RESIDENTIAL—5 units or more
z RESIDENTIAL—over commercial or industrial

AREAS 25% SOUND HOUSING (1960)
AREAS 25-50% SOUND HOUSING (1960)
AREAS 50-67% SOUND HOUSING (1960)

# EXHIBIT 5-15

## RESIDENTIAL TAX ARREARAGE (1971) BY SAMPLE AREA OF THE CITY, NEWARK (1971)

| 1971 Tax Arrears by Area | In Arrears | Not In Arrears | Total |
|---|---|---|---|
| Area 1 (less than 25 percent sound housing) | 32 | 153 | 185 |
| Area 2 (25-50 percent sound housing) | 26 | 158 | 184 |
| Area 3 (51-67 percent sound housing) | 42 | 157 | 199 |
| Total | 100 | 468 | 568 |
| PERCENT DISTRIBUTION | | | |
| Area 1 (less than 25 percent sound housing) | 17.3 | 82.7 | 100.0 |
| Area 2 (25-50 percent sound housing) | 14.1 | 85.9 | 100.0 |
| Area 3 (51-67 percent sound housing) | 26.7 | 73.3 | 100.0 |
| Average | 21.3 | 78.7 | 100.0 |
| $\chi^2 = 0.025$ | | | |

Source: Newark Area Resurvey, spring 1972

6.8 percent to a high of 34.2 percent. (See Appendix 1 for detail.) It is evident from the exhibit, therefore, that tax delinquency in 1971 was, in part, predictable, based on the 1960 housing and racial characteristics, with the latter clearly playing a formidable role. In a later section of this chapter other factors will be considered which may underlie this relationship.

## TAX DELINQUENCY AND PUBLIC PROGRAMS

### Urban Renewal and Model Cities

The probability that a property is located in an urban renewal area was inversely related to the degree of tax delinquency. Ninety-two out of the 340 nontax delinquent, or 27 percent, were in areas specifically defined as urban renewal areas. The same holds true for only seven out of 100 (7 percent) of the parcels that were two or more periods in arrears. This is a difficult finding to interpret. On the one hand, to the degree that tax delinquent parcels are those which are in the most trouble, urban renewal, at least as it has been mapped and practiced in Newark, simply has not dominated the group. On the other hand, there is some indication that parcels in urban renewal areas do not necessarily suffer tax delinquency. This may be a minor blessing but not a completely indifferent one.

There is some indication that owners faced with tenantry problems and the like in an urban renewal area may permit their buildings to become vacated and for that matter even board them up while still maintaining the tax payments in the hope of an urban renewal taking. This may account for some of the variations shown here.

In Model City areas there was a greater incidence of tax delinquency than outside these boundaries. Seven percent of the nondelinquents were in the Model Cities area versus 15 percent of the delinquent parcels.

Both delinquent and nondelinquent owners were equally unsure on whether their parcels were in an urban renewal area. The delinquent parcel owners in general, however, were much more sanguine in 1971 about getting their money back if there were a taking with 40.4 percent versus 30.9 percent of the nondelinquents certain that an urban renewal taking would be adequately recompensed.

### Demolition

Thirteen percent of the two or more period tax delinquent structures in 1971 had been demolished by some form of Newark public authority. Of the 340 nondelinquent parcels, 104 had been demolished. Note that this finding may be somewhat imprecise since it cannot be assumed that none of the tax delinquencies on the 104 zero period delinquent demolished structures had been wiped off prior to the title search. In any case, the attrition rate is substantial.

## TAX DELINQUENCY AND CHARACTERISTICS OF BOTH PARCEL AND NEIGHBORHOOD

### Level of Interior Furnishings

In 1964, 4.5 percent of the zero period delinquencies and 8.5 percent of the two or more period tax delinquencies, but less than 1 percent of the no period tax delinquencies, were rooming houses. But the relationships had reversed by 1971. By this date 9.4 percent of the zero period delinquent parcels were furnished in whole or part versus 4.2 percent of the two or more period delinquents. This may indicate that generalizations on the linkage between market weakness and furnished units based on the initial study are spurious.

### Size of Parcel

There was no distinction in size of parcel and tax delinquency, the latter's incidence was relatively smooth across the board. And similarly, there was little variation as a function of type of construction — frame, masonry, and the like — allowing for the relative proportions of such structures in the area as a whole.

### Quality of Structure

It is difficult to generalize by quality of structure given the relatively small set of tax delinquent parcels (59) for the 1964 data. *There is some indication, however, that, in general, the parcels which were later to become tax delinquent were in poor condition.* In terms of absolute quality rating, 21.3 percent of the 174 parcels rated as average in 1964 were tax delinquent seven years later; for the poorly kept parcels, however, the equivalent figure was 48.7 percent, while for the seventy-one well kept parcels only 4.2 percent were tax delinquent later. The criteria used here were such elements as garbage facilities, health hazards (dirty halls, broken stairs, and the like), and deficient safety measures (frozen fire escapes, cluttered porches and stairs, and so on). (See Exhibit 5-16.) While the comparisons with neighbors in terms of better, same, poorer, were not quite so marked, the basic trends were similar.

The findings are paralleled in 1971. Only 11.5 percent of the zero period delinquent parcels in 1971 were rated as poorer than their neighbors; the same held true for 17 percent of the two or more period delinquent. This trend was confirmed by the absolute quality ratings.

When owners in 1971 were asked whether they felt their buildings were in good operating condition, 37.3 percent of those forty-seven owners whose buildings were two or more periods tax delinquent, either said *no* or specifically described them as *very poor*. Among the zero period delinquent owners the equivalent response was only 7.7 percent. At the same time 79 percent of the zero delinquent in 1971 said their parcels were either in very good or moderately good condition versus only 34.1 percent of the two or more period delinquents.

EXHIBIT 5-16
PERIODS OF TAX ARREARAGE (1971)
BY ABSOLUTE QUALITY OF THE STRUCTURE (1964)

| | Absolute Quality | | | |
|---|---|---|---|---|
| Periods of Arrears | Reasonably Kept | Poorly Kept | Well Kept | Total |
| Zero | 89 | 10 | 54 | 153 |
| One | 48 | 10 | 14 | 72 |
| Two to Twenty | 37 | 19 | 3 | 59 |
| Total | 174 | 39 | 71 | 284 |
| PERCENT DISTRIBUTION | | | | |
| Zero | 51.1 | 25.6 | 76.1 | 53.9 |
| One | 27.6 | 25.6 | 19.7 | 25.4 |
| Two to Twenty | 21.3 | 48.7 | 4.2 | 20.8 |
| Total | 100.0 | 100.0 | 100.0 | 100.0 |

$\chi^2=0.001$

Source: Newark Area Resurvey, spring 1972

## Proximity of Nuisances

In the earlier survey mention was made of the proximity of bars, junk yards, factories, heavy traffic, and other generalized nuisances of mixed land use. It is interesting to note that while consideration must be given to the degree of subjective judgement which is always involved in these rating procedures, none of them was useful as predictive functions for tax delinquency.

## Commercial Occupancy

Only 19.3 percent of the 249 structures which had no commercial occupancy in 1964 were tax delinquent seven years later. The total number of buildings with some measure of commercial occupancy is only thirty-five, but no less than eleven (31.4 percent) of them were tax delinquent. Certainly one of the major problems in central cities is the disposition of parcels whose basic economic viability is dependent on commercial facilities which are no longer of any use.

## Actual Rent Levels

In general, actual rent levels of tax delinquent parcels in 1971 were substantially under those for the nondelinquent ones. Half of the tax delinquent parcels had rents of $90 or less versus approximately a quarter of the delinquent parcels.

## Availability of Rent Increases

When owners were asked in 1971 what level of rent increase they would require to make their parcels a good investment, regardless of tax status the response range was very wide, perhaps too much so for generalization. On the other hand, when they were asked whether they could get this increase, 42 percent of the two-or-more period tax delinquent parcel owners answered in the negative versus half that for the zero period tax delinquent.

## Vacancy Rates

In general, the owners of parcels which were later to be tax delinquent were much more negative on the question of vacancy rates. In 1964 when asked about general area vacancy rates, 69.5 percent of the owners of parcels which were later to be delinquent believed that they had gone up in the area versus 37 percent of the zero period delinquents. When asked specifically about their own parcel, the variation was less obvious, but still significant, with 28.6 percent of the future nondelinquent parcel versus 52.5 percent of those that were later to be two or more periods delinquent answering that they had gone up.

Variation in vacancy rate responses by owners as a function of the tax status of their properties by 1971 had blurred substantially. While still skewed slightly on the upwards side in those parcels two or more periods tax delinquent, the level of variation was no longer significant.

## Race of Tenantry

Of the 154 nondelinquent parcels, 27.9 percent had all white tenantry in 1964, which contrasts with only 1.7 percent of the fifty-nine parcels which were later to be two or more period tax delinquent. Conversely, 61.7 percent of the zero period delinquent, but 84.7 percent of the two or more period delinquent had all black tenantry. Again, this aspect clearly is not completely deterministic. There are obviously many parcels with equivalent tenantry groups on both sides of the tax delinquency picture. From a statistical base, however, there is no question of the skew.

The variation had blurred by 1971. The proportion of all white tenanted structures was so small as to make generalizations of dubious value. It should be noted, however, that none of the fifteen structures with such tenantry were two or more periods delinquent. The sample, however, is too small for positive conclusion. The proportion for other ethnic groups was constant. There was no clear-cut variation in the degree of welfare tenantry as of 1971 that in itself could account for tax delinquency *per se*.

# TAX DELINQUENCY AND OWNER/OPERATING CHARACTERISTICS

## Characteristics of Parcels

Are there any characteristics of owners and their operating patterns which are linked with tax delinquency? In a previous work (*The Urban Housing Dilemma*, New York, 1971) analysis was undertaken of the question of the levels of sophistication of the owners of tax delinquent buildings in New York City. There the hypothesis was tested that tax delinquency was a sophisticated way of borrowing money at a relatively low rate of interest. This hypothesis was rejected based upon analysis of owner characteristics. What is the pattern in Newark?

## Owner

### *First Entrance Into Real Estate*

There is little substantial variation on this score though some indication that parcels that later became delinquent, back in 1964, had owners of greater longevity than those parcels that did not become delinquent, i.e., the more recent experience in real estate was negatively linked to tax delinquency seven years later. As in abandonment, this seems to defy one hypothesis, that of newcomers to the market being the source of the problem.

The 1971 survey data were consistent in results with that obtained in 1964.

Neither in 1964 nor in 1971 was there any systematic variation in date of title to account for, or to serve, as a predicator of future abandonment.

### *Size of Holding*

Half of the 154 nondelinquent parcel owners in 1964 were owners of no other parcel versus 30.5 percent of the fifty-nine tax delinquent-to-be parcels. Similarly, only 20.8 percent of the nondelinquent parcel owners derived a substantial part of their income, i.e., a third up to full incomes, from real estate operation versus 37.2 percent of the parcels which were later to be two or more periods in arrears. This pattern continued through the 1971 interviews.

### *Motivation For Purchase*

Of the 151 owners in 1964 who had parcels which were not tax delinquent seven years later, 37.7 percent had purchased their buildings for homes. Among those parcels which were one period tax delinquent, it was fourteen out of seventy-one, or 19.7 percent, while for those parcels which were two or more periods delinquent, it was seven out of fifty-seven, or 12.3 percent. Again, *the purchase-for-home reason seems to be a very good predicator of the future health of a parcel.* The single largest reason for purchase among the owners of parcels which were later to become tax delinquent was the approximately 60 percent who had bought for rental return as contrasted with the 30 percent equivalent for the nondelinquent parcel owners.

The linkage was, if anything, even stronger when the results for 1971 are appraised. Here 43.4 percent of the nondelinquent parcel owners had bought for the purpose of a home while the same held true for barely a quarter (25.5 percent) of the two or more period delinquent owner (Exhibit 5-17).

In general, when parcels were in the hands of owners who had the same motivation for holding their parcels as for their purchase, they tended to be nondelinquent. Seventy percent of the 154 nondelinquent parcel owners gave the same reason for keeping as for purchasing versus only 45.8 percent of the two or more period delinquencies.

By 1971 an increasing number of owners basically want to sell regardless of the tax status of their properties. Despite this decline of esprit in terms of owner motivation for keeping their parcels, 51.4 percent of the zero period owners versus 30.4 percent of the two or more period delinquent owners were still positive in maintaining their original motivation for purchase.

### *Age of Owner*

Nearly half of the 154 nondelinquent parcel owners for whom there are data were under the age of fifty (48.7 percent) while among the two or more period delinquent-to-be owners the equivalent figure was 23.8 percent. Older owners are more prone to tax delinquency, and this pattern continues into 1971.

### *Owner's Residence*

More than half (52.6 percent) of the owners of parcels which were later not delinquent were resident owners versus 18.6 percent for the two or

## EXHIBIT 5-17

### OWNER'S REASON FOR PROPERTY PURCHASE (1971) BY CURRENT PERIODS OF TAX ARREARS (1971)

| Why Did You Buy . . .? | Area 1 | Area 2 | Area 3 | Total |
|---|---|---|---|---|
| Home | 79 | 19 | 12 | 110 |
| Rental return (investment) | 66 | 48 | 28 | 142 |
| Speculation | 1 | 1 | 0 | 2 |
| Inheritance | 12 | 4 | 2 | 18 |
| Debt | 1 | 1 | 0 | 2 |
| Commercial purposes | 7 | 3 | 0 | 10 |
| Home plus income | 6 | 0 | 1 | 7 |
| Other | 9 | 7 | 2 | 18 |
| Mortgage foreclosure | 1 | 2 | 2 | 5 |
| Total | 182 | 85 | 47 | 314 |

PERCENT DISTRIBUTION

| Why Did You Buy . . .? | Area 1 | Area 2 | Area 3 | Total |
|---|---|---|---|---|
| Home | 43.4 | 22.4 | 25.5 | 35.0 |
| Rental return (investment) | 36.3 | 56.5 | 59.6 | 45.2 |
| Speculation | 0.5 | 1.2 | 0.0 | 0.6 |
| Inheritance | 6.6 | 4.7 | 4.3 | 5.7 |
| Debt | 0.5 | 1.2 | 0.0 | 0.6 |
| Commercial purposes | 3.8 | 3.5 | 0.0 | 3.2 |
| Home plus income | 3.3 | 0.0 | 2.1 | 2.2 |
| Other | 4.9 | 8.2 | 4.3 | 5.7 |
| Mortgage foreclosure | 0.5 | 2.4 | 4.3 | 1.6 |
| Total | 100.0 | 100.0 | 100.0 | 100.0 |

$\chi^2=0.05$

Source: Newark Area Resurvey, spring 1972

more period delinquent owners. Of the zero period delinquents 27.2 percent lived outside of Newark versus 44.1 percent of the owners of two or more period delinquent-to-be parcels.

It should be recalled here that the samples used comparing 1964 and 1971 data are not precisely identical since the overall success level in interviews was dissimilar in the two periods. The basic shape of the variation in residence patterns, however, continues, with 37.6 percent of the zero period delinquent versus 15.2 percent of the two or more period delinquent parcel owners resident in their parcels in the latter period.

### *Ethnicity of Owner*

Given the variation in residence patterns there was surprisingly little variation in owner ethnicity as a function of later-to-be tax delinquent. While 37 percent of the 154 nondelinquent parcels were owned by blacks in 1964, the equivalent figure for two or more period delinquents was 34 percent. There was little variation in location of employment or income levels in general to act as a predictor.

In 1971 the variation in owner ethnicity and tax delinquency grew larger based upon the sample findings. Nearly half (45.5 percent) of the zero period tax delinquent parcels were in the hands of blacks versus only 35.6 percent of the two or more period delinquents. *This tends to generate a picture of white disinvestment in Newark residential properties.*

## Operating

### *The Use of A Manager*

Of the fifty-eight parcels that were tax delinquent in 1971, 22.4 percent as of 1964 used a manager or rent collector in contrast to half that proportion for the nondelinquent-to-be.

Slightly over one-fifth (20.3 percent) of the fifty-nine parcels later to be delinquent had full-time operators, and an additional 10.2 percent had half-time operators. This contrasts with 7.8 percent and 7.1 percent respectively for the 154 zero period delinquent of the future.

There has been a rising utilization of managers regardless of tax status. By 1971 the gap narrowed, with 19.9 percent of zero tax delinquent status owners using rent collectors versus 23.3 percent of the two or more period delinquents. The variation, therefore, is no longer significant.

### *Rent Collection Procedures*

There was some tendency for parcels that were later tax delinquent to have more frequent rent collection procedures than was true of the nondelinquent parcels, with 10.2 percent of the former owners as against only 4.5 percent of the latter collecting weekly. A slightly higher proportion of the former nominally collected their rents on a monthly base but realistically collected them whenever they could.

By 1971 the variation similarly had blurred between the zero period delinquent owners and those two or more periods delinquent. The variation was still toward a greater level of monthly collection on the part of the zero period owners; the differences, however, were no longer significant.

## Financing

### *Mortgage Sources*

Mortgage sources as of 1964 were definitely skewed as a function of later tax status. Savings banks, commercial banks, and savings and loan companies held the basic mortgages on 38.6 percent of the nondelinquents-to-be, while similar sources accounted for only 15.8 percent of the two or more periods delinquents to be. In this latter case, individual grantees and/or prior owners played a major role, accounting for more than half the mortgages versus only 20 percent of the nondelinquents.

Absence of a mortgage, however, did not deter later tax delinquency with 29.8 percent of the delinquents-to-be versus 15 percent of the nondelinquents having no mortgage.

The variation in mortgage sources had blurred substantially by 1971 with the majority of parcels both delinquent and nondelinquent having no mortgage shown on the deed. There was, however, the same basic variation with 11.6 percent of the nondelinquent parcels having mortgages given by individual grantees, including previous owners versus 28.5 percent of the delinquent ones.

This is based on the total sample of 563 for which there are data. If one assumes that the *no mortgage parcels* include all those which have been demolished, taken by the city, and so on, *this would indicate that a third of the zero period delinquent parcels had institutional mortgages versus seven out of forty-seven or less than half that proportion (14.9 percent) of the nondelinquents.*

Does this indicate merely foresight on the part of institutional lenders, or is the absence of their support a key input into tax delinquency?

When owners were asked in 1971 whether they could sell their parcels now and get a mortgage from a lending institution to facilitate the sale, the nondelinquent owners were much more sanguine than the delinquent ones, with 28.1 percent of the former answering yes, without any elements of difficulty, versus 21.3 of the latter. In contrast, 28.8 percent of the former, but 51.1 percent of the latter, said they either doubted it or were sure they couldn't.

## PROBLEM AREAS FOR TAX DELINQUENT PARCEL OWNERS

### Tenants

Tenants were given the top rating in 1964 as the key problem in maintenance by 22.3 percent of the nondelinquent-to-be owners, and as the second most important by 12.8 percent. This contrasts very sharply with the pattern among those owners whose parcels were later to be two or more periods delinquent where the respective figures were 32.8 and 27.6 percent. (See Exhibit 5-18.)

### Tax Level/Reassessment

The reverse was the case when the tax level was considered, with 52.7 percent of the zero period delinquent parcel owners rating this as the primary problem; it was number one for only 32.8 percent of the fifty-eight two-or-more period delinquent parcels. When questioned, however, specifically about taxes there seemed to be little variation in response, though a slightly higher fear of reassessment was shown by to-be-delinquent owners.

*This is particularly interesting in that tax delinquency is evolving not as a function of taxes as the primary operating problem but rather evolving from variation in attitudes toward tenantry. The former consideration, i.e., of taxes per se, is practically inverse to later delinquency patterns.*

When asked what improvements they would make if there were no fear of reassessment, the owners of parcels which were later in delinquency were much more negative about their neighborhood characteristics and their parcels not being worth additional capital investment. This negative result involved roughly 30 percent of the responses versus an equivalent of less than 12 percent for the zero period delinquent parcels. The latter group, in turn, had 38.3 percent of their owners replying that their parcels didn't need additional improvements versus 15.3 percent of the parcels later to be delinquent.

## EXHIBIT 5-18

### RELATIVE IMPORTANCE OF VARIOUS INHIBITORS TO PARCEL MAINTENANCE AND IMPROVEMENTS (1971) BY TAX ARREARAGE (1971)

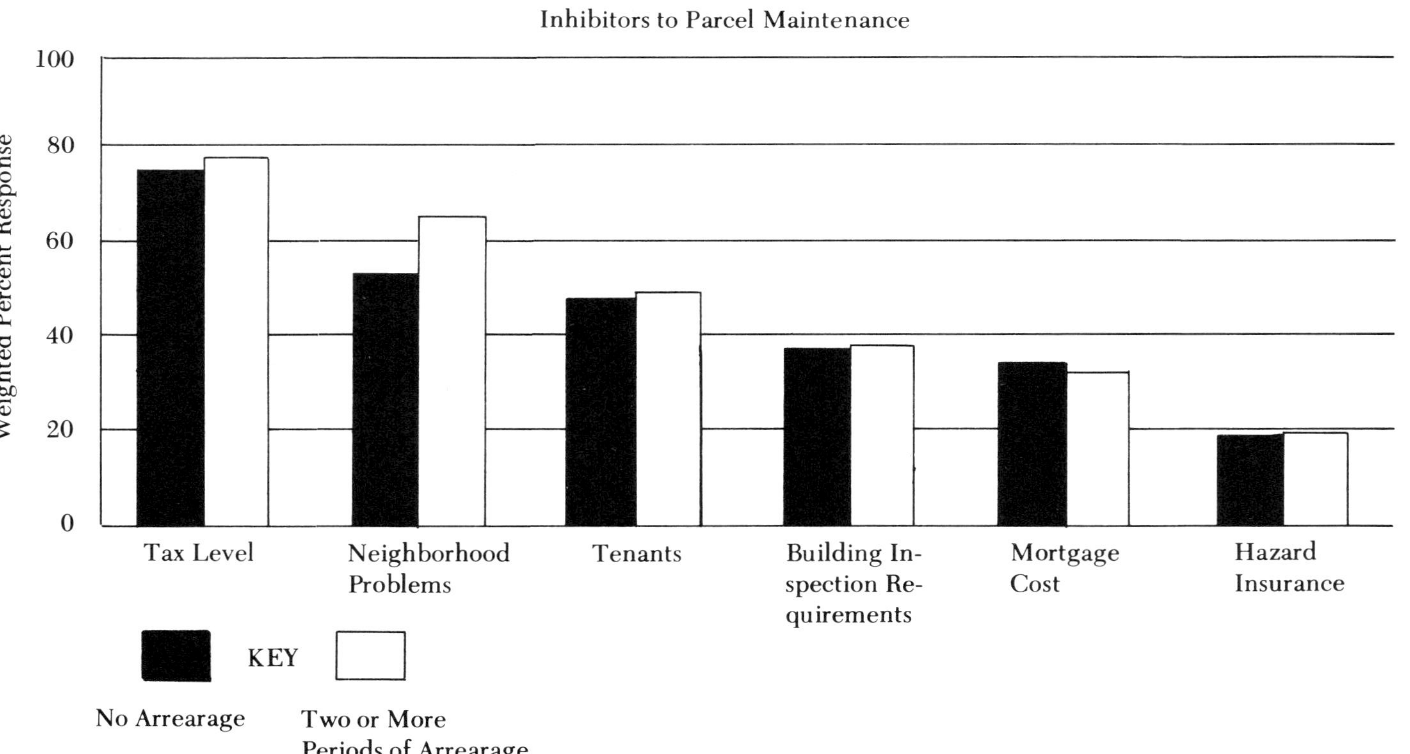


Source: Newark Area Resurvey, spring 1971

In general, later to-be-delinquent parcel owners were much less sanguine about their capacity to pass on tax increases to their tenantry than was true of the zero period delinquent. Nor were the owners of tax delinquent parcels sanguine about getting their money back on a resale if they did make improvements, with 61.7 percent saying *definitely not* versus 45.3 percent of the nondelinquent owners.

The variation in priority of problem areas shown in the 1964 responses again had diminished substantially by 1971. While 26.4 percent of the zero period delinquent parcel owners indicated tenants as their number one or number two problems, the equivalent response was a significant but not overwhelming 38.3 percent of the forty-seven parcel owners who were two or more periods tax delinquent.

## Neighborhood Problems

Neighborhood problems began to bulk much more significantly involving 27.7 percent of the two or more period tax delinquent parcel owners versus 17.8 percent of the zero tax delinquent parcel owners.

The imbalance in the response to tax levels, shown earlier, continued with this being of prime importance as a problem to 44.3 percent of the zero period delinquent owners versus only 31.9 percent of the two or more period tax delinquent parcel owners.

## Impact of Building Inspectors

One out of seven (14.3 percent) of the future nondelinquent owners but 33.9 percent of the later-to-be-delinquent parcel owners felt strongly that visits by building inspectors were a continual problem and unreasonable. Whether this variation can be attributed to individual variations in inspection procedures or to the realities of the parcel is far from ascertainable based on the data, but there is some indication that it may well be the latter rather than the former.

By 1971 the variation in response had blurred to the point of being practically identical from a statistical point of view.

# COROLLARIES OF TAX DELINQUENCY: THE SIGNIFICANCE OF TAX DELINQUENCY AND VARIOUS BEHAVIORAL AND ENVIRONMENTAL VARIABLES

## THE BEHAVIORAL ASPECTS OF RESIDENTIAL TAX DELINQUENCY

In order to test the statistical significance of the relationships previously discussed in the cross tabulation presentations, a one by one analysis of variance will be employed between the dependent variable tax delinquent/nontax delinquent and each of twenty-three 1971 independent variables. In terms of the analysis of variance model the dependent variable is a 0-1 dichotomous choice while the independent variables are grouped data usually having 4-7 intervals. Supplementing this, for ease of presentation, a multiple regression of dichotomous (both dependent and independent) dummy variables will be utilized again to present degrees and directions of association when *all* of the parcel variables above some chosen level of significance interract simultaneously. This then is nothing more than a one by thirteen analysis of variance used to gauge strength and direction of association of the complete variable array. It should be realized that using these analyses no attempt is being made to predict either current tax delinquency in other cities or future tax delinquency in this city from the characteristics of buildings observed in Newark at a single point in time. What is being attempted initially is to develop patterns of association between 1971 characteristics of buildings and buildings currently classified as tax delinquent. In a subsequent analysis with a larger body of data, tax delinquency will be linked to social characteristics of neighborhoods.

## Statistical Significance via the Analysis of Variance

Employing the analysis of variance, Exhibit 5-19 shows that in six out of the twenty-three cases specific parcel variables explain an amount of variance in tax delinquency sufficiently in excess of what would have been expected from sampling variation and thus may be adjudged to have a significant effect on the sample data (F statistic — 0.05 level).

The most clearly linked factors (significant at the F 0.01 level) appear to be the relationships of increased tax delinquency and: (1) poorer initial absolute quality of the residential structure, (2) parcels upon which a mortgage has been taken back by an individual (yet who is not the prior owner).

Of somewhat less significance (0.01-0.05), yet still strongly linked, are the one to one relationships of a tax delinquent parcel and: (1) poorer relative quality of the structure (compared to others nearby), (2) an increasing neighborhood vacancy rate, (3) owners who are nonresident, (4) location within the most deteriorated areas of the city and (5) the presence of an increasing welfare tenantry.

Perhaps most interesting in 1971, however, is the lack of linkage in the singular relationships of tax delinquency and: (1) whether the parcel was purchased for rental income or obtained through inheritance, (2) whether the owner employed a professional manager or performed repair work himself, (3) the number of other parcels which the owner simultaneously held, (4) whether he currently wants to sell the property or not. These latter relationships, which might have served as predictors of tax delinquency if 1964 characteristics had been used, are now blurred to the point of nonrecognition.

## Statistical Significance and the Relative Effect of Variables via Multiple Regression

If the F test at the 0.10 level is chosen for significance it may be seen that when all statistically significant variables are simultaneously taken into account, tax delinquency is explained most significantly by association of this phenomenon with: (1) buildings of poorer absolute quality in terms of an interviewer's comparison of the condition of other residential structures with which he/she is familiar, (2) to be operated by landlords who have higher proportions of tenants who

## EXHIBIT 5-19
### SIGNIFICANCE OF 1971 PARCEL COROLLARIES OF TAX DELINQUENCY
### ANALYSIS OF VARIANCE

029. DEPENDENT VARIABLE: NON-TAX DELINQUENT(0)/TAX DELINQUENT STRUCTURE(1)

| Variable Number | Variable Name | Direction of Coding | Individual Significance | Direction of Significance |
|---|---|---|---|---|
| 001 | Size of parcel | (Increases with size) | No | |
| 002 | Type of construction | (Increases toward masonry) | No | |
| 003 | Absolute quality | (Increases with better quality) | Yes | — |
| 004 | Relative quality | (Increases with better quality) | Yes | — |
| 005 | Commercial occupancy | (Increases with degree of occupancy) | No | |
| 006 | Nuisances nearby | (Increases with various nuisances) | No | |
| 007 | Length of experience in real estate | (Increases with length) | No | |
| 008 | Why purchased | (Increases with inheritance, rental income, etc.) | No | |
| 009 | Want to sell | (Increases with desire to sell) | No | |
| 010 | Professional manager | (Increases with professional management) | No | |

| | | | | |
|---|---|---|---|---|
| 011 | Size of holding | (Increases with size) | No | |
| 012 | Make living from real estate | (Increases with percent of real estate involvement) | No | |
| 013 | Race of tenants | (Increases toward black) | No | |
| 014 | Neighborhood vacancy rate | (Increases with larger) | Yes | + |
| 015 | Problem tenants | (Increases with severity rating) | No | |
| 018 | Residence of owner | (Increases with nonresidency) | Yes | + |
| 019 | Race of owner | (Increases toward white) | No | |
| 022 | Type of owner | (Increases with nonindividuals) | No | |
| 023 | Length of ownership | (Increases with term) | No | |
| 026 | Location in urban renewal area | (Increases with location in U.R. area) | No | |
| 027 | Multiple mortgages | (Increases with multiple mortgages) | No | |
| 028 | Location of parcel | (Increases with better locations) | Yes | — |
| 029 | Mortgage source | (Increases with noninstitutional lenders) | Yes | + |
| 030 | Welfare tenantry | (Increases with number on welfare) | Yes | + |

Source: Newark Area Resurvey, spring 1972

are on welfare, (3) to have higher vacancy rates, (4) to be one of multiple parcels owned by a landlord and (5) to be of less relative quality than surrounding neighbors (Exhibit 5-20).

This particular group of associations seems to dominate both the single and multi-variate analyses. Poor quality parcels whose neighborhood occupancy rate is low and whose current and potential occupants most likely are service-deficient welfare recipients cannot be looked upon as examples of rental situations where there is an excess of cash flow. Perhaps to maintain the building as a viable entity, additional money must be invested. The owner "borrows" from his taxes. He turns to municipal tax delinquency, an avenue of "illegal" credit engendering the slowest and least severe form of reprimand. Obligations often go unpaid for a period of up to four years with little censure and almost complete assurance that ultimately, due to waning private market interest, there will be no property loss.

## ENVIRONMENTAL ASPECTS OF RESIDENTIAL TAX DELINQUENCY

### Environmental Corollaries (The Static Case)

Having initially examined the *parcel* corollaries of residential tax delinquency, it is now necessary to view potential environmental conditions existing in areas in 1970 which may have contributed to 1971 tax delinquency.

Equally prevalent in tax delinquency, as in the abandonment case, is the positive* association of this phenomenon with black poverty (Race and Resources) and its negative association with white affluence (Social Status). These are the only two indices which prove to have statistically significant associations with tax delinquency at the F—0.05 level (Exhibit 5-21).

Residential tax delinquency in terms of location appears to be more prevalent in areas which in 1970 had significantly high black concentrations. Areas of low education/income, with an absence of sufficient housing space occasioned for the most part by the prevalence of children, seem to be characteristic environmental precursors to

* Poverty within the factor loaded negatively (—X— = +)

## EXHIBIT 5-20
### PARCEL COROLLARIES OF RESIDENTIAL TAX DELINQUENCY

DEPENDENT VARIABLE: TAX DELINQUENT STRUCTURES

| Variable Number | Variable Name | Regression Coefficient | F Statistic | F to Reject Randomness |
|---|---|---|---|---|
| 003 | ABSQAL | —0.195 | 13.67 | 2.74 |
| 022 | INDOWN | —0.101 | 3.88 | 2.74 |
| 004 | RELQAL | 0.091 | 2.75 | 2.74 |
| 017 | WELTEN | 0.100 | 4.09 | 2.74 |
| 014 | VACRAT | 0.128 | 2.91 | 2.74 |
| | | F = 0.10 | | |

Source: Newark Area Resurvey, spring 1972

## EXHIBIT 5-21
### STATIC ENVIRONMENTAL PRECURSORS OF RESIDENTIAL TAX DELINQUENCY

DEPENDENT VARIABLE: PERCENT STRUCTURES TAX DELINQUENT PER CENSUS TRACT

| Variable Number | Variable Name | Regression Coefficient | F Statistic | F to Reject Randomness |
|---|---|---|---|---|
| Factor 1 | Black poverty | —5.61 | 57.64 | 3.99 |
| Factor 2 | White affluence | —1.83 | 6.87 | 3.99 |
| | $R^2 = 0.50$ | F = 0.05 | | |

Source: Newark Area Resurvey, spring 1972

eventual tax delinquent neighborhoods. On the other hand, where income and education levels are high, there is an absence of tax delinquency.

## Environmental Corollaries (The Dynamic Case)

### *The Factored Set*

When one compares the dynamic predictors of tax delinquency to those previously analyzed for abandonment over an essentially similar building set, they appear identical both in direction of association and in order of importance (Exhibit 5-22).

Tax delinquency, like abandonment, is *less likely* to take place in areas whose decade change profile may be characterized as one of stability (high owner occupancy, housing value, percent married, percent foreign born); or of rejuvenation—areas of new, publicly assisted multi-unit construction which serve the female labor force.

Tax delinquency, on the other hand, is accentuated in areas whose change resembles one of age succession, i.e., heavy transition within oversized structures where the elderly occupant, frequently an owner, is replaced by a young, large family which often is a rental tenant. Tax delinquency is also accentuated by the staging phenomenon specifically associated with young blacks. Housing serving black families with large numbers of young children frequently is overcrowded; the structure experiences severe use and when income can no longer cover the cost of constant repair, payment of taxes ceases. The local property tax appears to be the expense most easily severed by the owner with the least jeopardy to his sustained flow of rental incomes.

## EXHIBIT 5-22
### DYNAMIC ENVIRONMENTAL PREDICTORS OF TAX DELINQUENCY: THE FACTORED VARIABLE SET

DEPENDENT VARIABLE: PERCENT STRUCTURES TAX DELINQUENT PER CENSUS TRACT

| Factor Number | Factor Name | Regression Coefficient | F Statistic | F to Reject Randomness |
|---|---|---|---|---|
| $X_5$ | Ethnic neighborhoods | —4.41 | 46.04 | 3.99 |
| $X_1$ | Age succession | —2.80 | 33.84 | 3.99 |
| $X_4$ | Black poverty | —2.14 | 20.33 | 3.99 |
| $X_6$ | Female employment | —2.82 | 18.76 | 3.99 |
| $X_3$ | Young blacks | 1.42 | 11.09 | 3.99 |
| | $R^2 = 0.69$ | $F = 0.05$ | | |

Source: Newark Area Resurvey, spring 1972

Finally, tax delinquency is accentuated in areas of black poverty. These areas are noted for both a preponderance of incomes below \$3,000 and an absence of incomes in excess of \$10,000.

The predictive equation which expresses the relationship between percent tax delinquency and the array of independent variables is detailed below:

$$\text{Percent Tax Delinquency} = 7.28—4.41X_5—2.80X_1—2.14X_4—2.82X_6 + 1.42X_3$$

where:

$X_1$ = Age Succession
$X_3$ = Young Blacks
$X_4$ = Black Poverty
$X_5$ = Housing Stability
$X_6$ = Female Employment

If one views this equation and also the subsequent one for abandonment, it may be seen that only in the case of the *housing stability* dimension is there any notable difference between the coefficients representing factored dynamic predictors of abandonment and those of tax delinquency. In this instance, for every unit increase in the Housing Stability factor, *residential abandonment decreases* by 7.8 percent whereas residential *tax delinquency* only *decreases* by 4.4 percent.

### The Unfactored Set

Using the unfactored set of variables in stepwise regression, after simple correlations of 0.80 or greater have been removed, nine variables exhibit statistically significant associations with tax delinquency at the F—0.05 level (Exhibit 5-23). This phenomenon, like abandonment, appears to be a function of neighborhood stability. Tax delinquency *decreases* in areas whose population exhibits both *high married percentages* and significant *concentrations of the elderly*. Similarly tax delinquency wanes in new, quasi-public, multi-family construction areas which house the female employed.

In reverse fashion, tax delinquency apparently *increases* in other low-end core areas. These are areas typified by massive multi-family demolitions which renders their single family percentages higher in 1970 than in 1960. These neighborhoods have also experienced significant private nonprofit residential development. Resulting cooperatives and high rise structures now house many of Newark's resident, young, black upward mobiles.

Finally, tax delinquency is also more prominent in neighborhoods which serve as a repository for the abject poor. This is evident in relationships of tax delinquency and low rent areas undergoing demolition.

In terms of prediction, the following equation shows tax delinquency to be a "best estimated" linear function of these previously discussed variables.

$$\text{Percent Tax Delinquency} = 10.0 - 16.1X_1 + 4.3X_2 - 5.8X_3 + 1.4X_4 - 9.3X_5 - 2.7X_6 - 8.0X_7 - 1.6X_8 - 3.3X_9$$

where:
$X_1$ = percent of the population married
$X_2$ = percent of the housing units single family
$X_3$ = median age female
$X_4$ = percent of the population with incomes >$10,000

## EXHIBIT 5-23
### DYNAMIC ENVIRONMENTAL PREDICTORS OF TAX DELINQUENCY: THE UNFACTORED VARIABLE SET

DEPENDENT VARIABLE: PERCENT STRUCTURES TAX DELINQUENT PER CENSUS TRACT

| Variable Number | Variable Name | Regression Coefficient | F Statistic | F to Reject Randomness |
|---|---|---|---|---|
| 012 ($X_1$) | Percent of the population married | —16.10 | 8.42 | 4.06 |
| 009 ($X_2$) | Percent of the housing units single family | 4.26 | 15.55 | 4.06 |
| 004 ($X_3$) | Median age female | — 5.78 | 5.78 | 4.06 |
| 029 ($X_4$) | Percent of the population with incomes over $10,000 | 1.42 | 7.99 | 4.06 |
| 016 ($X_5$) | Percent of the labor force female | — 9.27 | 5.99 | 4.06 |
| 005 ($X_6$) | Percent of the housing units with no bath or share | — 2.66 | 2.55 | 4.06 |
| 007 ($X_7$) | Median contract rent | — 7.95 | 5.34 | 4.06 |
| 006 ($X_8$) | Percent of the housing units with over 1.01 persons per room | — 1.62 | 4.33 | 4.06 |
| 011 ($X_9$) | Percent of the white population in excess of 65 years | — 3.28 | 4.07 | 4.06 |
| | $R^2 = 0.83$ | $F = 0.05$ | | |

Source: Newark Area Resurvey, spring 1972

$X_5$ = percent of the labor force female
$X_6$ = percent of the housing units with no bath or shower
$X_7$ = median contract rent
$X_8$ = percent of the housing units with >1.01 persons per room
$X_9$ = percent of the white population in excess of 65 years

When subsequently compared to the unfactored predictors of abandonment in Chapter 7, the two have four of eight dimensions in common at similar coefficient strength. Both abandonment and tax delinquency are reduced in areas of: high percent married, large elderly populations, and SRO neighborhoods. These two phenomena increase, however, in areas of considerable neighborhood change; most characteristically in neighborhoods where extensive multi-family demolition has taken place.

## The Relationship of Abandonment to Tax Delinquency

Exhibit 5-24, which compares tax delinquency and abandonment in selected cities other than Newark, reveals a lack of clear linkage between the two phenomena. For example, Detroit, St. Louis, and Washington, D. C., while evidencing a *growing* abandonment problem as of 1970, all reported *decreasing* tax delinquency in the period from 1965 to 1970. Gross statistics point to a closer relationship between levels of mortgage foreclosure and abandonment than between either tax delinquency and mortgage foreclosure or tax delinquency and abandonment.

Contributing to this apparent lack of association between tax delinquency and abandonment is the factor of the *time* at which tax delinquency is measured. If it is measured after municipal foreclosure, the parcels have already been removed from the category of taxable property; the effect is a reduction in the denominator (i.e., taxes levied) with a corresponding increase in the collection percentage. In municipalities allowing only a short period of redemption before municipal foreclosure many of the standing vacant properties may be classified as *abandoned* but they are not listed on municipal records as *tax delinquent*.

Also broadening the gap between tax delinquency and abandonment is the continued payment of taxes by an insured mortgagor (many secured by the FHA) even though the building is vacant and produces no income. This oversight may explain why Newark's increasing tax delinquency parallels its increasing abandonment, i.e., most of the abandoned structures are those without insured mortgages; the reverse is true in Detroit, where decreasing tax delinquency in the midst of increasing abandonment reflects a situation where most of the abandoned structures are insured and therefore continue to bring in tax revenues from the FHA.

In pursuing the relationship between abandonment and tax delinquency in Newark, one sees that, even here, by eliminating from

## EXHIBIT 5-24

### MORTGAGE FORECLOSURES (1970-1971) AND TAX COLLECTION PERCENTAGES (1965-1970) OF SELECTED CITIES

| Levels of Mortgage Foreclosure | Mortgage Foreclosures Per 100,000 Population and Tax Collection Percentages of Selected Cities | | | |
|---|---|---|---|---|
| | Mortgage Foreclosures (1970-1971) and Percentage Change from Previous Years† | | Tax Collection Percentages (1965 and 1970)‡ | |
| Areas in Excess of 400 (1970) | Mortgage Foreclosures in 1970 | Mortgage Foreclosures in 1971 | Tax Collection Percentage 1965 | Tax Collection Percentage 1970 |
| °Kansas City, Mo. | 637 (+17) | 650 (+ 2) | 97.8 | 97.6 |
| °Trenton, N.J. | 403 (+ 5) | 526 (+31) | — | — |
| °Philadelphia | 582 (+10) | 460 (—21) | 97.4 | 95.6 |
| °Detroit | 474 (+80) | 667 (+41) | 94.3 | 97.8 |
| Tulsa | 400 (+15) | 510 (+28) | 98.1 (1962) | 100.5 |
| Kansas City, Kansas | 406 (+29) | — | — | — |
| Areas with 200-400 (1970) | | | | |
| Indianapolis | 315 (+38) | 387 (+23) | 96.0 (1961) | 97.4 |
| °St. Louis | 240 (+17) | 251 (+ 5) | 92.5 (1962) | 94.7 |
| Oakland, Cal. | 206 (+19) | — | 98.5 (1969) | 97.4 |
| °Newark, N.J. | 201 — | 203 — | 89.4 | 87.4 |
| Richmond Borough, N.Y. | 329 (+ 6) | 159 (—32) | 95.6 | 95.0 |
| Areas with 100-200 (1970) | | | | |
| °Washington, D.C. | 182 (+14) | 141 (—23) | — | — |
| Toledo | 140 (+24) | 147 (+ 5) | 97.0 | 97.3 (1968) |
| °Brooklyn Borough, N.Y. | 102 (+24) | 105 (+ 3) | 95.6 | 95.0 |
| Syracuse, N.Y. | 129 (+34) | 108 (—16) | — | — |
| Elizabeth, N.J. | 147 (+ 7) | 151 (+ 3) | — | — |

Note: Cities preceded by an asterisk (°) are those that indicated an increasing problem with residential abandonment in their response to the Rutgers Center for Urban Policy Research Survey (1968).

Sources: (†) Roy Wenzlick Research Corp., *The Real Estate Analyst 1970-1971.*
(‡) *Moody's Municipal and Government Manual*, 1972.

consideration those abandoned parcels whose taxes are continuing to be paid by FHA, *an abandoned property is likely to be a tax delinquent property in at least two out of every three cases.*

## CONCLUSIONS

Previous analyses have shown that tax delinquency is a growing urban phenomenon, at least in the Northeastern and Midwestern areas of this country. The hypothesis of a definite link between abandonment and tax delinquency will be tentatively established by demonstrating the widespread existence of delinquency as a precursor to residential abandonment. Finally, the disinterest of private investors in core-city delinquent parcels has been demonstrated and some of the reasons for the lack of private investor participation have been explored.

The salient conclusion from all of the foregoing is that the city, through tax default, is becoming the unwilling owner of an increasing share of urban realty. Since the city ultimately steps in to purchase abandoned structures, it unwittingly encourages owners to *destroy through nonimprovement.* In other words, tax delinquency becomes the incentive for abandonment.

Through tax delinquency the landlord is in effect guaranteed a selling price equal to or greater than he could obtain through the private market. A landlord stands to benefit further by failing to improve his property, thereby being able to pocket the savings. Specifically, there is no indication that a well-maintained property in Newark would bring its owner substantially more money than a property in a state of disrepair. Why then should a landlord bother maintaining a property for ultimate sale if he knows that only a limited market exists and that he can do as well in an unlimited market (municipal purchase) with no further outlay of cash for improvements?

If the city were to accelerate the process whereby abandoned parcels are acquired, it could at least reduce its acquisition cost. If speedy demolition were to accompany this procedure, the city could further improve its position; instead of deriving no revenue from a parcel and having to provide services it would still derive no revenue but it would no longer have to provide services.

# ASPECTS OF THE TAX DELINQUENCY PROCESS

## ADMINISTRATIVE PROCESS

The administrative process which the municipal authority undergoes prior to an annual tax sale (November 1971) is to group all properties missing any single or combination of the February, May, August, or November 1970 tax payment dates for the previous tax period.

Delinquent owners are sent letters of notice and lists of parcels are published at multiple instances prior to tax sale.

If there is no interest on the part of the owner to bring taxes up to date, a lien on the parcel is sold at tax sale. Whether the parcel is purchased privately or by the city, the former owner is allowed a redemption period prior to the initiation of foreclosure procedures. Once foreclosure takes its course and the parcel is sold at sheriff's sale, an additional brief redemption period remains; however, for all practical purposes the former owner has lost all interest in the property.

Currently in Newark about 800 parcels, or 2 percent of the city's residential/nonresidential stock, are sold for tax purposes each year. When the list of tax delinquent parcels is initially published it may contain as many as 3,000 parcels. In the course of the preceding and following procedures the list is reduced to approximately one-fourth of its original total.

The written procedures for owner notification of outstanding tax delinquency leading to tax sale are city-originated letters sent in September and early November preceding a scheduled tax sale in late November. These letters contain a description of the property, the amount of outstanding taxes for which the property will be sold, the date of tax sale, and the procedures to be followed to avoid lien purchase.

In late October through mid-November the property is additionally advertised in local newspapers with similar information, once a week for four consecutive weeks.

Following the date of tax sale the owner has an additional ten days to forestall lien purchase. If the property is reclaimed subsequent to this period the owner must currently pay 8 percent annual interest on the amount of the lien up to $1,000 and 12 percent annually on that portion in excess of $1,000. An additional $5 is charged for administrative costs associated with lien processing. If the lien is purchased at tax sale by someone other than the city, however, the maximum allowable annual interest rate chargeable to the original owner by the lien purchaser is 8 percent. Competing potential purchasers may bid this rate downward.

If the property's taxes are brought up to date within the specified time period the costs to the previously delinquent owner are a similar "8-12" interest charge and $5 processing fee. Thus, other than the credit stigma of having real property officially sold for tax purposes, the owner receives no more financial censure for allowing his property to run the gamut of municipal operations through tax sale than he would by immediately reclaiming his property once delinquent.

## Generalizations

Exhibit 5-25 indicates the lengthy and expensive legal processes that dissuade private investors from purchasing tax title liens. In the specific example at hand a residential parcel assessed at $15,000 with a sales to assessment ratio of 0.40 (based on sales of 150 buildings within the sample set over the period 1964 to 1971) is worth $6,000 if acquired through the private market. Via the tax title acquisition procedure, it will cost the purchaser at least 25 percent more and will entail an additional time input of four and one-half years to secure the property.

Not only does this system afford no cash benefit to tax sale purchasers, but it necessitates the endurance by the new owner of a four-to-five year waiting period before being able to exercise full rights to the property. The waiting period is largely a legacy of the 1930s when foreclosure moratoriums were enacted, statutory periods for redemption were introduced or lengthened, and other foreclosure delaying procedures and requirements were adopted, basically for the mortgagor's protection.[2]

Today in core areas parcels are being abandoned by the owner, not taken from him. Yet the same set of laws which once protected his remaining interest now binds him to a property that he finds an encumbrance. The effect of the law in this instance may actually diminish any remaining private interest in center-city land development.[3]

## EXHIBIT 5-25
## COSTS TO THE LIEN HOLDER OF A PROPERTY BOUGHT AT TAX SALE, NEWARK, 1972

| | *In-Persona* Foreclosure Process | |
|---|---|---|
| Date | Delinquency, Tax Sale, and Foreclosure Actions | Cost to Lien Holder |
| November 1969 | Property* becomes delinquent | |
| November 1971 | Tax sale is held† and private tax lien purchaser pays 1970 delinquent taxes, "8-12" interest rate, and processing fee | $1,309 |
| November 1971 | To keep tax lien current tax lien purchaser pays 1971 taxes at escalating rate | $1,320 |
| November 1971 — November 1973 | Tax lien purchaser pays escalating property taxes during two-year period of redemption | $3,049 |
| November 1973 — May 1974 | *In persona* foreclosure proceedings are conducted entailing a legal expense of $1,000. The procedure takes six months and the tax lien purchaser additionally pays property taxes for one-half year. | $1,878 |
| | Total | $7,556 |

*Two and one half frame, two-family dwelling. Assessed value $15,000 annual property tax $1,200.

†New Jersey law requires, before a tax sale can be held, at least a six-month waiting period after the close of the calendar year in which levied taxes became delinquent.

Source: Newark Tax Collection Department, spring 1972

Referring again to Exhibit 5-25, if an owner loses interest in a residential parcel and misses any payment of taxes during 1970, his property is placed on the list for tax sale in November 1971. Assuming the owner missed paying all 1970 taxes,° the cost to the tax title lien holder at step 1 would be one year's taxes plus interest of 8 percent (12 percent over $1,000) and a $5 processing fee. In this case $1,200 + $104 + $5 = $1,309.

In order to maintain his interest in the property, the private lien holder must bring any outstanding 1971 taxes up to date. If he neglects to do this, the property would be sold again the following year for 1971 tax nonpayment and the new purchaser would have the same interest in the property as the prior lien holder. At this juncture (step two) the lien holder must pay $1,320, another full year's taxes (This higher figure reflects an estimate of an average annual property tax increase of 10 percent in Newark). His total financial input to date is $2,629. The private lien holder then enters a mandatory two-year redemption period (step three) before *in-persona* foreclosure procedures may begin.

This waiting period costs the lien purchaser two years' taxes at an increasing rate or an additional $3,049. At this point he has spent $5,678 and four years have passed since the owner last paid taxes on his property. Still the private lien purchaser cannot maintain or improve the property at his own expense except with the permission of the tax delinquent owner.[4]

The final six month foreclosure period costs the lien holder another half year in taxes — $878 — plus $1,000 in litigation fees. At the end of four and one-half years the private lien holder has paid $7,556 for a property which could have been purchased for $6,000 via conventional acquisition with unencumbered title passing within two weeks. In terms of initial equity, under conventional financing with 20 percent down payment, $1,200 is invested initially giving the owner full rights to the property. In the case of lien purchase, the 100 percent down payment invested over time, allows the lien holder no property rights.[5] [6]

---

°Taxes in Newark may be paid quarterly (February, May, August, and November). For our definition and in accordance with city hall recordkeeping procedures, two quarters equal one period of tax arrears.

Given the decline in capital value of central city property it no longer remains necessary to speculate why urban tax delinquent parcels remain unclaimed.

## WHY TAX DELINQUENCY OCCURS: COST/BENEFIT TO THOSE WHO PURCHASE TAX DELINQUENT PROPERTIES

### The Extent of Cash Flow Available to Residential Property Owners

Exhibit 5-26 depicts the typical cash flow posture of a two-family parcel in Newark. The two and one-half story frame dwelling is held by a nonresident owner. Each of its two apartments provides a monthly rental of $140, for a total annual income of $3,360.

Annual expenses assume a 1967 mortgage with 6 percent/thirty-year terms on a principal of $13,500. Water, electricity, heating, and maintenance are assumed to be paid by the landlord.

Another assumption is that the residential structure carries hazard insurance available from the local insurance pool (FAIR) at an annual cost of approximately $300 for a two-family structure mortgaged to 90 percent of a $15,000 appraised value. Even in the absence of hazard insurance the owner would be unlikely to receive a positive annual return since the full occupancy and 100 percent rent collections assumed in the example are both improbable in Newark's current rental market.

These income/expense indices point to the impossibility of the continuation of this cash flow picture. Yet the owner has few avenues of escape; buyers for residential properties within core areas cannot be found and $1,000-$2,000 demolition costs for a frame dwelling eliminate all hopes of turning the structure over for even a limited return. As a matter of fact, the property cannot even be given away as deeding to the city incurs a mandatory $200 fee in addition to proof of unencumbered title.

It does not seem unreasonable in light of these obstacles for an owner to transfer title to a dummy corporation. Such a transfer effectively removes the owner from both the potential liability resulting from hazards within the structure and from the additional liability accompanying continuous violation of multiple code standards. Furthermore, fraudulent transfer may even prove to be an avenue of eventual investment return, for if a personal mortgage is given on an inflated "paper" sale, upon default the amount of the mortgage may be deducted by the former owner as a bad debt loss.

EXHIBIT 5-26

CASH FLOW OF A TYPICAL RESIDENTIAL PROPERTY°
NEWARK (1972)

| | |
|---|---|
| INCOME | |
| Two Apts. @ $140/mo (assuming no vacancy) | $3,360/yr |
| EXPENSES | |
| Amortization/interest (6 percent, thirty yrs $13,500) | $ 930 |
| Maintenance | 200 |
| Heating | 400 |
| Insurance (risk pool) | 300 |
| Electricity | 290 |
| Water | 40 |
| | $2,160/yr |
| CASH FLOW (before taxes) | +$1,200 |
| Annual property tax | 1,200 |
| Net cash flow | 0 |

°Two and one-half story frame dwelling, two-family nonresident owner, parcel assessed value $15,000, market value $6,000,†, annual property tax $1,200.
†Sales/Assessment Ratio 0.40 (Noninsured Property Turnovers 1964-1972)
Demolition costs $1,500

Source: Newark Tax Department, spring 1972.

# NOTES

1. For a similar problem in New York, see: Edward S. Godfrey "Enforcement of Delinquent Property Taxes in New York," *Albany Law Review*, Vol. 24 (June, 1960), 271-316; 25 (January, 1961), 39-66; (June, 1961), 212-237; 26 (June, 1962), 201-230.

2. See H. K. Allen "Collection of Delinquent Taxes by Recourse to the Taxed Property" *Law and Contemporary Problems* 3 (June 1936), 397-405; Herbert D. Simpson "Tax Delinquency," *Illinois Law Review*, Vol. 28 (June 1933), 147-176; Frederick L. Bird "Extent and Distribution of Urban Tax Delinquency," *Law and Contemporary Problems*, 3 (July 1936), 337-346; Wade S. Smith "Recent Legislative Indulgences to Delinquent Taxpayers" *Law and Contemporary Problems*, 3 (July 1936), 371-381; for those who think this era is not over, see: Howard C. Emmerman "Revenue and Taxation — Collection of Delinquent Real Estate Taxes — Legislating Protection of the Delinquent Property Owner in an Era of Super-Marketable Tax Titles," *De Paul Law Review* Vol. XIX (1969), 348-376.

3. William J. Legg "Tax Sales and the Constitution," *Oklahoma Law Review*, 20 (November, 1967), 365-379.

4. What can the owner do and how good is title? See: George E. Harbert "Tax Foreclosures and Tax Titles" *University of Illinois Law Forum* (Summer 1952), 209-225; Richard E. Young "The Tax Deed — Modern Movement Towards Respectability," *Rocky Mountain Law Review* 34 (1962), 181-197.

5. See Charles Handler "In Rem Tax Foreclosure in New Jersey," *Municipalities and the Law in Action* NIMLO (1951), 290-295.

6. For model tax collection laws under varying priorities, see: Henry Brandis, Jr. "Tax Sales and Foreclosure under the Model Tax Collection Law," *Law and Contemporary Problems* 3 (June 1936), 406-415; Roger J. Traynor, "Legislation — The Model Real Property Tax Collection Law," *California Law Review* 24 (1935-1936), 98-107.

APPLIANCES
SNOW ROUTE
NO PARKING

FOUNTAIN SERVICE
DRINK
Coca-Cola
WE INSTALL
RADIATORS
REPAIRED
Coca-Cola

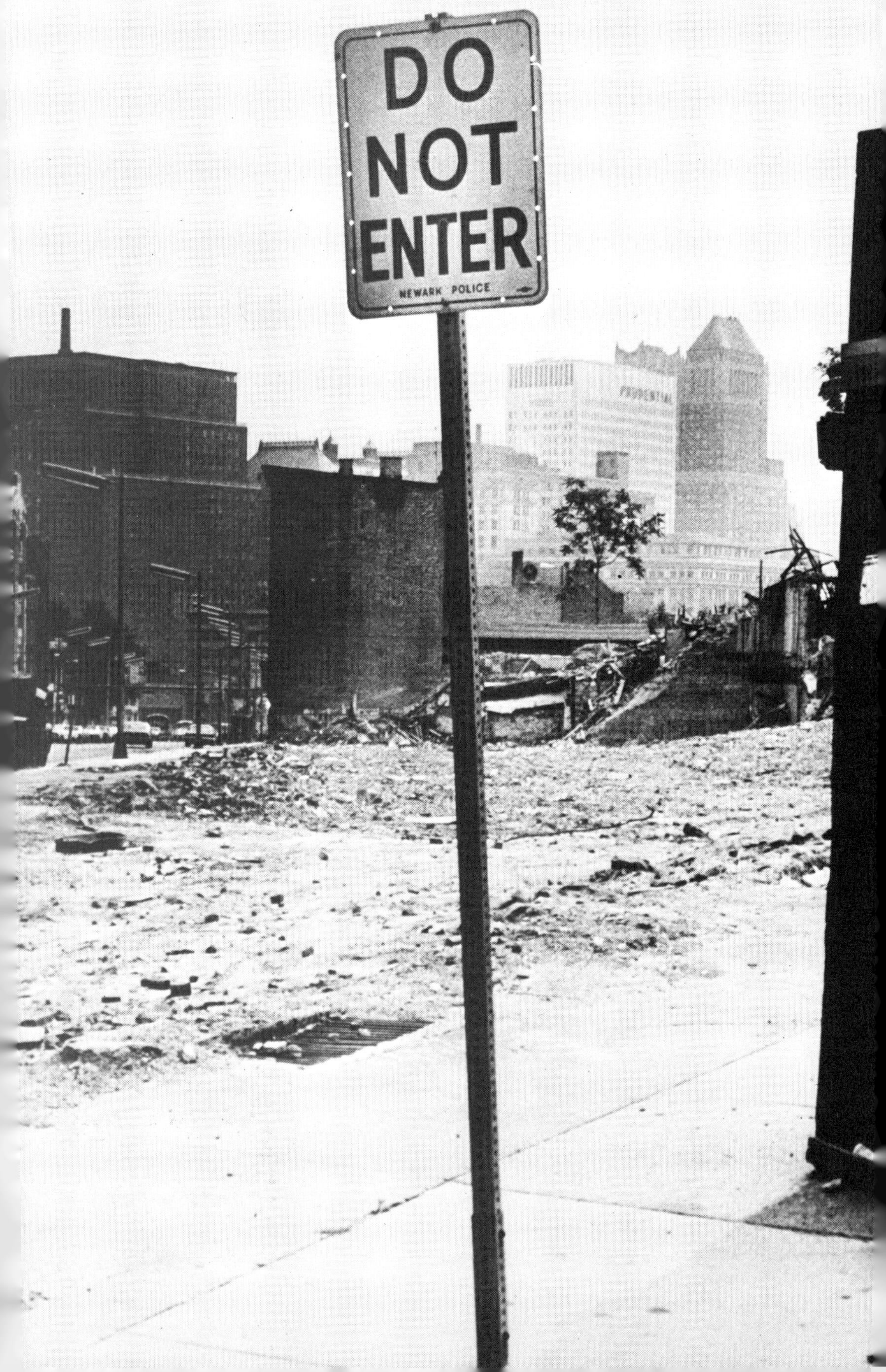
DO
NOT
ENTER
NEWARK POLICE
PRUDENTIAL

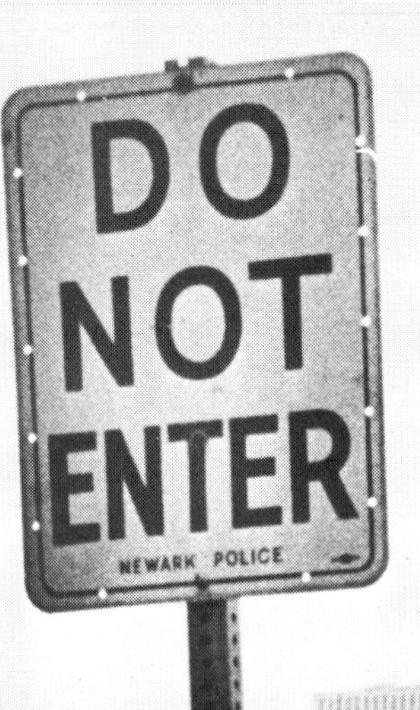

# 6

# THE "LOW-END" REAL ESTATE SECTOR

The availability of institutional financing is one of the major determinants of the health and vitality of the real estate market. If the banks, savings and loan companies, insurance companies, and the like are willing to lend in an area, then owners can have confidence that their investments in properties are redeemable through ultimate resale or remortgaging. Without this assurance, landlords become locked-in; they know that capital improvements and investment will add little to the ultimate value of their properties; they may very well view even positive cash flows and operating profits from their properties as nothing more than the liquidation of capital values. The latter without financing are simply not redeemable.

## BACKGROUND

### The Role of Purchase Money Mortgages

The vacuum left by the departure of institutional financing is filled only by so-called purchase money mortgages. These are mortgages typically granted by the seller in order to facilitate the sale. In the course of interviews when owners were asked whether they could get an appropriate return on capital improvements on resale, even those who answered in the positive pointed to the necessity of taking back a purchase money mortgage. As one professional operator pointed out, "You get a little cash and a lot of paper. And who wants paper? Particularly when the collateral is buildings in these areas."

The owner who has paid down an outstanding institutional mortgage may not want to sell. He may be entirely satisfied with the operation of his building, but want to reclaim some of the equity he has built up in the course of reducing his mortgage. The usual process is for such an individual to remortgage his building, not infrequently with the same bank which holds the remnant of the older indenture.

If there is no institution which is willing to go through this process, the landlord's investment is locked into the building. It is very easy to see how the feeling can evolve that the only way to secure the return of this investment is by decreasing improvements and by slowly draining the building of its capital value through poor maintenance procedures and generalized exploitation.

Potential buyers of such properties fall into two categories, the first are the speculators interested only in minimizing their cash investment and insistent on the balance being made up by purchase money mortgages; these the extant owner must fear since they have no personal liability for the loans which they require, and may very well completely ravage the building which serves as collateral on the purchase money mortgage. The second category are people who may have very limited options on where they can invest, and where they can find resident ownership. These typically are members of the minority groups. Since conventional financing frequently is not available in these areas, it is federally insured or guaranteed loans which permit this packaging. This process will be examined later in some detail in this chapter.

The case in Newark is a very simple one. The institutions are fleeing the market. Presently it is individual guarantees and private owners that bulk most large in Area 1 with 57.2 percent of the extant mortgages as compared with 44.4 percent of the Area 2 mortgages, and 38.5 percent of the Area 3 mortgages (Exhibit 6-1). It is only in these latter two areas that savings and loan companies and banks begin to make some significant presence felt.

Depressing as the data are, they understate the present reality. Mortgages typically are written for lengthy periods of time; many of the extant mortgages, for example, date back more than a decade. Of more significance is the present potential for institutional financing by area. As indicated in Exhibit 6-2, only 14.1 percent (less than one in seven) of the parcel owners in Area 1 felt they could get institutional mortgaging on a present sale of their sample property. This compares with one out

EXHIBIT 6-1
MORTGAGE SOURCE FOR RESIDENTIAL PARCELS BY AREA

| MORTGAGE SOURCE | Area 1 | Area 2 | Area 3 | Total |
|---|---|---|---|---|
| Banks | 0 | 11 | 8 | 19 |
| Mortgage company | 1 | 7 | 9 | 17 |
| Insurance company | 1 | 1 | 0 | 2 |
| Prior owner | 4 | 11 | 14 | 29 |
| Individual | 2 | 4 | 2 | 8 |
| TOTAL | 8 | 34 | 33 | 75 |

Source: Newark Area Resurvey, spring 1972.

of three of the owners in Area 2, and nearly that same proportion in Area 3. Conversely, 59 percent of the owners in Area 1, as compared with 35.6 percent of the owners in Area 2, and 24.8 percent in Area 3, said they definitely could *not* get institutional mortgages.

## Owner Knowledge of Financing Possibilities

The responses to a later series of questions on possible terms, length of mortgages, and the like, revealed that the potential for any form of substantial financing was so vague that owners were quite unfamiliar with what might be secured. More than half the black owners, for example, weren't sure what interest rates they would have to pay for improvement money — 54.9 percent, as compared with 43.3 percent of the whites. Nearly four out of five of the blacks (77.9 percent) and two-thirds of the whites had no idea of the length of terms they could secure on borrowing. The few positive responses clustered at the three- to five-year level.

About a quarter of the black respondents believe that if they had to make improvements they would use their own resources. This answer was given by 47.4 percent of the whites. A fifth of the total group said that they simply would not know where to turn if they needed money for improvements.

It is interesting in this context to note that statements about prejudice on the part of lenders were volunteered much more frequently by whites than by blacks. The former felt that what few

## EXHIBIT 6-2

### 1971 OWNER'S VIEW AS TO POTENTIAL FOR ACQUIRING A MORTGAGE FROM A LENDING INSTITUTION BY SAMPLE AREA OF THE CITY (1971)

| Are You Able To Obtain A Mortgage? | Area 1 | Area 2 | Area 3 | Total |
|---|---|---|---|---|
| Yes, easy to get | 3 | 9 | 11 | 23 |
| Yes, but with difficulty | 2 | 5 | 4 | 11 |
| Yes | 6 | 25 | 22 | 53 |
| Could go either way | 2 | 6 | 12 | 20 |
| Doubt it | 4 | 6 | 6 | 16 |
| Definitely not | 46 | 42 | 29 | 117 |
| Other | 0 | 0 | 1 | 1 |
| NA | 3 | 2 | 0 | 5 |
| DK | 12 | 23 | 32 | 67 |
| Total | 78 | 118 | 117 | 313 |

PERCENT DISTRIBUTION

| | Area 1 | Area 2 | Area 3 | Total |
|---|---|---|---|---|
| Yes, easy to get | 3.8 | 7.6 | 9.4 | 7.3 |
| Yes, but with difficulty | 2.6 | 4.2 | 3.4 | 3.5 |
| Yes | 7.7 | 21.2 | 18.8 | 16.9 |
| Could go either way | 2.6 | 5.1 | 10.3 | 6.4 |
| Doubt it | 5.1 | 5.1 | 5.1 | 5.1 |
| Definitely not | 59.0 | 35.6 | 24.8 | 37.4 |
| Other | 0.0 | 0.0 | 0.9 | 0.3 |
| NA | 3.8 | 1.7 | 0.0 | 1.6 |
| DK | 15.4 | 19.5 | 27.4 | 21.4 |
| Total | 100.0 | 100.0 | 100.0 | 100.0 |

$\chi^2 = 0.01$

Source: Newark Area Resurvey, spring 1972.

mortgages were available were more easily secured by black owners, particularly through the FACE Rehabilitation Program. In any case, certainly neither group was at all sanguine about the potential for this vital input.

## Would They Borrow?

It should be made clear here that the mere availability of financing is a necessary but not sufficient condition to get the market moving. It must be coupled with owners' energy and drive to improve their holdings. *Owners in areas for which they see no future are not owners who are going to invest, regardless of the availability of money.*

It is sometimes difficult to evaluate an owner's response on financing. One operator of a rooming house purchased in 1968 said, when asked whether he would improve his property if he were given a long term mortgage, "No, absolutely not, it doesn't need improvement. I'd never get my money back." Which is the governing condition: the adequate quality of the parcel or is it merely that the future prospects are so bleak?

The fear of going into debt and the crumbling market are not the sole prerogatives of small owners.

> Parcel number 60 is a twenty-family, brick and frame structure on a major traffic artery owned by a substantial realty operator headquartered in Florida. It has been in the same hands since the 1930s. The owner, when questioned as to whether he would make repairs given a mortgage, said, "We're of the old school. This parcel isn't going anyplace. We can hang on to it as long as we don't have a mortgage to service."

Again it should be noted that later in the interview he said that regardless of his desires, there was no institutional financing available in the area in which he was located.

In the material which follows, analysis is undertaken of the realities both of involvement and of attitude on the part of the housing finance institutions of the city. Attention is focused on the roles of realtors, of financial institutions, of individuals and mortgage companies in the process. The role of the speculator and the major governmental programs extant at the time of the interviews — 235 and 236 — will be touched on in some detail.

## HOUSING FINANCE INSTITUTIONS

This portion of the study is devoted to an overview of inner-city mortgage practices. An open ended interview technique was used in the spring of 1972 with the firms who do the bulk of real estate transactions and mortgage lending in Newark's core as reported by the annual summaries of the *Essex County Real Estate Directory*.[1] In essence, these companies represent a sampling of Newark's housing finance sector. They are composed of nine real estate agencies, ten savings and loan associations, mutual savings and commercial banks, a major insurance company, and eight mortgage companies. They are joined in support by regional HUD-FHA offices and to a limited extent by the housing counseling agencies of local charitable and other public groups.

The questionnaire probed trends in types of mortgage financing available to prospective urban homeowners and was specifically directed to different stages of the home purchase process. Information giving a prospective of both past and present conditions of the local real estate market was obtained.

### The Housing Finance Sector

The members of the local housing finance sector are those firms responsible for the location, sale, and financing of both single and multi-family residential units. It is usually made up of a realtor who brings buyer and seller together within mutually acceptable financial parameters and an institutional lender, i.e., a savings and loan, savings bank, commercial bank, or a mortgage company, which makes possible the mortgage indenture.[2]

#### *Realtors*

The realtor, besides bringing prospective buyers and willing sellers together, additionally may help the buyer by providing assistance in obtaining a mortgage through a primary mortgage source with whom he (the realtor) may have a long-standing relationship. In Newark three or four realtors dominate the low-end housing market. Their *For Sale* signs dot the neighborhoods and sometimes seem to dominate whole blocks. It is not unusual for a single parcel to have two or three signs of different realtors. Nor is it surprising to find realtors' signs on a parcel which is abandoned; the result of an owner who could no longer wait for a buyer and had to walk away from his property. The parcel then may have been gutted by fire originated by a "squatter," transient, drug addict, or young vandal who may have set the building ablaze by accident or design.

To say the least, the real estate business in Newark is not one of growth or vitality; few of the realtors interviewed claimed increasing sales for the period since 1967, the year of the riots. It is much more likely for realtors to claim barely equal or decreased volume compared with pre-1967. Many of Newark's realtors now supplement their business in the nearby communities of the Oranges, Irvington, Maplewood, and the Belleville-Bloomfield area.

### *Financial Institution Lenders*

Primary lenders, those providing the initial mortgage indenture, are divided into several groups: savings and loan associations, mutual savings banks, commercial banks, insurance companies, pension funds, mortgage companies, and a few other groups. This study, as a reflection of demonstrated lending patterns, will concern itself with two financing sources: banks and mortgage companies.

The essential difference between these two groups is found in the areas of processing of mortgages and maintenance of mortgage portfolios. Banks traditionally have been reluctant to initiate FHA/VA insured mortgages because of the intricacies of processing and additionally because they retain most of the mortgages they originate and are concerned with increased rates of default. Conventional, uninsured, suburban mortgages, those with traditional 20 percent down payments are welcomed by banking institutions, who process and retain these mortgages in their investment portfolios.

Mortgage companies specialize in a type of processing the primary lenders prefer not to do. The mortgage company is a financial service specializing in the processing and subsequent sale of insured mortgage indentures. They do not maintain mortgage investment portfolios, but rather sell these mortgages to secondary financial institutions.

Exhibit 6-3 shows Newark's mortgage patterns for a ten-year span over the period 1961 to 1971. The basic pace of the market has slowed drastically. Far fewer mortgages are being initiated regardless of their source. Within this declining sphere there has been a reversal of positions by banking institutions and mortgage companies in terms of the proportion of total mortgage loans processed. Since the mid-sixties

## EXHIBIT 6-3
## RESIDENTIAL/NONRESIDENTIAL MORTGAGES ISSUED IN NEWARK (1961-1971) BY TYPE OF LENDING INSTITUTION

| Fiscal Year | Savings & Loan, Mutual Savings, Commercial Banks (1) | Mortgage Companies (2) | Insurance Companies (3) | Individuals (4) | Total (1-4) |
|---|---|---|---|---|---|
| 1961-1962 | 2,685 | 202 | 23 | 1,591 | 4,501 |
| 1963 | 1,280 | 535 | 11 | 1,049 | 2,875 |
| 1964 | 1,556 | 413 | 8 | 975 | 2,652 |
| 1965 | 1,428 | 338 | 10 | 834 | 2,610 |
| 1966 | 1,211 | 353 | 7 | 751 | 2,322 |
| 1967 | 512 | 455 | 2 | 791 | 1,760 |
| 1968 | 495 | 685 | 4 | 655 | 1,839 |
| 1969 | 468 | 1,012 | 8 | 580 | 2,068 |
| 1970 | 417 | 1,298 | 7 | 425 | 2,147 |
| 1971 | 316 | 1,097 | 6 | 337 | 1,756 |

Source: *Essex County Real Estate Directory*, Annual Summaries Section, 1961-1971.

savings and loans, mutual savings, and commercial banks have lost their position as the number one mortgage lenders in the city, and have been replaced by mortgage companies as a source of funds. Also evident is a noted reluctance on the part of individuals to take back mortgages.

### *Savings and Loans*

The trends appear to be the result of two factors: the first is the declining social and physical environment in which housing in Newark is located, the second is a reported change in lending policy by the FHA. In the first case banking institutions have suffered substantial financial losses on mortgage investments due to the general decline of property values in Newark. Additionally, the period after the 1967 riot was characterized by numerous withdrawals from institutions' demand deposit accounts upon which residential mortgage loans would have normally been originated. Through conventional practice Newark savings and loan associations retained their originated mortgages in their investment portfolios; the bulk of these mortgages being on Newark properties. Subsequent defaults on mortgages and eventual abandonment of properties saw many of Newark's savings and loans retaining wasting assets. Additionally, the withdrawal of funds severely limited the number of mortgages the savings and loans could potentially initiate in local suburban areas. The situation became acute, ultimately forcing several of the larger institutions to borrow from the Federal Home Loan Bank and the smaller ones, facing both existing insolvency and eventual bankruptcy, to merge with larger institutions.

At this point in time many savings and loan associations had to reappraise their lending practices. Policy changes involved the marketing of services in suburban areas and the reduction of risk by simultaneously limiting loans in the Newark area. For example, one savings and loan in 1965 had over 800 Newark residential mortgages in its portfolio. Today it has only 400. Another savings and loan located in what was once a predominantly middle class Jewish neighborhood has only begun to recover from the problems it faced during the last five years. It has, however, changed its locus of operations from Newark to an upper middle class suburban area a half hour away from the city.

> Parcel number 584 illustrates the attitude of the lending officer of one major savings and loan association in Newark toward investing there. This is a four-story, masonry, eight-family house that has just been foreclosed by a savings and loan association on

> the basis of its mortgage. The owner had gone into default. A loan officer said: "He had problems collecting rents from his tenants. The situation is getting worse; the reason is that when an apartment becomes vacant the drug addicts move in and their habits force other tenants out and there are a large number of drug addicts in the area. . . . The owners are forced to let their properties go back to the bank because they simply don't have enough money to make improvements in the face of violations."
>
> When the official was asked how much of a rent increase he would need to make the parcel a good investment, he stated, "Nothing is going to help here, there is too much to be done. Basically there is no improvement money for this kind of parcel. The Newark situation is continuing to degenerate."

And this portrait could be replicated in dismal detail over and over again. Another example is the attitude of the lending officer of yet another savings and loan toward an abandoned building which they have just foreclosed because of a default on payments.

> This is parcel number 593. It is a three-story, three-family frame building. The owner said: "It was empty when we got it. We have a conventional mortgage, no guarantee. We tried to give it to the city but they wouldn't take it. At the moment we're keeping up the taxes, but we are about ready to rip down the building, there is no point to it. We tried to sell it; there are no buyers. We're going to take a $17,000 bath."

In the group of local savings and loans, one exception to this general trend was noted. The institution is located in the "Ironbound" area, a peninsula-like area bordered by Newark's neighboring communities on three sides, and set off from the rest of Newark by the Penn Central railroad tracks. Its current inhabitants are largely of Spanish, Portuguese, and Eastern European ethnic origin. Its shopping area remains essentially vital, its residential streets are perceptibly cleaner, and its crime rate one of the lowest in the city. The manager of the savings and loan which services only the Ironbound area reported that conventional mortgages rather than FHA/VA insured mortgages are standard practices. He pointed out that there is a market for housing in this sub-community with enough vigor to ensure both the maintenance of value and regular repairs. This is the one area of the city which has a significant surge in the number of recent nongovernment guaranteed mortgages.

### *Mutual Savings Banks*

An interview with an officer of a major mutual savings bank in New Jersey, a primary mortgage source, characterized the position of this type of institution. Much like the savings and loans, its lending activities are restricted by law. The mutual savings bank, however, is permitted more diversity than the savings and loans and has committed more funds to industrial, commercial and institutional, and nonresidential investments. This particular bank was reluctant to process its own FHA/VA mortgages, preferring instead to buy packages of processed residential mortgages from mortgage companies. When the bank had funds it wanted to invest, in order to maintain a particular portfolio balance, it called upon several mortgage correspondents to supply packages of mortgages purchased at discount/volume rates. Other elements of its investment portfolios were multi-million dollar nonresidential commitments encompassing hospitals, religious institutions, shopping centers, and industrial complexes, most of which are located outside of Newark. On the whole the mutual savings bank's lending structure seems to enable the institution to be better balanced and better able to pit higher risks against essentially stable investments.

### *Insurance Companies*

The insurance company included in the interviews, which is the only one active in Newark residential lending, had an investment policy of not lending money from insurance premiums on single family mortgage loans. It confined itself to the development of community facilities and multi-family dwellings; an area where it felt it played a significant role in helping a city to "come back."

In 1970 the company granted mortgages to seven multi-family projects, promoted by churches and limited dividend companies, totaling 570 dwelling units. It has also been granting mortgages to a nonprofit sectarian agency which rehabilitates houses insured by this company.

This respondent had committed the largest single amount, i.e., $300 million, to the insurance industry's billion dollar urban commitment.[3] Of that sum, $10 million was committed to encouraging homeownership amongst low income persons in Northern New Jersey core areas. The money was to purchase mortgages for one-to-four-family residences within these urban areas. A three-year agreement was drawn up between the insurance company and a mortgage company which would first process and then sell the mortgages to the insurance company. Of the $10 million commitment, only 80 percent of the funds could be allocated, as the insurance company could not continue as a competitive buyer. The point structure became more than the company could pay for the mortgage investments. Of the mortgages that were purchased, the insurance company initially experienced a high mortgage default rate (5 percent) but now the rate has dropped to the point where the remaining mortgages are as stable as most other residential commitments (3 percent default rate).

### *Individuals*

Another category of lender is that of an individual granting a mortgage. Usually it is done by a landlord or homeowner who is anxious to "get out from under" his parcel. It occurs when a potential buyer is present but a mortgage from an institutional lender or secondary source is either unavailable or of inadequate size. The owner of the parcel, seeing the chance to rid himself of a no longer desired asset with at least partial financial return (the other alternative now appears increasingly to be abandonment), grants the prospective buyer a mortgage. The risk is great because of the problems of both property and neighborhood. In addition, the cash exchange is frequently nominal. The mortgage reflects this risk by usually having a face value greater than what the local market would normally bring.

The "kited" mortgage, in its most legitimate sense, has a face value greater than the market value of the property, because the usury laws of the state under certain stipulations limit the amount of interest that can be charged regardless of lending risk. The inflated face of the mortgage, therefore, represents a realistic capitalization of the limited dependability of the collateral of the property involved. In the less than legitimate situation there is an inflated price *with no reasonable bounds*. This is the case in some of the federal guaranteed indentures discussed here as well as some of the nominal transfers discussed earlier. Even when institutional mortgages are available, the proportion of the transfer price which the lender is willing to extend is small. The semi-institutionalized second mortgage has disappeared from the urban scene, notwithstanding potential gains available to individual lenders. Purchase money mortgages, therefore, are required to fill the vacuum.

### *Mortgage Companies*

FHA's policy of mortgage commitment to urban areas under reduced credit standards has probably benefited mortgage companies as a group more than any other primary lender. Actual and potential volume has increased for the mortgage company since the bulk of mortgages on one-to-four family homes in the urban core must be insured to be marketable. The mortgage companies' specialization in the processing of FHA/VA mortgage loan applications, their ability to pass along these higher risk mortgages to the secondary market rather than retain them, and finally, their quickly-growing economies of scale have given institutional lenders reasons not to enter the government insured mortgage area directly. The mortgage company, thus, is also an integral part of the low-end housing finance sector — the link between the seller and prospective buyer of a core-area home and the investment portfolio of a large financial institution or the secondary market.

## THE OPERATION AND COST/REVENUE ASPECTS OF MORTGAGE COMPANIES

The mortgage company is typical of the growing American service sector. Its capital requirements are moderate, its labor demands intensive with volume production the key to success. The mortgage company's only essential financial assets are the dollars necessary to provide interim initial commitments for mortgages held by the company before subsequent reimbursement through sale to large financial institutions in whose portfolios the mortgages ultimately reside. The mortgage company's liability is also limited, as the mortgages in which it deals are either governmentally or privately insured (this study concerns itself with governmentally insured mortgages only).* The insured nature of the mortgages and active secondary market participation by FNMA/GNMA provides the marketing impetus needed to make otherwise high risk urban properties desirable investments. The mortgage company maximizes its return by turning over its funds for initial commitments as quickly as possible.

---

*These generalizations hold for the Newark residential market but are not applicable necessarily to the broader area of activities of mortgage companies outside it.

Mortgage companies are frequently called upon by real estate brokers to provide insured mortgages for homes to be sold to low-income buyers. If the real estate agency is active locally, it can provide a substantial market for the mortgage company. The latter in some cases attempts to encourage this relationship by returning to the broker an equivalent of one point (1 percent of the mortgage) charged to the buyer in the form of a fee. In essence the buyer may pay the broker on at least two separate occasions, once in the form of a sales commission (7 percent locally) and again in the point given to the realtor by the mortgage company.

## Initial Commitment Cost/Revenues

The mortgage company's revenue for initiating a mortgage is derived from the charging of points. The fee from the buyer is limited to one point by law while the seller is currently being charged between one and seven points. The mortgage is then sold as close as possible to full par value for maximum profit. A hypothetical sale of an $18,000 home in Newark may serve to clarify the process.

Initially a real estate broker brings together an able buyer and willing seller. In low-cost properties the mortgage company is then contacted by the broker to arrange for an insured mortgage. FHA is then requested to conduct an inspection as a first step in making the building acceptable for insurance. If the unit is appraised by FHA as equal to or in excess of the mortgage value and any structural or other deficiencies suitably corrected, then a mortgage commitment will be granted by FHA. When FHA issues the mortgage commitment, the mortgage company continues the processing. The mortgage company charges one point to the purchaser of the house and six points to the seller, a total of seven points. In this specific example, the computations are the following:

| | | | | | |
|---|---|---|---|---|---|
| Price | $18,000 | Buyer | $17,250 | Seller | $17,250 |
| Down payment | 750 | Charge | .01 | Charge | .06 |
| Mortgage | $17,250 | | $172.50 | | $1035.00 |

When the mortgage is subsequently auctioned by the mortgage company, points are again charged, this time, however, by the institutional buyer at the expense of the mortgage company. At the time of these interviews a total of seven points were being required by the mortgage company, yet the institutional market would buy at 95 percent of par, leaving a gain of two points or $355 to the mortgagor.

Time, of course, is extremely crucial to the mortgage company. If the FHA responds slowly to a request for structure inspection and eventual mortgage approval, time is lost and the trading atmosphere may no longer warrant the initial commitment made by the mortgage company. Again, this is where the speedier, privately insured mortgages are making their presence felt.

To return once more to the cash flow situation sketched above, the specific transaction yielded a gross revenue of $355.

Mortgage companies were asked in the course of this survey what the costs of initiating an FHA/VA insured loan were. Most responded that initiation costs were in the area of $300 to $350 per loan, although admittedly substantially reduced by economies of scale. Thus, in terms of cost versus revenue in the initiation of insured loans, mortgage companies handling only a moderate number barely break even.

## Subsequent Servicing Cost/Revenues

Mortgage companies, once final mortgage commitments are secured, continue to service these loans after they are sold to institutions or to FNMA/GNMA. This servicing includes the monthly collection and processing of mortgage payments and annual credit checks and structure inspections. For this the mortgage company annually charges between one-fourth and three-eights of 1 percent of the original mortgaged amount. In the case just shown the fee would be under $65. According to mortgage companies this is their mainstay; marginal processing costs under insured loan conditions are less than $20 per loan. Mortgage companies actively compete for initiation of loans for the subsequent profit available in processing.

# THE FHA 235 PROGRAM

## Background: Income Limitations

The FHA 235 program since its inception in 1968 has been geared to providing home ownership* opportunities through interest reduction payments for families whose incomes are too high for public housing but too low for housing available in the private, unassisted market.

In the specific case of existing, single-family housing for families with incomes of $4000 to $8000, the 235 program assists in the payment of interest on FHA insured mortgages by providing a subsidy which may cover up to all but 1 percent of the applicable loan interest. Currently this may be the difference between 1 and 7.5 percent on new mortgages and is paid by FHA directly to the mortgagee (Exhibit 6-4).

The 235 program seeks to limit a family's monthly mortgage payment (principal, interest, taxes, fire insurance, and FHA insurance) to 20 percent of its adjusted gross income; this forms the basis for the ultimate extent of the subsidy. In no case, however, at this writing is the government permitted to pay more than the difference between monthly payments under prevailing mortgage interest rates and what the monthly payments would be if the mortgage were at a 1 percent interest rate.

Maximum incomes of families qualifying for subsidies are currently set at 135 percent of public housing income admission limitations although up to 20 percent of the allocated funds may go to families whose incomes are as high as 90 percent of the 221d(3) income limitations. In the Newark area, the upper levels of income permitted under the 235 program for a family of four are approximately $8,000 and $10,000 respectively.

For families making minimum $200 down payments in HUD defined "low cost" areas, mortgage amounts are restricted to $18,000 and $21,000, depending upon room count. Ceilings in "high cost" areas are only slightly higher at $21,000 and $24,000.

---

*Several assets of the 235 program other than its home ownership programs have been recounted in numerous other studies and include: (1) its wider sweep of income eligibility which encompasses a range from public housing to 221d(3); (2) its applicability to existing as well as new housing; and (3) its freedom of operation by not being tied to local approval through the adoption of a "workable program."

# EXHIBIT 6-4
## LOW INCOME HOME OWNERSHIP VIA VARIOUS FEDERAL PROGRAMS

| Schedule of Costs | FHA-203 | FHA 221d(2) | FHA-235 |
|---|---|---|---|
| | Specific Programs | | |
| 1. Appraised value | $18,750 | $18,750 | $18,750 |
| 2. Down payment | $ 800 | $ 560 (3%) | $ 200 |
| 3. Insured mortgage | $17,900 | $18,750 | $18,750 |
| 4. Prepayables (Four months' taxes, one year's hazard insurance, one month's MIP°) | $ 848 | $ 848 | $ 848‡ |
| 5. Closing costs | $ 800 | $ 800† | $ 800† ‡‡ |
| 6. Amortization period | 25 years | 25 years | 25 years |
| 7. Interest rate | 7% +1/2% MIP° | 7% + 1/2% MIP° | 7% + 1/2% MIP° |
| 8. Monthly amortization | $127 + $8 | $133 + $8 | $133 + $8 |
| 9. Monthly taxes | $ 150 | $ 150 | $ 150 |
| 10. Monthly hazard insurance | $ 20 | $ 20 | $ 20 |
| Total | $ 305 | $ 311 | $ 311 |
| Maximum monthly subsidy | 0 | 0 | $ 133 |
| Initial investment of recipient | $1,698 (Items 2+4 +$50 or Item 5) | $1,458 (Items 2+4 +$50 or Item 5) | $ 200 (Item 2) |
| Monthly expense borne by recipient | $ 305 | $ 311 | $ 178 |
| Gross income required to support | $12,600 | $12,800 | $ 6,780 |

° MIP = Mortgage Insurance Premium
† Closing costs become part of the mortgaged principal.
‡ FHA 235 closing costs and prepayables paid by seller.

Source: Newark Area Resurvey, spring 1972

## FHA 235: National Impact

Nationally, by the end of 1969, approximately one year after the program's inception, 15,000 units of existing housing had been purchased under the 235 program. This was joined by an additional 10,000 units of new and rehabilitated housing. These initial 25,000 insured units were increased to 107,000 in 1970 and 144,000 in 1971. Only slightly more than 6 percent of these units, however, were in the Northeast region with the bulk in the Southeast and Southwest.

According to the U.S. Commission on Civil Rights, the great majority of new 235 houses have been constructed in the suburbs while close to 70 percent of the existing housing has been insured within central city areas. Those who tenant new housing are primarily white and their geographic distribution is random throughout metropolitan areas; those who tenant existing 235 housing are black or Spanish-speaking and appear to cluster in core areas or suburban zones of emergence.

FHA data indicate that in the period 1969 to 1971 approximately 220 of FHA 235 mortgages were issued in Essex County, New Jersey. Over this period these represent under 2 percent of the total mortgages issued annually and less than 4 percent of those issued that were of the insured variety (Exhibit 6-5).

In the program's heyday (1970-1971) only 100 loans had been financed annually under the 235 program in Essex County; however, this figure has currently dropped by nearly 50 percent.

The reason for this decrease in volume is due to a lack of recovery from a temporary suspension of funds in January 1971 after initial deficiencies in the program's structure and weaknesses in FHA appraisal practices allowed speculators to pick up houses for minimal amounts, perform a so-called paste up or cosmetic rehabilitation which, in many cases, amounted to only a few hundred dollars, and then resell the properties under FHA 235 for a profit of thousands of dollars. The result of this in some cases was that buyers paid more than for identical houses that were financed conventionally, i.e., interest rate subsidies were being capitalized into higher sales prices.

While the criticism no doubt contains a good deal of truth, examples of which are in the earlier chapters, perhaps a look at gross statistics will place this program in a somewhat different perspective.

## EXHIBIT 6-5
## FHA INSURANCE WRITTEN IN ESSEX COUNTY, NEW JERSEY, AND CURRENT LEVELS OF DEFAULT, 1969-1971

| | FHA Program | | | |
|---|---|---|---|---|
| Insurance Written/Defaults | 203 | 221d(2) | 235 | Total/Avg. |
| Total FHA insurance written | | | | |
| Essex County,[1] N.J. (1969-1971) | 3378[2] | 2501[3] | 220[4] | 6099 |
| Total FHA acquisitions | | | | |
| Essex County, N.J. (1969-1971) | 127 | 85 | 11 | 223 |
| Newark[5] | 91 | 60 | 10 | 161 |
| All other municipalities | 36 | 25 | 1 | 62 |
| Default rate | | | | |
| Essex County (Percent) | 3.8 | 3.4 | 5.0 | 3.7 |
| Newark's defaults as a percent of total defaults | 74 | 71 | 90 | 73 |

Notes:
1. Newark break-out not available.
2. Includes two units new construction.
3. Includes five units new construction.
4. Includes one unit new construction.
5. Unofficial data secured from FHA.

Source: HUD-FHA Offices: Newark, N.J. and Washington, D. C.

In Newark, as noted, during 1969, 1970, and 1971, 220 FHA 235 mortgages were given on existing one to four-family housing units. Although the default rate associated specifically with the 235 program is over twice the suburban uninsured rate, the fact remains that 209 of 220 families are currently residing in housing which they now own and have replaced families who, for the most part, no longer cared to remain within the city.

It will be shown in a later chapter that one of the parcel predictors of abandonment within the sample is a desire on the part of the owner of the 1971 abandoned parcel to sell the property in 1964. In 1964 owners who wanted to get out complained that there were no takers. In 1971 there are even fewer! If one applies an actuarial standard to the 235 program, a prudent lender might view it as a disaster. If, however, one views the program as a vehicle whereby the natural flow of residential stock is assisted by bringing together a buyer and a seller, in the former case by expanding the potential buyer market, in the latter by making it profitable for real estate brokers to locate and retain sellers, then perhaps the program is saving a large portion of the residential stock which might otherwise ultimately have been abandoned. In this case the program may be viewed as having a definite positive societal function.

The ideal situation is one which would expand the buyer market sufficiently to allow an increment of buyers who would then be able to operate and *maintain* these properties with only a moderate increase in the rate of default. The ideal situation must also mandate realistic levels of profit for the speculator. The situation of a $7,000 parcel undergoing cosmetic repairs and being resold for $18,000, while not unique, is a dysfunctional element of the private market, and cannot be tolerated in the publicly assisted sphere in view of the difficulty the ultimate recipient will have in running the parcel, even with mortgage subsidies, at this selling price level. In addition, the potential for accumulation of capital through ultimate resale is stymied by the inflated purchase price. The sections which follow detail the role of 235 more clearly and present the lenders' views toward the program and its problems.

## FHA 235: Local Reaction

### *Blockages*

When local funds for 235 became available after the initial suspension in January 1971, the number of inspections specified by HUD/FHA, city ordinances, and local social service agencies cost realtors and mortgage companies valuable time. The house being considered had to be initially inspected by a licensed plumber and electrician who did what work had to be done in order to repair and improve the property prior to mortgage commitment. The City of Newark sent building and fire inspectors who inspected the building for various code violations. If a welfare family was to be moved into the house, the city's Department of Social Welfare also sent its inspectors to the property. Of course the unit was inspected by the FHA. The process was time consuming, extending the closing of a deal on the house in some cases for four to six months.

The inspection problem was compounded by the fear and resistance of the inspectors to perform their duties in certain areas of the city. Plumbers, electricians, and appraisers went to the houses in groups of two. The threat of physical violence and/or theft of equipment necessitated the assignment of one man to work inside the building and one to watch the truck. Where equipment replacement was made it was not unusual for it to be removed from the house within the week as a result of vandals working against or with specific repair crews.

### *Abuses*

The most publicized abuses of the program appear to be in the inspection process. FHA requirements placed the responsibility and cost of repair upon the seller. The house has to meet FHA specifications before it can be sold, i.e., the electrical, plumbing, and heating system must be in working order, and the house structurally sound before final mortgage approval. If a house does not meet these specifications a commitment for an insured mortgage is not supposed to be given. Currently it has been suggested that short-term owners of these homes, often brokers, paid FHA appraisers a portion of the selling price for certification that repairs which had not been made were completed. This certification gained for the property a mortgage guarantee and an attendant inflated price.[4]

The 235 program in a less publicized manner also ran into problems with its target group. Many of those serviced in the central city are of a rural-agrarian background, making the transition into an industrial-urbanized community. Compounding the problems of transition is the fact that in many cases families had personal problems, i.e., no male head of household and dependency upon public assistance for a substantial part of their income. For some, homeownership was a novelty, little understood except for the increased space and perhaps the single-family environment it provided. Interviews conducted with the coopters in one Newark housing rehabilitation effort indicate that many of them thought of their down payments as essentially illicit payoffs for the purpose of securing "rooms." Budgetary and maintenance problems and a lack of understanding of the concept of a mortgage were considerations which came up on many occasions during the interviews.

One mother with a large family reported that her house's boiler cracked because she didn't realize it needed water. When mortgage payments were late or unmet another owner would call, saying he could not "pay the rent." Maintenance problems occasioned calls to the FHA or to the mortgage company who processed the mortgage rather than directly to repairmen. For those who budgeted, the unexpected repair bills of a large, old house made this planning a meaningless exercise; for those who did not, the budgeting itself became an unachievable end. Often unfamiliarity necessitated a call for a repairman for the slightest of problems; this problem is especially acute for welfare families without male heads of households.

### *Origination/Processing Costs*

In terms of volume, most of the local 235s were originated by mortgage companies, while institutional lenders processed only a negligible number. Most mortgage company officials agreed that both initial commitments and subsequent processing were more costly under the 235 program than standard FHA 203 loans. In several cases poor credit histories had to be researched and corrected. If, in the past, a claim had been unjustly placed against a prospective 235 buyer resulting in property repossession, the marred credit record had to be cleared prior to mortgage commitment.

The servicing aspect of the loan also cost the originator more because subsequent credit checks had to be made semi-annually rather than annually as had been originally planned. The processing of monthly mortgage payments involved not only the forwarding of the owner's mortgage stipend but also the simultaneous processing of the interest above 1 percent assumed by the government. Despite this most mortgage companies were not negative toward the program, nor did they report a default rate noticeably higher than the traditional FHA mortgage program.

### *Local Housing Potential*

Few of the realtors interviewed had sold any houses under the 235 program. Curtailment of funds occasioned by malpractice had made realtors reluctant to utilize the program as a marketing vehicle. (A subsequent requirement that 5 percent of the selling price be held in escrow for fourteen months to cover the cost of recurring repairs made sellers also shy away from the program.) In an attempt to judge impact, realtors were asked whether FHA 235 made houses turn over faster in a core area. Most replied *no;* not because of the nature of the program but rather because the program had not had enough time. Most realtors interviewed, however, felt that the market of potential homeowners was greatly increased under the provision of the 235 program, but the current amount of processing time and required inspections held up sales for an additional sixty to ninety days. One realtor claimed he could sell two homes under more conventional programs in the time it took him to sell one 235, yet he needed the lower down payments and the assumption of closing costs which 235 offered for the type of client he was trying to place.

The range of interviews finally brought to the surface the sentiments and ideas held by the Newark housing finance sector toward the 235 program. Some expressed a belief that the initial equity or down payment requirements of the program were insufficient and made it easy for a family to walk away from a property if there was a problem they could not handle. The $200 down payment was not enough to keep the family there, while the mortgage payments were comparable to the rent that they had been paying previously. Some respondents also felt that the program was unable to operate successfully in older housing. The problems of wear and tear, the necessity of rehabilitation, and the accompanying FHA approval of work done were problems found infrequently in northern 235 new construction efforts. Most respondents further noted that regular counseling was essential if an answer was to be found to the maintenance and budgetary problems of the low income homeowner. In this vein it was suggested that the efforts of the local Mount Carmel Guild in counseling new low and moderate income homeowners be expanded and copied by other groups.

## HOUSING COUNSELING SERVICES

### A Specific Source

The Mount Carmel Guild of Newark is a nonprofit sectarian organization which devotes its activities to housing and health. It is part of the archdiocese of Newark. The Guild is certified by HUD to counsel prospective low and moderate income homeowners in the "do's and don'ts" of purchasing a home, and in credit aid if the homeowner should require these services.

### Users of Counseling Services

A typical counseling session is recounted below. The session was held at the Guild's headquarters in downtown Newark on a weekday at 10 a.m. A total of seven people were in attendance:

> 1. A disabled black woman in her early fifties living on social security with a yearly income of $3000. She was enrolled in another training program provided by the Guild and had there been directed to housing counseling service. This woman desired to purchase a home for herself and her aging mother, an arrangement which would provide a rent saving to both. Ultimately she was told that her income was too low to qualify for home ownership. The Guild aided the woman in finding senior citizen housing in one of its own projects for both herself and her mother.
>
> 2. A Spanish-speaking couple with two children and a combined yearly income of $14,000. The Guild's instructor found that their applications for the 235 program had been improperly completed by the real estate broker. They lacked date of sale, signature of the seller, etc. The instructor said she would call the realtor involved and have the papers placed in order prior to any further action by the couple in pursuit of the sale.

3. A Spanish-speaking man with ten children and an annual income of $6,730 composed of both wages and welfare assistance. He spoke no English and came with an interpreter from a community agency. The house he and his family were living in was to be razed for urban renewal in ten days. The Guild advisor said the purchase of a home was not a proper remedy and offered the Guild's aid in finding large temporary quarters for the man and his family until more permanent lodgings could be found.

4. A black couple with four children had purchased a home a year and one-half earlier and were facing foreclosure. Their mortgagee had sent them to the Guild for credit counseling. The family had a yearly income of $8,000 which was subject to seasonal fluctuations. The Guild advisor set up a budgeting program for this family based upon what they could count on as steady income throughout the year. A stay of foreclosure was also obtained.

## The Counseling Session

The counseling began with a presentation to the group explaining the terms and contractual obligations of a mortgage. Each aspect was gone over slowly and carefully. A few pointers on how to select and inspect a house were offered. The prospective homeowners were told what to look for in a home in terms of both amenities and structural deficiencies. The prospectives were also made aware of potentially unsavory practices of real estate brokers. All but the last of these subject areas were dull and dry. There was some question on the part of the observer whether in most cases the material was not completely over the head of the entire audience.

Of unquestionable value, however, is extensive *individual* attention to both prospective and deficient homebuyers. After the formal presentation individual cases were discussed privately and questions were answered. The counselor went around the room to hear and reply to each individual case. Where the Guild could be of further assistance, the offer was made and usually accepted.

## Future Success

This latter situation seems to be the level at which housing counseling must operate. The value of the formal instruction was questionable; individual attention was badly needed, however, and quite well received.

This precis serves to illustrate the level of pathos involved in low income home ownership. The available counseling services which were observed seem to be ill-attended and even then, for the most part, by people who cannot qualify for the house under discussion.

The problems of the owners were complex, and mortgage facts do not lend themselves to easy simplifications. If housing counseling is to have the impact on mortgage default rates that lenders in the financial sector hope for, it must be conducted on a basic — and costly — individual level. Before success is achieved in this area many home ownership tasks will have to be performed for these new low income buyers.

## THE ROLE OF THE SPECULATOR

### Speculator Defined

The speculator plays a very fundamental role in the free enterprise system, that of bringing together a buyer and a seller. Most basic to the speculator and the market mechanism is the risk/reward concept. For every transaction the amount of risk to be taken is directly related to the amount of reward expected. If the amount of reward is deemed unwarranted or illicit by members of society, the speculator is taken to task and his function questioned. In the 235 housing program he is defined as the taker of interim title to a one- to four-family home in hope of immediate sale with substantial capital gain. His risk is his investment in terms of time, purchase price, improvements, interim taxes, and incidental expenses. His reward is the amount he receives for the property in resale less his initial costs.

### The Speculator's Publicity

At the time of this study investigations in Newark and indictments in New York City and other urban communities are being undertaken involving speculators who exceed prudent risk/reward returns. The scenario at question is often repeated. A speculator, usually affiliated with a real estate broker, finds a prospective seller, often white and aged, owning a house in a changing neighborhood. An offer is made to the seller by the broker well below the actual market value of the parcel. In the owner's desperation to leave the deteriorating neighborhood the offer is accepted, and the property is taken over by the speculator. Improvements which must be made in order to qualify under the 235 program are not made yet an inspection approval is granted from FHA and the parcel receives a kited mortgage reflective of both substantial profits to the broker and the inclusion of closing costs for the buyer. The latter in the central city is frequently a member of a minority group in many cases with numerous children. Within a short period of time the building is found to be in a gross state of disrepair.

### The Real Question

The pathos of the act and the illegitimate actions of its participants tend to mask the real question, i.e., what is the level of profit to be afforded a legitimate low-end, housing speculator? This question was put to the members of the housing finance sector. The most frequent reply was 25 percent, in view of the possible expenses and risks taken by the speculator. With regard to the specific functional role of the speculator, several lenders claimed that in terms of on-going property transfer, in many cases requiring rehabilitation, the speculator was essential. If his profit was severely limited the local market would slow, possibly increasing residential abandonment. Respondents further pointed out that much of the *excessive* profits available through 235 could be substantially reduced given *realistic* FHA appraisals.

It was also noted that if good appraisals were to be made, better quality and thus better paid appraisers would have to be the order of the day. One mortgage company official claimed that he could not make an appraisal for less than $100; FHA appraisers receive $35 per appraisal.

## THE LOW-END LANDLORD

### Can Black Replace White?

In addition to questioning Newark's housing financial sector about center city mortgage lending practices, inquiries were made concerning the disappearance of the typical white professional multi-parcel landlord and the emergence of the small black owner. The questions inquired into ways to stem the total disappearance of the white professional, at least before he could impart his skill to his black replacement, and also whether it was possible for this black replacement to sustain himself in low-end rental real estate where the white landlord had previously failed.

There seemed to be a definite consensus on the part of those surveyed that the white landlord was leaving the inner-city, yet some serious question remained as to whether the black owner could successfully take his place. While there was some doubt as to whether a small scale black owner could run his properties more efficiently than his white predecessor, there was a definite feeling that the black owner had fewer investment alternatives and thus would be more highly motivated to retain his investment than the earlier ownership group.

### A Case in Point

One respondent, a long-time resident of Newark and a prototype of the classic tenement landlord, had been a holder of over one hundred low-end properties in the early and mid-sixties. Today he is in the process of simultaneously changing both the mode and locale of his operations. This realtor is now moving significantly into the management of housing for the elderly for nonprofit organizations within core areas and the purchase of rental housing in noncore, suburban areas. He has sold, given away, or abandoned most of his previous holdings.

His successful replacement is a large scale, black landlord, who as of the moment seems to be able to make a profit and is willing to stay. Interestingly enough, one cannot distinguish his management practices from those of his predecessor. He appears similarly cold and businesslike and is just as concerned with both the irresponsibility of tenants and potential danger to collection agents and repair crews. His present levels of profit are principally a function of reduced overhead, in terms of temporary rather than full time employees and a lower wage scale.

## CONCLUSION

The continuing presence of the government insured loan has seen mortgage companies evolve into a dominant force in the urban mortgage market.

Their "middleman" structure which allows them to take an almost risk-free posture in a high risk situation has enabled them to fill a void left by the decreasing participation of more familiar institutional lenders.

Without excusing criminal excesses, the disappointing experience of one program participated in heavily by mortgage companies, i.e., FHA 235 in Newark, seems to be a function of the more general problems of low income realty and areas.

## NOTES

1. *Essex County Real Estate Directory* (East Orange, New Jersey, Annual Supplements 1960-1970).
2. See Robert W. Burchell, James W. Hughes and George Sternlieb, *Housing Costs and Housing Restraints: Newark, N.J.* (New Brunswick, N.J.: Center for Urban Policy Research, Rutgers University, May 1970), 187-201.
3. See Eric Stevenson, "A Commitment Made and Kept . . . The Urban Investment Program," *The Mortgage Banker* (May 1970), 18-27; Robert H. Wilson, "Another Tool to Fund Life Insurance Companies' Urban Investment Program," *The Mortgage Banker* (May 1971), 98-104; "Mortgages for the Slums," *Fortune* (January 1968), 162-163.
4. See William Lilley III and Timothy B. Clark, "Federal Programs Spur Abandonment of Housing in Major Cities," *National Journal,* January 1, 1972, 26-33; Gurney Breckenfeld, "Housing Subsidies Are a Grand Delusion," *Fortune* (February 1972), 136-138+; Fred Fenitti, "U.S. Looks into Profits on Homes," *The New York Times,* February 20, 1972, 118; U.S. Departments of Housing and Urban Development, *HUD Clip Sheet,* March 9, 1972; "Profits Reaped in Sale of Homes to Help Poor," *Newark Sunday Star Ledger,* February 13, 1972, 1+; "Mayors Urge U.S. Probe of Home Buying Program," *Newark Sunday Star Ledger,* February 20, 1972, 1+; "Neighborhood Uplift Projects Stir Complaints," *Newark Sunday Star Ledger,* April 30, 1972, 1+.

439

# 7

# ABANDONMENT

The great English historian Henry Maitland once pointed out that simple explanations of social or natural phenomena are products of sophistication; of understanding what is truly essential and important as against those elements which are not really central to the act. In primitive societies phenomena are seen as one of a kind, each of them unique — so much so that each occurrence must be viewed as an entity together with all of the specific minutia that seemingly adhere to it. In a sense, the study of residential abandonment is still at this latter stage of analysis.

Detailed scholarship and thoroughgoing analysis have lagged behind reality. The phenomenon is just being recognized as one of importance and of broad sweep, not confined to a few discreet areas in a very few cities. Little comparative analysis in depth exists which permits distinguishing between the noise — the one of a kind elements that are not central to the phenomenon — and those factors which are truly related.

In the following material some of these difficulties will become evident. However, it is hoped that the data incorporated here will serve as a base line for future more sophisticated research.

## ABANDONMENT: THE UNEVEN FIT OF THE THEORETICAL BASE

One of the principal reasons for concern with abandonment is its devastating concentration in individual neighborhoods. The dynamics of neighborhood evolution are poorly understood. Conventional economic concepts of supply and demand lose much of their defining power at this level. Nevertheless, some researchers have approached the analysis of abandonment using this framework to illuminate the abandonment decision of individual landlords. This approach is fruitful because from the point of view of the landlord the characteristics of a neighborhood are relatively independent of his actions alone. As a result, the landlord's decision to abandon can be set against a well-defined background, and the macro-determinants of the decision identified.

In these analyses, supply factors are those affecting landlord costs of providing some level of housing services. Examples of factors producing these cost differentials are "problem tenants," often accused of wearing out housing faster than do normal tenants. These problem tenants are usually assumed to be poor, and unwilling or unable to recompense landlords sufficiently to allow adequate maintenance.

Another closely related argument emphasizes problem neighborhoods, where high rates of crime and vandalism enhance both operating and maintenance costs. A third and perhaps the most important example of supply side variation in the cost of providing housing is the possibly vast differences among neighborhoods in the characteristics of the housing stock. Though some versions of this latter argument are almost indistinguishable from demand factors, on the simplest level it is apparent that maintenance and operating costs differ with structure and unit design. Older structures typically require greater maintenance outlays, for instance.[1]

Demand factors affect the landlords' gross revenues secured by providing housing services. Neighborhood quality and the levels of public services are often emphasized here. The race of neighborhood residents has also been highlighted. Some empirical evidence has been developed indicating that the segregation of black households in urban ghettoes maintains these often obsolete neighborhoods beyond their normal limits. A final important factor is the location of housing within urban areas. Accessibility to jobs and services of various kinds is an important determinant of housing value. The secular decentralization of metropolitan areas obviously is markedly changing patterns of accessibility.[2]

Though this approach to the analysis of abandonment offers potentially important insight, it is fundamentally limited. It leaves out the factors producing neighborhood change. In large part, landlord decisions are important in producing these changes. At the same time, they undoubtedly react powerfully to these changes. This type of dynamic system can be quite difficult to predict or understand. Despite its complexity, overly simplified life cycle models are often proposed.

One early example of such a scheme of neighborhood evolution suggested:

> "In its life cycle, the residential area begins with the need of a growing city for additional homes and the consequent development of a new urban community. It then passes through a considerable and often comparatively long period of normal use, marked by reasonable maintenance. It next begins to suffer from advancing age, accelerating obsolescence, and structural neglect. As the process of decay continues, investment and rent values gradually fall; since these values no longer justify proper maintenance, repairs are progressively scaled down or are wholly neglected; one by one individual residential units — and presently the district as a whole — show marked evidence of important deterioration. And finally, the district emerges as a slum area, wherein depreciated property values reflect a tremendous investment loss and physical structures have become unfit for decent human habitation."[3]

Edgar Hoover and Raymond Vernon offered a more explicit five-stage model of neighborhood evolution in the classic New York stage model of neighborhood evolution in the classic New York Metropolitan Region Study. Five evolutionary stages were hypothesized:[4]

*Stage 1:* The transformation of undeveloped rural land to residential use. The building boom of the 1920s defined this stage for most of the Newark study area — frame multi-dwelling units responsive to the needs of that era.

*Stage 2:* This stage comprises a time of apartment construction. Many of the development sites are either patches of open space, bypassed in the first building wave for various reasons, or obtained through the demolition of the oldest single family homes. This stage is most evident in the inner rings of metropolitan areas.

*Stage 3:* Can occur several years later, and is a time of housing down-grading and conversion. Population and density increase through the crowding of existing structures by the newest in-migrants to the region. The growth of young families generates additional strains on an aging infrastructure. This down-grading stage is often associated with the "slum invasions" by segregated ethnic and minority groups.

*Stage 4:* Occurs after the in-migrant couples have settled down. This "thinning out" stage is characteristic of slum areas some time after they have been turned over to slum use. This is mainly a phenomenon of household size shrinkage as children and boarders move out. Large portions of Newark appear to be in this development stage.

*Stage 5:* Is the renewal stage, where the obsolete areas of housing arriving at Stage 4 are replaced by new multifamily units. Most often this has either been subsidized, moderate, or low income housing, or luxury apartments. In almost every case, this stage depends on public intervention.

Hoover and Vernon optimistically assumed renewal of some type followed the neighborhood collapse of stages 3 and 4. The characteristics of renewed land uses and the process accomplishing the renewal were largely unspecified, however. Some public intervention was assumed, apparently along the lines of community renewal programs. The place of private housing abandonment in this scheme is unclear. It has been suggested that so long as public and private demolition programs are adequate, abandonment may act as a sort of piecemeal land clearance program. Private abandonment on a sufficient scale might work to make private renewal of slum neighborhoods possible. It might supplement existing public renewal programs, and substitute for inadequacies in their scale.

Anthony Downs in a preliminary report to the U.S. Department of Housing and Urban Development was one of the few early researchers to recognize abandonment as the ultimate fate of housing and to suggest programs to be introduced at various stages which might possibly counteract the abandonment process. He described neighborhood evolution in five basic steps and various repetitions of these parameters.[5]

1. Racial Transition — from white to black
2. Declining average resident's income as a result of the "filtering" process
3. Declining levels of security as the number of low-income households rises.

4. Rising difficulty with tenants involving rent payment, maintenance of the parcel, and turnover.
5. Inability to obtain loans through normal mortgage channels.

The remaining steps in the process are essentially repetitions or combinations of 2 through 5 as they interact with each other to produce steadily worsening conditions.

6. Physical deterioration
7. Declining tenant quality
8. Psychological abandonment by the landlord
9. Final tenancy decline and departure — the physical abandonment of the structure.

Downs further outlines the problem of abandonment as one reflected by the inability of decaying *neighborhoods* (1) to attract households with steady incomes and (2) to reduce significantly the level of local insecurity. He further notes that important aspects of the abandonment process are specific actions of the *landlord* in terms of (1) his ability to secure financing, (2) his regular performance of maintenance and (3) his on-going relationships with his tenants.

The approach employed in this study may well be criticized in terms similar to those advanced in earlier efforts. However, an attempt will be made to cull what theory exists in this area and document the resulting hypotheses empirically. Similarly inductive reasoning will be used to develop the method of examining the abandonment phenomenon yet only a limited model of landlord behavior or housing demand will be employed.

In terms of the supply or behavioral aspect of residential abandonment, characteristics of landlords and buildings both statically and over time will be examined via the anecdotal as well as the statistical approach. The sample data on landlords and structures which will be used are a rich body of data consisting of in-depth interviews with landlords who have currently either abandoned their properties or retained them, yet who were all reasonably solid owners of real estate some eight years previous. This is particularly significant given the recent policy orientations directed to the area of changes in ownership and management practices.

The *gross abandonment data* obtained not by sample but rather for the city as a whole from fire and planning department tallies are somewhat less rich in terms of the depth of information which is available for each parcel. In the case of the *sample* this information was extensive including for instance: the type of structure, whether the owner occupied the structure, the condition of the structure, the management techniques employed by the owner etc.

The gross abandonment data contain only the address of the structure and the fact that it has been abandoned. Yet while these data are limited in depth, linked with census variables tabulated on a tract basis, their breadth enables one to view in the static case the *characteristics* of neighborhoods in which heavy abandonment took place and in the dynamic case, the *changes in the characteristics* of these similarly heavy abandonment areas. Hopefully this will ultimately lead to the isolation of early indicators of residential abandonment.

Before delving any further into the abandonment problem it is necessary first to define what this study terms an abandoned building and second, to gauge the presence of this phenomenon both locally and nationally.

## ABANDONMENT: DEFINITION AND SCOPE

As noted, the crisis of housing abandonment has received relatively little hard analysis, or quantification, despite the concern it has generated. Nor has it received a broadly acceptable definition. Two principal attempts have been made to suggest the magnitude of the national problem. In the first of these, the Urban League defined abandonment as follows (Exhibit 7-1):

> "When a landlord no longer provides services to an occupied building and allows taxes and mortgages to go unpaid, it is clear that the building is uninhabitable by all but desperation standards. We consider such buildings to be finally abandoned. On the other hand, when a building is temporarily unoccupied or is to be demolished for another socially or economically useful purpose, it cannot be considered finally abandoned."[6]

Using this definition, informed persons in seven cities were querried on the nature, extent, and causes of abandonment in their areas. The included cities were New York, Hoboken, Cleveland, St. Louis, Atlanta, Chicago, and Detroit. Housing abandonment was found to be a serious problem in all except Detroit and Atlanta. Detroit was

## EXHIBIT 7-1
### A DEFINITION OF THE ABANDONMENT PROCESS/HOUSING TYPES ACCORDING TO SEVERAL AUTHORS

| Sternlieb: *Some Aspects of the Abandoned House Problem*[a] | National Urban League: *National Abandonment Survey*[b] | Linton, Mields, and Coston: *Problems of Abandoned Housing and Recommendations for Action*[c] |
|---|---|---|
| 1. A reduction in maintenance procedures | 1. Decline in an area's socio-economic status | 1. Vacant and derelict<br>a. Vandalized (e.g., doors and windows knocked out, walls kicked in, paint sprayed mischievously on exterior, wiring and fixtures stripped, gutters stripped)<br>b. Boarded (i.e., openings into buildings secured by nailing closures over them)<br>c. Deteriorated (an intermediate state of disrepair)<br>d. Dilapidated (having one or more critical defects in sufficient number to require extensive repair on building)<br>e. Unmaintained Grounds (a combination of trash and garbage accumulation, uncut grass or weeds, broken fence) |
| 2. Permitting the structure to become tax delinquent | 2. Racial or ethnic change | |
| 3. The virtual abandonment of all reinvestments for maintenance usually coupled with increased tax delinquency | 3. Property speculation and exploitation | |
| 4. The cessation of vital services to the structure, particularly utility elements and heating | 4. Weakened market conditions | |
| 5. The landlord arranging through a paper sale to avoid any level of legal liability for the structure | 5. Disinvestment | |

Sources:

a. Sternlieb, George. *Some Aspects of the Abandoned House Problem* (New Brunswick, N.J. Rutgers University, Center for Urban Policy Research, 1970).

b. National Urban League. *The National Survey of Housing Abandonment* (New York, N.Y. The Center for Community Change, 1971).

c. Linton, Mields & Coston. *A Study of Abandoned Housing and Recommendations for Action by the Federal Government and Localities* (Washington, D. C., 1971 mimeo.).

found to have an incipient problem. Numerically, it was estimated that in New York City as a whole, approximately 2 percent of structures had been abandoned. In the most afflicted sections of St. Louis approximately 16 percent of structures were abandoned. In the East New York section of Brooklyn, abandonment rates ranged between 6 percent to 10 percent. Finally, it was estimated that abandonment rates in the Woodlawn and Lawndale sections of Chicago approached 20 percent.

A second survey of national patterns of abandonment employed a somewhat different definition of abandonment. In this study, Linton, Mields, and Coston defined structures as abandoned if they were *unoccupied* and (Exhibit 7-1):

1. vandalized;
2. boarded up;
3. deteriorated or dilapidated; or
4. had unmaintained grounds.[7]

Survey methods were used to measure the extent of housing abandonment in neighborhoods of four metropolitan areas. This study reported that in January, 1971, the City of St. Louis counted 3,500 vacant and derelict buildings containing approximately 10,000 housing units. This amounted to approximately 4 percent of the city's housing stock. Moreover, 1,444 of these 3,500 structures had been abandoned between July, 1970, and January, 1971, a seven-month period. Though it was concluded that abandonment was concentrated in the poorest neighborhoods (abandonment rates exceeded 20 percent in one neighborhood), abandoned structures were found to be located in virtually all areas of the city. In the North Lawndale area of Chicago it was discovered that during a two-month period between September and November 1970, fully 2.6 percent of the area's housing units were abandoned. In the city as a whole it was found that during the same short period, 0.4 percent of the housing stock was abandoned. This abandonment was concentrated in seven inner city neighborhoods. By contrast with these two cities, it was found that abandonment is not a serious problem in Oakland or New Orleans.

These two studies offer dramatic evidence that abandonment is devastating neighborhoods in several metropolitan areas. They also suggest it is a phenomenon concentrated in neighborhoods dominated by poor, principally black households. While they document the proportions of the crisis of abandonment, the evidence they provide is far too fragmentary to offer insight into the process. Neither do they offer the understanding necessary for the design of ameliorative policy.

The study which follows examines two differing bodies of data and attempts to segregate abandoned residential parcels via similar criteria. It then attempts to link these buildings with certain social and economic characteristics of owners, tenants, and neighborhood. Subsequently the operating patterns of abandoned versus nonabandoned buildings are viewed.

An abandoned building, at least initially, is defined solely as *one which has been removed from the housing stock for no apparent alternative profitable reason and for which no succeeding use occurs on the land*. Thus, the study is concerned with *standing*, vacant, residential or residential/commercial buildings which serve no housing function and, additionally, with those that have been *demolished* due to the owner's fear of continued economic loss and therefore have also ceased to perform their "shelter" function. This is a more expansive definition than that posed by Linton, Mields, and Coston which includes only the vacant and standing category. Hopefully this expansion will sufficiently widen the study area so that stronger predictive relationships may be observed. Two basic data sources are used.

1. Within the sample of buildings previously studied in 1964, eighty-four buildings out of the total of 569, over 15 percent, were found to be abandoned by late 1971. These consist of: thirty-eight which are vacant now but were not vacant in 1964; twelve which are currently occupied, but from which the owner derives no income and thus provides no housing services; twenty-seven which were demolished privately over the period 1964-1971 due to lack of income and potential owner liability for personal injury; and seven which were demolished by the municipal government for reasons of health or hazard (Exhibit 7-2).

2. In similar fashion, *gross citywide* abandoned structures, drawn from fire inspectors' recurring surveys of their respective districts, have been defined as those residential or residential/commercial structures which cease to provide basic housing services, but are currently standing without alternate use, and those which once provided housing services but since have been removed from the existing stock for reasons other than a scheduled urban renewal project (Exhibit 7-2).

Thus, within the sample, this study is viewing abandonment as synonymous with *housing loss occurring as a result of a failing local housing market which, for the most part, is incapable of regeneration.*

## EXHIBIT 7-2
## THE DEFINITION OF ABANDONMENT BOTH WITHIN THE SAMPLE SET AND FOR CITYWIDE TOTALS

| Gross Totals (Residential/Commercial) | | Sample Totals (Residential/Commercial) | |
|---|---|---|---|
| 1. Observed as vacant and *open* in violation of fire inspection standards over the period 1967-1971 | 652 | 1. Observed vacant in 1971 and not in 1964 | 38 |
| 2. Observed as vacant and *secured* meeting fire inspection standards over the period 1967-1971 | 820 | 2. Observed partially occupied in 1971 but owner derives no income and claims parcel is vacant | 12 |
| 3. Observed initially as vacant and subsequently removed from housing stock by non-urban renewal demolition or fire over the period 1967 to 1971 | 1081 | 3. Demolished *privately* for reasons of hazard with no succeeding use occurring on the land | 27 |
| | | 4. Demolished *publicly* for reasons of hazard with no succeeding use occurring on the land | 7 |
| 4. Total gross residential abandonment over period 1967 to 1971 | 2553 | 5. Total sample residential abandonment over period 1964-1971 | 84 |
| 5. Percent of total stock (4 years) | 8.0 | 6. Percent of sample (7 years) | 15.0 |
| 6. Abandoned gross residential structures standing in 1971 | 1472 | 7. Abandoned sample residential structures standing in 1971 | 50 |

Source: Newark Area Resurvey, spring, 1972

In this case private demolitions for reasons of commercial gain are not considered *abandonments,* nor are structures which are removed from the housing supply as part of either a scheduled urban renewal program or a planned transportation change.

In like fashion within the larger citywide glimpse at abandonment, subject to the limitations of the data, essentially the same criteria pertain. A building is not considered abandoned if it has the potential for replacement, even though it is temporarily lost as a result of scheduled demolition by the Newark Housing Authority or by the New Jersey Department of Transportation. It is considered abandoned if it is vacant and standing or has been removed for reasons of hazard with no replacement forthcoming.

Thus, in terms of Sternlieb's earlier definition (Exhibit 7-1), this study is viewing abandonment as occurring *after* the cessation of housing services by the owner; occasioned by, or sometimes occasioning, housing vacancy. It may or may not occur before local municipal records necessarily indicate tax delinquency as a significant problem and further may or may not occur before the owner, via paper sale, absolves himself from complete responsibility for the building.

*Abandonment is not an orderly process. It is a pipeline phenomenon, from useful structure to a discarded one.* The stage of the process to be isolated under the particular term is highly subjective. There are a great many inconsistencies in the behavior of owners which prevent the abandonment process from being documented accurately. Also present, though, in a small proportion, is the return to the housing stock, often through philanthropic rehabilitation, of residential parcels which seemed to have ceased their housing function and reached the end of their economic life.

## Is Abandonment Exclusively A Residential Phenomenon?

While abandonment is most frequently seen in residential terms, it is clear that abandonment definitely has nonresidential elements. Exhibit 7-3 represents citywide loss of structures over the period 1967 to 1971. The total loss of structures in this period is approximately 4,500 structures of which 1,165 of those included under the category "type not indicated" are structures demolished for urban renewal (1,053) or realigned/new automobile transportation routes (112).

EXHIBIT 7-3

GROSS CITYWIDE LOSS OF STRUCTURES BY TYPE OF STRUCTURE, ULTIMATE STATUS, AND TYPE OF CONSTRUCTION
NEWARK, 1967-1971

LOSS OF STRUCTURES BY TYPE OF STRUCTURE

| | Residential | Commercial | Residential / Commercial | Industrial | Industrial / Commercial | Type Not Indicated | Total |
|---|---|---|---|---|---|---|---|
| Type of Structure | | | | | | | |
| (number) | 1621 | 235 | 165 | 213 | 2 | 2246 | 4482 |
| (percent) | 36.2 | 5.2 | 3.7 | 4.8 | 0.0 | 50.1 | 100.0 |
| Percent within Newark's population of structures° | 7.29 (35,356) | 8.47 (7,078) | — | 20.98 (1531) | — | — | 7.54 (43,965) |

LOSS OF STRUCTURES BY ULTIMATE STATUS

| | Currently Standing | | | | Currently Demolished | | |
|---|---|---|---|---|---|---|---|
| | Private Ownership | | | Public Ownership | Private/Public Ownership | | |
| | Open | Secured | Rehabilitated | Status Not Indicated | Razed Publicly | Razed Privately | Total |
| Ultimate status | | | | | | | |
| (number) | 873 | 1244 | 225 | 118 | 1254 | 767 | 4482 |
| (percent) | 19.5 | 27.8 | 5.0 | 2.6 | 28.1 | 17.0 | 100.0 |

LOSS OF STRUCTURES BY TYPE OF CONSTRUCTION

| | Frame | Masonry | Frame/Masonry | Construction Not Indicated | Total |
|---|---|---|---|---|---|
| Type of construction | | | | | |
| (number) | 1311 | 894 | 10 | 2267 | 4482 |
| (percent) | 29.3 | 19.9 | 0.3 | 50.5 | 100.0 |

°To calculate this percentage 1081 of "type not indicated" structures were redistributed among "types" of structures according to the existing distribution. These were structures which were not taken for urban renewal or transportation purposes.

Source: Newark Fire Department, Division of Combustibles, Vacant and Razed Building Card File, 1971.

However, of the remaining 3,500 structures which this study considers "abandoned," 1,320, or 40 percent, are nonresidential, assuming equal redistribution of the 1,081 structures remaining in the "type not indicated" category. (Combined uses, in similar fashion as zoning classifications, are assigned the high-order use.)

While proportionately, *commercial* uses are being retired at roughly the same rate as residential uses, i.e., approximately 2 percent annually, *industrial* land uses are being abandoned at two and one-half times this residential/commercial rate. Over a four-year period (1967-1971) Newark alone lost 213 industrial structures out of its 1969 citywide total of 1,531, or 5.2 percent annually.[8]

If citywide, multiple, land use abandonment is limited to residential and residential/commercial abandonment (Exhibit 7-4), trends in the status of the property and type of construction of abandoned structures prove quite insightful.

Comparing Exhibits 7-3 and 7-4, it is evident that "the most hazardous and fire-prone" open properties exist in larger proportion in residential and residential/commercial uses than when they are within the multiple use (i.e., residential, commercial, and industrial) abandonments.

Similarly, and quite logically, frame construction is associated with residential abandonment more than it is with multi-use buildings. Most residential abandonment in Newark is taking place in turn-of-the century, two and one-half story, frame dwellings which are substantially representative of the city's basic housing stock. More detail on size characteristics is presented later.

Another stage of the abandonment cycle is the small proportion of the stock being rehabilitated as housing (Exhibit 7-3 middle). In most cases the specific phenomenon which is evident here is private rather than public rehabilitation. In specifically designated, peripheral, public rehabilitation areas, buildings are usually in better condition than those in core urban renewal areas and owners apparently retain parcels longer when they know that the area is designated for public support. Abandonment is thus less likely to take place initially due to the above average quality of the parcels and as a result of the owner's slowing down of the process.

In any analysis of abandonment in which there is a time delay between sampling and data analysis some portion of abandoned structures may be returned to the standing stock. But this number is small.

EXHIBIT 7-4

1967-1971 REFINED GROSS RESIDENTIAL ABANDONMENT BY TYPE OF CONSTRUCTION, STATUS OF SECURITY, AND TOTAL NUMBER OF STORIES NEWARK, 1971

Residential Abandonment By Type Of Construction

| | Frame | Masonry | Frame/Masonry | Construction Not Indicated | Total |
|---|---|---|---|---|---|
| Type of construction | | | | | |
| (number) | 1047 | 409 | 5 | 11 | 1472 |
| (percent) | 71.1 | 27.8 | 0.3 | 0.8 | 100.0 |

Residential Abandonment by Status of the Property

| | Open | Secured | Total |
|---|---|---|---|
| Status of security | | | |
| (number) | 652 | 820 | 1472 |
| (percent) | 44.3 | 55.7 | 100.0 |

Residential Abandonment By Number Of Stories

| | One | Two | Three | Four | Five or More | Stories Not Indicated | Total |
|---|---|---|---|---|---|---|---|
| Number of stories | | | | | | | |
| (number) | 42 | 511 | 804 | 97 | 4 | 14 | 1472 |
| (percent) | 2.9 | 34.7 | 54.6 | 6.6 | 0.2 | 1.0 | 100.0 |

Source: Newark Fire Department, Division of Combustibles, Vacant and Razed Building Card File, 1971

## Geographic Dispersal of Abandonment within a Local Area

The geographic impact of abandoned residential parcels varies considerably. At first glimpse it may be seen to be synonymous with blight infestation.[9] As has been shown in an earlier chapter, abandonment does have a geographical element and is also related to other indices of decay, i.e., tax delinquency, fire, and crime. However, relationships between owner and tenant also seem to be keys to the loss or retention of a residential parcel. Therefore, it may be premature to conclude that abandonment is exclusively a function of generally deteriorating areas. Exhibit 7-5 shows the levels of abandonment, by the three categories of tracts used in the sample. Because of urban renewal clearance, however, the pattern is obscured.

In Newark as a whole residential abandonment is taking place at rates of 0.4 to 3.5 percent annually when the city is partitioned according to voting ward structure (Exhibits 7-6, 7-7, and 7-8). It is highest in the Central Ward, moderately high in the East and South Wards, and least evident in the West and North Wards. Historically, the white flight to the suburbs took place initially and most noticeably in the Central and East Wards, is currently far-advanced in the South Ward, and has been retarded somewhat in the Northern and Western Wards due to ethnic solidarity. The extra-market forces at work in these latter two wards make for an abandonment rate which is one-sixth of the Central Ward's and one-half of the Eastern Ward's.

## Summary

Thus, in gross number of abandonments, Newark today is losing approximately 2 percent of its combined residential, commercial, and industrial stock annually. Although in many cases Newark must be viewed at the leading edge in terms of urban decay, certainly St. Louis, Chicago, Philadelphia, Baltimore, and New York fall within a similar classification. Although there is little evidence on which to base an estimate of gross numbers of units, there is increasing evidence of the growing presence of abandonment in these areas.

Within the city of Newark itself, there is great variation as to types of properties which are being abandoned and areas where this abandonment is concentrated.

## EXHIBIT 7-5
### RESIDENTIAL ABANDONMENT BY SAMPLE AREA OF THE CITY, NEWARK, 1971

| | Nonabandoned | Abandoned | Other | Total |
|---|---|---|---|---|
| Area 1 (less than 25% sound housing) | 71 | 34 | 81 | 185 |
| Area 2 (25-50% sound housing) | 122 | 27 | 35 | 184 |
| Area 3 (51-67% sound housing) | 149 | 23 | 27 | 199 |
| Total | 342 | 84 | 143 | 569 |

PERCENT DISTRIBUTION

| | Nonabandoned | Abandoned | Other | Total |
|---|---|---|---|---|
| Area 1 (less than 25% sound housing) | 20.8 | 40.5 | 56.6 | 32.7 |
| Area 2 (25-50% sound housing) | 35.7 | 32.1 | 24.5 | 32.3 |
| Area 3 (51-67% sound housing) | 43.6 | 27.4 | 18.9 | 35.0 |
| Total | 100.0 | 100.0 | 100.0 | 100.0 |

$\chi^2 = 0.01$

Source: Newark Area Resurvey, spring 1972

# EXHIBIT 7-6

## GEOGRAPHIC DISPERSION OF RESIDENTIAL ABANDONMENT BY STATUS OF STRUCTURE WITHIN THE SAMPLE SET

LEGEND

DEFINITION OF ABANDONMENT

● VACANT AND STANDING (OBSERVED)
○ VACANT AND STANDING (LANDLORD)
✱ PRIVATE DEMOLISHMENTS
* PUBLIC (NON-U.R.) DEMOLISHMENTS

ZONES

-·-·-·- AREAS 25% SOUND HOUSING (1960)
- - - - - AREAS 25-50% SOUND HOUSING (1960)
-/-/-/- AREAS 50-67% SOUND HOUSING (1960)

## EXHIBIT 7-7
### RESIDENTIAL ABANDONMENT BY CITY WARD LOCATION
### NEWARK, 1967-1971

| | Ward (Non-Razed Structures) | | | | | |
|---|---|---|---|---|---|---|
| Type of structure | North | West | Central | South | East | Total |
| Residential | | | | | | |
| (number) | 100 | 189 | 449 | 291 | 308 | 1337 |
| (percent) | 7.5 | 14.1 | 33.6 | 21.8 | 23.0 | 100.0 |
| Residential/commercial | | | | | | |
| (number) | 20 | 11 | 23 | 12 | 69 | 135 |
| (percent) | 14.8 | 8.1 | 17.0 | 8.9 | 51.1 | 100.0 |
| Total | | | | | | |
| (number) | 120 | 200 | 472 | 303 | 377 | 1472 |
| (percent) | 8.2 | 13.6 | 32.1 | 20.6 | 25.6 | 100.0 |
| 1967-1971 non-razed residential abandonment as a percent of total 1970 residential structures within each ward | 1.45 (8070) | 2.60 (7695) | 12.36 (3819) | 3.62 (8359) | 5.09 (7413) | 4.16 (35,356) |
| $\chi^2 = 0.01$ | | | | | | |

Source: Newark Fire Department, Newark Area Resurvey, spring 1972

# EXHIBIT 7-8
## 1970 CENSUS TRACTS AND WARD DISTRICT MAP

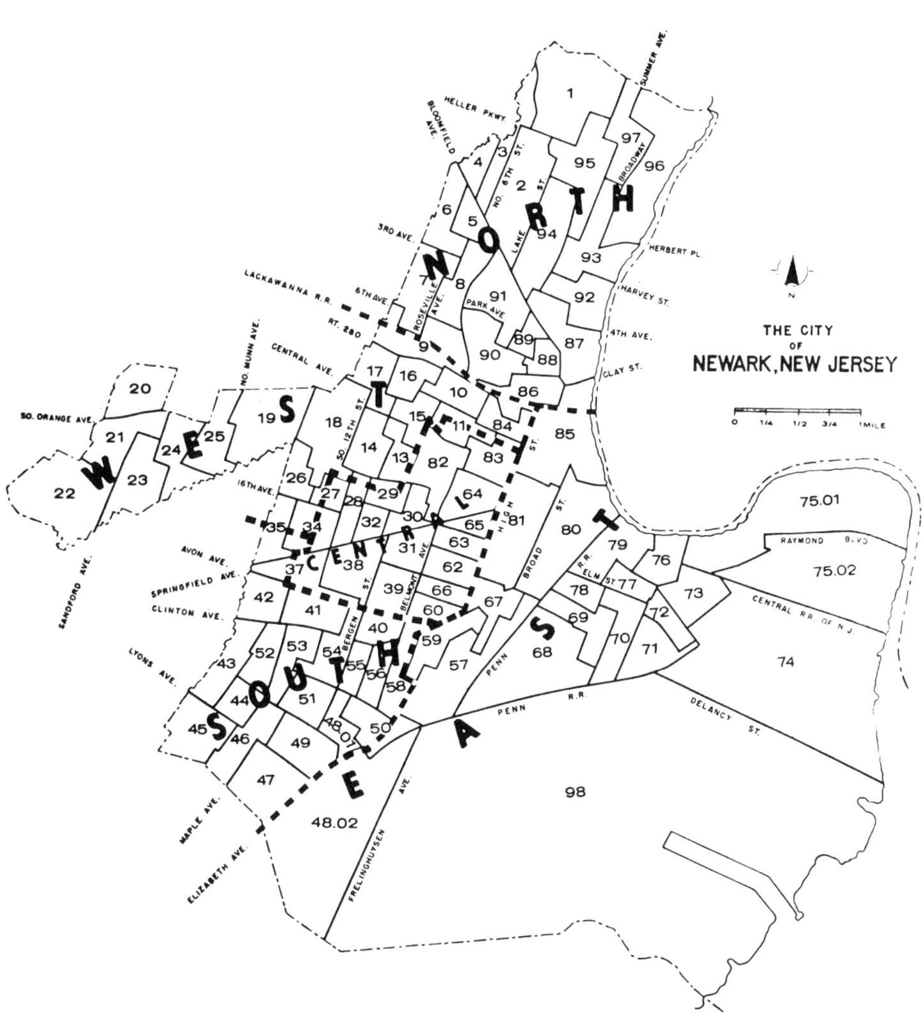

EXHIBIT 7-9
GROSS ABANDONMENT LEVELS
NEWARK, NEW JERSEY, 1967-1971

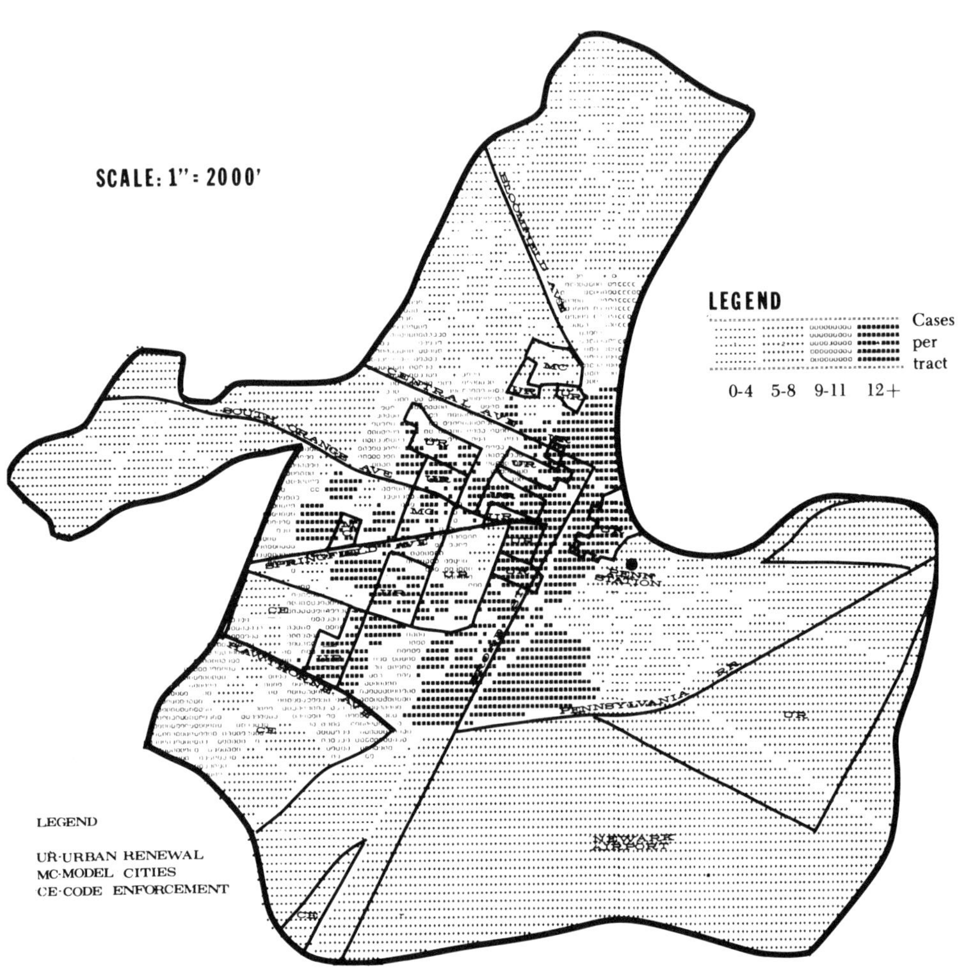

# THE DYNAMICS OF ABANDONMENT

## A Myriad of Specific Occurrences

Why is a parcel abandoned? The reasons are numerous, varied, and, sometimes, obscure. For example:

> Parcel number 108P is a three-story frame structure with four apartments. It was purchased by the present landlord's father in 1900. The present owner, an aged white who lives in one of the fringe areas of Newark, is retired from his job as a machine shop worker. When interviewed in 1965 he had just completed renovating his building, yet it is now vacant and open to weather after two fires. The landlord is not interested in any additional efforts or investment in the structure. His whole hope is to get the ground cleared and "hold it for speculation." The last time that he had the house refinished "before the tenants could move in all my plumbing, the pipes, the sinks, the toilets were stolen. Before that I couldn't even collect rents. Even if I'd fix it up, I can't get good tenants to move in." The parcel is now one tax period in arrears and with carrying costs of over $700 for taxes, will probably be left to the city.

Another case illustrates the vagueness of holding:

> Parcel number 89 is a four-story masonry building with three apartments on the upper floors and a store on the lower floor. It was part of an estate involving more than twenty parcels in Newark. Even in 1964, at the time of our earlier interview, it was vacant, the last tenant just having left at the time of the survey. The owner's responses to why he had abandoned the parcel, assessed at $9,200 including land, was: "I gave it up because I couldn't maintain it. To tell the truth, I don't think I even own it anymore. A lot of the tenants owed rents and they just left. We [the receivers of the estate] weren't going to put our own money into it; if repairs had to be made they'd have to come from rents; we just couldn't handle it anymore. The fire insurance was cancelled a long time ago after a little fire — a $100 claim. But that's it, they just got up and cancelled." The nominal owners have dickered with a non-profit corporation on its sale, but this seems to be hanging fire. In the meantime the parcel gapes open to the weather.

Even the date at which a building is abandoned becomes unclear.

> The three-story masonry building, parcel number 1T is in an area of mixed land use in Newark. Its three apartments have been vacant

> for three years. Its owner, an elderly suburban widow, purchased it fifteen years ago. In her own words: "I never go down there anymore." In the last several years when the building was operative, her involvement with it was negligible, all rents that were received were received by mail. When asked about the potential of rehabilitating the building, her answer was very emphatic, under no circumstances would she borrow. The taxes continue to be paid, the buildings around and peripheral to it are burning down, but her insurance is current; the potential for redevelopment under present tenure negligible.

And certainly one of the complaints voiced by this owner, of problems with tenants (if not with one's own, then with those surrounding the parcel) are close to a common denominator.

Another case in point is the response of a white owner of a two-family masonry parcel, both apartments of which are vacant.

> The owner indicated that for $5,000 they could both be made usable, and that they could conceivably rent for as much as $140 a month each. Though she had heard vaguely of some HUD programs in Newark she had not looked into them as yet; had no specific information on their potential support for rehabilitation investments. According to her, no mortgage money would be available. When asked whether if she made improvements the resale market would support the cost, she said "Never." In the meantime in the midst of the housing shortage the apartment languishes.
>
> It should be noted that on the occasion of our first interview six years earlier the same owner had pointed to the lack of total revenue derived from the property as making it unworthy of basic inputs. At the time, however, she had some intentions of subdividing the two relatively large apartments. Her present feeling is that the neighborhood conditions are so serious as to make it impractical to repair.

The basic comments of owners echo those of the previous holder of a parcel in one of the core slum areas just transferred to a large professional operator management firm. It is assessed for $10,200, had no mortgage, and had been in the same hands since 1932. It is now standing vacant, open to the weather. In 1965 it was owned free and clear and was occupied. The owner has just completed a transaction for a nominal sum to a shell corporation to avoid legal liabilities. Why did he give up?

"The taxes were too high and the rents too low. We haven't tried to rent it in five years, the place is just boarded up. It's an old parcel and needs many, many repairs. The tenants weren't helping and we had trouble with the insurance on the parcel. I don't know what we are going to do about the parcel, we haven't paid taxes for over two years, we'd like the city to take it over. No one would buy this kind of parcel; who would buy a white elephant?"

There is no insurance on the parcel. The owner pointed out that no insurance company would insure a vacant parcel in that particular area.

Sophisticated and unsophisticated owners frequently answer in the same fashion:

Parcel number 35 is a frame six-family house in the hard core slum area of Newark; it is held by a large scale management firm which owns and operates many slum properties. Though there has been a nominal transfer in the last two years, it has basically been in the same hands for at least fifteen years. The windows are smashed, the building is vacant. The owner estimates that it would cost $10,000 to $15,000 to put it into habitable condition, and he has no intention of doing so. Before the firm stopped collecting rents, the rental was from $80 to $120 for four to six rooms respectively.

"There is no resale market in Newark; you can't give property away. If we fix it up the tenants would destroy it, and even if we wanted to do it, there is no place you could turn to for money." The owner was familiar with the federal "312" loan program and noted that the building did not qualify because of its location. The building was vandalized when a number of tenants moved out. The balance of the tenants left, and it simply deteriorated beyond repair within the present economic framework, or at least the landlord's perception of that economic framework.[10]

Nor are complaints about neighborhood influences and problems restricted to white owners:

Parcel number 525, for example, is a three-story, three-apartment frame structure in the semi-industrial area of Newark. It is owned by a black, one man contracting firm who purchased it in 1970 for $500 in anticipation of rehabilitation. The land assessment alone is $1,500, the building assessment $7,800. In 1944 the building was purchased by a resident owner for $3,000. At the time he secured a $2,000 first money mortgage from the seller. The next entry in the title is a sale for $13,000 in 1965 with 100 percent mortgage from the local savings and loan. This mortgage, guaranteed by the VA, was foreclosed in 1969. By this time it had arrived in the sad state in which it presently stands. It was sold to a local speculator for $300 in early 1970 and by him to the present owner for $500. The statement of the present owner is as follows: "I bought three houses (the other two are in the near neighborhood) to rehabilitate and rent. I'm a contractor and I've a permit to do rehab work. I'm currently using them as warehouses — they're not occupied and everything I do there just gets wrecked. I've made some improvements with a view toward renting them, but everything has been broken down."

"I paid for the houses in cash and lowered my cash reserve, I can't get a mortgage until the houses are occupied and until they're improved. And I can't get insurance until the units are occupied. And even then the rate will be very high."

"The police don't come into the area no matter how many times they are called. The big problem, however, is the neighborhood. They wreck all my improvements — everything I've put in has been ripped out. The building inspectors have said either I start work on the properties or I'll have to board them up and the vandals will only break in if that's done. So what am I going to do?"

And in the meantime this building and its peers molder. *There is no financing without insurance, and there is no insurance without rehabilitation, and there can't be any rehabilitation until there is financing; and all of this has to be done in an environment that is difficult and very hostile. Repairs must be made and completed and tenants secured in very short order to safeguard any level of capital investments. But within the framework of needs and necessities, this is practically impossible.*[11]

And it must be remembered that all of this takes place in an old city with an old residual white population whose children may have little interest in either occupying or owning the housing of their parents.

For example, parcel number 089 has been in the same family for sixty years. There are ten descendents of the original owner who are in possession of the parcel. It is a masonry four-story, six-family plus stores building on a major avenue of Newark. The parcel is vacant. No taxes have been paid for more than three years. According to the individual who had nominally managed the parcel, "We had trouble getting the tenants to pay the rent, and there is none of us who had enough serious interest in the building to really pursue them."

In any large sample of humanity (including owners of properties) there will always be some who have severe personal problems whether mental or physical. Parcel number 115 is a case in point. It was purchased in 1959 for $9,000 but has now been shattered beyond repair. Its owner suffered a nervous breakdown because his repair business, among other things, had failed, and, according to his brother-in-law, he simply didn't look after the parcel. Elderly owners, non-caring heirs, personal misfortunes, health difficulties, problems with tenantry — these are constants in any large population of housing units and their owners. What is important here, however, is that *there is no recuperative power based on the independent market for the parcels in question. In Newark and cities like Newark, because of the fragility of the market, what elsewhere would be a trivial happening yielding a bargain to the speculator and to the new buyer, now often proves fatal to the building in question. There is not enough value inherent in the parcel.*

## The Decline of Capital Values[12]

The decline in capital values can be viewed in several ways. First is the reality of current yield together with the multiplier placed on that yield to determine overall value. The variation in the multiplier may be more significant than even the realities of current profitability. And clearly that multiplier is a compound of alternative investment yields, the security of future expectation, as well as a difficult to define, but very significant, negative utility function: *How much of a reward must an owner or potential owner be given for possession and operation of tenement properties over and above equivalent investments in time or money in areas which society may look on with more approval?*

Certainly in the last generation the incentives and status given the landlord, particularly of lower class properties, have diminished substantially. The term landlord, meaning someone of significance in the community, has become synonymous with slumlord, i.e., someone little better than a criminal, an exploiter of the poor, etc.

Clearly, given these pejoratives, the financial rewards of holding must be commensurately increased. *To the extent that stronger negative attitudes exist toward whites owning parcels occupied by minority groups than toward minority group members being landlords and housing their own, white landlords may require more rewards to stay in business than minorities do.*

Even without alterations in the multiplier, extended current yield, and future expectation, the situation in Newark's core areas and in other similar cities is one of a genuine and real decline in capital values. And as shall be noted later in more detail, this may account for the relatively higher level of abandonment on the part of large-scale operators than of small ones. The former have a clearer analysis of the economic function of their structures with no ancillary values attached to them. Their attitudes were characterized by the response of a large-scale operator who owns a four-story, frame structure in the sample. It has been in his family since the 1930s. It is one of the few still held of more than one hundred properties owned in Newark at that time. He said very simply:

> "If you make money, you keep property, if you don't — you drop it. There was no use for us doing anything with that parcel. I couldn't visualize any new or forseeable improvement. The neighborhood's changed drastically and the whole section is so bad that people are afraid. No one would want to live there. So we walked away. Why pay taxes when there's no income. Let the city take it over. What else can I do?"

This building is owned free and clear and it should be noted that the particular landlord has abandoned at least two other parcels in this sample.

> The speed with which property can lose value was illustrated by the experience of parcel number 242. This is a six-family, frame house in an area which, until about twenty years ago, was considered an upper middle class section of the city. The parcel is a large one containing slightly more than 5,000 square feet of living space. It is assessed at $3,600 for the land and $21,800 for the building. In 1961 it was sold for $25,000 with the seller taking back a $19,000 mortgage. The buyer was a grocery store operator in the area. In 1969 it was sold to a small real estate dealer in a nearby suburb for a total of $8,500 with 90 percent taken back by the seller. It is now gutted; the surrounding lawn littered with glass. Three of the apartments are still in use; three are completely vandalized. The current owner said, "I'd give the building away, if only somebody would take it." He estimated that it would cost $20,000 to repair the building and given the high rate of local vandalism, such an action would be "useless." He added, "The area is bad and there's no investment deal possible here." While he was familiar with a variety

of funding mechanisms as well as federal programs, he said, "They'd never give me money for a building in Newark. I have no faith in restoration by urban renewal in Newark."

Examples of this type of attitude seem to be endless:

Parcel number 252, for example, is in a fringe area. In 1965 the brick five-family house with its 4,500 square feet of lot was assessed at $3,000 for land, $21,100 for the building. It had been purchased in 1948 for $11,500 by an experienced, small-scale real estate operator who owned four similar parcels in the city. In 1964, while the owner reported some level of vacancies, including some recent tenants who had skipped out without paying rent, the parcel was in good condition. Even at this time, however, the owner reported that he would not improve the parcel even if given a long-term mortgage because the neighborhood did not warrant it. The building now is vacant and vandalized. The owner has stopped paying taxes. He once owned four or five buildings in Newark but has essentially sold or abandoned all of them. The owner's summary of the reasons was very simple. "Area conditions got so bad, the building was deteriorating and the atmosphere became violent. We closed it up. We abandoned." The building has been vacant for four years. The owner reports no future interest in the parcel, and although he was familiar with government programs, he was not interested in pursuing them. The city, which had an asset which once paid nearly $2,000 in taxes and provided housing for its citizens, has suffered a loss as has the private owner.

Tenement ownership has historically been one of the classic methods whereby relative newcomers to the city acquired capital. Can it serve this purpose for the present group? The previous chapter on minority group owners has centered on this question; and certainly the total results are not in.

Parcel number 544 owned by a Puerto Rican family since December 1964 is a chastening example of some of the problems. The owner was first interviewed shortly after he had purchased the structure. At that time he glowed with enthusiasm. "Since we got married we wanted to buy our own place. Finally our ship came in. We got a little money in the lottery [Puerto Rican Lottery] and decided the time had come for us to own our own place." The owner and his wife were putting in central heat and were bubbling over about their three-story masonry building. The words of our interviewer at that time were as follows: "This is a young couple: the husband has been here for a while and speaks some English, his wife speaks

> none. They have a one year old child and they take her to a relative while they both work. They don't seem to have knowledge of the housing laws and regulations involving real estate and don't have much in the way of management skills, but they are both working."

They secured the building, which was assessed at $10,800, for a not unreasonable $9,500 aided by a $6,500 institutional mortgage. Now the owner is carrying three jobs. He bought a second building in the immediate area but it is vacant and abandoned. He had welfare families in the building but "they destroyed it." Speaking of his own beautifully maintained residence he said, "If you built this building it would cost you double what I paid for it. If you sold it, you'd get half."

## The Impact of Financing Patterns and Acquisition Prices

A fairly common ploy observed when the professionals abandon buildings is for a paper sale to be completed with a very large mortgage being held by the seller. The idea here is that if by some stroke of good fortune the government becomes interested in acquiring the land, this paper sale establishes a base price for an inflated condemnation proceeding.

Perhaps a cursory analysis of an abandoned structure, after the fact, gives the impression that heavy financing requirements have caused the deterioration of the structure. However, the reverse may be the case. The buildings may degenerate to the point where the owner of substance decides to get out from under the title with a failsafe of a large mortgage. *In other words, the very large purchase money mortgage may be the result of the abandonment process rather than the cause of it.*

> An illustration is parcel number 447, a seventeen-family, four-story masonry building owned since 1958 by a major slum operator in Newark. In 1962 the parcel was sold for approximately $46,000 to a shell corporation with the seller, a professional mortgage operator, taking back the $38,000 mortgage. After some nominal transfers, the parcel was sold in 1971 on an all purchase money mortgage deal to a black owner who lives in an adjoining suburb. Ten of the seventeen tenants are behind in their rents. The black couple who own the property are trying to sell, but there are no buyers. They owe $7,000 for plumbing and oil bills. The basic mortgage

> apparently is held by a savings and loan institution which dates back to 1961. When interviewed, officers of the company anticipated the foreclosure of the building shortly.

There is little evidence that the black speculator who sold the building actually made any money on it. In 1971 he essentially abandoned his equity by taking back the second mortgage with no cash on the transfer. The building appears to be shattered beyond repair. The speculator admitted that he had no idea who owned the building and wasn't interested since he no longer had any title or any hopes for it, although he holds the second mortgage.

Despite this, there is no question that unsophisticated buyers are frequently victimized by speculators. This pattern is exemplified by parcel number 582. The parcel was purchased in 1964 for $18,000, the first mortgage was secured from a savings and loan for $10,000, and the parcel was appraised at $12,500. At the time it was a handsome, three-family, frame house; it now gapes open, with a large "*For Sale*" sign on it. The owner was first interviewed shortly after he purchased the structure.

The owner is Puerto Rican and the interview which follows is translated from the Spanish in which it was conducted.

> "I've never owned property; I had an accident, I got hit by a truck. I got some money, and friends and relatives advised me to invest in buying a house. I bought it to use the rent and maybe some day eventually sell. This way I get my rent free and maybe when my son grows up I will sell it and move to Puerto Rico." When questioned about improvements, at that time of our interview in 1964, he said, "Until I pay off the mortgage I cannot think of any major improvements — to buy this house took every penny I had."

The owner at that time was working at an electronics assembly plant in Newark. He had the feeling that he had probably over paid for the building but it was difficult for him to admit it to our female interviewer. The taxes on the house are now almost $1,200; the owner is desperately trying to sell it since he cannot maintain the mortgage. (Note: in this case there was a large down payment and no government program was involved.)

The pattern of members of minority groups, particularly, paying inflated prices precedes the recent FHA debacle. In 1963 a young black mechanic bought the house in which his mother was living because he and his wife were working and the mother needed a place to live while she, in turn, cared for the children. The house was assessed at $8,400, but was sold for $13,469. The first mortgage was taken back by the real estate dealer for $7,469, and a $4,500 second mortgage was held by the previous owner. The buyer's down payment was about $1,500. The new owner had some personal problems which involved his employment. In February, 1971, the holder of the first mortgage foreclosed on what had become empty property. In turn it was sold to a black rehabilitation firm for $2,872. The building now needs complete reconstruction.

As noted in the chapter on minority group owners, there is no question that homes sold to unwary buyers have been substantially overpriced, particularly with government financed or guaranteed mortgage help. Unfortunately, these overpayments are *not* necessarily central to the abandonment phenomenon. Declining capital values are so pervasive that they clearly show the need for more penetrating analysis.

Adequate information on sales prices over time was not always available because of the difficulty of reconstructing extant mortgages and blanket sales, i.e., two or more parcels at one transfer. There is some indication, however, that in general over the last eight to ten years there has been an absolute reduction in price of approximately 40 percent on a large number of parcels for which sales data could be assembled.

The impact of the decline in value cannot be overstated in accounting for owner insecurity in improving parcels. In 1963, for example, a three-family, frame home in a fringe area was purchased for $17,500 by an elderly nonresident white who "Bought it to supplement my social security when I retired." In 1969, one of the last large scale speculators in Newark bought the same parcel for half the price.

The decline in value frequently has been so abrupt as to outrun the speculators.

> For example, parcel number 588 is a three-story, masonry structure. The building is assessed for $13,000, the land at $2,200, with a tax bill of about $1,400. In 1952 it was sold to an absentee landlord for $16,000, a savings and loan association took the first mortgage of $9,000, a second mortgage of $3,900 was taken by the seller, with a mortgage broker in turn taking his commission as part of the selling price in a third mortgage of $680. Although, the owner made some improvements in the property, by 1963 the building was taken over by a professional speculator "as a favor to the previous owner." The

mortgage, which was open-ended, was restated at its original amount of $9,000, the second and third mortgages were wiped off. Over and above the first mortgage, the speculator paid $3,500, i.e., a decline in the selling price of $16,000 to $12,500 from 1952 to 1963, which, nationally, were years of great inflation in real estate values. The building now, eight years later, in the speculator's own words is "in the process of being abandoned. No rents are collected, there are three tenants there but I don't know who they are or what they are. They are probably black." No repairs have been made for ". . . a long time. I wouldn't even try to put it in good condition; I just want to let it go." The taxes aren't paid and the boiler is not working. "The tenants blew it up. I'm finished with it."

*In sum, the problem of the inflated sales price is a serious one and has a considerable impact on the abandonment rate. However, to assume that abandonments would stop if transfers were made at a more legitimate level is a drastic oversimplification.*

## Urban Renewal and Abandonment

Earlier chapters discussed in detail the substantial extent of urban renewal designations in Newark, landlord attitudes toward the equity of land taking under the programs, and so on. But what is the impact of urban renewal and other forms of governmental land taking on abandonment? The urban renewal program and other forms of governmental land taking are grouped together because in the public mind, as reflected in the interviews, they tended to be thought of as synonymous. Whether land is being taken as part of the urban renewal program or for a new highway is irrelevant to owners and tenants. It is "all urban renewal." It should be noted that until fairly recently the public considered the less adequate forms of notification and indemnification under land taking programs, other than those for urban renewal, sins of renewal itself. Certainly in the landlords' minds there is a very real problem in that rumors of land taking for any form of governmental program result in an evacuation of tenantry with concomitant vandalization and abandonment.

This refrain is repeated in a large number of interviews:

Parcel number 288 was a four-family house that lost all of its tenantry, according to the owner, three years ago when it was announced a highway interchange (Route 75) was going through.

The building was vandalized and has since been demolished by the city. The property still has not been taken for the highway and there is some question about whether the highway will ever be built. The problems of the parcel left over after land taking has begun can be horrendous.

Parcel number 145 is a small three-story house with a store on the ground floor and two apartments on each of its other floors. The apartments rent at approximately $50 to $55 per month, only $5 more than in 1965. The owner, who formerly operated the fish store on the ground floor, has moved both his business and residence to an adjoining, older suburb. The building was owned by the same individual for more than twenty years. It is in the path of the much anticipated, but now cancelled Route 75. The area around it was aptly described by the owner as "looking like the Gaza Strip." The apartments are very shoddy and need real repair. The owner, however, when asked about making improvements if he was sure of not getting a boost in taxes, pointed out that the building is too old — over eighty years — and besides the highway was going to be built there. For the moment that does not seem to be occurring; the owner isn't sure of the future of the parcel; and there are no potential alternative buyers. One apartment is vacant; the other seems near to going; the store is closed; and the parcel is clearly on the road to abandonment — its future disposal hopelessly caught up in the path of stymied highway construction.

These cases are numerous. On the other hand, a number of owners said that they can only get their money out of the properties if taken by urban renewal, and then only if the building looks functional, i.e., not boarded up at the time of taking. The hope for an urban renewal taking as one of the few ways of "getting your money out" was a frequent refrain, though sometimes an inadequate one to insure appropriate maintenance.

Parcel number 259 is a four-apartment plus two-store frame structure on one of the old shopping streets of the city. Its windows are broken and the building abandoned by tenants, though not boarded up. Vandalized and littered with garbage, it has been standing in the same condition for three years. As far back as 1965 its owner reported it to have been a very poor buy. He bought it in 1963 for $9,000, securing a first mortgage of $5,000 from a savings and loan. The parcel is assessed at $13,300. He reported that he is keeping it because he can't sell it. It is in a distressed area that nobody wants and he is waiting for the city to take the parcel (though it is not in an urban renewal area).

The same owner still has the same parcel; it has not been taken. Tenants left when they heard that the area was going to be cleared for urban renewal. At the second interview it was clear that the owner had bought the building intending to get a fast return on an urban renewal taking which he had been assured was forthcoming.

There is a mixed picture in terms of urban renewal and the dynamics of abandonment. Some owners cling to property, though sometimes in poor condition or unlivable, hoping for a windfall from the federal taking procedures. At the same time tenants frequently feel that the lifetime of their residence is short because of rumored taking and leave, with the resultant harm to the building and the neighborhood.

> For example, parcel number 107 is a masonry four-story structure with stores on the bottom floor and six rental units above it. It is now in the hands of the Newark Housing Authority. It was purchased in 1951 for $9,500, with a first mortgage retained by the seller for $5,500. Even then this price compared with a land assessment of $1,800 and a building assessment of $14,800. The owner in the 1964 interview pointed to difficulties in collecting rent and stated that though he wanted to sell the parcel he simply couldn't because of the blighted area "where people don't want to live; up until three years ago the parcel showed 20 to 25 percent return but now there's no return. But I don't want to sell because of the possibilities of takeover by the federal or city authorities." Even in 1965 he could not get insurance except at a very high rate. By 1971 the building was empty; the owner's wait for urban renewal had not paid off. The parcel had been foreclosed by the city.

Much more analysis and improvement of the implementation of urban renewal and other land taking programs are required not only for Newark, but all across the country. Better forms of land taking, perhaps with greater safeguards against speculation, must be devised. The use of relatively secretive acquisition procedures, in order to minimize costs and complaints, is much too costly in other ways to be permitted by public authorities. Unless there is confidence in precisely where urban renewal and other governmental taking are to take place and strict adherence to a schedule for them, the results are chaotic and scarcely in accordance with federal policies and objectives.

## The Problem of Insurance

In the last case interview, the owner of parcel number 107 had considerable difficulty, as far back as 1965, in getting insurance. He claimed that normal fire insurance at that time would have been $61. He was paying $275 to a foreign company and not securing full coverage. This was on a building which with full occupancy had a rent roll of under $4,000.

The prevalence and significance of fires in Newark as both the cause and consequence of abandonment is sufficient enough to deserve a chapter by itself. Certainly, however, despite the FAIR plans which became operative after the 1968 riots, there is still considerable dissatisfaction about the availability and costs of insurance, particularly for fire coverage, in the core area. The complaint of one black owner, who has owned the same property since 1961, typifies some of the responses. "We can't get insurance, either fire or accident. We never had any problem all these years. We've been married, and had our own house even before we owned this one, since 1935. But our insurance was cancelled because we live in a bad neighborhood." A large number of parcels do not have any insurance at all.

As described earlier, when landlords were given a list of possible problems in operating and maintaining their properties to rate, insurance was the single largest volunteered response to the question of whether there were any other problems. Obviously, insurance affects financing parcels. Without insurance institutional financing is precluded unless the bank is caught on a mortgage which it simply can't get out of. Even in that case, bank examiners usually will not permit as collateral improved real estate which does not have appropriate forms of fire insurance. Some improvements have been made under the FAIR plan to enable owners to secure proper insurance. Still more must be done.

The broad sweep of forces that lead to maintaining a parcel or abandoning it operate through the filter of owners and their attitudes. Do the 1964 interviews yield predictors of later abandonment?

## THE ABANDONED BUILDING OWNER[13]

In the analysis which follows, the characteristics of owners of parcels with whom successful interviews were concluded in 1964 are split into two categories: those parcels which were abandoned by 1971 and those which were not. Each of the characteristics of owners i.e., experience, ethnicity, motivation for purchase, and the like, are examined separately. Later in the work these are brought together in both factor analysis and multiple regression work. It is important, however, particularly considering the interrelationships of some of these characteristics such as scale of holding and ethnicity, that they be examined separately.

It should be noted that parcels taken for public purposes, as well as other factors which seem extraneous to the functional analysis are excluded. This leaves a residue of 286 parcels of which 59 were abandoned by 1971.

### Owner Experience

As Exhibit 7-10 illustrates, there is a tendency for those buildings which have been abandoned (the 59 shown in column two) to be in the hands of long-term buyers; while the folklore of the field generally is that new, less-experienced participants in the market are those who abandoned properties. That is not the finding of this study. For example, of the 286 owners for whom there are 1964 data, 23.3 percent of the nonabandoners entered the market from 1960 to date as compared with 11.9 percent of the abandoned parcel owners. More than half (50.9 percent) of the abandoned structures were in the hands of owners who had entered the market before 1950, as compared with 39.2 percent of the nonabandoned parcel owners.

### Scale of Operation

Exhibit 7-11 shows that there is a mixed pattern for the scale of operation as a function of abandonment. The strongest holders clearly are owners who own no other parcel. As will be shown later, this is linked to residency. Over half, 54.2 percent, of the nonabandoned parcels, but only 18.6 percent of the abandoned parcels, were in the hands of people who owned no other real estate in 1964. The greatest

## EXHIBIT 7-10
### OWNER'S DATE OF ENTRANCE TO THE RENTAL REAL ESTATE MARKET (1964) BY DEFINITION OF ABANDONMENT

| First Owned Real Estate | Nonabandoned | Abandoned | Total |
|---|---|---|---|
| Pre 1930 | 19 | 8 | 27 |
| 1930-1940 | 13 | 5 | 18 |
| 1940-1950 | 57 | 17 | 74 |
| 1950-1955 | 39 | 14 | 53 |
| 1955-1960 | 38 | 8 | 46 |
| 1960-1964 | 53 | 7 | 60 |
| No Answer | 8 | 0 | 8 |
| Total | 227 | 59 | 286 |
| PERCENT DISTRIBUTION | | | |
| Pre 1930 | 8.4 | 13.6 | 9.4 |
| 1930-1940 | 5.7 | 8.5 | 6.3 |
| 1940-1950 | 25.1 | 28.8 | 25.9 |
| 1950-1955 | 17.2 | 23.7 | 18.5 |
| 1955-1960 | 16.7 | 13.6 | 16.1 |
| 1960-1964 | 23.3 | 11.9 | 21.0 |
| No Answer | 3.5 | 0.0 | 2.8 |
| Total | 100.0 | 100.0 | 100.0 |

$\chi^2$ n/s @ 0.05

Source: Newark Area Resurvey, spring, 1972

level of discontinuity is in the middle range operators, those who own one or two to those who own from six to twelve additional parcels. They bulk most substantially in the hands of abandoners as against nonabandoned parcel owners with a ratio of two to one. When the relatively small sample of owners who own twelve or more parcels is analyzed, however, their level of abandonment does not seem to be skewed one way or the other. They own the same proportion of abandoned as nonabandoned structures. Interestingly, when the degree of involvement in real estate generally was studied, this pattern continued, with the proportion of full-time real estate operators nearly

EXHIBIT 7-11
OWNER'S SIZE OF HOLDING (1964) BY DEFINITION OF ABANDONMENT

| Number of Other Parcels | Nonabandoned | Abandoned | Total |
|---|---|---|---|
| No other | 123 | 11 | 134 |
| Other (1 or 2) | 39 | 17 | 56 |
| 3-6 | 19 | 11 | 30 |
| 7-12 | 10 | 8 | 18 |
| 13 plus | 31 | 8 | 39 |
| Used to own more than 2 but no more | 0 | 1 | 1 |
| Used to own 1 other but no more | 2 | 1 | 3 |
| NA/DK | 3 | 2 | 5 |
| Total | 227 | 59 | 286 |

PERCENT DISTRIBUTION

| | Nonabandoned | Abandoned | Total |
|---|---|---|---|
| No other | 54.2 | 18.6 | 46.9 |
| Other (1 or 2) | 17.2 | 28.8 | 19.6 |
| 3-6 | 8.4 | 18.6 | 10.5 |
| 7-12 | 4.4 | 13.6 | 6.3 |
| 13 plus | 13.7 | 13.6 | 13.6 |
| Used to own more than 2 but no more | 0.0 | 1.7 | 0.3 |
| Used to own 1 other but no more | 0.9 | 1.7 | 1.0 |
| NA/DK | 1.3 | 3.4 | 1.7 |
| Total | 100.0 | 100.0 | 100.0 |

$\chi^2 = 0.001$

Source: Newark Area Resurvey, spring, 1972

the same in abandoned and nonabandoned structures, while owners who made from one-third to three-quarters of their income from real estate comprise 12.3 percent of the owners of nonabandoned parcels but 20.3 percent of the abandoned parcels. Other than that there was no major division here.

## Occupation of Owner

The patterns of owner occupation are shown in Exhibit 7-12. It is the housewives as owners who have a high propensity toward abandonment; 8.5 percent versus 4.8 percent. On inspection these often turned out to be owners by inheritance, etc., rather than residents. Lawyers and real estate brokers bulk twice as large in the abandoned parcel group as in the nonabandoned, while basic blue collar skills were underrepresented in the abandonment group.

## Residence and Age of Owner

There is little variation in age of owner between abandoned and nonabandoned parcel holders of record in 1964. Exhibit 7-13 shows the place of residence of the owners as a function of abandonment. The skew is evident: *46.3 percent of the nonabandoners were resident owners as contrasted with 11.9 percent of the abandoned parcel owners.* By way of contrast, 47.5 percent of the abandoned parcel owners lived outside of Newark, though within a twenty-mile radius, as compared with 29.1 percent of the nonabandoned parcel owners. The significance of this pattern is evident. *Despite some of the delinquency problems under FHA mortgage programs for new resident owners, resident ownership has been ownership which has not abandoned. And, to the degree that this is a predictive as well as an historic fact, there seems to be little alternative except to continue to encourage this pattern, assuming that the pace of abandonment is to be slowed.*

## Motivation for Purchase

Of the nonabandoned parcels, 33.8 percent were in the hands of people who had bought strictly for the purposes of residence as compared with only 5.2 percent of the abandoned structures. In the latter case, 69 percent of the owners had bought for rental return as compared with 36 percent of the nonabandoned. Even considering the home plus income response, it too is skewed toward the nonabandoned parcels with 14 percent of the owners of such parcels giving this response as compared with 10.3 percent of the abandoned.

EXHIBIT 7-12
OCCUPATION OF OWNER (1964) BY DEFINITION OF ABANDONMENT

| Job Description | Nonabandoned | Abandoned | Total |
|---|---|---|---|
| Housewife | 11 | 5 | 16 |
| Lawyer | 12 | 7 | 19 |
| Real estate broker | 19 | 9 | 28 |
| Real estate manager | 20 | 4 | 24 |
| House oriented craftsman | 8 | 1 | 9 |
| Craftsman, other | 77 | 6 | 83 |
| Other professions and managerial | 17 | 10 | 27 |
| Retired | 31 | 6 | 37 |
| NA/DK | 32 | 11 | 43 |
| Total | 227 | 59 | 286 |
| PERCENT DISTRIBUTION | | | |
| Housewife | 4.8 | 8.5 | 5.6 |
| Lawyer | 5.3 | 11.9 | 6.6 |
| Real estate broker | 8.4 | 15.3 | 9.8 |
| Real estate manager | 8.8 | 6.8 | 8.4 |
| House oriented craftsman | 3.5 | 1.7 | 3.1 |
| Craftsman, other | 33.9 | 10.2 | 29.0 |
| Other professions and managerial | 7.5 | 16.9 | 9.4 |
| Retired | 13.7 | 10.2 | 12.9 |
| NA/DK | 14.1 | 18.6 | 15.0 |
| Total | 100.0 | 100.0 | 100.0 |

$\chi^2$ n/s @ 0.05

Source: Newark Area Resurvey, spring 1972

## Number of Units in Structure by Definition of Abandonment

As shown in Exhibit 7-14 there is some skew in size of parcel and abandonment. Of the nonabandoned structures, 78 percent are three- to six-unit buildings as compared with only 64.4 percent of the abandoned ones. In the latter case 23.7 percent are seven- to twenty-four units as

## EXHIBIT 7-13
## OWNER'S ADDRESS OF RECORD (1964) BY DEFINITION OF ABANDONMENT

| Place of Residence | Nonabandoned | Abandoned | Total |
|---|---|---|---|
| Same house | 105 | 7 | 112 |
| Within study area | 20 | 6 | 26 |
| Balance of Newark | 29 | 9 | 38 |
| Within 20 mile radius of Newark | 66 | 28 | 94 |
| Balance of New Jersey | 1 | 1 | 2 |
| New York City | 1 | 2 | 3 |
| Elsewhere | 1 | 2 | 3 |
| NA | 2 | 2 | 4 |
| DK | 2 | 2 | 4 |
| Total | 227 | 59 | 286 |
| PERCENT DISTRIBUTION | | | |
| Same house | 46.3 | 11.9 | 39.2 |
| Within study area | 8.8 | 10.2 | 9.1 |
| Balance of Newark | 12.8 | 15.3 | 13.3 |
| Within 20 mile radius of Newark | 29.1 | 47.5 | 32.9 |
| Balance of New Jersey | 0.4 | 1.7 | 0.7 |
| New York City | 0.4 | 3.4 | 1.0 |
| Elsewhere | 0.4 | 3.4 | 1.0 |
| NA | 0.9 | 3.4 | 1.4 |
| DK | 0.9 | 3.4 | 1.4 |
| Total | 100.0 | 100.0 | 100.0 |

$\chi^2 = 0.001$

Source: Newark Area Resurvey, spring, 1972

compared with 10.6 percent of the nonabandoned ones. It suggests that this too is linked to the new ownership groups who are least likely to abandon structures; for whom residence is more significant, perhaps, than immediate return. It may also indicate the decline of management firms which are practically essential for nonresident owners of larger parcels.

EXHIBIT 7-14
NUMBER OF UNITS IN STRUCTURE (1964)
BY DEFINITION OF ABANDONMENT

| Units | Nonabandoned | Abandoned | Total |
|---|---|---|---|
| 3 to 6 | 177 | 38 | 215 |
| 7 to 12 | 17 | 13 | 30 |
| 13 to 24 | 7 | 1 | 8 |
| Sleeping rooms | 8 | 1 | 9 |
| Other | 2 | 0 | 2 |
| Less than 3 units | 14 | 4 | 18 |
| NA | 1 | 1 | 2 |
| DK | 1 | 1 | 2 |
| Total | 227 | 59 | 286 |
| PERCENT DISTRIBUTION | | | |
| 3 to 6 | 78.0 | 64.4 | 75.2 |
| 7 to 12 | 7.5 | 22.0 | 10.5 |
| 13 to 24 | 3.1 | 1.7 | 2.8 |
| Sleeping rooms | 3.5 | 1.7 | 3.1 |
| Other | 0.9 | 0.0 | 0.7 |
| Less than 3 units | 6.2 | 6.8 | 6.3 |
| NA | 0.4 | 1.7 | 0.7 |
| DK | 0.4 | 1.7 | 0.7 |
| Total | 100.0 | 100.0 | 100.0 |

$\chi^2 = 0.05$

Source: Newark Area Resurvey, spring, 1972

## Forms of Ownership

The relationship between small-scale ownership and nonabandonment is indicated by the fact that 89.4 percent of the buildings not abandoned in the original sample were held by individual ownerships, including husband and wife. This compares with 76.3 percent of those that were abandoned. While corporate holdings were roughly similar, only 4.8 percent of the nonabandoned, but 13.5 percent of the abandoned were partnerships with two different names represented. Though personal holding, including husband and wife, was far from a guarantee of nonabandonment, the patterns are obvious.

## Owner Ethnicity

In Exhibit 7-15 owner ethnicity is shown as a function of abandonment. The pattern speaks for itself; while 15.3 percent of the abandoned parcels were owned by blacks in 1964, 38.3 percent of the nonabandoned ones were similarly held. A substantially different finding occurs when white ownership is considered. Here 85.7 percent of the abandoned parcels were in such hands as compared with 56.8 percent of the nonabandoned ones. It is in this area that the link with residence patterns and, as will be seen later, landlord's attitudes toward municipal problems and the future, becomes clear.

Some of the nominal black ownership of abandoned structures follows the case of parcel number 013.

> This three-family, frame house, windows gaping, is a wreck. It illustrates the nebulous nature of some of the ownership data. It had been purchased in 1956 for $5,500 with subject mortgage of $4,000 and purchase money mortgage of $1,275. At the time of the 1964 interview, the parcel was reported in good condition. It had relatively low taxes, with land assessment of $1,500 and the building assessment of $5,000. By 1967, its white owners had turned it over to a local black resident. While the title indicates a sale for a nominal $1,000, the new owner, when interviewed, indicated that she had paid $1.00. All the mortgages had been wiped off. The parcel, however, was tax delinquent by $400. The interview with the new owner, a middle-aged, black woman follows.
>
> Question: "Why did you give up the structure?"
>
> "I didn't have money, I didn't have much money to start with. People knew the place was vacant; they'd go in and steal. The winos, the drug addicts, even the plumber will go back and take whatever he put in. When I bought it, it had just become vacant. I had troubles with the fire department. They said I'd have to board it up and clean it up. I did it twice and I was finished. They wouldn't leave it clean and then they took everything out."
>
> The new owner paid half of the $400 in back taxes and then stopped. The parcel has now been transferred for a nominal payment to the NAACP, but in the eight months that have followed this last sale, nothing has been done and the parcel from outward appearances looks fit only for the wrecker's ball.

# EXHIBIT 7-15
## OWNER'S ETHNICITY (1964) BY DEFINITION OF ABANDONMENT

| Owner Ethnicity | Nonabandoned | Abandoned | Total |
|---|---|---|---|
| Black | 87 | 9 | 96 |
| White | 129 | 50 | 179 |
| Spanish-speaking | 4 | 0 | 4 |
| Other | 1 | 0 | 1 |
| DK | 6 | 0 | 6 |
| Total | 227 | 59 | 286 |

PERCENT DISTRIBUTION

| Owner Ethnicity | Nonabandoned | Abandoned | Total |
|---|---|---|---|
| Black | 90.6 | 9.4 | 100.0 |
| White | 72.1 | 27.9 | 100.0 |
| Spanish-speaking | 100.0 | 0.0 | 100.0 |
| Other | 100.0 | 0.0 | 100.0 |
| DK | 100.0 | 0.0 | 100.0 |
| Total | 79.4 | 20.6 | 100.0 |

PERCENT DISTRIBUTION

| Owner Ethnicity | Nonabandoned | Abandoned | Total |
|---|---|---|---|
| Black | 38.3 | 15.3 | 33.6 |
| White | 56.8 | 85.7 | 62.6 |
| Spanish-speaking | 1.8 | 0.0 | 1.4 |
| Other | 0.4 | 0.0 | 0.3 |
| DK | 2.6 | 0.0 | 2.1 |
| Total | 100.0 | 100.0 | 100.0 |

$\chi^2 = 0.01$

Source: Newark Area Resurvey, spring, 1972

## Income

The response to income questions is unquestionably one of the least trustworthy in studies of this kind. There seems to be some distinct skew (Exhibit 7-16), however, which, despite the substantial number of no answers, don't knows, and misinformation that was given, indicates that in general, owners with higher incomes had a greater tendency to abandon than their equivalent among the owners of nonabandoned parcels. Of those owners who abandoned parcels, 20.3 percent had incomes of over $20,000 as compared with less than a third (6.2 percent) that of the owners of the nonabandoned parcels. Even allowing for the weakness in the response rate and the distortion that creeps into responses on sensitive questions such as this, the pattern is evident.

EXHIBIT 7-16

OWNER'S INCOME (1964) AND ABANDONMENT

| Income Categories | Nonabandoned | Abandoned | Total |
|---|---|---|---|
| $3,000-$5,000 | 37 | 6 | 43 |
| $5,000-$8,000 | 38 | 8 | 46 |
| $8,000-$11,000 | 36 | 10 | 46 |
| $11,000-$20,000 | 20 | 8 | 28 |
| Over $20,000 | 14 | 12 | 26 |
| Less than $3,000 | 24 | 7 | 31 |
| NA | 52 | 7 | 59 |
| DK | 6 | 1 | 7 |
| Total | 227 | 59 | 286 |
| PERCENT DISTRIBUTION | | | |
| $3,000-$5,000 | 16.3 | 10.2 | 15.0 |
| $5,000-$8,000 | 16.7 | 13.6 | 16.1 |
| $8,000-$11,000 | 15.9 | 16.9 | 16.1 |
| $11,000-$20,000 | 8.8 | 13.6 | 9.8 |
| Over $20,000 | 6.2 | 20.3 | 9.1 |
| Less than $3,000 | 10.6 | 11.9 | 10.8 |
| NA | 22.9 | 11.9 | 20.6 |
| DK | 2.6 | 1.7 | 2.4 |
| Total | 100.0 | 100.0 | 100.0 |

$\chi^2 = 0.05$

Source: Newark Area Resurvey, spring 1972

# OPERATING, INSPECTION, AND TAXATION PROCEDURES AND TENANT-OWNER CHARACTERISTICS IN RELATION TO ABANDONMENT

## The Use of a Manager

Of the fifty-seven parcels which were abandoned by 1971 and for which data were collected on this point in 1964, eighteen (31.6 percent) had owners who used rent collectors or managers as against 9.4 percent of the nonabandoned parcels. In simpler terms, nine out of ten of the nonabandoned parcels had owners who collected their own rents versus barely two out of three of the abandoned ones.

## Frequency of Rent Collection

The pattern of rent collection may be the most useful advance indicator of parcels which are highly vulnerable. In Exhibit 7-17 the pattern of rent collection frequency is shown as a function of abandonment. Note that 79.3 percent of the nonabandoned structures, as compared with 67.8 percent of the abandoned structures, have purely monthly rent collection. The variation is made up by the pattern of nominal monthly collection procedures. In this group the landlord, though he nominally charges by the month, in effect, collects when he can, whether by the week, two weeks, or taking whatever he can get while keeping the balance as an account receivable. This pattern made up 6.6 percent of the nonabandoned structures. It made up fully 22 percent, three times as much, in the abandoned ones.

## Tenant Ethnicity as a Predictor of Abandonment

As shown in Exhibit 7-18 there is a significant deviation in the pattern of abandonment as a function of tenant ethnicity. Nearly a fourth, 23.3 percent, of the parcels which were not abandoned had all white tenantry, compared to 6.8 percent of the abandoned ones. The complement of this was the 62.1 percent of the nonabandoned structures which were all black in tenantry as compared with 86.4 percent of the abandoned ones. Unfortunately the other subsets of mixed buildings and those with Puerto Rican or Spanish-speaking tenantry, were too small for any type of generalization.

EXHIBIT 7-17
OWNER'S FREQUENCY OF RENT COLLECTION (1964) AND ABANDONMENT

| Collect Rent | Nonabandoned | Abandoned | Total |
|---|---|---|---|
| Weekly | 13 | 4 | 17 |
| Monthly | 180 | 40 | 220 |
| Partly each | 11 | 2 | 13 |
| Other | 2 | 0 | 2 |
| Nominal monthly | 15 | 13 | 28 |
| No tenants, but house partly occupied | 2 | 0 | 2 |
| NA/DK | 4 | 0 | 4 |
| Total | 227 | 59 | 286 |
| PERCENT DISTRIBUTION | | | |
| Weekly | 5.7 | 6.8 | 5.9 |
| Monthly | 79.3 | 67.8 | 76.9 |
| Partly each | 4.8 | 3.4 | 4.5 |
| Other | 0.9 | 0.0 | 0.7 |
| Nominal monthly | 6.6 | 22.0 | 9.8 |
| No tenants, but house partly occupied | 0.9 | 0.0 | 0.7 |
| NA/DK | 1.8 | 0.0 | 1.4 |
| Total | 100.0 | 100.0 | 100.0 |

$\chi^2$ n/s @ 0.05

Source: Newark Area Resurvey, spring 1972

## Owner Confidence in the Future

The mood of apathy that permeates many of the interviews with owners is difficult to exaggerate.

> Parcel number 090 is a three-story, three-family, frame house in a formerly Italian area of Newark. The present owner inherited it in 1958 from his father who had lived there more than thirty years. The three apartments were all occupied by black welfare recipients. When asked why he kept the parcel the owner said, "We can't sell it, we might as well keep it for land value, the building is becoming

## EXHIBIT 7-18
### TENANT ETHNICITY (1964) AND ABANDONMENT

| Tenant Ethnicity | Nonabandoned | Abandoned | Total |
|---|---|---|---|
| Black | 141 | 51 | 192 |
| White | 53 | 4 | 57 |
| Mixed | 18 | 3 | 21 |
| Spanish-speaking | 1 | 0 | 1 |
| Black and Spanish-speaking | 6 | 0 | 6 |
| Spanish-speaking and other | 3 | 0 | 3 |
| All three | 3 | 0 | 3 |
| NA/DK | 2 | 1 | 3 |
| Total | 227 | 59 | 286 |
| PERCENT DISTRIBUTION | | | |
| Black | 62.1 | 86.4 | 67.1 |
| White | 23.3 | 6.8 | 19.9 |
| Mixed | 7.9 | 5.1 | 7.3 |
| Spanish-speaking | 0.4 | 0.0 | 0.3 |
| Black and Spanish-speaking | 2.6 | 0.0 | 2.1 |
| Spanish-speaking and other | 1.3 | 0.0 | 1.0 |
| All three | 1.3 | 0.0 | 1.0 |
| NA/DK | 0.9 | 1.7 | 1.0 |
| Total | 100.0 | 100.0 | 100.0 |

$\chi^2$ n/s @ 0.05

Source: Newark Area Resurvey, spring, 1972.

worthless — let it rot." The owner is a blue collar worker who lives in one of the fringe areas of Newark. And while he pointed to the fact that the housing shortage meant that there were few vacancies, the apartments were in such bad repair that the present rents of $60 per month were all that they were worth. Under no circumstances would he "mess with the mortgage." While the apartments are still occupied, many of the windows are smashed. He feels that there is no resale market, so what's the point in making any repairs. "Even when you want to make repairs, there's nobody that's willing to go into this area."

Even among more recent owners there is a basic feeling of disillusionment that comes through the interviews, particularly with white owners who purchased shortly before the first survey. Parcel number 375 is a three-family frame house with large apartments renting for an average of $125 a month. The white purchaser in 1964 paid $18,000, $5,500 cash above a $12,500 mortgage secured from a savings and loan association. In 1964, during a lengthy interview with him, he said that this was the first of a series of acquisitions of "undervalued" Newark real estate. He had developed a systematic method of projecting operating statements and was self-described as embarking on a series of acquisitions. By 1971 he seemed most interested in getting rid of the parcel and he agreed that if he did he would have to provide the financing.

But this is a reflection of current fact and outlook. What other advance indicators were there in 1964 from which some of this could have been predicted?

## Would You Improve If You Were Given a Mortgage?

As shown in Exhibit 7-19, there is a substantial variation between the responses of parcel owners who were later to abandon their parcels as against the nonabandoners. A third of the nonabandoned parcel owners said that their parcels did not need improvement as against 18.6 percent of the abandoned ones. The response rates that indicated such feelings as "neighborhood no good," "rentals too limited," "tenants not worthy of it," were more than double among the owners of later to be abandoned parcels than their representation among the nonabandoned ones. The "parcel not worthy of improvement" secured a 10.6 percent response among the nonabandoners; it was half again as large among the abandoned ones.

The pattern of response is not so clear cut to the question of whether the resale market as of 1964 would adequately support extensive structural improvements. As shown in Exhibit 7-20, certainly the pattern even among the nonabandoners was far from sanguine. However, 19.4 percent of this group felt that the market definitely would support extensive improvements on their parcel in terms of resale. The abandoned owner response was only 13.6 percent.

EXHIBIT 7-19
1964 RESPONSE TO:
"WOULD YOU IMPROVE IF GIVEN A MORTGAGE?"
AND ABANDONMENT

| Would You Improve? | Nonabandoned | Abandoned | Total |
|---|---|---|---|
| I can't afford it | 11 | 1 | 12 |
| Parcel doesn't need it | 76 | 11 | 87 |
| Neighborhood no good | 13 | 6 | 19 |
| Rental too limited | 8 | 5 | 13 |
| Tenants not worthy of it | 6 | 4 | 10 |
| Not worth it | 24 | 9 | 33 |
| NA/DK | 89 | 23 | 112 |
| Total | 227 | 59 | 286 |
| PERCENT DISTRIBUTION | | | |
| I can't afford it | 4.8 | 1.7 | 4.2 |
| Parcel doesn't need it | 33.5 | 18.6 | 30.4 |
| Neighborhood no good | 5.7 | 10.2 | 6.6 |
| Rental too limited | 3.5 | 8.5 | 4.5 |
| Tenants not worthy of it | 2.6 | 6.8 | 3.5 |
| Not worth it | 10.6 | 15.3 | 11.5 |
| NA/DK | 39.2 | 39.0 | 39.2 |
| Total | 100.0 | 100.0 | 100.0 |

$\chi^2 = 0.05$

Source: Newark Area Resurvey, spring, 1972

Conversely, the negatives were evident in both groups, but made up 35.2 percent of the nonabandoned parcel owners as against 47.5 percent of the abandoned ones.

## Sources of Funds for Improvements

There is presently a drastic atmosphere of loss of confidence in the future expressed by many of the Newark owners. Even if funds were available their attitude would seem negative toward their use.

> Parcel number 296 was purchased in 1968 after a series of speculators and operators had traded it for a period of four years previous, following a foreclosure by a home improvement company

# EXHIBIT 7-20

## OWNER'S EVALUATION OF STRENGTH OF RESALE MARKET IN LIGHT OF EXTENSIVE STRUCTURAL IMPROVEMENTS (1964) AND ABANDONMENT

| Is Market Strong Enough to Make Improvement Worthwhile | Nonabandoned | Abandoned | Total |
|---|---|---|---|
| Yes — definitely | 44 | 8 | 52 |
| Yes — maybe | 21 | 8 | 29 |
| Toss-up | 17 | 6 | 23 |
| Probably not | 33 | 4 | 37 |
| Definitely not | 80 | 28 | 108 |
| NA | 4 | 0 | 4 |
| DK | 28 | 5 | 33 |
| Total | 227 | 59 | 286 |
| PERCENT DISTRIBUTION | | | |
| Yes — definitely | 19.4 | 13.6 | 18.2 |
| Yes — maybe | 9.3 | 13.6 | 10.1 |
| Toss-up | 7.5 | 10.2 | 8.0 |
| Probably not | 14.5 | 6.8 | 12.9 |
| Definitely not | 35.2 | 47.5 | 37.8 |
| NA | 1.8 | 0.0 | 1.4 |
| DK | 12.3 | 8.5 | 11.5 |
| Total | 100.0 | 100.0 | 100.0 |

$\chi^2$ n/s @ 0.05

Source: Newark Area Resurvey, spring, 1972

on a bad debt. The parcel is appraised at $11,700. The present owner, when asked what source he would turn to if he needed money to make improvements said, "My own savings, if the requirements were minor. If it required major improvements, I'd drop it." Note that his actual cash investment in the parcel seems to be less than one year's rent roll. This type of tenuous equity position and its impact on the longevity of an owner faced with any kind of difficulty needs little elaboration.

For all three of the questions which we asked about sources of mortgage financing, i.e., in terms of the cost, the length of mortgages, and the sources of financing, there was relatively little variation. If anything, the abandoners were somewhat more sophisticated; their level of "don't know" response lower than that of the long-term property holders. There was little deviation in the pattern of dominance of bank financing which could have forecast the levels of abandonment which later were to take place.

## Building Inspection and Abandonment

Are there differences in owners' 1964 attitudes on inspection which would have forecast abandonment? As shown in Exhibit 7-21, there are small but meaningful differences in responses of owners in the earlier interviews as a function of whether their buildings were later abandoned. In general, the buildings that were to be abandoned were in the hands of owners in 1964, who felt much more negative about municipal inspection procedures, and who much less frequently indicated that their buildings were above criticism than did owners of buildings that were not abandoned by 1971. Again, in this response as in all of the others, there are enough people on both sides of the fence as to make this far from an absolutely deterministic phenomenon. But certainly the statistical weight is there.

To what degree in reality have inspection procedures led to abandonment and, if they have, to what degree should they be altered, if at all? This certainly is an area that needs some study.

## The Owner's View of Problems and Maintenance Improvement

In Exhibit 7-22 landlords' responses to a list of operational parameters in terms of their impact on maintenance procedures are shown. The owners were asked to put these in rank order. For the purposes of summarization they were then weighted with the most important problems in the landlord's reckoning being given a grade of six, the next most important, five, and so on. The responses are divided between those coming from owners of buildings which were abandoned between 1964 and 1971 and those which remained in operation.

Nearly half (45.8 percent) of the abandoned parcels in 1964 had owners who said tenants were their number one problem; conversely, only 23.4 percent of the nonabandoned structures had a similar

## EXHIBIT 7-21
## OWNER'S VIEWS AS TO THE EFFECT OF BUILDING INSPECTIONS ON MAINTENANCE (1964) AND ABANDONMENT

| Building Inspections have . . . | Nonabandoned | Abandoned | Total |
|---|---|---|---|
| No effect — visits rare | 62 | 13 | 75 |
| No effect — building above criticism | 61 | 8 | 69 |
| Occasional — good but worthwhile | 16 | 3 | 19 |
| Occasional — good but meaningless | 22 | 9 | 31 |
| Continual problem — unreasonable | 38 | 16 | 54 |
| Significant factor — no value judgments | 16 | 7 | 23 |
| Payoff | 3 | 2 | 5 |
| NA/DK | 9 | 1 | 10 |
| Total | 227 | 59 | 286 |

PERCENT DISTRIBUTION

| | | | |
|---|---|---|---|
| No effect — visits rare | 27.3 | 22.0 | 26.2 |
| No effect — building above criticism | 26.9 | 13.6 | 24.1 |
| Occasional — good but worthwhile | 7.0 | 5.1 | 6.6 |
| Occasional — good but meaningless | 9.7 | 15.3 | 10.8 |
| Continual problem — unreasonable | 16.7 | 27.1 | 18.9 |
| Significant factor — no value judgments | 7.0 | 11.9 | 8.0 |
| Payoff | 1.3 | 3.4 | 1.7 |
| NA/DK | 4.0 | 1.7 | 3.5 |
| Total | 100.0 | 100.0 | 100.0 |

$\chi^2 = 0.05$

Source: Newark Area Resurvey, spring 1972

LLB
R.C
Mc

EXHIBIT 7-22

RELATIVE IMPORTANCE OF VARIOUS INHIBITORS TO PARCEL MAINTENANCE AND IMPROVEMENTS (1964) BY DEFINITION OF ABANDONMENT

| | Tax Level | | Tenants | | Building Inspection Requirements | | Mortgage Cost | | Tax Reassessment | | Mortgage Length | |
|---|---|---|---|---|---|---|---|---|---|---|---|---|
| Rank | Non-Abandoned | Abandoned | Non-Abandoned | Abandoned | Non-Abandoned | Abandoned | Non-Abandoned | Abandoned | Non-Abandoned | Abandoned | Non-Abandoned | Abandoned |
| | UNWEIGHTED DISTRIBUTION (PERCENT) | | | | | | | | | | | |
| 1 | 48.2 | 25.4 | 23.4 | 45.8 | 10.1 | 16.9 | 7.3 | 5.1 | 16.5 | 10.2 | 3.2 | 1.7 |
| 2 | 23.4 | 23.7 | 16.1 | 25.4 | 10.6 | 13.6 | 7.3 | 6.8 | 21.1 | 8.5 | 4.6 | 5.1 |
| 3 | 11.0 | 13.6 | 15.6 | 10.2 | 8.7 | 18.6 | 5.5 | 8.5 | 13.8 | 16.9 | 5.0 | 1.7 |
| 4 | 3.7 | 10.2 | 4.6 | 3.4 | 17.9 | 11.9 | 7.3 | 15.3 | 9.6 | 13.6 | 7.3 | 8.5 |
| 5 | 0.9 | 5.1 | 3.2 | 1.7 | 2.8 | 3.4 | 14.2 | 10.2 | 5.5 | 5.1 | 6.4 | 18.6 |
| 6 | 0.0 | 0.0 | 5.5 | 0.0 | 7.3 | 10.2 | 0.5 | 1.7 | 2.8 | 13.6 | 11.5 | 6.8 |
| NA | 12.8 | 22.0 | 31.7 | 13.6 | 42.7 | 25.4 | 57.8 | 52.5 | 30.7 | 32.2 | 61.9 | 57.6 |
| Total | 100.0 | 100.0 | 100.0 | 100.0 | 100.0 | 100.0 | 100.0 | 100.0 | 100.0 | 100.0 | 100.0 | 100.0 |

| Weight | WEIGHTED DISTRIBUTION (PERCENT) | | | | | | | | | | | |
|---|---|---|---|---|---|---|---|---|---|---|---|---|
| 6 | 289.2 | 152.4 | 140.4 | 274.8 | 60.6 | 101.4 | 43.8 | 30.6 | 99.0 | 61.2 | 19.2 | 10.2 |
| 5 | 117.0 | 118.5 | 80.5 | 127.0 | 53.0 | 68.0 | 36.5 | 34.0 | 105.5 | 42.5 | 23.0 | 25.5 |
| 4 | 44.0 | 54.4 | 62.4 | 40.8 | 34.8 | 74.4 | 22.0 | 34.0 | 55.2 | 67.6 | 20.0 | 6.8 |
| 3 | 11.1 | 30.6 | 13.8 | 10.2 | 53.7 | 35.7 | 21.9 | 45.9 | 28.8 | 40.8 | 21.9 | 25.5 |
| 2 | 1.8 | 10.2 | 6.4 | 3.4 | 5.6 | 6.8 | 28.4 | 20.4 | 11.0 | 10.2 | 12.8 | 37.2 |
| 1 | 0.0 | 0.0 | 5.5 | 0.0 | 7.3 | 10.2 | 0.5 | 1.7 | 2.8 | 13.6 | 11.5 | 6.8 |
| Weighted Average | 77.2 | 61.0 | 51.5 | 76.0 | 35.8 | 49.4 | 25.5 | 27.8 | 50.4 | 39.3 | 18.1 | 18.7 |

Source: Newark Area Resurvey, spring, 1972

response. Tax level secured 48.2 percent of the first priority responses of nonabandoners with an additional 23.4 percent giving it second priority versus 25.4 percent and 23.7 percent, respectively, for the abandoners. No other factor got a 20 percent response in the lead slot.

## Taxes

When the 1964 responses of owners were analyzed in terms of what improvements they would make if they were sure of not getting a tax boost, there is a distinct variation. The owners of parcels that were to be abandoned felt much more negative about the impact of tax rates and tax assessment levels than did the balance of the group. This finding held true even though in their rank ordering the tax problem generally was less important to them than it was to the nonabandoners. It is important that this be studied in context. Note particularly their response to parcels not worthwhile versus parcels in good condition, of neighborhood problems and the like; these bulked much more heavily among the future abandoners than the rest of the group.

To this degree, therefore, the observations can be generalized in terms of the rank ordering and the specific problems as seen by owners. *A much less positive attitude toward the future exists among owners of parcels that were later to be abandoned. A skewed distribution of their primary negative feelings toward tenantry is evident and several other probes (taxes, tax assessment, attitudes toward building inspectors, etc.) evoked far more negative responses than those among owners of parcels which remained in business.*

One of the interesting variations in this level of response is that there was no discernible difference in respondents' opinions as to whether or not they were in an urban renewal area. If anything, the abandoners were even more confident of securing an adequate return if their parcels were taken for urban renewal. The variations, however, were slight.

## The Character of Tenantry

It is difficult to distinguish the fantasies of owners, who are specific in their own rationalizations of failure in operating a building (either in terms of personal profit or from an overall societal point of view), from the realities. *Certainly, however, one of the patterns which emerges consistently in the case studies is the decline in the socio-economic status of the possible tenant pool. This, it should be pointed out, is not a function of ethnicity.* In dealing with Newark, racial shifts were largely a *fait accompli* in much of the area which is under discussion here. Perhaps a vignette or two will clarify this.

> This is a three-story, masonry structure with five families. The parcel was bought in 1948. It is assessed at $21,000 for building; $3,000 for land. In 1964 its condition was described as better than its neighbors with the owners a long-established real estate firm. Yet by 1971 the building was abandoned. The reasons for this summarized the woeful state of the art. "We own the building free and clear, but our problems started when our better black families moved out because they didn't like the environment and the area. And even though this was a nice structure, fairly well maintained, and we had a nice group of people even though they may have been poor, its condition got worse. We were forced to accept a lower grade tenant. We started to settle for tenants who were more rough: drunks, low morals, and so on. These people have lots of problems. They won't pay the rent and they did more damage, more than you can believe. You just can't keep up with that kind of tenant. The repairs became so outrageous we just stopped paying our taxes and dropped the property because the city kept squeezing us to maintain it.
>
> "Selling it is out of the question, no one wants to buy that kind of environment. Even with conscientious landlords you just can't maintain these parcels. I think of myself as being reasonably intelligent and basically liberal and I can appreciate the importance of the city saying the place is rat-infested and that I should have it exterminated and fix the plumbing, and wiring. That's reasonable, but we couldn't rent it at a cost that would enable us to meet the demands of the city. We just couldn't maintain it. You get to a point, somewhere, in which the cost just becomes ridiculous. A landlord could spend thousands in fixing up a parcel; inside of a couple of months the place would be wrecked by the tenants.
>
> "We had an old black man who had been living there for thirty years and he maintained the building and we gave him an apartment rent free and a few bucks. He acted as a supervisor. He would have all the repairs made and send me the bill. He also used to interview all the tenants. When he died the property began to go downhill."

The changing patterns of acceptable housing often mean that old buildings require substantial investments to be brought up to current standards. Given a failure of faith in area or parcel this leads only one way and that is to abandonment.

> Parcel number 107 characterizes this phenomenon. It is a four-story, masonry building with six families above a series of stores. The parcel was bought in 1950 for $9,500, the first mortgage taken back by the seller for $5,500. It was assessed for $16,600. At the time of the 1967 riots, it was owned free and clear. The owner's words were as follows:
>
> "When I bought the building it had no central heat. My colleagues said that it would be worth $10- to $15,000 to put in a system. I was going to do it — then came the 1967 riot. I'd of had to reinvest; people just don't want to live in cold water flats and the welfare department wouldn't put them in there because of a lack of service. There's just too much vandalism to make it worthwhile. We thought about the central heat. If we put in the central heat, the rents would have to be doubled. For that kind of money the tenants could go uptown to a better area. I'd have to take a loan and who wants to do it? A friend of mine put in heat in one of his buildings not too far away and two months later the furnace was closed. The pipes were pulled out. There is an atmosphere of cannibalism. We stopped paying real estate taxes because there is no income. We boarded up the building and are going to give it to the city unless they foreclose before then. There is nobody interested in buying these kinds of properties.'

While much of this may be self-serving rationalization, it is not confined solely to white professionals:

> For example, parcel number 112 is an eight-family, masonry structure, now abandoned. It was purchased in 1965 by a real estate speculator who had secured it from the previous owner who "got along so badly with his tenants, he had to get out." The speculator in turn sold it to a black real estate management firm which also has a side line of rehabilitating properties. They purchased it "because we hoped to renovate the building. We put in heat, improved the structure. We wanted to get decent tenants and we thought we could if we did these things, however, they wouldn't move into this area. We had less desirable tenants and it became impossible to maintain the building."
>
> The firm paid $5,000 for the parcel in addition to the speculator taking back a $12,500 mortgage. Their own estimates currently are that the building is in such bad condition, after being abandoned,

that it would cost a minimum of $35,000 to $40,000 to improve it. "People around here don't know how to maintain property and respect property."

There is no one clear road to abandonment — nor equivalently one clear cut solution. In this section, responses and attitudes of owners have been examined individually. In the next section, more rigorous examination is given to the facets of data collectively.

## COROLLARIES OF ABANDONMENT: THE SIGNIFICANCE OF ABANDONMENT AND VARIOUS BEHAVIORAL AND ENVIRONMENTAL VARIABLES

The research reported here is exploratory. The analysis focuses on the city of Newark. Abandonment in that city has been approached from two directions. First, a sample of 567 buildings originally surveyed in 1964 were revisited in 1972. Over the period a portion of these buildings had become abandoned; some were taken for public purposes, while others remained viable within the existing housing stock. Using the buildings that were abandoned and those that were retained, an effort was made to explain a parcel being abandoned in 1972 by delving deeply first into the physical characteristics of the abandoned parcels, second into their operating procedures, and finally into relations between owners and tenants that were taking place some eight years previously at the time of the original interview. In effect, the question to be answered was whether there were any early warning indicators which could be isolated that might signal sometime in advance the future abandonment of a residential structure.

Second, the relationships between neighborhood characteristics and change and aggregate levels of abandonment will be examined. This analysis will attempt to determine whether there were changes taking place within the city's environment that would lessen its desirability, stimulate housing obsolescence, and promote residential abandonment. To answer this question, 1960 and 1970 socio-economic data, as well as abandonment levels, were tabulated on a census tract base. The basic questions to be answered are: What were the dominant characteristics of neighborhoods in 1960 in which abandonment was rampant in 1970? Were there changes which these neighborhoods had undergone from 1960 to 1970 that might have contributed to the high abandonment statistic evident in 1970?

Within the analyses which follow there are three sets of data considered:

(1) The sample of 286 parcels, for which 1964 data are present on characteristics of owner and tenant and on the condition and maintenance procedures of the building, is an excellent device to obtain some indication of structural corollaries of residential abandonment.

(2) Gross abandonment data, plus socio-economic variables tabulated on a census tract base, provide an input of stronger and wider scope. These form indicators of environmental conditions which may be present in an area of high abandonment. The link between these two initial bodies of data is a housing deterioration measure which gauges the importance of location as a criterion of abandonment.

(3) Probably the most robust of all, if one can really ever get to the point of prediction, is the employment of dynamic changes taking place in neighborhoods over time as indicators of residential abandonment. Changes in 1960 and 1970 census variables are used to provide insight into the abandonment phenomenon.

The analysis proceeds from specific information on residential parcels to general information on neighborhood change. In the initial examinations, statistical significance is of prime importance. As the universe widens, the percent of the variance explained becomes much more important. The study moves from general corollaries or associations of abandonment to some type of limited predictors.

## THE BEHAVIORAL ASPECTS OF RESIDENTIAL ABANDONMENT

### Statistical Significance via the Analysis of Variance

Having viewed individual cross tabulations for specific patterns of association, it is now necessary to attempt to develop general corollaries of abandonment. To gauge simple statistical significance and direction of association of the one-by-one relationships, analysis of variance is employed. The relationship of nonabandoned/abandoned parcels and twenty-eight variables are compared using the F statistics at the 0.05 level. The dependent variable (nonabandoned/abandoned) is a dichotomous choice (0-1), while the independent variables are grouped data of 4-7 intervals (Exhibit 7-24).

On an individual basis, fifteen of the twenty-eight variables explain an amount of variance in abandonment sufficiently in excess of what would have been expected from sampling variation and thus may be viewed as having a significant effect on the sample data (F statistic — 0.05 level).

Of highest statistical significance (F — 0.01 level) are the relationships between increasing abandonment and: (1) previous tax arrearage, (2) having to employ a professional manager or rent collector, (3) being located in the worst areas of the city, (4) tenants who evoke severe criticism from their landlords, (5) properties which have no mortgage, and finally, parcels (6) owned by whites which have (7) large proportions of black tenantry.

Of somewhat less statistical significance (0.01 to 0.05), but still linked in a fashion which is greater than sample variance, are the relationships between abandoned buildings and (1) owners who wanted to sell their properties in 1964 but couldn't, and (2) owners of more, rather than less, income.

Once again, perhaps the most incisive analysis may be made by examining lack of relationships. There appears to be no significant variation outside, as opposed to within, variable cells between abandonment and (1) specific involvement or length of involvement in real estate, (2) the age of the owner and his current participation or lack of participation in the labor force, and (3) the relative quality of the building and its type of construction.

## Statistical Significance and the Relative Effect of Variables via Multiple Regression

As indicated in Exhibit 7-24, twenty-eight variables were originally selected for entrance to the multivariate analysis according to the listed partitions. The dependent variable is "abandoned/nonabandoned residential structures in 1971" viewed individually and collectively with

EXHIBIT 7-23
SIGNIFICANCE OF 1964 PARCEL COROLLARIES OF ABANDONMENT—
ANALYSIS OF VARIANCE

016. **Dependent Variable**: Nonabandoned/abandoned(1)structure

| Variable Number | Variable Name | Direction of Coding | Individual Significance (F—0.05) | Direction of Significance |
|---|---|---|---|---|
| 001 | Size of parcel | (Increases with size) | No | |
| 002 | Type of construction | (Increases toward masonry) | No | |
| 003 | Absolute quality | (Increases with better quality) | Yes | — |
| 004 | Relative quality | (Increases with better quality) | No | |
| 005 | Commercial occupancy | (Increases with degree of occupancy) | No | |
| 006 | Nuisances nearby | (Increases with various nuisances) | No | |
| 007 | Length of real estate experience | (Increases with length) | No | |
| 008 | Why purchased | (Increases with inheritance, rental income, etc.) | Yes | + |
| 009 | Want to sell | (Increases with desire to sell) | Yes | + |
| 010 | Professional manager | (Increases with professional management) | Yes | + |
| 011 | Size of holding | (Increases with size) | Yes | + |
| 012 | Make living from real estate | (Increases with percent real estate involvement) | No | |

| | | | | |
|---|---|---|---|---|
| 013 | Race of tenants | (Increases toward black) | Yes | + |
| 014 | Neighborhood vacancy rate | (Increases with larger) | Yes | + |
| 015 | Problem tenants | (Increases with severity rating) | Yes | + |
| 017 | Age of owner | (Increases with age) | No | |
| 018 | Residence of owner | (Increases with nonresidency) | Yes | + |
| 019 | Race of owner | (Increases toward white) | Yes | + |
| 020 | Labor force participation | (Increases with participation) | No | |
| 021 | Income of owner | (Increases with income) | Yes | + |
| 022 | Type of owner | (Increases with nonindividuals) | Yes | + |
| 023 | Length of ownership | (Increases with term) | No | |
| 024 | Presence of mortgage | (Increases with mortgage) | Yes | — |
| 025 | Value of parcel | (Increases with value) | No | |
| 026 | Location in urban renewal area | (Increases with location in urban renewal area) | No | |
| 027 | Multiple mortgages | (Increases with multiple mortgages) | No | |
| 028 | Location of parcel | (Increases with better locations) | Yes | — |
| 030 | Tax arrearage | (Increases with more arrearage) | Yes | |

Source: **Newark Area Resurvey**, spring 1972

## EXHIBIT 7-24
## LISTING OF REGRESSION VARIABLES FOR MULTIVARIATE PARCEL COROLLARIES

Dependent Variable: Abandoned Parcels (1)*

Regression Statistics

| Variable Number | Name | Abbreviation | Mean | S.D. |
|---|---|---|---|---|
| 030 | Tax arrears(1)no tax arrears in 1964 | TAXARR | 0.45 | 0.40 |
| 013 | White(1)/nonwhite tenantry | WTETEN | 0.20 | 0.40 |
| 010 | Professional/nonprofessional repairs(1) | NONPRF | 0.86 | 0.35 |
| 019 | White(1)/nonwhite owners | WHTOWN | 0.63 | 0.48 |
| 007 | Pre(1)post 1960 real estate involvement | ERLOWN | 0.76 | 0.42 |
| 024 | Mortgage(1)/no mortgage | NOMORT | 0.19 | 0.40 |
| 021 | Owner incomes $8,000(1) | LESINC | 0.31 | 0.46 |
| 009 | Want(1)/not want to sell | WANTSL | 0.23 | 0.42 |
| 015 | Tenants are(1)/not a problem | BADTEN | 0.27 | 0.45 |
| 025 | Value parcel $15,000(1) | HIVALU | 0.24 | 0.43 |
| 006 | Adjacent (1)/nonadjacent nuisances | NUISNR | 0.58 | 0.50 |
| 011 | Other/no other real estate holdings(1) | OTHPRP | 0.48 | 0.50 |

| | | | | |
|---|---|---|---|---|
| 002 | Frame(1)/masonry construction | FRMCON | 0.86 | 0.34 |
| 023 | Owned parcel four years(1) | SHTOWN | 0.30 | 0.46 |
| 027 | Multiple(1)/no mortgages | MNYMTG | 0.15 | 0.36 |
| 012 | Minor/substantial(1)living from real estate | MIREAL | 0.31 | 0.46 |
| 014 | Vacancy rate up(1)/down | VACRAT | 0.37 | 0.48 |
| 003 | Parcel well kept(1)/not | ABSQAL | 0.86 | 0.35 |
| 005 | Commercial Occupancy(1)/no commercial occupancy | COMOCC | 0.12 | 0.33 |
| 022 | Individual(1)/institutional owner | INDOWN | 0.82 | 0.38 |
| 026 | Urban renewal(1)/not urban renewal area | URAREA | 0.18 | 0.39 |
| 004 | Quality of block same(1)/poorer | RELQAL | 0.90 | 0.30 |
| 001 | Number units: 4+(1)/3— | NUMUNT | 0.76 | 0.43 |
| 017 | Age owner-middle(1)/old | AGEOWN | 0.71 | 0.45 |
| 018 | Resident(1)/nonresident landlord | RESLAN | 0.39 | 0.49 |
| 008 | Buy property-voluntary(1)/involuntary | BUYPRP | 0.19 | 0.39 |
| 028 | Location of property in increasing(1)/decreasing areas of deterioration | LOCATN | 0.25 | 0.43 |

°Indicates a coding running in the same direction as abandonment.

Source: Newark Area Resurvey, spring 1972

groupings of independent variables to gain appreciation for relative directions and strengths of association.

An F test at the 0.10 level was used as an indication of initial significance. The specific level, not necessarily robust, and actually lower than that for individual variable significance, has been specifically chosen so as not to be overly restrictive at a time when theory building is of prime importance.

The sample of 567 structures, for which owner interview data were obtained in 391 cases, is subdivided into a trichotomous grouping of abandoned, nonabandoned, and other structures in accordance with definitions explained earlier in this section. Exhibit 7-25 summarizes the components of each of these groupings.

As is indicated, the two sets of buildings which are of prime importance are the abandoned and nonabandoned structures. The third set has been completely eliminated from the regression. It would appear

EXHIBIT 7-25

ELEMENTS OF THE DEFINITION OF ABANDONMENT

| | Abandoned | Nonabandoned | Other | Total |
|---|---|---|---|---|
| | 1. Observed vacant in 1971 and not in 1964<br>2. Reported by owner as vacant although viewed partially occupied in 1971<br>3. Demolished publicly for hazard<br>4. Demolished privately with no use occurring on the land | 1. Occupied<br>2. Partially Occupied | 1. Demolished publicly for funded urban renewal programs<br>2. Demolished privately for another use<br>3. Vacant both in 1964 and 1971 | |
| Parcels having 1964 interview | 59 | 227 | 105 | 391 |
| Parcels within the sample | 84 | 342 | 141 | 567 |

Source: Newark Area Resurvey, spring 1972

then that of the 567 residential buildings rented and occupied in 1964, eighty-four, or 15 percent, had become abandoned by 1971. Among those who answered the 1964 questionnaire, the figure is fifty-nine of 392, or 14.5 percent. In the latter case, if parcels demolished for public and private purposes are eliminated, 1971 abandonments represent 20 percent of the 1964 residential stock which is not being claimed for reuse.

## Individual Indicators

As indicated in Exhibit 7-26, by the magnitude of the coefficients* a key to the abandonment process, at least at the 0.10 significance level, appears to be prior tax arrearage (030). The coefficient of this index alone is three times that of any other corollary. Also contributing to the

*For convenience and ease of presentation, regression coefficients are used to show trends which normally would be evident in the difference of intercellular means of the analysis of variance.

EXHIBIT 7-26

PARCEL COROLLARIES OF RESIDENTIAL ABANDONMENT

Dependent Variable: Abandoned Structures

Regression Statistics

| Variable Number | Name | Regression Coefficient | F Statistic | F to Reject Randomness |
|---|---|---|---|---|
| F = 0.10 | | | | |
| 030 | TAXARR | 0.586 | 30.62 | 2.74 |
| 013 | WTETEN | (—) 0.218 | 8.70 | 2.74 |
| 010 | NONPRF | (—) 0.206 | 8.07 | 2.74 |
| 028 | LOCATN | 0.156 | 7.15 | 2.74 |
| 024 | NOMORT | 0.124 | 3.97 | 2.74 |
| 019 | WHTOWN | 0.121 | 3.21 | 2.74 |
| 007 | ERLOWN | 0.116 | 3.45 | 2.74 |
| 015 | BADTEN | 0.112 | 3.92 | 2.74 |
| 009 | WANTSL | 0.096 | 2.80 | 2.74 |
| 021 | LESINC | (—) 0.092 | 2.96 | 2.74 |

Source: Newark Area Resurvey, spring 1972

abandonment process is the heavy presence of nonwhite tenants (013) in structures which were either professionally managed or at least in those employing a professional rent collector (010). Possession of either of these latter two characteristics increases the probability of the abandonment of a parcel by an amount approximately equal to the average rate of abandonment in the sample (20 percent).[10]

Following this selection criteria in order of importance is the locational variable which expresses abandonment as a function of areas of increasing adjacent housing deterioration (028). While this matter will be discussed subsequently, notice that once the tax arrearage, business aspects, and residency profile of rental urban housing have been established as corollaries of abandonment, then location of the parcel seems to be of primary import.

Two other important relationships with increasing abandonment appear to be white ownership of the subject parcel (019)[°] and the lack of a mortgage or significant monetary interest in the property (024). Heavy loading on these two variables alone would equal the average probability of abandonment across all variables. It appears after examining these and the two previous indices, that abandonment is the nail in the coffin of the fabled tenement landlord. The reality is that the white owner in an urban core area increasingly is unable to rent his mortgage-free structures to poor blacks and still derive necessary profit. It may well be, however, that the tenants themselves have caused the dissolution of this market, for it can neither be said that these structures were initially in relatively worse condition in 1964 than their surrounding neighbors nor were they of a certain "tenement type" in terms of either construction or number of units. Their owners were not particularly aged nor did owners display any notable lack of real estate know how. Each of these latter four indices proved to be statistically insignificant.

It further does not hold that succeeding waves of tenement landlords are milking parcels and deriving substantial income. It seems that if there were once a tenement landlord, in the classic sense, he is fast disappearing. There appears to be a greater tendency for 1971

---

[°] It was originally thought that due to the moderate correlation between white/nonwhite owners, other/no-other holdings and resident/nonresident landlords that in the stepwise program the former is masking the two latter indices. When run separately, however, white/nonwhite owner remains significant while the other two indices prove to be statistically nonsignificant.

abandoned parcels to be owned by people who had at least ten years experience in the real estate market (007) and also to have had incomes in 1964 of more than $8,000 (021). The owner in 1964 wanted to sell the building and couldn't (009), and bitterly complained that the tenantry (015) and not taxes or other city ills was preventing him from improving upon or recouping all or a portion of the parcel's value (025).

## THE ENVIRONMENTAL ASPECTS OF RESIDENTIAL ABANDONMENT

Environmental corollaries of abandonment will be analyzed by initially grouping twenty-five socio-economic variables, via factor analysis, which were originally tabulated individually on a census tract base in 1960. This, hopefully, may be of use when attempting to foresee abandonment by supplementing the parcel data or replacing them when they are not available.

Factor analysis is used here to reduce somewhat the overlapping patterns of variation present in many of the variables and thus makes possible more concise statements about the "abandoned structure" population under consideration.

Factor score, i.e., the value of each tract on a factor, will serve as prime input to the regression equation. The dependent variable, "percent residential structures abandoned 1967 to 1971," then becomes a function of these factor scores.

### Methodology

Thirty variables summarizing the dimensions contained in Exhibit 7-27 were reduced to six factors via the initial factor analysis. To provide independent dimensions to the regression equation, the orthogonal rotational scheme was chosen with factors being selected for rotation if their eigenvalue exceeded unity. The resulting factor structure explaining 78 percent of the variance is also set forth in Exhibit 7-27.

### Factors Underlying Newark's Neighborhoods

The six factors derived from the census which interpret Newark's urban structure in 1960 are not unlike those which have been found in other cities similarly reaching their systemic end-state. To review briefly and

## EXHIBIT 7-27
## FACTOR ANALYSIS OF SELECTIVE 1960 SOCIO-ECONOMIC VARIABLES EMPLOYING NEWARK CENSUS TRACTS AS A DATA BASE

| | Factor | | | | | |
|---|---|---|---|---|---|---|
| Variable | Race and Resources 1 | Social Status 2 | Stage in Life Cycle 3 | Puerto Rican Segregation 4 | Housing Stability 5 | Male Unemployment 6 |
| 1. Percent housing units: occupied | | | | | .723 | |
| 2. Percent population: Negro | —.919 | | | | | |
| 3. Median age female | .807 | | | | | |
| 4. Median age white female | | .471 | | | | —.616 |
| 5. Percent housing units: no bath or share | | | | | —.713 | |
| 6. Percent housing units: >1.01 persons/rm | —.767 | —.413 | | | | |
| 7. Median contract rent | | .775 | | | .422 | |
| 8. Median house value | | .732 | | | | |
| 9. Percent housing units: single family | .444 | | | | | |
| 10. Percent population: >65 years of age | .771 | .400 | | | | |
| 11. Percent white pop.: >65 years of age | .872 | | | | | |
| 12. Percent population: married | .685 | | | | | |
| 13. Percent population: <5 years of age | —.837 | —.400 | | | | |
| 14. Percent housing units: owner occupied | .705 | | | | .458 | |

| | | | | | | |
|---|---|---|---|---|---|---|
| 15. Median rooms/unit | | | | .658 | .488 | |
| 16. Percent labor force: female | | | | .684 | | |
| 17. Percent population: Puerto Rican parentage | | | | —.736 | | |
| 18. Median education | | .774 | | | | |
| 19. Median family income | .579 | .401 | | | | |
| 20. Percent labor force:male unemployed | | | | | | —.787 |
| 21. Percent labor force: female clerical | .722 | | | | | |
| 22. Percent labor force: professional, managerial | | .777 | | | | |
| 23. Percent population: foreign born | .817 | | | | | |
| 24. Population per household | | —.458 | .472 | | | |
| 25. Percent population: elem. school enrollment | | | .776 | —.463 | | |
| 26. Percent population: h.s. graduate | | .746 | | | | |
| 27. Percent population: college graduate | | .849 | | | | |
| 28. Percent population: income < $3,000 | —.646 | | | | | |
| 29. Percent population: income > $10,000 | .609 | .595 | | | | |
| 30. Percent labor force: manufacturing | | —.787 | | | | |
| Variance explained by factor (percent) | 29.6 | 21.5 | 8.9 | 8.3 | 5.3 | 4.6 |

< less than
> greater than

extend the analysis somewhat, there are three principal factors appearing in two dichotomous sets: (1) A qualitative, *Social Status* factor (white affluence) demonstrating high professional/managerial employment, income, education, rents, and housing value, and low crowding/population per household and manufacturing employment for a portion of the city's census tracts and (2) two complementary city-structure indices which express location in terms of (a) a lower quality *Race and Resources* factor (black poverty), i.e., areas of high nonwhite population, structural crowding, and low income and (b) a *Puerto Rican Segregation* factor (Puerto Rican poverty) somewhat less forcefully, yet nonetheless indicative of low income, more frequent participation in the female labor force, and requiring a larger number of rooms in their housing accommodations.

These three factors are joined by three other lesser indices of the city (in terms of the amount of variance explained) which depict areas of (1) *Housing Stability* in terms of low occupancy, the availability of basic housing services, high rental levels, and significant owner occupancy; (2) concentrations of residential areas for large families and school-age children; and finally, (3) areas represented by both high male unemployment and high proportions of white, female elderly.

## Environmental Corollaries (The Static Case)

The factor scores of each census tract contributing to these resulting factors were then entered into the regression equation as independent indices representing 1960 socio-economic characteristics used to interpret "percent residential abandonment" by tract in 1971.

As shown in Exhibit 7-28, only two of the three primary factors proved to be meaningful at the F. 0.05 significance level, with no other factor significant even at the 0.15 level. Residential abandonment, in terms of location, increases in areas of high black and Puerto Rican concentration and thus becomes a part of the dismal social and environmental conditions which are normally associated with these subpopulations, i.e., persons in these areas suffer loss of housing through abandonment in addition to poor educational quality, low resources, crowding, high birth rate, etc. If one lowers considerably the level of significance (0.20), areas of high housing stability (low vacancy, normal housing services, etc.) seem to slow the abandonment process.

EXHIBIT 7-28
STATIC ENVIRONMENTAL PRECURSORS OF
RESIDENTIAL ABANDONMENT

Dependent Variable: Percent Structures Abandoned Per Census Tract

| Variable Number | Name | B | F | F to Reject Randomness |
|---|---|---|---|---|
| Factor 1 ($X_2$) | Black poverty | —5.49 | 32.93 | 3.99 |
| Factor 2 ($X_3$) | Puerto Rican poverty | —2.15 | 4.39 | 3.99 |
| Factor 3 ($X_4$) | White affluence | —1.21 | 2.13 | 3.99 |
| Factor 4 ($X_5$) | Housing stability | —1.44 | 1.68 | 3.99 |

$R^2 = 0.78$ $F = 0.05$

Source: Newark Area Resurvey, spring 1972

Also at a lower level of significance the presence of affluence, expressed in terms of area resident's income, education, and monthly housing cost, is associated with a lack of abandonment. Basically residential abandonment occurs more frequently in areas of general urban decay — those areas judged socially and economically substandard regardless of specific criteria. Conversely, it is less frequent in areas where people of higher socio-economic status reside and, consequently, where housing is more stable.

## The Relationship of Behavioral to Environmental Aspects of Abandonment

Now it is necessary to return to the parcel corollaries of abandonment to gain a perspective for the relationships in evidence between these two indices. Within the parcel corollary set, the locational variable seems to be of demonstrable secondary importance to those variables representing characteristics of both tax arrearage and those of the owner and tenant (based on strength of coefficients and differences in means). Thus, while it is easy to surmise that "slums breed abandonment," or vice-versa, it may be true that this may be said only to the degree that both tax arrearage and owner/tenant characteristics vary significantly across these areas. That is, as one traverses from "good" to "bad" areas of the city, one is statistically more likely to find increased tax arrearage and the combination of a white owner/black tenant in a housing relationship where structural repairs are contracted and heavily dependent on a smooth and continuous flow of rental income.

If one moves from "good" areas of the city to a pocket within a generally designated "bad" area where tax delinquency is low as a result of white tenants occupying a structure in an acceptable leasing arrangement which is heavily supported by "sweat equity," while the environmental predictors of abandonment may be present, there is a good chance that the structure will remain part of the city's housing stock.

## Environmental Corollaries (The Dynamic Case)

The object of this section is to relate abandonment to indicia of change. What city-structure dynamics have occurred over the decade 1960 to 1970 and how are they related to the residential abandonment which was rampant at the end of this period?

Earlier it was stated that until this level of generality had been reached no attempt would be made, via a regression equation, to predict abandonment. Now with a dynamic measure (i.e., change: 1960 to 1970 in census variables) it may be possible to isolate leading indicators of the dynamic abandonment phenomenon based on the approximately 3,500 parcels abandoned in the city over the last five years. (See Appendix 1 for details of the origins of this figure.) This may be approached in several ways, two of which will be discussed here.

## Predicting Abandonment with a Limited Number of Factored Indices

In the initial chapter, using factor analysis, the city was pictured as having multiple dimensions of decennial change (Exhibit 7-29). These are repeated here in the order of the percent variance they explain:

| Designation | Factor Name | Percent Variance Explained in the Factor Analysis |
|---|---|---|
| $X_1$ | Age Succession | 18.2 |
| $X_2$ | Social Status | 12.9 |
| $X_3$ | Young Blacks | 10.1 |
| $X_4$ | Black Poverty | 9.7 |
| $X_5$ | Ethnic Neighborhood | 6.8 |
| $X_6$ | Multi-unit/Female Employment | 5.5 |
| $X_7$ | Service Labor | 5.0 |
| $X_8$ | Young Puerto Ricans | 4.5 |

In summary, changes in the city over time can be explained by an area's continuous reorientation to: the phenomenon of young blacks replacing aging whites ($X_1$), increasing and decreasing income ($X_2$), young blacks moving up and out of the city ($X_3$), immobile blacks being forced to remain in the city ($X_4$), ethnic stability in time of change ($X_5$), the growth of newer residences for the female employed ($X_6$), small increases in incomes due to the growth of a resident service labor force, and, finally, young Puerto Ricans moving up and being assimilated into the city's social structure.

If each of these isolated dimensions of change are subsequently regressed against the dependent variable percent of structures abandoned per census tract* it may be possible to explain a large proportion of the variance surrounding residential abandonment within these tracts. In this and the subsequent analysis, the stepwise mode is used with reported results being statistically significant at the 0.05 level (F statistic).

The dimensions of change which explain the greatest amount of variance in residential abandonment and remain statistically significant are: the *Ethnic Neighborhood* factor ($X_5$), the *Age Succession* factor ($X_1$), the *Black Poverty* factor ($X_4$), the *Female Employment* factor ($X_6$), and the *Young Black* factor ($X_3$). Together these five variants explain in

*Census tracts with large amounts of urban renewal occurring from 1960 to 1970 have been removed from this analysis.

# EXHIBIT 7-29
## FACTOR ANALYSIS OF SELECTIVE CHANGE VARIABLES (1960-1970) EMPLOYING NEWARK CENSUS TRACTS AS A DATA BASE

| | FACTOR | | | | | | | |
|---|---|---|---|---|---|---|---|---|
| Variable* | Age Succession | Social Status | Young Blacks | Black Poverty | Ethnic Neighborhoods | Female Employment | Poverty | Young Puerto Ricans |
| 1. Percent housing units: occupied | | —.856 | | | | | | |
| 2. Percent population: Negro | | | —.676 | .522 | | | | |
| 3. Median age female | .743 | | .406 | | | | | |
| 4. Median age white female | .428 | | | | | | | .683 |
| 5. Percent housing units: no bath or share | | | | .624 | | | | |
| 6. Percent housing units: >1.01 persons/rm | | | —.872 | | | | | |
| 7. Median contract rent | | —.792 | | | | | | |
| 8. Median house value | | | | | .601 | .401 | | |
| 9. Percent housing units: single family | | | | | | —.711 | | |
| 10. Percent population: 65+ years of age | .864 | | | | | | | |
| 11. Percent white population: 65+ years of age | .897 | | | | | | | |
| 12. Percent population: married | .579 | | | | .619 | | | |
| 13. Percent population: <5 years of age | —.472 | | —.786 | | | | | |
| 14. Percent housing units: owner occupied | | | | | .841 | | | |

| | | | | | | | | |
|---|---|---|---|---|---|---|---|---|
| 15. Median rooms/unit | —.585 | | | | | | | |
| 16. Percent labor force: female | | | | | | .683 | | |
| 17. Percent population: Puerto Rican parentage | | | | | | | | .740 |
| 18. Median education | —.416 | —.632 | | | —.476 | | | |
| 19. Median family income | | | | | | | .761 | |
| 20. Percent labor force: male unemployed | | | | | | | .600 | |
| 21. Percent labor force: female clerical | | | | | —.697 | | | |
| 22. Percent labor force: professional, managerial | | —.821 | | | | | | |
| 23. Percent population: foreign born | .652 | | | | .501 | | | |
| 24. Population per household | —.764 | | | | | | | |
| 25. Percent population: elem. school enrollment | —.689 | | | | | | | |
| 26. Percent population: high school graduate | | —.632 | | | | | | |
| 27. Percent population: college graduate | | —.821 | | | | | | |
| 28. Percent population: income < \$3,000-\$4,000 | | | | .754 | | | | |
| 29. Percent population: income > \$10,000-\$12,000 | | —.416 | | —.495 | | | | |
| 30. Percent labor force: manufacturing | | | —.808 | | | | | |
| Variance explained by factor (percent) | 18.2 | 12.9 | 10.1 | 9.7 | 6.8 | 5.5 | 5.0 | |

°Change Quotient: The ratio of the 1970 percentage to the 1960 percentage for each variable characteristics.

excess of *65 percent* of the variance in the intercorrelation matrix (Exhibit 7-30).

In the first case residential abandonment is *less* likely to take place in areas of high owner occupancy, high percent married, high housing value, and high percent foreign born. There appears to be less residential housing loss in areas of the city which have continued to serve as immigrant staging areas for white ethnics. In these areas, which, incidentally, reflect both a somewhat lower female participation in the labor force and lower median education level,* there seems to be a retention of housing for individual use as well as to possibly supplement income. The now aging, foreign born immigrant, living in a neighborhood which at this glimpse of time is characterized by an absence of large numbers of children, is a force which is associated with a housing retention rate vastly different than is found in other parts of the city.

Abandonment also seems to be related to other indicia of change. The first is an *Age Succession* phenomenon in which abandonment increases in areas of high age structure transition. The most frequent case is large, principally black families replacing a dwindling proportion of elderly whites. As two of the housing stability dimensions fall negatively within this factor, it appears clear that abandonment increases as *in*-migrants replace earlier immigrants. The housing is subjected to much greater wear and receives less funds to perform routine maintenance when large, rental families follow previous elderly, owner-occupants.

Housing loss is a corollary of yet a third dimension of decennial change, i.e., *Black Poverty*. It appears that abandonment is found more frequently in residential areas which serve the most impoverished. These are areas where for the most part there is both a notable absence of incomes in excess of $10,000 and a preponderance of incomes below $3,000. These areas which cater to transiency frequently possess housing units in which a bath does not exist or must be shared. In Newark, although there is a significant step function in the price of housing in which a sharp increase is noted between those residential accommodations which lack and provide a bath, even this rent differential does not significantly deter abandonment.

---

*As a portion of the second generation follows the family rearing practices and apprenticeship service characteristic of their forebearers.

## EXHIBIT 7-30
### DYNAMIC ENVIRONMENTAL PREDICTORS OF ABANDONMENT: THE FACTORED VARIABLE SET

Dependent Variable: Percent Structures Abandoned Per Census Tract

| Factor Number | Name | B | F | F to Reject Randomness |
|---|---|---|---|---|
| $X_5$ | Ethnic neighborhoods | —7.79 | 68.92 | 3.99 |
| $X_1$ | Age succession | —2.94 | 18.15 | 3.99 |
| $X_4$ | Black poverty | —2.51 | 13.43 | 3.99 |
| $X_6$ | Female employment | —2.48 | 6.98 | 3.99 |
| $X_3$ | Young blacks | 1.46 | 5.65 | 3.99 |

$R^2 = 0.65$ $F = 0.05$

Source: Newark Area Resurvey, spring 1972

Residential housing loss through abandonment appears less, however, in areas where there are greater proportions of newer multifamily units serving the female employed. These accommodations contribute to a higher median housing value for an area and seem to engender sufficient confidence in owners to both retain and maintain their properties.

Finally, abandonment may be keyed by forces emanating from a *Young Black* factor. Abandonment appears to increase in areas which serve as staging grounds for young black families. These are areas whose resident head of household may frequently be employed in manufacturing, and which are characterized by severe housing usage occasioned by high proportions of children and greater-than-average overcrowding.

If now each of these dimensions is placed in an explanatory equation which attempts to interpret abandonment,

Percent of residential abandonment per census tract $= 8.54 - 7.79X_5 - 2.94X_1{}^{*} - 2.51X_4{}^{*} - 2.48X_6 + 1.46X_3$

$X_5$ = *Ethnic Neighborhood*
$X_1$ = *Age Succession*
$X_4$ = *Black Poverty*
$X_6$ = *Female Employment*
$X_3$ = *Young Blacks*

it is possible to say that abandonment *decreases* by 7.8 percent for every unit *increase* in the *Ethnic Neighborhood* factor and by 2.5 percent for every unit increase in the *Female Employment* dimension. Abandonment *increases* by 2.9 percent, 1.5 percent, and 2.5 percent, respectively, for unit *increases* in the *Age Succession, Young Black,* and *Black Poverty* factors.

## Predicting Abandonment Using Unfactored Indices

If now the change variables are employed directly,† after initially removing variables of unduly high intercorrelation, we can see why the *Ethnic Neighborhood* factor predominated. Of the seven variables which are significant at the F—0.05 level, four were originally part of the *Ethnic Neighborhood* factor (Exhibit 7-31).

According to this analysis, which explains approximately 85 percent of the variance which surrounds housing loss via abandonment, the phenomenon takes place less frequently in areas where the change in the percent of the population married is increasing or conversely takes place more frequently where increased numbers of children replace previously resident elderly (concurrently reducing the percent married population). This point is further accentuated by abandonment's negative relationship with areas which have an increasing percent of the population in excess of sixty-five years.

Abandonment also seems to wax in areas of decreasing housing value and decreasing owner occupancy. The latter variable in terms of

---

*Note internal loadings on these dimensions are negative making their overall effect positive.

†Entered directly into the regression equation without first grouping via factor analysis.

## EXHIBIT 7-31
## DYNAMIC ENVIRONMENTAL PREDICTORS OF ABANDONMENT: THE UNFACTORED VARIABLE SET

Dependent Variable: Percent Structures Abandoned Per Census Tract

| Variable Number | | Name | B | F | F to Reject Randomness |
|---|---|---|---|---|---|
| 012 | ($X_1$) | Percent of the Population Married | —17.50 | 6.00 | 4.05 |
| 008 | ($X_2$) | Median House Value | — 6.99 | 5.79 | 4.05 |
| 014 | ($X_3$) | Percent of the Housing Units Owner Occupied | —20.29 | 16.78 | 4.05 |
| 009 | ($X_4$) | Percent of the Housing Units Single Family | 3.62 | 6.59 | 4.05 |
| 021 | ($X_5$) | Percent of the Labor Force Female Clerical | — 1.68 | 5.09 | 4.05 |
| 005 | ($X_6$) | Percent of the Housing Units w/no bath or Share | — 2.31 | 5.80 | 4.05 |
| 011 | ($X_7$) | Percent of the White Population in Excess of 65 Years | — 4.62 | 4.59 | 4.05 |

$R^2 = 0.85$ $F = 0.05$

Source: Newark Area Resurvey, spring 1972

individual statistical significance is by far the most robust. This may lend additional evidence to the superficiality of the importance of the black/white ownership characteristics (parcel corollaries) in light of likeness to the resident/nonresident categories. Whether this may be extended to the individual parcel or not, owner-occupancy seems to be a powerful element of neighborhood stability. Its impact on abandonment is obvious.

According to Newark's specific change over the decade, abandonment also seems to increase in inner-city areas characterized by an increase in their single family percentages. For core areas, realistically speaking, what is being said is that abandonment increases in central city areas where multi-family demolition exceeds that of single family.

If each of these separate variables are now used to predict abandonment it is evident that given the equation below:

$$\text{Percent abandonment per census tract} = 58.84 - 17.50X_1 - 6.99X_2 - 20.29X_3 + 3.62X_4 - 1.69X_5 - 2.31X_6 - 4.62X_7$$

where

$X_1$ = Percent Married
$X_2$ = Median House Value
$X_3$ = Percent Owner Occupied
$X_4$ = Percent Housing Units Single Family
$X_5$ = Percent of the Labor Force Female Clerical
$X_6$ = Percent of the Housing Units — No Bath or Share
$X_7$ = Percent of the White Population in Excess of 65.

residential abandonment *decreases* by: 17.5 percent for every percent increase in the married population, 7 percent for each $1,000 increase in median housing value, 20 percent for each percent increase in owner occupancy, 1.7 percent for each percent increase in female clericals in the labor force, 2.3 percent for each percent increase in units which have no bath or must share, and 4.6 percent for each percent increase in the white population in excess of 65 years. Abandonment *increases* 3.6 percent with each percent increase of single family units as a result of massive multifamily demolition.

## Summary

What may be said then about residential abandonment? Residential abandonment seems to be much more a function of tax delinquency, owner-tenant interplay, and neighborhood location than of physical characteristics of the building itself.

Tenants with large numbers of children, no matter how well behaved, demand more from and contribute less to a building than can an elderly couple. If there is sufficient disregard by tenants for the property of the owner to occasion the owner to cite this as an operating problem, a potentially volatile abandonment situation exists. If the relationship is further compounded by racial differences generating mistrust or noncooperation, abandonment may be imminent.

In their rental relationships the owners of the buildings have responsibilities to which they too must adhere. They should attempt to screen tenantry, to maintain high occupancy levels, to provide basic housing services, and to maintain their tax commitments. The owners for the most part are not poor, not encumbered by mortgages, and seem to know rental real estate. Their basic personal assets should retard rather than encourage abandonment: but the reverse is the case.

In terms of the location of the building, the static environmental precursors stated that abandonment is a function of poor areas, principally black and Puerto Rican. Yet, this glimpse (1960) may have been too early and too "one shot" to assess the phenomenon adequately.

In looking at abandonment through the dynamics of change, somewhat more of the unexplained variance could be interpreted. The change variables noted that not only did residential abandonment appear to be a function of poor areas but also of changes occurring within these areas.

The last remnants of European ethnic staging/ownership seem to retain housing. Black staging in the presence of white owners, as does the need for shelter for a growing population of urban immobiles, seems to increase housing abandonment. Inner city residential growth to accommodate the clerical labor force again seems to retard abandonment.

In terms of numbers, the in-migrant population appears to have the most significant impact on housing abandonment. Any measure which would improve the relationship between renter/owner, increase owner-occupancy, and curtail transiency would then retard abandonment. Although currently under fire, it would appear that one program, black home ownership, is at least a step in this direction.

## Notes

1. Gregory K. Ingram and John F. Kain, "A Simple Model of Housing Production and the Abandonment Problem" (Proceedings of the American Economics Association and the American Real Estate Urban Economics Association, Vol. 5, 1972)
2. Ibid., p. 4.
3. Federal Home Loan Bank Board, *Waverly: A Study in Neighborhood Conservation* (Washington, D.C.: FHLB, 1940), p. 3.
4. Edgar Hoover and Raymond Vernon, *Anatomy of a Metropolis* (Cambridge, Mass.: Harvard University Press, 1959), pp. 190-207.
5. Anthony Downs, "Possible Program for Counteracting Housing Abandonment" (Preliminary Report) (Chicago, Ill.: Real Estate Research Corporation, 1971), pp. 13-20 (unpublished).
6. National Urban League, *The National Survey of Housing Abandonment* (New York, 1971), p. 12.
7. See Linton, Mields & Coston, *A Study of the Problems of Abandoned Housing and Recommendations for Action by the Federal Government and Localities* (Washington, D.C.: 1971 mimeo.), pp. 19-20.
8. For abandonment in other areas see: Citizens Budget Committee, Inc., *Abandoned Buildings: A Time for Action* (New York, February 1970); "The Wildfire of Abandonment: Entire Blocks Are Rotting as Landlords Claim: 'We Can't Make a Buck,'" *Business Week,* April 4, 1970, p. 57+; "In the Inner Cities: Acres of Abandoned Buildings: Landlords Are Now Fleeing the Inner City . . .," *U.S. News and World Report,* January 26, 1970, pp. 54-56; "No Vacancy: Shortage of Housing in N.Y. City Gets Worse with Every Day; Abandonments, Withdrawal of Capital and an Old Law Exacerbate City's Crisis," *Wall Street Journal* December 2, 1970, p. 1+; Sandra Conchado and William P. Nolan, "Building Abandonment in New York City," *New York Law Forum,* Vol. 16, No. 4 (February 1970), pp. 798-862.
9. See Art Silbergeld, "Abandoned Housing," *Planning Comment* (Spring 1971), p. 5.
10. See similar conclusions for St. Louis in *Urban Decay in St. Louis* (St. Louis, Missouri: The Institute for Urban and Regional Studies, Washington University, March 1972), pp. 40-74.
11. For the HUD director's view, see George Romney, "Statement before the Subcommittee on Housing of the House Committee on Banking and Currency on Settlement Costs, Mortgage Foreclosure, Housing Abandonment and Site Selection Policies," February 22, 1972.
12. See Frank S. Kristof, "Housing: Economic Facts of New York City's Housing Problems," in *Agenda for a City,* eds. Lyle Fitch and A. Walsh (Beverly Hills, California: Sage Publications, 1970).
13. For a fullsome description of the abandoned building owner see "Walk Aways: A Growing Threat to Cities," *The Realtors Quarterly Magazine,* Vol. 37 (April 1970).

# *Appendix 1*

# METHODOLOGY

Two basic data sources have been employed through the bulk of this study: *gross statistics* on the City of Newark, obtained either from the U.S. Census or local and state records and *sample statistics* obtained from interviews of Newark property owners in 1964 and 1971. The methodology which follows presents the procedural processes of gathering and manipulating these data. This appendix proceeds from a discussion of data available for the city at large to how these varying bodies of data were refined via regression and factor analyses. Further on, the sample data are discussed as well as the interview instrument and the training of interviewers.

## GROSS CITYWIDE DATA AT A POINT IN TIME

### Abandonment Data

In order to obtain gross figures on citywide abandonment in Newark, recurring fire department surveys of vacant buildings, prepared by fire inspectors within the Division of Combustibles, were utilized. The fire department's inventory of vacant buildings is kept current through the initiation of a Kardex file card for every structure observed vacant on a fire inspector's daily rounds and the refiling of this card in a "razed building file" if the structure is demolished publicly or privately, or completely destroyed through fire. To this list were added a small number of additional abandoned buildings observed by the Newark Planning Department in a survey in 1970, which were not already included on the fire department's list of vacant buildings.

For accuracy, this combined list was visually checked by field teams in areas of high, moderate, and low concentrations of structure abandonment. The field teams were asked to gauge not only the gross levels of estimated abandonment but also the accuracy of the fire department in specifying exactly which structures were or were not undergoing this process. This was done by selecting a square block in each of the three areas and, via visual inspection, listing exactly what was taking place in each area. The results of the comparison for each area appear in Exhibit A1-1.

In general the fire department list was found to be quite accurate. If anything, viewing the exhibit, it appears to be somewhat of an *understatement* of the magnitude of the abandonment problem. In the most severe areas of abandonment, it was also apparent that the fire department data could age quite quickly. Fire department records were simply unable to keep up with the continuing change that was taking place in these rapidly decaying neighborhoods.

One of the most heartening aspects of the data was the fire department inspectors' ability, through a series of regular card filings, to document adequately block areas of residential decay. As has been noted previously, in several cases specific addresses were dated; yet the *neighborhoods* to which the data directed the study group were definitely areas of substantial structure abandonment, significantly different from "unblighted" areas where no listings were filed by inspectors.

On the whole it was felt that the data, though far from ideal, did present across an area (in this case a census tract) a reasonable estimate of structure abandonment. If one were to use fire department data on a structure by structure basis it would have to be sifted and tested much more deliberately than was the case for the gross analysis. On an area base, however, it is possible to use the data, given recurring accuracy checks, with a good deal of confidence.

When the data on abandonments were used in subsequent regression or factor analyses the base was refined according to this study's definition of abandonment. Essentially these consisted of residential and residential/commercial standing, vacant structures and similar residential, residential/commercial structures which had been demolished either privately or publicly for reason of hazard over the period 1967-1971.

## EXHIBIT A1-1
## ACCURACY OF THE FIRE DEPARTMENT "OBSERVED VACANT" DATA AS AN INDICATOR OF THE LEVEL OF CITYWIDE RESIDENTIAL ABANDONMENT

| Areas of Residential Abandonment In Order Of Severity | Within A Contiguous Four Block Sample: Reported by the Fire Department as "Observed Vacant" and Found to be Correct | Not Reported by the Fire Department Yet Found to be Observed Vacant[1] | Reported by the Fire Department as Observed Vacant Yet Found to be Occupied[2] |
|---|---|---|---|
| Area I (Most Severe Area of Abandonment) | 68 | 12 | 1 |
| Area II | 23 | 7 | 5 |
| Area III | 10 | 2 | 3 |
| Area IV (Least Severe Area of Abandonment) | 1 | 0 | 0 |
| TOTAL | 101 | 21 | 9 |

1. This figure includes inaccurate street addresses within the same block.
2. With no visible evidence of rehabilitation.

Source: Newark Area Resurvey, spring 1972.

## Crime Data

The data on crime were obtained from the files of the Newark Police Department and represent over 90,000 incidents of police activity during 1971. While many of the noncrime-related activities of the police department may be just as pertinent in terms of services rendered to decaying areas, this study, for reasons of expediency, concerned itself for gross analysis with the more serious of general police activities.

Crimes against the person (murder, negligent manslaughter, forcible rape, and aggravated assault), crimes against property (robbery, burglary, larceny, and auto theft), and the presence of suspicious or disorderly persons within a neighborhood, constitute this study's definition of *crime*. When instances of *crime* appear as a variable in the Symap program or in the regression and factor analyses it is an unweighted summation of these previous subsets.

As instances of crime had to be assigned to census tracts manually, a selected sample of approximately 1,000 were chosen from approximately 30,000 annual occurrences of serious crime. Three heightened crime periods were selected for this purpose. Historical data were utilized to partition: first, the most active crime months; second, the most active crime days; and third, the most active crime periods within these days.

In Newark over a four-year observation period this appears to be respectively: (1) the summer months of May, June, July, and August and the seasonal theft periods of April (Easter) and December (Christmas); (2) the days of Saturday and early Sunday, and (3) the specific time periods of 8-12 p.m. and 0-4 a.m.

Each of the Saturdays was numbered starting with one in April and ending with twenty-four in December and a table of random numbers was used to select a profile of crime during six of these heightened crime periods. The number of instances of serious crime observed via this refining process was 861.

For the analysis dealing specifically with crimes within vacant/abandoned buildings police activities were expanded to include *both* less than major offenses and instances of police assistance. For the years 1965 and 1971 lists of vacant buildings were prepared. In each case the entire year's police activities were screened according to their appearance within buildings of the designated abandoned building set. From this it was possible to compare relative police activity both within and without abandoned buildings and within abandoned buildings over a monitored time period. No refining process was employed here; 90,000 incidents of police activity were analyzed as to their occurrence within or around abandoned buildings.

## Fire Data

The fire data were obtained from Newark Fire Department records for the period 1970 and 1971. These represent serious fires and are designated *Signal 11 Fires* and *Multiple Alarm Fires* in increasing order of severity. In a Signal 11 Fire all major fire apparatus from a specific district responds to the call; in a Multiple Alarm Fire major apparatus from several districts respond.

Seven hundred fifty instances of serious fires were noted in the city during 1970 and 1971. Each of these were checked with buildings appearing on the abandoned building list and a comparison made between the frequency of fire in unoccupied versus occupied buildings. In addition, data maintained specifically by the fire department on fires within vacant buildings were also analyzed. Finally, each building appearing as abandoned within the sample set was viewed over time to estimate whether fire indeed had a causal influence on abandonment or whether the instance of fire occurred after the fact. In each of these buildings the phenomenon of recurring fires was also examined.

## Tax Delinquency Data

Data for tax delinquencies were taken from the city's annual list of properties offered in sale for tax purposes, after all periods of prior owner-warning had expired. This list, in excess of 700 parcels annually, was employed for the period 1967 through 1971 (five years), each year reflecting the previous calendar year's tax delinquency. Additional information sought and subsequently utilized was property classification and purchase price. The latter was available for each of the five years while the former, although available for 1971, had to be reconstructed for 1967.

It should be realized that there is a definite lag between sustained tax delinquency, notification of tax sale, and an owner losing interest in a parcel as measured by nonpayment of taxes. While the last situation is of course what should be measured, data limitations limit us to the first two. Thus observed, correlations or regressions are as a conequence weaker due naturally to an absence of almost a complete year's tax data.*

## Mortgage Lending Data

Gross citywide financial data were obtained by tracing property transfer records over a ten-year period using the Essex County Real Estate Directory as a data base. From this, trends in mortgage lending within the city were developed and a sample of active or once-active lenders generated. In addition, several managers of slum realty were interviewed as well as real estate brokers who deal heavily in low-end property transfers. In *total,* thirty lenders and realtors were interviewed.

The questionnaire employed, which is presented in the appendices, sought to probe in depth lender and realtor views toward the trends in center city mortgage originations that the study group had unearthed as a result of viewing the real estate directory over time. Supplemental questions also explored the scope of insured mortgage lending in general and specific impact of the local FHA 235 program.

## Relationships Among the Data

Using the abandoned building data set as a base, each of the other bodies of data, i.e., crime, fire, and tax delinquency, was simultaneously screened to isolate the occurrence of multiple indicators of decay within the same building. In this way it was possible to estimate both degrees of association and potential linkage between the various phenomena.

The study further employed several common statistical tools to derive relationships between these data and other socio-economic indicators available for Newark, on a census tract basis. In each case, where regression analysis was used, the stepwise mode was employed. Similarly when factor analysis was called upon to aggregate data, the orthogonal solution was chosen. Within specific sections the rationale

*Sufficient information was not available on the gross list of abandoned parcels to categorize them by time of abandonment, thus one of the few ways of avoiding the above problem (i.e., comparing tax delinquency and abandonment specifically by time period) could not be used.

for the various statistical selection processes is more fully documented. A brief description of data manipulation follows the discussion of the tenement landlord sample.

## SAMPLE DATA OVER TIME

### Housing Condition and Demographic Partitions (1960)

The basic sample target was a representative sample of Newark slum tenements (parcels with three or more rental units) selected in 1964 according to several categories of blighted areas as reported in the 1960 U.S. Census of Housing.

Originally there were three basic waystations on the road toward ultimate parcel choice. The first of these was the question of what criterion should be used to measure the degree of blight; the second was the question of what geographical subsets were to be used in describing areas; and the third was the question of what degree of blight to use as sample partitions.

Although not available for 1970, the census in 1960 presented data on housing units by three categories of decay: sound, deteriorating, and dilapidated. Obviously the subjective judgements of the field survey groups used by the census played a major role in determining the categories in which the housing units were placed. In 1960 alone there were a number of discrepancies between the census data and studies done both by the Newark City Planning Board and the Newark Housing Authority. Since then, subsequent studies performed by the Bureau of the Census have shown great statistical unreliability across cities and the housing quality measure has been discontinued. Nevertheless, for general purposes the data (1964) proved to be reasonably reliable. When the proportion of sound housing for each of the city's census tracts* was listed in an array from those tracts with the least sound

*Definition of census tract: "Census tracts are small areas into which large cities and adjacent areas have been divided for statistical purposes. Tract boundaries were established cooperatively by local committees and the Bureau of the Census, and generally designed to be relatively uniform with respect to population characteristics, economic statuses, and living conditions. The average tract has about four thousand residents. Tract boundaries are established with the intention of being maintained over a long time so that comparisons can be made from census to census."[1]

housing to those with the most, in 1960, there were two obvious clusters. Exhibit A1-2 shows there were seven census tracts with less than 25 percent of their housing units sound.

Yet another cluster was present for the eleven tracts with less than 50 percent of sound housing. In 1964, to see whether there would be significant differences in landlord opinion and reaction to areas which had considerable pockets of blight, but which overall were still basically sound, a third set of tracts was chosen from the next twenty-one. The very best of these tracts had 66.7 percent of its housing classified as sound.

For the purposes of later analysis, another partition was found worthy of note. This is the proportion of housing occupied by nonwhites. In 1960 for Group 1, this ran from a low of little less than half, 48.7 percent, to a high of 92.9 percent. Current opinion indicates a comparative homogenization of the Group 1 tracts. Both for Groups 2 and 3, however, in 1960 there were decided dichotomies (Exhibit A1-3).

In Group 2A, for example, the proportion of nonwhites in 1960 ran from a low of 56.2 percent to a high of 84.4 percent, with a relatively even distribution through the eight tracts concerned. Group 2B goes from a low of 22.1 percent to a high of 42.4 percent. Similarly, when tract Group 3 was prepared in a rank ordering, there was an obvious division into two different subgroups with eleven census tracts running from 41.2 percent to 95.1 percent nonwhite occupancy and ten tracts running from a low of 6.8 percent to a high of 34.2 percent. The exhibits in the main body of the 1964 work were based, therefore, at least in part, on five subsets composed of a combination of housing characteristics and also nonwhite occupancy. By 1971, however, the dominance of minority group occupancy found earlier in Group 1 had spread to Groups 2 and 3. In the current volume, therefore, data presented by area will usually be presented in three rather than five subsets.

## Block and Parcel Choice (1964)

The Newark census tracts within each of the three housing sets were then detailed in terms of the number of the census blocks they contained which had twenty or more renter-occupied dwelling units. For each tract enough blocks were chosen using a random number table to secure approximately forty to fifty blocks per set. The number of

EXHIBIT A1-2
FREQUENCY DISTRIBUTION OF TRACTS BY PROPORTION OF SOUND HOUSING IN NEWARK, N.J. 1960

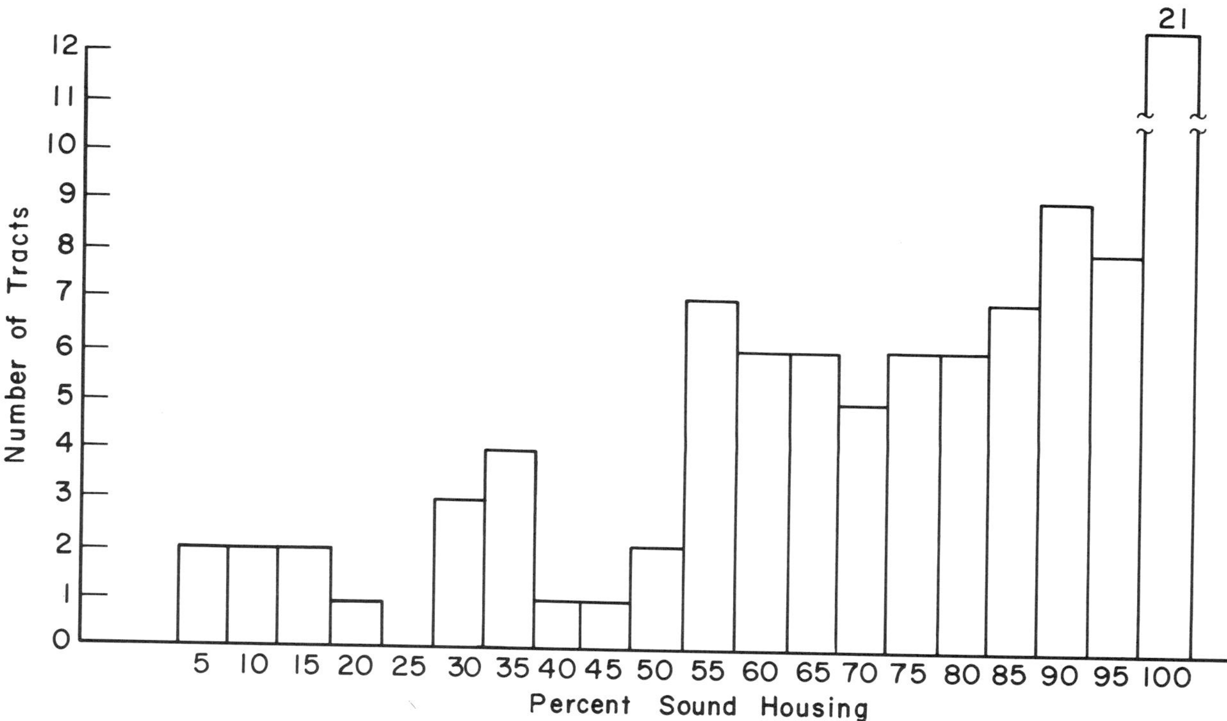

## EXHIBIT A1-3
### TRACT GROUP CATEGORIES — HOUSING QUALITY/RACE NEWARK, N.J. 1960

| Group | Number of Tracts | Housing Characteristics Percent Sound | Proportion of Occupied Housing Units Occupied by Nonwhites (1964) | Proportion of Occupied Housing Units Occupied by Nonwhites (1971) |
|---|---|---|---|---|
| 1 | 7 | 2.3-17.7 | 48.7-92.9 | 74.4 |
| 2 (A | 8 | 29.1-46.8 | 56.2-84.4 | 82.2 |
| (B) | 3 | 26.7-38.0 | 22.1-42.4 | 82.2 |
| 3 (A | 11 | 50.2-66.7 | 41.2-92.6 | |
| (B | 10 | 51.2-66.8 | 7.9-31.1 | 52.1 |

Source: U.S. Census of Housing 1960, Newark, New Jersey.

blocks per tract, however, regardless of the paucity or abundance of blocks with twenty or more renter-occupied dwelling units within the tract, was limited to five by means of a random number table. The parcel surveyors were then sent out to the chosen blocks. (The instructions for the parcel surveyors and the parcel check list were the same in both 1971 and 1964 and follow in the appendices.) Originally in 1964, starting at a designated corner of the specified block, the field surveyor counted all parcels on the block which had three or more rental units. He then used a random number table to determine which of those parcels were to be incorporated into the sample. For no block were more than five parcels chosen. In theory this should have yielded 200 to 250 parcels in each area. Because of blocks which contained fewer than five appropriate parcels, this was not the case. In addition, three parcels were discovered to be in tax-exempt hands and were, therefore, dropped from the sample. In 1964 for Area 1 there were 186 parcels; for Area 2 there were 182; and finally for Area 3 there were 198; for a total of 566 parcels. Exhibit A1-4 summarizes the numbers involved. The same parcels were surveyed in 1971.

## The Field Survey Parcel Check List

The basic goal of this portion of the field survey was to gain a basic description of the parcel, its condition, and its maintenance.

EXHIBIT A1-4

SUMMARY OF BLOCK AND PARCEL CHOICE, 1964 and 1971

| | Number of Tracts | Number of Blocks Chosen | Total Parcels Counted | Parcels in Sample |
|---|---|---|---|---|
| Area 1 | 7 | 39 | 609 | 186 |
| Area 2 | 11 | 42 | 622 | 182 |
| Area 3 | 13 | 52 | 829 | 198 |
| | | | | 566 |

Source: Sternlieb, George, *Tenement Landlord* (New Brunswick, Rutgers University Press, 1966).

Three categories of occupancy were specified: those dwellings which were described as occupied, those which were partially occupied, and those which were vacant. If the categories are taken in reverse order, the vacant parcels were those parcels which were completely vacant. The reasons for this, as was later discovered, were various: a number of the parcels were burned out; some were in the process of being restored, and several were boarded up, with no signs of tenancy. The partially occupied category required much more judgement on the part of the field surveyors. These were parcels which showed signs of substantial vacancy. In a number of cases a part of the parcel had been either demolished or obviously vandalized. An additional group included parcels which had been substantially rebuilt and were in the process of being rented. The occupied parcels, on the other hand, although they had the normal quota of *For Rent* signs, exhibited none of the characteristics of the other two sets.

In 1971 a new category of occupancy had to be added to document Newark's growing squatter population. This category, "partially occupied but reported as vacant by the owner," indicates the presence of tenants who draw very few housing services, i.e., barely shelter, yet pay nothing for them. For American cities in advanced stages of residential abandonment this is a growing phenomenon of the 70s.

Exhibit A1-5 shows the size of parcel and the number of apartments as noted by the field surveyors in both 1964 and 1971. As is indicated, the bulk of Newark tenements are relatively small with six or fewer units. A very few ran in the thirteen and over categories. This obviously is a factor of considerable significance in terms of the costs of maintaining and supervising rental units in Newark. Larger units can more easily afford the services of a full-time resident janitor or superintendent. Smaller units, on the other hand, can have only part-time supervision at best. Area 1, the hard-core slum area, has the largest number of parcels with more than six units. The number of apartments observed required a considerable degree of judgment on the part of the field surveyors, and obviously there was much room for error.

The size of parcel was checked out in the personal interviews. By adding back in the "less than three units" to the three- to six-unit figure, it can be seen that the field survey universe and interviews have roughly the same size of unit proportions.

## EXHIBIT A1-5
### SIZE OF PARCEL
### NUMBER OF APARTMENTS OBSERVED

1964

| | AREA 1 | | AREA 2A | | AREA 2B | | AREA 3A | | AREA 3B | | TOTAL | |
|---|---|---|---|---|---|---|---|---|---|---|---|---|
| | Number | Percent | Number | Percent | Number | Percent | Number | Percent | Number | Percent | Number | Percent |
| 3-6 Units | 159 | 85.5 | 111 | 86.7 | 52 | 96.3 | 105 | 91.3 | 75 | 91.5 | 502 | 88.8 |
| 7-12 Units | 23 | 12.4 | 10 | 7.8 | 1 | 1.9 | 7 | 6.1 | 6 | 7.3 | 47 | 8.3 |
| 13-24 Units | 4 | 2.2 | 7 | 5.5 | 1 | 1.9 | 2 | 1.7 | 1 | 1.2 | 15 | 2.7 |
| 25 or More | — | — | — | — | — | — | 1 | 0.9 | — | — | 1 | 0.2 |
| Total | 186 | 100.0 | 128 | 100.0 | 54 | 100.0 | 115 | 100.0 | 82 | 100.0 | 565 | 100.0 |

1971

| | AREA 1 | | AREA 2 | | AREA 3 | | TOTAL | |
|---|---|---|---|---|---|---|---|---|
| | Number | Percent | Number | Percent | Number | Percent | Number | Percent |
| 3-6 Units | 77 | 82.8 | 116 | 82.3 | 146 | 90.7 | 338 | 85.9 |
| 7-12 Units | 13 | 14.0 | 15 | 10.6 | 9 | 5.6 | 37 | 9.4 |
| 13-24 Units | 3 | 3.2 | 6 | 4.3 | 4 | 2.5 | 13 | 3.3 |
| 25 or More | 0 | 0.0 | 4 | 2.8 | 2 | 1.2 | 6 | 1.5 |
| Total | 93 | 100.0 | 141 | 100.0 | 161 | 100.0 | 395 | 100.0 |

Source: Newark Area Resurvey, spring 1972

## Condition of Parcel (1964 and 1971)

The next category in the field survey directions was aimed at defining the quality of the parcel being surveyed. This is obviously a difficult task involving a variety of subjective elements. There were three questions which were directed to this end. The first of them appraised the quality of external appearance. The field surveyors were asked to compare the parcel to its immediate neighbors. Was it poorer than its neighbors, the same as its neighbors, or better than its neighbors?

The field surveyor was then asked to define the absolute quality of the landlords' maintenance of such elements as garbage facilities, halls, stairs, fire escapes, porches, and steps. This too was categorized by reasonably kept, poorly kept, and well kept.

The surveyors were then directed to compare the street upon which the parcel being rated was situated with the general area. A word of definition is in order here. By the street was meant the block frontage on which the parcel was located. By the general area was meant the frontage across the street upon which it faced and the several blocks in the immediate area, with greatest weight being placed upon the facing frontage.

## Nonresidential Uses (1964 and 1971)

One of the most striking characteristics of the slums is the number of parcels which have commercial occupancy to some degree. This can be the small grocery store, the automobile repair shop, the plumbing and roofing contractors' headquarters, and so on. Two measures of commercial occupancy were defined. The first was a minor degree — occupancy which would generate in the surveyor's opinion less than 30 percent of the total parcel rent roll. The second was rated as a *significant category*, i.e., over 30 percent of parcel rent. Obviously, these are rough judgments on the part of the surveyors. They were spot checked, however, by the authors and only one substantial discrepancy was noted.

## Ownership (1964 and 1971)

Defining the ownership of slum tenements is a far from easy task. In the case of Newark the researchers in both 1964 and 1971 were fortunate in having the *Essex County Real Estate Directory* available. This is a service which compiles frequently updated ownership lists which include transaction data. Unfortunately, the prevalence of nominal transfers, i.e., transfers usually without consideration as between members of the same family or between holding corporations, must be researched in order to find last bonafide sales. With the help of title experts, headed by Ms. Dorothea Kaas, this difficulty was overcome.

Titles for the original study were researched back to 1939, those for the period between the two studies to 1964. In all cases that were not clear, actual title deeds were researched. Although initially data were obtained on nominal ownership by deed, this is far from indicative of the true owners of the parcels in question. It was found, for example, that many major holders held parcels individually, and, conversely, that the existence of a corporation did not necessarily mean a multiple holder. Similarly, the addresses of owners, as obtained from the title search and by the cooperation of the Newark tax authorities, was far from adequate. Many owners use addresses of convenience, which are not indicative of their real residences. These addresses, however, did provide a first lead for the next stage of the research, contacting the individual landlords.

The difficulties in finding owners are exemplified by parcel number 113.

> This is a four-story masonry structure with five apartments plus a store on the first floor. The latter is presently occupied by a revivalist church. The parcel, presently assessed for $13,500, was purchased in 1946 by one of the old line large scale slum operators in Newark for $6500.
>
> In 1969, the bank which held the first mortgage of $4,142 foreclosed. [Note that this mortgage was a blanket including another building of comparable size, thus indicating how little value this corner property retained.] The bank, in turn, sold it for $500 to a management company with an address in Jersey City.
>
> Search of that city's directories and a visit to the nominal address indicated that the company was essentially a fiction. The last address, in the words of our field searcher, "is an abandoned building that is condemned and according to a neighborhood store keeper has been vacant for over two years." The management company seemed to have existence only in the Newark city tax records.
>
> By dint of a number of efforts the owner was finally discovered in a nearby suburb. Though he had purchased the building for $500, his current feeling was that the area simply doesn't make any

sense for additional investment. He had been hopeful of a quick resale and since this has not come through, given his feeling of insecurity on the future of the area, had let the building slip into tax delinquency. It is presently in the process of being foreclosed by the city.

### Tax Delinquency of the Parcel (1964 and 1971)

In 1971, as a result of earlier explorations of the relationship of abandonment and tax delinquency in a study of rent control in New York City, it was deemed necessary to examine the tax status of each parcel.

Specific parcels were checked against the records of the Newark Tax Department for any recorded period (six months) of tax delinquency. Since subsequent payment of taxes once in the tax delinquent stage will allow a parcel to appear on the most current records as "paid to date," an additional search for outstanding delinquency regardless of current status was conducted in the title tax lien file. For both current and outstanding delinquencies total periods of tax arrears were summed for each parcel.

The linkage of tax delinquency and abandonment became so obvious that it seemed imperative to look at the presence of this phenomenon in 1964. This had not been investigated in the earlier study but it now appeared that the phenomenon could well be a lead indicator of abandonment. These relevant tax delinquency data were retrieved from storage and the tax status of each parcel was checked as if the parcel was being investigated in 1964.

The investigation proved extremely worthwhile, for ultimately it was found that prior tax delinquency was in fact a dominant characteristic of buildings classified as abandoned.

### The Interview Pattern

### The Nature of the Instrument (1964 and 1971)

The interview pattern, which was decided on in 1964 and reused in 1971, was a personally administered, structured one. In 1964 there were thirty-one substantive questions plus an additional number of personal classification questions. In 1971 both the number of substantive and personal questions were increased to include data inspired by studies conducted during the interim period. These mainly had to do with the effect of welfare tenantry on maintenance procedures. It is obvious that securing reliable responses in sensitive areas is most difficult. In order to meet this problem, the pattern of the interview rotates relatively innocuous questions with the basic important ones, i.e., those concerning capacity and will to improve, given certain concessions. On such questions as vacancy rates and goals of property ownership, projective techniques were used, i.e., what do most owners do, etc. A substantial degree of redundancy was introduced in order to check out difficult areas.

Newark residential structures typically have relatively few dwelling units. The ownership pattern with few exceptions is one either of single parcel owners or relatively small operators. Few of the resident owners as detailed in Chapter 3 own other real property. Under these circumstances questions on investment return or on potential of higher rents were frequently *non sequiturs*.

A case in point is parcel number 143P, whose black owner, having purchased it nearly twenty-five years ago, holds the parcel free and clear.

> When asked about investment patterns her response was that she simply couldn't answer some of these questions because she does not look at her home as an investment and therefore questions relating to that aspect were irrelevant. All of her tenants were long term, and she would not consider a rent increase or whether there was any potential for one since "I'm satisfied with the tenants, they give me no problems, and I wouldn't like to bring strangers in."

In 1964 the interview instrument went through a number of permutations in dry runs conducted by the authors among owners in other New Jersey municipalities, such as Jersey City and Hoboken, before being stabilized in its final form. It can be observed that a number of the questions are essentially open ended. This provided the interviewer with an opportunity of jotting down the wealth of information that was often offered which would not have been encompassed in a completely structured instrument.

## The Interviewers

Sixteen individual interviewers worked on the survey in 1964, twelve on the 1971 study. In both cases two to four of them contributed nearly two-thirds of the total responses. Spot-checking by phone was conducted in both years among those interviewed to assure the continuity of the performance. The interviewers had a variety of backgrounds; most, however, were law and city planning students drawn from the Rutgers Law School and from the Planning Department at Livingston College. In areas where the resident landlords typically were black, every effort was made to assure that the interviewer was also black. Interviews with Puerto Rican owners were done in Spanish by Spanish-speaking students from the Newark area. All interviewers, prior to doing any interviewing, went through training sessions. In addition, an interviewer's manual was prepared and the interviewers were tested on its contents. All interviews were checked in detail with the individual interviewer. A typical interview lasted roughly one and one-half hours.

## Finding the Owners

As mentioned earlier, the addresses given in title records are far from adequate for the purpose of finding slum tenement owners. Cooperation of the Newark tax authorities was secured, but even their data were not completely adequate. Exhibit A1-6 presents a summary of response activity in 1971.

## Respondents versus Nonrespondents

Is there any skew in the nonrespondents distribution which would make generalizations dangerous? Can generalizations be made on the basis of the 70 plus percent of the sample who permitted themselves to be interviewed in both years as to the conduct and attitudes of the nonrespondents? This is a difficult question to answer.

Based upon interviewers reporting on their failures, the nonrespondents are perhaps weighted in the direction of elderly owners, typically of immigrant stock.

The bulk of the nonrespondents, in both studies, were not multiple owners of parcels within the sample area. In asking major real estate dealers who were the significant owners of parcels in 1964, none of the persons mentioned were in the nonrespondent group. The same is true of 1971.

On the whole, therefore, it is the authors' opinion that reasonable generalizations for the whole sample can be made on the basis of the successful interviews secured.

## EXHIBIT A1-6

### FINAL SAMPLE STRUCTURE BY AREA OF SURVEY

| SAMPLE STRUCTURE | AREA OF CITY | | | |
|---|---|---|---|---|
| | CORE | INNER RING | OUTER RING | TOTAL |
| TOTAL | 186 | 184 | 199 | 569 |
| A. Non-Assignments[1] (owned by public body) | 85 | 41 | 31 | 157 |
| B. Interviews Assigned | 101 | 143 | 168 | 412 |
| 1. Completions | 79 | 117 | 118 | 314 |
| 2. Non-Completions | 22 | 26 | 50 | 98 |
| a. Refusal | 7 | 12 | 25 | 44 |
| b. Owner No Contact[2] | 5 | 4 | 6 | 15 |
| c. Owner Address Unknown[3] | 10 | 10 | 19 | 39 |

Notes: 1. Non Assignments:

| | |
|---|---|
| 3 | Veteran's Administration |
| 5 | Board of Education (Newark) |
| 4 | Board of Education (Vocational Schools) |
| 4 | Essex County College |
| 4 | Essex County |
| 104 | Newark Housing Authority |
| 10 | New Jersey (State) |
| 20 | City of Newark |
| 3 | United Hospitals of Newark |
| 157 | Total |

2. No contact with owner at legitimate address after 3 callbacks.
3. Address of owner is nonexistent or owner was resident in now-demolished building and current address is unknown.

Source: Center for Urban Policy Research, Resurvey, fall 1971

As stated earlier, essentially complete interviews were secured with the owners of 392 parcels in 1964 and 313 owners in 1971. This does not mean, however, that there were 392 or 313 individual interviews. In a number of cases there were owners who had more than one parcel in the sample.

Multiple parcel owners were asked about their parcels individually. The answers that are tabulated in this work are weighted in proportion to the 392 or 313 parcels owned.

### The Subset Interview: Questioning the Abandoned Parcel Owner (1971)

According to this study's definition of abandonment, eighty-four sample owners whose buildings were lost to the housing stock over the period 1964 to 1971 were sought for interview both as to why and how they gave up the structures. Thirty owners of abandoned buildings were ultimately interviewed. Once reason and process were determined these owners were subsequently asked whether or not they were paying taxes on the structures, whether they had any trouble in maintaining their fire insurance, and finally, why if they wanted to get rid of the buildings, did they not use the city's program for the taking of vacant structures.

## DATA MANIPULATION

### Basic Strategy

The strategy followed throughout this study has been, where possible, to provide simultaneous analysis from both micro and macro levels. The report proceeds from the anecdotal through sample data, ultimately to statistical analysis on information which is reflective of the city's entire population.

In the case of abandonment and tax delinquency, it was felt that both are situations which depend on environmental as well as behavioral characteristics, i.e., of owner/parcel/tenant influences. Thus, in each case, when the development of early warning indicators is attempted, the methodology of moving from the specific case to the more general, statistical manipulation of data will be employed, recognizing the parcel's immediate and nonimmediate influences. The strength of prediction also builds as the steps of this methodology are traversed. Degrees and directions of association are the products of initial analyses. Prediction is diffidently attempted in later efforts.

## A Statement on Analysis of Variance

Analysis of variance is employed here to establish strength and direction of association between a dependent variable and singular independent variables. The object of the analysis of variance is to investigate both the variation within the sample and the variation among sample means ultimately to test the hypothesis that the subpopulation means are equal. If $M_1 \neq M_2 \neq M_3$ then the sample means should also differ from each other and X by more than what may be attributed to chance. The null hypothesis (i.e., that there is no difference) may then be rejected.

An additional advantage of using the analysis of variance technique is that, as a by-product, the reliability of the sample means may be verified. The models chosen allow the dependent variable a 0 or 1 dichotomous choice while each independent variable has several intervals, in most cases, from four to seven.

## A Statement on Factor Analysis

Principal components factor analysis is utilized in this study to reduce many intercorrelated variables into a limited number of independent variables. The factor analysis routine is advantageous because it produces statistically independent factors which may be used to satisfy assumptions of independence in multi-variate regression analysis. Second, it produces a unique principal component's solution to a correlation matrix, insuring the repeatability of the routine and the reliability of the analytical procedure.

As a mathematical tool factor analysis has many uses ranging from classifying and reducing data to testing hypotheses and making inferences. For the purposes of this study it was used in its most basic and familiar form; i.e., as an "exploratory technique" to reduce data and isolate patterns of regularity. The patterns of regularity were initially identified, analyzed to determine the variables involved, and ultimately assembled and entered into the regression equation in the form of "factor scores" to attempt to predict the dependent variable as a function of several independent indices.

Basic to the concept of factor analysis is the idea that if several variables exist and are intercorrelated, the relationships which accrue may be due to the presence of one or more underlying factors. Those variables which are most highly correlated with a particular underlying factor (i.e., those which the factor loads heavily upon) should in such case be most highly related to each other. The high correlation between a factor and its associated variables produces independent clusters (if principal component's solution is chosen) of high intercorrelation. The theoretical assumption is made that the high intercorrelation within each cluster and the low relationship between clusters is due to the presence of a single factor representing the particular cluster. Factors are associated with clusters until all the clusters have been isolated. When this is complete, the variables within each cluster are examined to determine the presence of a common element. The common element among the indices is presumed to be the factor associated with the cluster and is named accordingly.

Via this process, the problem of linking empirical research and conceptual theory is approached on one front. It is assumed that the underlying theoretical indices, which actually explain a portion of the regularity of the object of inquiry, actually exist. Individual, yet readily accessible, operational variables only imperfectly measure this "regularity." The operational variables when subjected to statistical description evidence common elements which, when isolated, describe regularity in a more concentrated and broader framework. Kelley makes this point but is careful, also, to keep the limitations of factor analysis well in mind:

> "There is no search for timeless, spaceless, populationless truth in factor analysis; rather it represents a simple straightforward problem of description in several dimensions of a definite group functioning in definite manners, and he who assumes to read more remote verities into the factor outcome is certainly doomed to disappointment."[2]

## A Statement on Multiple Regression[3]

Regression analysis is a mathematical model designed to describe and measure the functional relationship between two variables. The regression equation permits the prediction of the value of the dependent variable, given a known value of the independent variable.

The basis for computation of this relationship is a regression equation which fits a curve to the distribution of observed data. This equation, using a least squares technique for a linear model, reduces to the smallest possible magnitude the sum of the squared deviations of the estimated values of the dependent variable that is analyzed from the observed values, to produce the best fitting equation "through" the observed data. The regression equation produces a coefficient with which to assess the magnitude of the independent variable's effect upon the dependent variable.

Linear multiple regression analysis is a further delineation of the regression technique which specifies as an assumption of the model, the form of the real relationship between the dependent and independent variables. The assumption of linearity dictates that there be a constant change in the dependent variable for every unit change in the independent variable, adjusting for the other independent variables, regardless of the initial magnitude of the independent variable. The basis for computation of these relationships is the multiple regression equation which takes the following form:

$$Y = a + b_1x_1 + b_2x_2 + b_3x_3 + \ldots\ldots + b_nx_n + e$$

where: *a* equals a constant generated in the regression; *b* equals the unnormalized regression coefficient constant or rate of change of the dependent variable per unit change in the independent variable holding *constant* the other independent variables. The *e* represents the error term associated with the equation; it is that portion of the variation in the observed data not "explained" by the regression equation and is attributable to the nature of the model. Or this variation may be a function of other variables not included in the regression equation. In any event, although the regression attempts to estimate the best fitting relationship through the observed data, it is, at best, only an approximation and necessarily includes randomized effects.

Stepwise regression analysis will be used in the regression analyses. It is a technique by which independent variables are accepted into the regression equation to provide the near-optimum prediction with the least number of independent variables. The stepwise method entails a recursive construction of regression equations starting with the first independent variable with the greatest power of "explanation" and then adding variables step-by-step, given the previously added variables, until no additional variable will make a significant addition to the regression equation. The use of such a technique is particularly convenient if the regression analysis is designed to provide understanding of variation in observed data, given little preliminary research in the field.[4]

## NOTES

1. U.S. Bureau of the Census, *U.S. Census of Population and Housing: 1960 Census tracts, Final Report PHC(1)-105.* (Washington, D.C.: Government Printing Office, 1962).
2. Truman L. Kelley, "Comments on Wilson and Worcester's Vote on Factor Analysis," *Psychology 5,* (1940), 117-120.
3. J. Johnston, *Econometric Methods* (New York, N.Y.: McGraw-Hill, 1963), 119-120.
4. Norman H. Nie et al., *Statistical Package for the Social Sciences* (New York, N.Y.: McGraw-Hill, 1970), 185.

# *Appendix 2*

# QUESTIONNAIRES AND CODING SHEETS

| Card No. | Subject | 1964 |
|---|---|---|
| 1 | Exterior maintenance check | |
| 2 | Landlord interview | |
| 3 | Title search | |
| 4 | Tax record | |
| | | 1971 |
| 5 | Exterior maintenance check | |
| 6 | Landlord interview | |
| 7 | Title search | |
| 8 | Tax record | |

**Notes on the Coding Process**

1. For both years (1964 and 1971) corresponding cards have the same sequence of variable.

2. Every parcel is represented by seven cards, even if some cards are blank, with only the I.D. and card number.

3. If there is no landlord interview completed in 1971, a computer card with only the I.D. and card number is included.

# 1964 EXTERIOR MAINTENANCE CHECK
# (CARD 1)

**ADDRESS:** ______________________________

______________________________

| Variable Number | Column | Row | |
|---|---|---|---|
| 1 | 1-2 | | Census tract number |
| 2 | 3-4 | | Census block number |
| 3 | 5-8 | | Tax block number |
| 4 | 9-11 | | Tax lot number |
| 5 | 12 | | Tract category |
| | | (1) | Less than 25 percent sound (pink) |
| | | (2) | 25-50% (blue contiguous) |
| | | (3) | 25-50% (blue free standing) |
| | | (4) | 50-68% (sound gray contiguous) |
| | | (5) | 50-68% (sound gray standing) |
| 6 | 13 | | Occupancy |
| | | (1) | Occupied |
| | | (2) | Partially occupied |
| | | (3) | Vacant |
| 7 | 14 | | Size of parcel—number of apartments (Each family represents a unit) |
| | | (1) | 3-6 units |
| | | (2) | 7-12 units |
| | | (3) | 13-24 units |
| | | (4) | 25 or more units |
| 8 | 15 | | Type of construction |
| | | (1) | Frame |
| | | (2) | Frame with reasonable to good condition siding |
| | | (3) | Frame with bad condition siding |
| | | (4) | Masonry |

| Variable Number | Column | Row | |
|---|---|---|---|
| 9 | 16 | | Quality of external appearance (Compare to neighboring parcel) |
| | | (1) | Poorer than neighbors |
| | | (2) | Same as neighbors |
| | | (3) | Better than neighbors |
| 10 | 17 | | Absolute quality (Landlord's maintenance) |
| | | (1) | Reasonably kept |
| | | (2) | Poorly kept |
| | | (3) | Well kept |
| | | | (Criteria) |
| | | | a. garbage facilities |
| | | | b. health hazards, (dirty halls, broken stairs) |
| | | | c. safety measures, i.e., fire escapes, sturdy porches, and stairs |
| 11 | 19 | | Quality of streets vs. block (Compare parcel to both sides of street) |
| | | (1) | Same as |
| | | (2) | Better than |
| | | (3) | Poorer than |
| 12 and 13 | 20 and 21 | | Exterior Maintenance Check |
| | | (1) | Storm windows (combination) |
| | | (2) | New porch and/or front steps |
| | | (3) | New siding/shingles (partial or total) |
| | | (4) | Newly painted |
| | | (5) | Trim painting only |
| | | (6) | Air conditioners |
| | | (7) | Other |
| | | (8) | None |
| | | (9) | No Answer/Don't Know (NA/DK) |
| 14 | 22 | | Degree of commercial occupancy (Specify type of business, if any) |
| | | (1) | None |
| | | (2) | Minor—less than 30 percent rent of parcel |
| | | (3) | Significant—30 percent |

| | | | |
|---|---|---|---|
| 15 and 16 | 23 and 24 | | Proximity of nuisances |
| | | (1) | Bars—in proximity to parcel |
| | | (2) | Loitering by undesirables |
| | | (3) | Junk yards |
| | | (4) | Factories |
| | | (5) | Heavy traffic |
| | | (6) | None |
| 17 and 18 | 25 and 26 | | General comments (Surveyors comments and evaluation of the parcel in general) |
| 19 and 20 | 31-33 | | Parcel I.D. number |
| 21 | 80 | (1) | Card number |

## 1964 LANDLORD INTERVIEW (CARD 2)

| Variable Number | Column | Row | |
|---|---|---|---|
| 23 | 1. When did you first become an owner of rental real estate? | | |
| | | (1) | Pre 1930 |
| | | (2) | 1930-1940 |
| | | (3) | 1940-1950 |
| | | (4) | 1950-1955 |
| | | (5) | 1955-1960 |
| | | (6) | 1960 to date |
| | | (7) | |
| | | (8) | No Answer (NA) |
| | | (9) | Don't Know (DK) |
| 24 | 2. Why did you buy property at ____________________? | | |
| | | (1) | Home |
| | | (2) | Rental return |
| | | (3) | Speculation |
| | | (4) | Inheritance |
| | | (5) | Debt |
| | | (6) | Commercial purposes |
| | | (7) | Home plus income |
| | | (8) | Other |
| | | (9) | Mortgage foreclosure |

25 3. Is this still your reason for keeping it?

(1) Yes
(2) Want to sell—not listed w/broker
(3) Want to sell—listed w/broker
(4) Want to sell—no buyers
(5) Want to sell—no use, no buyers
(6) Income
(7) Income plus capital appreciation
(8) Waiting for Urban Renewal
(9) NA/DK

26 4. Do you use a manager or rent collector?

(1) Manager
(2) Rent collector
(3) Self
(4) Other
(5) In part
(6) Employee
(7) Agent
(8) Superintendent
(9) NA/DK

27 5. Collect rent weekly or monthly?

(1) Weekly
(2) Monthly
(3) Partly each
(4) Other
(5) Nominal monthly (must collect more frequently)
(6) No tenants—but house partly occupied
(7) Vacant parcel
(8)
(9) NA/DK

28 6. Furnished or Unfurnished?

(1) Furnished
(2) Unfurnished
(3) Mixed
(4) Rooming House
(5) Other
(6)
(7)
(8)
(9) NA/DK

29 7. Size of Holding

(1) No other
(2) Other (one or two more)
(3) Three to six more
(4) Six to twelve more
(5) Twelve plus
(6) Used to own more than two but no more
(7) Used to own one other but no more
(8) Other
(9) NA/DK

30 7a. Other properties—location

(1) Owns no other
(2) Newark solely
(3) Newark plus other old New Jersey central city
(4) Wider geographical spread
(5) None Newark
(6)
(7)
(8) NA
(9) DK

31 7b. Other properties — condition

(1) Owns no other
(2) All same (i.e., slums)
(3) Great bulk slums—some others
(4) 50/50
(5) Bulk not slums
(6) Not usable
(7)
(8) NA
(9) DK

32 8. Make living from real estate

(1) Full-time R.E. Owner
3/4 or more income from
(2) Substantial 1/3—3/4 income from
(3) Minor supplement to income
(4) No income, self-sustaining
(5) Claims loss on operation
(6)
(7)
(8) NA
(9) DK

33 9. How many apartments at ____________________?

(1) Three to six
(2) Seven to twelve
(3) Thirteen to twenty-four
(4) Twenty-five or more
(5) Sleeping rooms
(6) Other
(7) Less than three units
(8) NA
(9) DK

34 10. Do you have Negro or white tenants?

(1) Negro
(2) White
(3) Mixed
(4) Puerto Rican
(5) Negroes and Puerto Rican
(6) Puerto Rican and white
(7) All three
(8) Vacant—no tenants
(9) NA/DK

35 11. Has the vacancy rate changed in general area?

(1) Yes—up
(2) Yes—down
(3) No
(4)
(5)
(6) People move to projects
(7) Unclassifiable other
(8) NA
(9) DK

36 12. Has vacancy rate changed in your property?

(1) Yes—up
(2) Yes—down
(3) No
(4)
(5)
(6)
(7) Unclassifiable other
(8) NA
(9) DK

37 13. Hire someone to do repair work or do it yourself?

(1) Practically all (self-done)
(2) About half and half
(3) Just a little done by self
(4) Rarely or none self
(5) Employee
(6)
(7)
(8) NA
(9) DK

38 14. How much times does operating rental properties take?

(1) Full time or nearly
(2) Half-time
(3) One-fourth time (one day a week with or without evenings)
(4) One-half time (one day a week with or without evenings plus other job)
(5) Less
(6) Two to three days a week
(7)
(8) NA
(9) DK

39 15. Would you say most owners . . . looking for return through rental or profit through sale?

(1) Rental—exclusively
(2) Profit from resale (rental mainly)
(3) 50/50
(4) Profit from resale (mainly)
(5) Profit from resale (exclusively)
(6) Other
(7)
(8) NA
(9) DK

40 16. Would you differ with this opinion? (Referring to question number 15)

(1) Rental (exclusively)
(2) Profit from resale (rental mainly)
(3) 50/50
(4) Profit from resale (mainly)
(5) Profit from resale (exclusively)
(6) Waiting for urban renewal
(7) Rental and place to live
(8) NA
(9) DK

17. Problems of maintenance and improvements.
(Order of importance: 1 to 6)

| | | |
|---|---|---|
| 41 | (1-6) | Tenants |
| 42 | (1-6) | Mortgage Cost |
| 43 | (1-6) | Mortgage length |
| 44 | (1-6) | Tax level |
| 45 | (1-6) | Tax reassessment |
| 46 | (1-6) | Builder requirements |
| 47 | (1-6) | No problems (punch [1] in Col. 29) |
| 48 | (1-6) | No answer (punch [1] in Col. 30) |
| 49 | | |

50 18. You did/did not mention taxes . . .

(1) Not impediment to improvements
(2) As above but with stress on tax limits on return
(3) Won't improve because of tax levels
(4)
(5)
(6)
(7) Strongly harmful to market—no reference to improvements
(8) Non sequitur
(9) NA/DK

51 18a. You did/did not mention taxes . . .

(1) Strong reference to reassessment
(2) Some reference to reassessment
(3) Reference to reassessment, but o.k.
(4) No reference to reassessment
(5) Unimportant
(6)
(7)
(8) NA
(9) DK

19. Which improvements . . . without reassessments

(1) Yes, will be reassessed
(2) No reassessment

52 1(Yes)—2(No) Electrical wiring, including additional electrical outlets

53 1(Yes)—2(No) Automatic hot water heater

54 1(Yes)—2(No) Installation of central heat

55 1(Yes)—2(No) Repairing and replacing porches and steps

56 1(Yes)—2(No) Outer refacing; i.e., shingles, etc.

57 19a. Which improvements . . . without reassessments

(1) Any outside yes, inside w/o permit, no.
(2) NA
(3) DK
(4) Other
(5) But some fear of reassessment in general
(6) Strong fear of reassessment

58 20. What improvements . . . w/o no tax boosts?

(1) Can't afford it—none
(2) Doesn't need it
(3) Neighborhood no good
(4) Would need refinancing
(5) Other requirements
(6) Rental too limited
(7) Tenants no good; don't warrant
(8) Not worth it
(9) NA/DK

59 20a. What improvements . . . without tax boosts?

(1) Internal minor
(2) External minor
(3) Internal major
(4) External major
(5) Few or none
(6) Doing it without regard for taxes
(7) Urban renewal
(8) Major internal and external
(9) NA/DK

60 21. Change in taxes as a percent of rent—change in income?

(1) No passing on tenants w/more
(2) Some passing on
(3) Matching increases
(4) Used to but can't any longer
(5) Matching increases but kills whole rental
(6) No passing on—other reason
(7)
(8) NA
(9) DK

61 22. Is the resale market such that . . .

(1) Yes—definitely
(2) Yes—maybe
(3) Toss-up
(4) Probably no
(5) Definitely no
(6) Other reasons
(7)
(8) NA
(9) DK

62 23. If improvements—fair return

(1) Yes—definitely
(2) Yes—maybe
(3) Toss-up
(4) Probably no
(5) Definitely no
(6) Definitely no—tenants can't pay
(7) No—Urban Renewal coming
(8) NA
(9) DK

63 24. Improve property if given long term mortgage?

( 1) Don't want to go in debt
( 2) Parcel isn't worth it
( 3) No return
( 4) Neighborhood doesn't warrant it
( 5) Urban Renewal is taking property
( 6) Property doesn't need it
( 7) Taxes
( 8) No money

( 9) NA/DK
(10) Parcel and neighborhood, no good
(11) Yes, no restrictions
(12) Taxes plus something else
(13) Yes, if mtg. payments equal increased revenue cost
(14) Too old

64 25. Know of any government programs for older properties?
(1) FHA General
(2) FHA Title I
(3) FHA 203, 220, 221
(4) VA
(5) Yes, but nothing specific
(6) No
(7) Not for this area (or parcel)
(8) NA
(9) DK

65 26. What would you have to pay for improvement money? (Interest payments)
(1) 5 percent or less
(2) 5 percent to 6 percent
(3) 6 percent to 7 percent
(4) 7 percent to 10 percent
(5) Over 10 percent
(6) Won't borrow
(7) Would not be able to get it
(8) NA
(9) DK

66 26a. What would you have to pay (terms)?
(1) Under three years
(2) Three to five years
(3) Five to ten years
(4) Ten years
(5) Ten plus to fifteen years
(6) More than fifteen years
(7) Won't borrow
(8) NA
(9) DK

67 27. What source . . . for improvement money?

(1) Mortgage—Savings bank
(2) Mortgage—broker
(3) Finance Company
(4) Personal loan and commercial bank
(5) Personal resources
(6) Second mortgage—no source
(7) Bank w/o details
(8) NA
(9) DK

68 28. Visits by building inspectors' effects

(1) No effect—visits rare
(2) No effect—building above criticism
(3) Occasional—good but worthwhile
(4) Occasional—good meaningless
(5) Continual problems—unreasonable
(6) Significant factor—no value judgments
(7)
(8) Payoff
(9) NA/DK

69 29. Are you in an area scheduled for Urban Renewal?

(1) No
(2) Yes—within one year
(3) Yes—one to five years
(4) Yes—five to ten years
(5) Yes—long term
(6) Not sure
(7)
(8) Other
(9) NA/DK

70 30. If property taken by Urban Renewal . . . get back investment?

(1) Yes
(2) Yes—but
(3) Maybe
(4) Probably not
(5) Definitely not
(6) Doesn't care—wants out
(7)
(8) NA
(9) DK

71 31. Why not? (If no for question number 30)

(1) Time lag between announcement and taking
(2) Authorities judge by area not by parcel
(3) Other
(4)
(5)
(6)
(7)
(8) Non sequitur
(9) NA/DK

72 32a. Points of additional information. (Businessmen) (Continuation of occupation)

(1) Small businessman
(2) House craft businessman
(3) Big businessman

73 32. Points of additional information (Occupation)

(1) Housewife
(2) Lawyer
(3) Real estate broker
(4) Real estate manager
(5) House oriented craftsman
(6) Craftsman, other
(7) Other profession—Mg't.
(8) Retired
(9) NA/DK

74 32. Age of owner.

(1) Minor
(2) 21 to 30
(3) 30 to 40
(4) 40 to 50
(5) 50 to 60
(6) 60 to 70
(7) 70 +
(8)
(9) NA—No observation

75 32. Place of residence

(1) Same house
(2) Within study area
(3) Balance of Newark
(4) Within twenty mile radius of Newark
(5) Balance of New Jersey
(6) New York City
(7) Elsewhere
(8) NA
(9) DK

76 32. Owner Ethnicity

(1) Negro
(2) White—Jewish
(3) White—Italian
(4) White—other
(5) White—unobserved
(6) Cuban
(7) Other
(8)
(9) DK

77 32. Work condition of owner (area of employment).

(1) Employed home
(2) Employed—Newark
(3) Employed outside Newark
(4) Not working—retired
(5) Not working—unemployed
(6)
(7)
(8) NA
(9) DK

78 32. Owner's income.

(1) $ 3,000 to $ 5,000
(2) 5,000 to 8,000
(3) 8,000 to 11,000
(4) 11,000 to 20,000
(5) Over 20,000
(6) Less than 3,000
(7)
(8) NA
(9) DK

79 32. Type of ownership.

(1) Individual; including man and wife
(2) Partnership
(3) Holding Co.
(4)
(5)
(6)
(7)
(8) NA
(9) DK

80 32. Owner's sex.

(1) Male
(2) Female
(3) Both
(4)
(5)
(6)
(7)
(8)
(9)

81 32. Residence/Non-residence of owner

(1) Resident in parcel
(2) Within a block of parcel
(3) In study area—outside "block"
(4) Newark—other
(5) New Jersey—twenty mile radius from Newark
(6) Balance of New Jersey
(7) New York
(8) Other
(9) NA/DK

82 32. Cooperation of owner in interviewing.

(1) None
(2) Poor
(3) Average
(4) Good
(5) Excellent

## 1964 TITLE SEARCH
## (CARD 3)

| Variable Number | Column | Row |
|---|---|---|
| 91 | 27 | Name of owner<br>(1) Individual (including joint ownership by husband and wife)<br>(2) Two or more individuals<br>(3) Realty corporations<br>(4) Financial institutions<br>(5) Nonfinancial institutions<br>(6) Estate<br>(7)<br>(8) |
| 92 | 28 | Address of owner<br>(1) Same address<br>(2) Same general area of Newark (i.e., within one mile)<br>(3) Newark other<br>(4) New Jersey other than Newark<br>(5) Outside New Jersey<br>(6) |
| 93 | 29 | Date of title<br>(1) 0 up to but not including 2 years old<br>(2) 2+ to 4 years old<br>(3) 4+ to 6 years old<br>(4) 6+ to 10 years old<br>(5) 10+ to 15 years old<br>(6) 15+ to 20 years old<br>(7) 20+ years old<br>(8) Not recorded<br>(9) |
| 94 | 30 | Property class<br>(1) 2<br>(2) 4A<br>(3) 4B<br>(4) 4C<br>(5) Other |
| | | Lot Size—(as stated, i.e., frontage x depth) include symbols |

95 31-33 Frontage (rounded to nearest foot)

96 34-36 Depth (rounded to nearest foot)

97 37-41 Land assessment
(in 100's of $)
(1)

98 42-47 Building assessment
(in 100's of $)
(1)

99 53 Mortgage source—by name
(1) Savings bank
(2) Commercial bank
(3) Savings and loan
(4) Individual grantee
(5) Prior owner
(6) Mortgage company
(7) No mortage shown
(8) Realty and construction company
(9) Not given
(0) Government agency

100 54-59 First mortgage amount $__________
(1)

101 60 First mortgage terms
(1) not listed
(2) —4 percent plus to 4.5 percent
(3) —4.5 percent plus to 5 percent
(4) —5 percent plus to 5.5 percent
(5) —5.5 percent plus to 6 percent
(6) 6 percent plus to 7 percent
(7) 7 percent plus to 8 percent
(8) 8 percent plus
(9) Bond
(0) Other

| | | |
|---|---|---|
| 102 | 61 | Mortgage types |
| | | (1) B (Blanket mortgage of consideration) |
| | | Blanket = more than one parcel in transit |
| | | (2) Clear cut first mortgage |
| | | (3) S (subject mortgage) |
| | | (4) Subj. (encumbrances on record) |
| | | (5) Other—note |
| | | (6) |
| 103 | 62-67 | Amount paid for property $ __________ |
| | | (Be careful to note method for determining this in book!) |
| | | (1) |
| 104 | 68 | Value category of property |
| | | (1) Up to $8,000 |
| | | (2) $8,000 up to but not including $10,000 |
| | | (3) $10,000 up to but not including $12,000 |
| | | (4) $12,000 up to but not including $15,000 |
| | | (5) $15,000 up to but not including $20,000 |
| | | (6) $20,000 up to but not including $30,000 |
| | | (7) $30,000 up to but not including $50,000 |
| | | (8) $50,000 up to but not including $100,000 |
| | | (9) $100,000 up to but not including $250,000 |
| | | (0) Not available |
| 105 | 69 | |
| | | (1) In Renewal Area |
| | | (2) Not in Renewal Area |
| 106 | 70 | Bona fide sale |
| | | (1) Previous nominal transfer |
| | | (2) No previous nominal transfer |
| | | (3) Nominal transfer |
| | | (4) |
| | | (5) |

| | | | |
|---|---|---|---|
| 107 | 71 | | |
| | | (1) | Sale price can't be determined |
| | | (2) | Blanket mortgages |
| | | (3) | Foreclosure—price unclear |
| | | (4) | Sale price can't be determined—last sale before record |
| | | (5) | Sales price n.g.—subject mortgage |
| 108 | 72 | Second Mortgage | |
| | | (1) | Yes |
| | | (2) | No |
| | | (3) | Third mortgage |
| 109 | 73 | Second Mortgage Source by Name | |
| | | (1) | Savings bank |
| | | (2) | Commercial bank |
| | | (3) | Savings and loan |
| | | (4) | Individual grantee |
| | | (5) | Mortgage company |
| | | (6) | Construction or home improvements |
| | | (7) | |
| | | (8) | |
| 110 | 74-78 | Second mortgage amount $__________ | |
| 111 | 79 | Second mortgage type | |
| | | (1) | B (Blanket mortgage of construction) |
| | | (2) | Clear cut second mortgage |
| | | (3) | S (subject mortgage) |
| | | (4) | Subj (encumbrances on record) |
| | | (5) | Purchase money |
| | | (6) | At time of transfer (within six months) |
| | | (7) | At time of transfer (more than six months) |
| | | (8) | Other |
| 112 | 77-79 | I.D. number | |
| 113 | 80 | (3) | |

# 1971 EXTERIOR MAINTENANCE CHECK (CARD 5)

**I D Number** ______________________________

**Parcel Address** ______________________________

| Variable Number | Column | Row | |
|---|---|---|---|
| 114 | 1-2 | | Census tract number |
| 115 | 3-4 | | Census block number |
| 116 | 5-8 | | Tax block number |
| 117 | 9-11 | | Tax lot number |
| 118 | 12 | | Tract category (leave blank) |
| | | (1) | Less than 25 percent sound (pink) |
| | | (2) | 25-50 percent (blue contiguous) |
| | | (3) | 25-50 percent (blue free standing) |
| | | (4) | 50-68 percent (sound gray contiguous) |
| | | (5) | 50-68 percent (sound gray standing) |
| 119 | 13 | | Occupancy |
| | | (1) | Occupied |
| | | (2) | Partially occupied |
| | | (3) | Vacant |
| | | (4) | Demolished |
| | | (5) | |
| | | (6) | Observed occupied, but vacant according to landlord |
| | | (7) | Privately demolished—building no longer of use |
| | | (8) | Privately demolished—building replaced by another use |
| 120 | 14 | | Size of parcel—number of apartments (each family represents a unit) |
| | | (1) | 3-6 units |
| | | (2) | 7-12 units |
| | | (3) | 13-24 units |
| | | (4) | 25 or more units |
| | | (5) | None |

| | | | |
|---|---|---|---|
| 121 | 15 | | Type of construction |
| | | (1) | Frame |
| | | (2) | Frame with reasonable to good condition siding |
| | | (3) | Frame with bad condition siding |
| | | (4) | Masonry |
| 122 | 16 | | Quality of external appearance |
| | | (1) | Poorer than neighbors |
| | | (2) | Same as neighbors |
| | | (3) | Better than neighbors |
| 123 | 17 | | Absolute Quality |
| | | (1) | Reasonably kept |
| | | (2) | Poorly kept |
| | | (3) | Well kept |
| | 18 | | (leave blank) |
| 124 | 19 | | Quality of street versus block |
| | | (1) | Same as |
| | | (2) | Better than |
| | | (3) | Poorer than |
| 125 and 126 | 20 and 21 | | Alterations and improvements |
| | | (1) | Storm windows (combination) |
| | | (2) | New porch and/or front steps |
| | | (3) | New siding/shingles |
| | | (4) | New paint for siding |
| | | (5) | Trim painting only |
| | | (6) | Air conditioners |
| | | (7) | Other |
| | | (8) | None |
| | | (9) | No Answer/Don't Know (NA/DK) |
| 127 | 22 | | Degree of commercial occupancy |
| | | (1) | None |
| | | (2) | Minor—less than 30 percent of total rent |
| | | (3) | Significant—30 percent or more of rent |

| | | | |
|---|---|---|---|
| 128 and 129 | 23 and 24 | | Proximity of nuisances |
| | | (1) | Bars—in proximity to parcel |
| | | (2) | Loitering by undesirables |
| | | (3) | Junk yards |
| | | (4) | Factories |
| | | (5) | Heavy traffic |
| | | (6) | Other—specify |
| | | (7) | |
| | | (8) | None |
| | | (9) | NA/DK |
| | 25 | | |
| | | (1) | if in "Project Rehab"—Breakthrough |
| 130 | 26 | | Urban renewal area (if any) |
| | | (1) | R 6 |
| | | (2) | R 32 |
| | | (3) | |
| | | (4) | R 72 |
| | | (5) | R 123 |
| | | (6) | R 141 |
| | | (7) | R 196 |
| | | (8) | |
| | | (9) | |
| 131 | 27 | | Model City area (if any) |
| | | (1) | Model city A |
| | | (2) | Model city B |
| | | (3) | Model city C |
| | | (4) | |
| | | (5) | |
| | | (6) | |
| | | (7) | |
| | | (8) | |
| | | (9) | |
| 132 | 28 | | Fire at building since January 1970 |
| | | (1) | while building was vacant |
| | | (2) | prior to demolition |
| | | (3) | if other with fire |

| | | | |
|---|---|---|---|
| 133 | 30 | | Demolished by Newark Housing Authority |
| | | (1) | demolished for redevelopment |
| | | (2) | to be rehabilitated |
| | | (3) | for new school |
| | | (4) | for highway construction |
| | | (5) | for other (Essex County, parking, federal building) |
| | | (6) | Hazardous |
| | | (7) | |
| | | (8) | |
| | | (9) | |
| 134 and 135 | 31-33 | | Parcel I.D. Number |
| 136 | 80 | | |
| | | (5) | Card Number |

## 1971 LANDLORD INTERVIEW (CARD 6)

| Variable Number | Column | Row | |
|---|---|---|---|
| 137 | | Code Number | |
| | | | (1-3) |
| 138 | 1. When did you first become an owner of rental real estate? | | |
| | | (1) | Pre 1930 |
| | | (2) | 1930-1940 |
| | | (3) | 1940-1950 |
| | | (4) | 1950-1955 |
| | | (5) | 1955-1960 |
| | | (6) | 1960 to 1965 |
| | | (7) | 1965 to 1967 |
| | | (8) | 1967 to date |
| | | (9) | No Answer/Don't Know (NA/DK) |

139 2. Why did you buy property at ____________________?

(1) Home
(2) Rental return
(3) Speculation
(4) Inheritance
(5) Debt
(6) Commercial purposes
(7) Home plus income
(8) Other
(9) Mortgage foreclosure

140 3. Is this still your reason for keeping it?

(1) Yes
(2) Want to sell—not listed w/broker
(3) Want to sell—listed w/broker
(4) Want to sell—no buyers
(5) Want to sell—no use, no buyers
(6) Income
(7) Income plus capital appreciation
(8) No
(9) NA/DK

141 4. Do you use a manager or rent collector?

(1) Manager
(2) Rent collector
(3) Self
(4) Other
(5) Mailed
(6) Employee
(7) Agent
(8) Superintendent
(9) NA/DK

142 5. Collect rent weekly or monthly?

(1) Weekly
(2) Monthly
(3) Partly each
(4) Other
(5) Nominal monthly (must collect more frequently)
(6) No tenants—but house partly occupied
(7) Vacant parcel
(8) Demolished
(9) NA/DK

143 6. Furnished or Unfurnished?
(1) Furnished
(2) Unfurnished
(3) Mixed
(4) Rooming house
(5) Other
(6)
(7)
(8)
(9) NA/DK

144 7. Size of holding
(1) No other
(2) Other one or two parcels more
(3) Three to six more
(4) Six to twelve more
(5) Twelve to seventy-five
(6) Seventy-six plus
(7) Used to own others but no more
(8) NA/DK

145 7a. Other properties—location
(1) Owns no other
(2) Newark solely
(3) Newark plus other old New Jersey Central city
(4) Wider geographical spread
(5) None Newark
(6)
(7)
(8) Other
(9) DK/NA

146 7b. Other properties—condition
(1) Owns no other
(2) All same
(3) Worse
(4) Some better, some worse
(5) Better than
(6) Not usable—vacant
(7) ANS—not code
(8) Other
(9) DK/NA

147 8. Make living from real estate

(1) Full-time real estate owner—three-fourths or more income from
(2) Substantial one-third—three-fourths income from
(3) Minor supplement to income
(4) No income, self-sustaining—No
(5) Claims loss on operation
(6)
(7)
(8)
(9) DK/NA

148 9. How many apartments at ____________________?

(1) Three to six
(2) Seven to twelve
(3) Thirteen to twenty-four
(4) Twenty-five or more
(5) Sleeping rooms—roominghouse
(6) Other
(7) Less than three units
(8) DK/NA

149 10. Do you have Negro or white tenants?

(1) Negro
(2) White
(3) Mixed
(4) Puerto Rican
(5) Negroes and Puerto Rican
(6) Puerto Rican and white
(7) All three
(8) Vacant—no tenants
(9) NA/DK

150 11. How many of them are on welfare?

(1) None
(2) Less than three
(3) Three to six
(4) Seven to twelve
(5) Thirteen to twenty-four
(6)
(7) All
(8)
(9) DK/NA

151 12. How do welfare tenants affect a property?

A. Behavior

(1) Very positive effect
(2) Slightly positive effect
(3)
(4) No effect
(5)
(6) Slightly negative effect
(7) Very negative effect
(8)
(9) DK/NA

152 B. Rent level

(1) Lower it very much
(2) Lower it a little
(3)
(4) No effect
(5)
(6) Raise it a little
(7) Raise it a lot
(8)
(9) DK/NA

153 13. Has the vacancy rate changed in general area?

(1) Yes—up
(2) Yes—down
(3) No
(4) Yes—due to fire and abandonment
(5) Yes—due to widespread demolition
(6) People move to projects
(7) Unclassifiable other
(8)
(9) DK/NA

154 14. Has vacancy rate changed in your property?

(1) Yes—up
(2) Yes—down
(3) No
(4) Vacant or abandoned for several years
(5) Demolished
(6)
(7) Unclassifiable other
(8)
(9) DK/NA

155 15. Hire someone to do repair work or do it yourself?

(1) Practically all (self-done)
(2) About half and half
(3) Just a little done by self
(4) Rarely or none self
(5) Employee
(6)
(7)
(8)
(9) DK/NA

156 16. How much time does operating rental properties take?

(1) Full-time or nearly
(2) Half-time
(3) One-fourth time (one day a week with or without evenings)
(4) One-half time (one day a week with or without evenings plus other job)
(5) Less—few hours a week
(6) Two to three days a week
(7) Other
(8)
(9) DK

17. Problems of maintenance and improvements. (Order of importance: 1 to 6)

157 (1-6) Tenants
158 (1-6) Mortgage cost
159 (1-6) Neighborhood problem
160 (1-6) Tax level
161 (1-6) Other
162 (1-6) Builder requirements
163 (1-6) Insurance
164 (1-6) No problems
165 (1-6) No answer—punch (1) in column 32

166 18. What improvements . . . w/o any tax boosts?

( 1) Can't afford it—none
( 2) Doesn't need it
( 3) Neighborhood no good
( 4) Would need financing
( 5) Other requirements

( 6) Rental too limited
( 7) Tenants no good; don't warrant
( 8) Not worth it
( 9) NA/DK
(11) All repairs made despite taxes
(12) Exterior main. (i.e., paint, shingles, siding)
(13) Interior remodeling (bath, kitchen, basement)
(14) Adding to structure (porch, room, fencing)
(15) Major repair/replace plumbing or electrical system
(16) General repair nonspecific—minor
(17) Total rehabilitation

167 19. Was a bank or savings and loan mortgage available?
(1) Yes, from a commercial bank
(2) Yes, from a savings and loan or mutual savings bank
(3) VA/FHA
(4) No, had to got to mortgage company
(5) No, had to take back mortgage
(6) Other
(7) Yes
(8) No—without details
(9) DK/NA

168 20. Sell parcel now . . . possible to get mortgage from a lending institution?
(1) Yes, easy to get
(2) Yes, but with difficulty
(3) Yes
(4) Could go either way
(5) Doubt it
(6) Definitely not
(7)
(8)
(9) DK/NA

169 21. If yes . . . would you have to take back a mortgage?

(1) No, mortgage covers sale price
(2) Yes
(3) Partial
(4)
(5) Yes, for 100 percent of sale price
(6) Other
(7)
(8)
(9) DK/NA

170 22. Do you feel your building is in good operating condition?

(1) Yes, very good
(2) Yes, moderately good
(3) Livable
(4) No
(5) Very poor
(6) Other
(7)
(8)
(9) DK/NA

171 23. Cost to be put in good condition.

(1) Less than $500
(2) $500 to $2000
(3) $2000 to $5000
(4) $5001 to $10,000
(5) $10,001 to $20,000
(6) Over $20,000
(7) Building is beyond any sensible investment
(8) No expenditures necessary
(9) DK/NA

172 24. How much of a rent increase for good investment?

(1) Up to $5 per tenant per month
(2) $6-$10 per tenant per month
(3) $11-$20 per tenant per month
(4) $21-$30 per tenant per month
(5) $31-$50 per tenant per month
(6) $51 and over

(7) Rent needed to maintain this building no one would pay!
(8) Satisfied with present level
(9) DK/NA

173 25. Could you get this increase?
(1) Yes, easily
(2) Yes, grudgingly
(3) Could go either way
(4) Not likely
(5) Definitely not
(6) Other
(7)
(8)
(9) DK/NA

174 26. Against current average monthly rents of:
(1) Under $45
(2) $45-$75
(3) $76-$90
(4) $91-$110
(5) $111-$135
(6) $136-$160
(7) $161-$185
(8) Over $185
(9) NA/DK

175 27. Is the resale market such that you can get your improvement money back?
(1) Yes—definitely
(2) Yes—maybe
(3) Toss up
(4) Probably not
(5) Definitely not
(6) Other reasons
(7)
(8)
(9) DK/NA

176 28. Would you improve property if given a long-term mortgage?
- (1) Parcel and neighborhood no good
- (2) Yes, no restrictions
- (3) Taxes plus something else
- (4) Yes, if mortgage payments equal increased revenue cost
- (5) Too old
- (6) Other
- (7) No

177
- (1) Don't want to go into debt
- (2) Parcel isn't worth it
- (3) No return—Won't improve
- (4) Neighborhood doesn't warrant it
- (5) Urban renewal is taking property
- (6) Property doesn't need it
- (7) Taxes
- (8) No money
- (9) NA/DK

178 29. Do you know of any government financial programs for older properties?
- (1) FHA General
- (2) FHA Title I
- (3) FHA 203, 220, 221
- (4) VA
- (5) Yes, but nothing specific
- (6) No
- (7) Not for this area (or parcel)
- (8) FACE
- (9) NA/DK

179 30. What would you have to pay for improvement money?

A. Interest Payments
- (1) 5 percent or less
- (2) 5 percent to 6 percent
- (3) 6 percent to 7 percent
- (4) 7 percent to 10 percent
- (5) Over 10 percent
- (6) Won't borrow
- (7) Would not be able to get it
- (8)
- (9) DK/NA

180 B. Terms

(1) Under three years
(2) Three to five years
(3) Five to ten years
(4) Ten years
(5) Ten to fifteen years
(6) More than fifteen years
(7) Won't borrow
(8)
(9) DK/NA

181 31. What source would you turn to for improvement money?

(1) Mortgage—savings bank
(2) Mortgage—broker
(3) Finance company
(4) Personal loan and commercial bank
(5) Personal resources
(6) Second mortgage—no source
(7) Bank w/o details
(8) Government
(9) DK/NA

182 32. Are you in an area scheduled for urban renewal?

(1) No
(2) Yes—within one year
(3) Yes—one to five years
(4) Yes—five to ten years
(5) Yes
(6) Not sure
(7)
(8) Other
(9) NA/DK

183 33. If property taken by urban renewal . . . get back investment?

(1) Yes
(2) Yes—but long term
(3) Maybe
(4) Probably not
(5) Definitely not
(6) Doesn't care—wants out
(7)
(8)
(9) DK/NA

184 34. Why not? (if no for question number 33)
- (1) One never receives full value of property
- (2) Authorities judge by area—property values in Newark on the decline
- (3) Authorities would not recognize value of improvements
- (4) Previous experience
- (5) Vacant building—MC only pay for functioning property
- (6) Deterioration of parcel due to age or fire damage
- (7) Loss income and capital appreciation
- (8) Other
- (9) NA/DK

185 35. Will your property be worth more or less five years from now?
- (1) Much more
- (2) More
- (3) Depends if improvements in parcel
- (4) Hold its own
- (5) Little less
- (6) Depends on future of Newark
- (7) Will not be standing
- (8) Other
- (9) NA/DK

186 35a. Why?
- (1) Present tenants effect
- (2) Area effect
- (3) Neglect of municipal services
- (4) Fire damage or age
- (5) Failure of administrative policies
- (6) General lack of interest in Newark
- (7) Other
- (8) Inflation
- (9) DK/NA

# SUMMARY SHEET

| Variable Number | Column | Row | |
|---|---|---|---|
| | A. (skip) | | |
| 187 | B. Sex of owner | | |
| | | (1) | Male |
| | | (2) | Female |
| | | (3) | Co-ownership |
| | | (4) | Corporation |
| | | (5) | |
| | | (6) | |
| | | (7) | |
| | | (8) | NA |
| | | (9) | DK |
| | C. (skip) | | |
| 188 | D. Place of residence | | |
| | | (1) | Resident in parcel |
| | | (2) | Within a block of parcel |
| | | (3) | |
| | | (4) | Newark—other |
| | | (5) | New Jersey—twenty mile radius from Newark |
| | | (6) | Balance New Jersey |
| | | (7) | New York |
| | | (8) | Other |
| | | (9) | NA/DK |
| 189 | E. Race—ethnicity | | |
| | | (1) | Negro |
| | | (2) | White—Jewish |
| | | (3) | White—Italian |
| | | (4) | White—other |
| | | (5) | White—unobserved |
| | | (6) | Puerto Rican |
| | | (7) | Cuban |
| | | (8) | Other |
| | | (9) | DK/NA |

190 F. Cooperation of owner in interviewing

(1) None
(2) Poor
(3) Average
(4) Good
(5) Excellent

## 1971 TITLE SEARCH
## (CARD 7)

ADDRESS OF PARCEL ______________________________

| Variable Number | Column | Row | |
|---|---|---|---|
| 195 | 1- 6 | _____ | Parcel identification number |
| 196 | 7- 9 | _____ | Census tract number |
| 197 | 10-11 | _____ | Census block number |
| 198 | 12-15 | _____ | Tax block number |
| 199 | 16-17 | _____ | Tax lot number |
| | | | Name of owner ______________________ |
| 200 | 18 | (1) | Individual (including joint ownership by husband and wife) |
| | | (2) | Two or more individuals |
| | | (3) | Realty corporations |
| | | (4) | Financial institutions |
| | | (5) | Nonfinancial institutions |
| | | (6) | Estates |
| | | (7) | City (detail) *Includes all public institutions* |

| | | | |
|---|---|---|---|
| | | | Address of owner ______________ |
| 201 | 19 | (1) | Same address |
| | | (2) | Same general area of Newark (i.e., within one mile) |
| | | (3) | Newark other |
| | | (4) | New Jersey other than Newark |
| | | (5) | Outside New Jersey |
| | | | Date of title ______________ (last bonafide transfer) |

Note: If above is prior to 1964, leave the rest blank, after Col. 20

| | | | |
|---|---|---|---|
| 202 | 20 | | |
| | | (1) | Zero-one year old |
| | | (2) | Two-four years old |
| | | (3) | Five-six years old |
| | | (4) | Seven-ten years old |
| | | (5) | Eleven-fifteen years old |
| | | (6) | Sixteen-twenty years old |
| | | (7) | Over twenty years old |
| | | (8) | Not recorded |
| | | | Property class |
| 203 | 21 | (1) | 2 |
| | | (2) | 4A |
| | | (3) | 4B |
| | | (4) | 4C |
| | | (5) | Other |
| | | | Lot size (to nearest foot) |
| 204 | 22-25 | ____ | frontage |
| 205 | 26-29 | ____ | depth |
| 206 | 30 | (1) | regular |
| | | (2) | irregular |
| 207 | 31-37 | $____ | land assessment |
| | 38-44 | $____ | building assessment |

| | | | |
|---|---|---|---|
| | | | Mortgage source by name ________ |
| 209 | 45 | (1) | Savings bank |
| | | (2) | Commercial bank |
| | | (3) | Savings and loan |
| | | (4) | Individual grantee |
| | | (5) | Prior owner |
| | | (6) | Mortgage company |
| | | (7) | No mortgage shown |
| | | (8) | Realty and construction company |
| | | (9) | Not given |
| | | (0) | Government agency |
| 210 | 46-52 | $________ | First mortgage amount (At time of purchase) |
| | | | First mortgage terms |
| 211 | 53 | (1) | Not listed |
| | | (2) | 4 percent plus to 4.5 percent |
| | | (3) | 4.5 percent plus to 5 percent |
| | | (4) | 5 percent plus to 5.5 percent |
| | | (5) | 5.5 percent plus to six percent |
| | | (6) | 6 percent plus to 7 percent |
| | | (7) | 7 percent plus to 8 percent |
| | | (8) | 8 percent plus |
| | | (9) | Bond |
| | | (0) | Other |
| | | | Mortgage types |
| 212 | 54 | (1) | B (blanket mortgage of consideration) Blanket-more than one parcel in transaction (Give detail if available) |
| | | (2) | Clear-cut first mortgage |
| | | (3) | S (subject mortgage) |
| | | (4) | Subject (Encumbrances on record) |
| | | (5) | Other—note (detail) |
| 213 | 55-61 | | $________ amount paid for property (Be careful to note method for determining this item.) |
| | | | Bonafide sale |
| 214 | 62 | (1) | Previous nominal transfer |
| | | (2) | No previous nominal transfer |

| | | | |
|---|---|---|---|
| 215 | 63 | (1) | Sale price can't be determined |
| | | (2) | Blanket mortgages |
| | | (3) | Foreclosure—price unclear |
| | | (4) | Sale price can't be determined—<br>last sale before record |
| | | (5) | Sales price n.g.—subject mortgage |
| | | | Second mortgage |
| 216 | 64 | (1) | Yes |
| | | (2) | No |
| | | (3) | Third Mortgage |
| | | | Second mortgage by name |
| 217 | 65 | (1) | Savings bank |
| | | (2) | Commercial bank |
| | | (3) | Savings and loan |
| | | (4) | Individual grantee |
| | | (5) | Mortgage company |
| | | (6) | Construction or home improvements |
| 218 | 66-72 | | $__________ second mortgage amount |
| | | | Second mortgage type |
| 219 | 73 | (1) | B (blanket mortgage of consideration) |
| | | (2) | Clear cut second mortgage |
| | | (3) | S (subject mortgage) |
| | | (4) | Subject (encumbrances on record) |
| | | (5) | Purchase money |
| | | (6) | At time of transfer (within six months) |
| | | (7) | At time of transfer (more than six months) |
| | | (8) | Other (detail) |
| 220 | | | Bonafide sales since 1964 |
| 220 | 74 | (1) | None |
| | | (2) | One |
| | | (3) | Two |
| | | (4) | Three |
| | | (5) | Four or more |
| | | | Detail |
| 221 | (77-79) | | I.D. |
| 222 | 80 | | |

# 1964, 1971 TAX RECORD

## 1964—CARD 4
## 1971—CARD 8

| Variable Number | Column | Row | |
|---|---|---|---|
| 223 | 1-6 | | Parcel Identification Number |
| 224 | 7 | (1) | If tax exempt<br>(Rest of card is blank) |
| 225 | 8-11 | | Block |
| 226 | 13-14 | | Lot |
| | 15 | (1) | If building is foreclosed<br>A. **REAL ESTATE TAX: for current year** |
| 227 | 16-20 | | First half amount (to nearest dollar) |
| 228 | 22-26 | | Second half amount (to nearest dollar) |
| 229 | 28 | | B. REAL ESTATE ARREARS: one Period or more |
| | | (1) | Yes |
| | | (2) | No |
| 230 | 29-30 | | Period (include fractions as one period) |
| 231 | 32-36 | | **Total** (to nearest dollar) |
| 232 | | | |

# CRIME CODE SHEET
# (CARD 11)

| Column | |
|---|---|
| (1-4) | Identification number |
| (6-9) | Time of call (twenty-four hour basis) |
| (11-13) | Duration of crime (in minutes) |
| (15-17) | Type of crime |
| (19) | Police precinct |
| (20) | Police beat |
| (22-24) | Census tract—location |
| (26-28) | New police district |
| (31) | Ward |
| (32-33) | Voting district |
| (79-80) | Card number |

# ABANDONMENT CODE SHEET
# (CARD 12)

| Column | Row |
|---|---|
| (1-3) | Census tract |
| (4) | Is the building on the Planning Department vacant building list?<br>1 Yes—sound list<br>2 Yes—unsound list |
| (5) | Status of building<br>1 open ("court," "dead end," etc.)<br>2 secured<br>3 rehabilitated |

4 publicly owned (state, NHA, etc.)
5 razed
6
7
8
9 NA/DK

(6) If razed, in what year?
1 1971
2 1970
3 1969
4 1968

(7) Type of use
1 residential
2 commercial
3 commercial/residential
4 industrial
5 industrial/commercial
6 service
7 industrial/residential
8
9 NA/DK

(8) If razed, by whom
1 privately
2 NHA
3 City of Newark
4 State of New Jersey

(9) Type of construction
1 frame
2 masonry
3 both
9 NA/DK

(10) Is the building on the city's tax sale list?
1 1971 list
2 1970 list
3 1969 list
4 1968 list
5 1967 list

| | |
|---|---|
| (11) | Total number of stories |
| (12) | Number of residential stories |
| (13-16) | Identification number |
| (17) | Ward |
| (18-19) | Voting district |
| (20) | Has a fire occurred in the building?<br>1 Multiple alarm in 1971<br>2 Multiple alarm in 1970<br>3 Signal 11 in 1971<br>4 Signal 11 in 1970 |
| (79-80) | Card number **12** |

## TAX SALE CODE SHEET (CARD 14)

| **Column** | **Row** |
|---|---|
| (1-4) | Identification number |
| (6) | Punch **1** if building was bought privately |
| (8) | Classification<br>1 Vacant land<br>2 Residential<br>3 4A—commercial<br>4 4B—industrial<br>5 4C—apartments (six families or more)<br>6 House and Lot<br>7<br>8<br>9 NA/DK |
| (10-15) | Amount (to nearest dollar) |
| (17-19) | Census tract |

| | | |
|---|---|---|
| (21) | Year of sale | 1 1971<br>2 1970<br>3 1969<br>4 1968<br>5 1967 |
| (79-80) | Card number **14** | |

## FIRE CODE SHEET
## (CARD 15)

| Column | | Row |
|---|---|---|
| (1-4) | Case number | |
| (6-8) | Census tract | |
| (9) | Occupancy | 1 occupied<br>2 partially occupied<br>3 vacant<br>4<br>5<br>6<br>7<br>8<br>9 NA/DK |
| (11-2) | Number of stories | (Leave blank if not known) |
| (14-15) | Number of units | (Leave blank if not known) |
| (17) | Type of use | 1 residential<br>2 commercial<br>3 residential/commercial<br>4 industrial |

| | | | |
|---|---|---|---|
| | | 5 | commercial/industrial |
| | | 6 | |
| | | 7 | |
| | | 8 | |
| | | 9 | NA/DK |
| (19) | Type of construction | 1 | frame |
| | | 2 | masonry |
| | | 3 | |
| | | 4 | |
| | | 5 | |
| | | 6 | |
| | | 7 | |
| | | 8 | |
| | | 9 | NA/DK |
| (21) | Type of Fire | 1 | multiple alarms |
| | | 2 | signal 11 |
| | | 3 | |
| | | 4 | |
| | | 5 | |
| | | 6 | |
| | | 7 | |
| | | 8 | |
| | | 9 | NA/DK |
| (23) | Ward | 1 | North |
| (24-25) | Voting district | 2 | West |
| | | 3 | Central |
| (80) | Card number | 4 | South |
| | **15** | 5 | East |

# IN-DEPTH ABANDONED BUILDING OWNER QUESTIONNAIRE

(Hand Tabulated)

1. Why did you give up the structure? (GET A STORY)

2. What was the turning point which made the structure no longer worthwhile for tenants?

3. How did you give up the structure? (WHAT PROCESS, i.e., WALK AWAY, STOP SERVICES, etc.)

4. Have you stopped paying taxes or are you continuing to pay them?

5. If you are paying taxes, why are you doing so if you derive no income from the parcel?

6. Do you annually claim the building as a tax loss?

7. Have you thought of selling the property to the City of Newark under its take-over program?

8. If not, what do you plan to do with the building?

9. Have you tried to sell the property?

10. Did you get any offers?

11. From whom?

12. How much?

13. What is the current mortgage payment, if any, and outstanding amount owned on the building?

14. Do you have fire insurance on the structure?

15. Have you had any trouble maintaining fire insurance on your structure?

16. Have you collected on your fire insurance policy for fires on the property?

17. How much money? Over what period of time?

# FINANCIAL—INSTITUTIONS—QUESTIONNAIRE

## (Hand Tabulated)

1. What reason do you give for these trends we have observed in the Newark mortgage market?
   (SHOW EXHIBIT—LIST SEVERAL REASONS IN ORDER OF PRIORITY)

2. Is this exclusively based on an increase in insured mortgages and the mortgage company's ability to handle these, or are primary lenders bailing out?

   Or is this a combination of both?

   Neither? (specify)

3. Is your firm currently doing more or less residential business in the core than it did prior to 1967?
   Yes No

4. Why?

5. Approximately how many VA/FHA loans on one to three family homes has your firm processed in Newark during 1970 and 1971?

   1970 1971

   Percent of each year's total residential activity.

   1970 1971

6. What are the advantages of securing and processing an insured loan on a one to three family home worth $18,000?
   (MAKE SURE YOU DOCUMENT HOW REVENUES ARE DETERMINED)
   Net points Annual servicing fee
   Note any additional advantages:

6a. What are the costs of such a transaction?
   (MAKE SURE YOU DOCUMENT HOW COSTS ARE CALCULATED)
   Initial processing cost
   Annual servicing cost

7. Given the essentially slim margin of profit demonstrated above, why do you continue to be active in this market?

8. How many homes in Newark financed under the 235 program has your firm handled annually for 1970 and 1971?

   1970 1971

9. How do your costs and revenue under the 235 program compare with the VA/FHA picture previously described?

10. What is the average time for homes in the same area as those processed under 235 to remain on the market before buyer and seller are brought together?
(TAKE FIVE TO TEN HOMES SOLD THROUGH 235 AND COMPARE TIME ON BOOKS WITH THOSE SOLD VIA FHA/VA)

11. What are the start-up and long-term costs to the buyer under the 235 program versus the FHA/VA programs? (ASSUME $18,000 PARCEL).

| | |
|---|---|
| Difference in down payments | $__________ |
| Difference in monthly cost as a function of differing interest rates | $__________ |
| Difference in principal paid up annually | $__________ |

11a. Does 235 housing program expand the potential residential market considerably?

11b. How does this compare with the increase in potential risk?

12. What is your specific relationship to the speculator* currently active in Newark's 235 program?
(*Speculator: Person who takes interim title between seller and prospective buyer, usually at considerable profit.)

13. If the speculator was not present and 235 not available, by how much (percent) would the turnover in one to three family residential units be cut?

14. We have observed in a parallel study the abandonment of structures by the multi-parcel, white professional landlord. Do you think there is any way of countering this trend?

15. What is your feeling towards the increase in black landlords? Can he make any money by owning urban-core, low-end rental properties?

16. If he can, why can he make it when the white owner cannot?

17. What policy recommendations would you make to continue a *healthy* turnover of residential parcels in Newark?

17 a. How can the speculator's profit be limited to keep him in the business yet stop potential buyers from being scalped?

18. Note: Ask for case history of the following parcels:
(SPECIALS)
Number 211 129 Arlington Street
Number 230 690 Hunterdon Street
Number 283 66 South Orange Avenue

(a) Did owner qualify under normal credit standards?
(b) What went wrong with the loan?
(c) How many similar situations? (Percent of your Newark residential portfolio)
(d) How has this affected your center-city lending policies?

# BIBLIOGRAPHY

## Books

Allihan, Milla. *Social Ecology*. New York: Columbia University Press, 1939.

Anderson, Martin. *The Federal Bulldozer*. Cambridge, Mass.: The M.I.T. Press, 1964.

Berry, Brian, and Horton, Frank E. *Geographic Perspectives on Urban Systems*. Englewood Cliffs, N.J.: Prentice-Hall, 1969.

Birch, David L. *The Economic Future of City and Suburb*. New York: Committee for Economic Development, 1970.

Burchell, Robert W.; Hughes, James W.; and Sternlieb, George. *Housing Costs and Housing Restraints: Newark, N.J.* New Brunswick, N.J.: Center for Urban Policy Research, Rutgers University, 1970.

Chernick, Jack,; Indik, Bernard; and Sternlieb, George. *Newark, New Jersey: Population and Labor Force*. New Brunswick, N.J.: Institute of Management and Labor Relations, Rutgers University, 1967.

Clark, Ramsey. *Crime in America*. New York: Simon and Schuster, 1971.

Dogan, Mattei, and Rokkan, Stein. *Quantitative Ecological Analysis in the Social Sciences,* Cambridge, Mass.: MIT Press, 1969.

Frieden, Bernard J. *The Future of Old Neighborhoods*. Cambridge, Mass.: The M.I.T. Press, 1964.

Grigsby, William G.; Rosenberg, L.; Stegman, Michael and Taylor, J. *Housing and Poverty*. Philadelphia, Pa.: University of Pennsylvania, Institute of Environmental Studies, 1973.

Hoover, Edgar M. and Vernon, Raymond. *Anatomy of a Metropolis*. New York: Doubleday Anchor, 1962.

Hoyt, Homer. *The Structure and Growth of Residential Neighborhoods in American Cities*. Washington, D.C.: Federal Housing Administration, 1939.

Hughes, James W. *Urban Indicators: Metropolitan Evolution and Public Policy*. New Brunswick, N.J.: Rutgers University, Center for Urban Policy Research, 1973.

Johnston, J. *Econometric Methods*. New York: McGraw-Hill, 1963.

Kristof, Frank S. "Housing: Economic Facts of New York City's Housing Problems," in Lyle Fitch and A. Walsh *Agenda for a City*. Beverly Hills, California: Sage Publications, 1970.

Murdie, Robert. *The Factorial Ecology of Metroplitan Toronto 1951-1961*. Chicago: University of Chicago, Department of Geography, 1969.

Nie, Norman A., et al. *Statistical Package for the Social Sciences*. New York: McGraw-Hill, 1970.

Nourse, Hugh O. *Urban Decay in St. Louis*. St. Louis, Mo.: Washington University, The Institute for Urban and Regional Studies, 1972.

O'Hagan, John T. *Fire Fighting During Civil Disorders*. New York: International Association of Fire Chiefs, 1968.

Rapkin, Chester and Grigsby, William G. *Residential Renewal in the Urban Core*. Philadelphia: University of Pennsylvania Press, 1960.

Robson, B. T. *Urban Analysis: A Study of City Structure*. London: Cambridge University Press, 1969.

Shevky, Eshref, and Bell, Wendell. *Social Area Analysis: Theory, Illustrative Application, and Computational Procedure*. Stanford, Calif.: Stanford University Press, 1955.

Schorr, Alvin L. *Slums and Social Insecurity*. Washington, D.C.: U.S. Government Printing Office, 1966.

Steffens, Joseph Lincoln. *The Autobiography of Lincoln Steffens*. New York: Harcourt, Brace and Company, 1931.

Sternlieb, George. *The Tenement Landlord*. New Brunswick, N.J.: Rutgers University Press, 1969.

Sternlieb, George, and Indik, Bernard P. *The Ecology of Welfare*. New Brunswick, N.J.: Transaction Press, 1973.

Sternlieb, George. *The Urban Housing Dilemma*. New York: New York City Housing Development Administration, 1972.

Timms, D. W. G. *The Urban Mosaic: Towards a Theory of Residential Differentiation*. London: Cambridge University Press, 1971.

## Periodicals

Abu-Lughod, Janet. "Testing the Theory of Social Area Analysis: The Ecology of Cairo, Egypt." *American Sociological Review* 34 (1969):198-212.

Ahern, John, and Morgan, Charles S. "The National Fire Profile." *Fire Journal* Vol. 66, no. 2 (1972):7-11.

Allen, H. K. "Collection of Delinquent Taxes by Recourse to the Taxed Property." *Law and Contemporary Problems* 3 (June 1936):397-405.

Bird, Frederick. "Extent and Distribution of Urban Tax Delinquency." *Law and Contemporary Problems* 3 (July 1936):337-346.

Blum, Edward. "Fire Service: Challenge to Modern Management." *Public Management* vol. 52, no. 11 (November 1970):4-7.

Blum, Walter, and Dunham, Allison. "Slumlordism as a Tort — A Dissenting View." *Michigan Law Review* (January 1968): 451-464.

Brandis, Henry. "Tax Sales and Foreclosure under the Model Tax Collection Law." *Law and Contemporary Problems* 3 (June 1936): 406-415.

Breckenfeld, Gurney. "Housing Subsidies Are a Grand Delusion." *Fortune*, February 1972, 136-138+.

Carey, George. "The Regional Interpretation of Manhattan Population and Housing Patterns through Factor Analysis." *Geographical Review* 56 (1966):551-569.

Clayton, Glenn. "Abandoned — That's the Fate of Housing and of Neighborhoods — In a Growing Number of American Cities; Survey Report Analyzes Causes: Recommends Action to Reverse the Trend." *Journal of Housing*, (June 1971): 271-276.

Conchado, Sandra, and Nolan, William P. "Building Abandonment in New York City." *New York Law Forum* 16, no. 4 (1970):798-862.

Cranker, Glenn. "Abandoned and Vacant Housing Units: Can They be Used During Housing Crises?" *New York University Review of Law and Social Change* 1 (Spring 1971):3-68.

Emmerman, Howard. "Revenue and Taxation — Collection of Delinquent Real Estate Taxes — Legislating Protection of the Delinquent Property Owner in an Era of Super-Marketable Tax Titles." *De Paul Law Review* 19 (1969):348-376.

Fenitti, Fred. "U.S. Looks into Profits on Homes." *The New York Times*, 20 February 1972, p. 118.

Godfrey, Edward. "Enforcement of Delinquent Property Taxes in New York." *Albany Law Review* 24 (June 1960):271-316; 25 (January 1961):39-66; (June 1961): 212-237; 26 (June 1962):201-230.

Greenberg, Michael R., and Boswell, Thomas D., "Neighborhood Deterioration As A Factor in Intraurban Migration: A Case Study in New York City." *The Professional Geographer* 24 (February 1972):11-16.

Greer, Scott. "Urbanism Reconsidered: A Comparative Study of Local Areas in a Metropolis." *American Sociological Review* 21 (February 1956):19-24.

Handler, Charles. "In Rem Tax Foreclosure in New Jersey." *Municipalities and the Law in Action* NIMLO (1951):290-295.

Harbert, George. "Tax Forelcosures and Tax Titles." *University of Illinois Law Forum* (Summer 1952):209-225.

"Housing Abandonment." *Architectural Forum*, April 1971, pp. 42-45.

"Housing: The Shell Game." *Newsweek*, 28 February 1972, pp. 60-61.

"How Washington Is Helping More People Buy Homes." *U.S. News and World Report*, 26 October 1970.

Hunter, Albert. "The Ecology of Chicago: Persistence and Change, 1930-1960." *American Journal of Sociology*, 77 (November 1971):425-444.

"In the Inner Cities: Acres of Abandoned Buildings: Landlords Are Now Fleeing the Inner City . . ." *U.S. News and World Report*, 26 January 1970, pp. 54-56.

Ingram, Gregory K. and Kain, John F. "A Simple Model of Housing Production and the Abandonment Problem." *Proceedings of the American Real Estate and Urban Economics Association* 5 (1972).

"Insurers Get Burned on Ghetto Policies." *Business Week*, 6 November 1971, p. 38.

James, Franklin J., Burchell, Robert W. and Hughes, James W. "Race, Profit, and Housing Abandonment in Newark." *Proceedings of the American Real Estate and Urban Economics Association* 5 (1972).

"Jersey's Relief Rolls Rose 2 ½ Times from '66 to '71." *The New York Times*, 23 April 1972, p. 61.

Jones, Richard. "Sponsorship of Subsidized Housing for Low and Moderate Income Families under the National Housing Act." *George Washington Law Review*, 38 (July 1970):1073-1090.

Kelley, Truman. "Comments on Wilson and Worcester's Vote on Factor Analysis." *Psychology* 5, (1940):117-120.

Kniesner, Thomas. "A Quantitative Analysis of Substandard Urban Housing in Ohio." *Bulletin of Business Research* 45 (September 1970):5-8.

Legg, William. "Tax Sales and the Constitution." *Oklahoma Law Review* 20 (November 1967): 365-379.

Lilley III, William, and Clark, Timothy B. "Federal Programs Spur Abandonment of Housing in Major Cities." *National Journal*, 1 January 1972, pp. 26-33.

"Mayors Urge U.S. Probe of Home Buying Program." *Sunday Star Ledger*, 20 February 1972, p. 1.

"Mortgages for the Slums." *Fortune* (January 1968), pp. 162-163.

Nachbaur, W. T. "Empty Houses: Abandoned Residential Buildings in the Inner City." *Harvard Law Journal* vol. 17, no. 3 (1971).

"Neighborhood Uplift Projects Stir Complaints." *Sunday Star Ledger*, 30 April 1972, p. 1.

"No Vacancy: Shortage of Housing in N. Y. City Gets Worse with Every Day; Abandonments, Withdrawal of Capital and an Old Law Exacerbates City's Crisis." *Wall Street Journal*, 2 December 1970, p. 1.

Phares, Donald. "Racial Change and Housing Values: Transition in an Inner Suburb." *Social Science Quarterly* 52 (December 1971):560-573.

"Profits Reaped in Sale of Homes to Help Poor." *Sunday Star Ledger*, 13 February 1972, p. 1.

Ross, Sid, and Kupferberg, Herbert. "The Undeclared War on the Nation's Firemen." *International Fire Fighter* 54, no. 11 (November 1971):18-22.

Sangstar, Robert Powell. "Abandonment of Inner City Properties." *Federal Home Loan Bank Board Journal* 5 (February 1972):15.

Sax, Joseph. "Slumlordism as a Tort — A Brief Response." *Michigan Law Review* (January 1968):465-468.

Schreiberg, Sheldon. "Abandoned Buildings: Tenant Condominiums and Community Redevelopment [Approaches that a Municipality Might Try] — New York City's Experience." *Urban Lawyer* 2 (Spring 1970):186-218.

Silbergeld, Art. "Abandoned Housing." *Planning Comment* (Spring 1971):5.

Simpson, Herbert. "Tax Delinquency." *Illinois Law Review* 28 (June 1933):147-176.

Smith, Wade. "Recent Legislative Indulgences to Delinquent Taxpayers." *Law and Contemporary Problems* 3 (July 1936):371-381.

Smith, Wallace F. "Forecasting Neighborhood Change." *Land Economics* (August 1963).

Spivak, Jonathan. "Pride of Ownership: Government Is Testing a Plan to Help Poor Buy Their Own Homes." *Wall Street Journal*, 23 October 1970, p. 1.

Sporn, Arthur. "Empirical Studies in the Economics of Slum Ownership." *Land Economics* (November 1960).

Stegman, Michael. "The Myth of the Slumlord." *American Institute of Architects Journal* (March 1970):45-49.

Sternlieb, George. "Abandoned Housing — What is to Be Done?" *Urban Land* 31, no. 3 (March 1972), p. 6.

Sternlieb, George, and Indik, Bernard P. "Housing Vacancy Analysis." *Land Economics* vol. 45, no. 1 (February 1969):117-121.

Stevens, Sally. "Low Income Co-Ops; A Solution to Abandonment" [of Slum Housing Buildings, N.Y., N.Y.] *New York Law Forum* 17 (November 1971): 148-206.

Stevenson, Eric. "A Commitment Made and Kept . . . The Urban Investment Program." *The Mortgage Banker* (May 1970), pp. 18-27.

Traynor, Roger. "Legislation — The Model Real Property Tax Collection Law." *California Law Review* 24 (1935-1936):98-107.

"Walk Aways: A Knowing Threat to Cities." *The Realtors Quarterly Magazine* 37 (April 1970).

"The Wildfire of Abandonment: Entire Blocks are Rotting as Landlords Claim: 'We Can't Make a Buck.' " *Business Week*, 4 April 1970, p. 57.

Wilson, Robert. "Another Tool to Fund Life Insurance Companies' Urban Investment Program." *The Mortgage Banker* (May 1971), pp. 98-104.

Ylvisaker, Paul N. "The Deserted City." *Journal of the American Institute of Planners* vol. 25, no. 1 (February 1959):1-2.

Young, Richard E. "The Tax Deed — Modern Movement Towards Respectability." *Rocky Mountain Law Review* 34 (1962):181-197.

## Other

Akahoshi, George, and Gass, Edna. *A Study of the Problems of Abandoned Housing and Recommendations for Action by the Federal Government and Localities.* Washington: Linton, Mields and Coston, 1971.

Center for Urban Policy Research Staff. "Suburban Office Space: The Continued Demise of the Central City." Mimeographed. New Brunswick, N.J.: Center for Urban Policy Research, Rutgers University, 1972.

Citizens Budget Committee, Inc. "Abandoned Buildings: A Time for Action." New York, February 1970.

*Essex County Real Estate Directory.* East Orange, N.J.: Annual Supplements 1960-1970.

Federal Home Loan Bank Board. *Waverly: A Study in Neighborhood Conservation.* Washington, D.C.: Federal Home Loan Bank Board, 1939.

Grigsby, William. *The Residential Real Estate Market in an Area Undergoing Racial Transition.* Ph.D. dissertation, Columbia University, 1958.

Hughes, James W. "Changing Urban Social Structure: Black Differentiation in Newark." New Brunswick, N.J.: Center for Urban Policy Research, Rutgers University, 1972.

Institute for Urban and Regional Studies. *Urban Decay in St. Louis.* St. Louis, Missouri: Washington University, March 1972.

National Housing Agency. *Who Owns the Slums? Where Does Money Spent for Slum Property Go?*" Washington: National Housing Bulletin 6, March 1964.

National Urban League. *The National Survey of Housing Abandonment.* New York, 1971.

Public Affairs Counseling. *HUD Experimental Program for Preserving Declining Neighborhoods: An Analysis of the Abandonment Process.* San Francisco, Cal.: Public Affairs Counseling 1973.

Romney, George. "Statement before the Subcommittee on Housing of the House Committee on Banking and Currency on Settlement Costs, Mortgage Foreclosure,

Housing Abandonment and Site Selection Policies." Washington: U.S. Government Printing Office, 22 February 1972.

Sternlieb, George. "Abandonment and Rehabilitation: What is to be Done." New Brunswick, N.J.: Rutgers University, Center for Urban Policy Research, 1971.

Sternlieb, George. *Some Aspects of the Abandoned House Problem.* New Brunswick, N.J.: Center for Urban Policy Research, Rutgers University, 1970.

U.S. Bureau of the Census, *U.S. Census of Population and Housing: 1960 Census Tracts, Final Report PHC(1)-105.* Washington: U.S. Government Printing Office, 1962.

U.S. Commission on Civil Rights. *Home Ownership for Lower Income Families: A Report on the Racial and Ethnic Impact of the Section 235 Program.* Washington, D.C.: U.S. Government Printing Office, 1970.

U.S. Congress. *Defaults on FHA-Insured Mortgages.* Hearings before a Subcommittee of the Committee on Government Operations, House of Representatives, 92nd Congress, 1st Session. Washington, D.C.: U.S. Government Printing Office, 1972.

U.S. Congress, *Defaults on FHA-Insured Mortgages (Part II).* Hearings before a Subcommittee of the Committee on Government Operations, House of Representatives, 92nd Congress, 2nd Session. Washington, D.C.: U.S. Government Printing Office, 1972.

U.S. Congress, *Defaults on FHA-Insured Home Mortgages—Detroit, Michigan. Fifteenth Report by the Committee on Government Operations.* House Report 92-1152. Washington, D.C.: U.S. Government Printing Office, 1972.

U.S. Congress, House of Representatives, Committee on Banking and Currency. *Housing and the Urban Environment.* Washington: U.S. Government Printing Office, 1971.

U.S. Congress, House of Representatives, Committee on Banking and Currency. *Interim Report on HUD Investigation of Low- and Moderate-Income Housing Programs.* Washington: U.S. Government Printing Office, 1971.

U.S. Department of Housing and Urban Development. *HUD Clip Sheet.* 9 March 1972.

U.S. Federal Bureau of Investigation. *Crime in the United States, Uniform Crime Reports — 1960.* Washington: U.S. Government Printing Office, 1961.

U.S. Federal Bureau of Investigation. *Crime in the United States, Uniform Crime Reports — 1970.* Washington: U.S. Government Printing Office, 1971.

U.S. National Advisory Commission on Civil Disorders. *Report.* Washington: U.S. Government Printing Office, 1968.

# INDEX